ASIAN STUDIES ASSOCIA

Southeast Asia Publications Series

HISTORY IN UNIFORM

Military Ideology and the Construction of Indonesia's Past

HISTORY IN UNIFORM

Military Ideology and the Construction of Indonesia's Past

Katharine E. McGregor

Asian Studies Association of Australia
in association with
UNIVERSITY OF HAWAI'I PRESS
HONOLULU

First published by:

NUS Press
National University of Singapore
AS3-01-02, 3 Arts Link
Singapore 117569

Published in North America by:

University of Hawai'i Press
2840 Kolowalu Street
Honolulu, Hawai'i 96822

Library of Congress Cataloging-in-Publication Data

McGregor, Katharine E.
 History in uniform : military ideology and the construction of Indonesia's past /
Katharine E. McGregor.
    p. cm. — (Southeast Asia publications series)
 "Asian Studies Association of Australia in association with University of Hawaii
Press."
 Includes bibliographical references and index.
 ISBN-13: 978-0-8248-3153-0 (pbk. : alk. paper)
  1. Indonesia—Armed Forces—History—20th century. 2. Indonesia—Armed
Forces—Public relations—History—20th century. 3. Indonesia—Armed Forces—
Political activity—History—20th century. 4. Civil-military relations—Indonesia—
History—20th century. 5. Indonesia—History—Coup d'état, 1965. 6. Indonesia—
History—1966–7. Notosusanto, Nugroho. I. Title.
 UA853.I5M25 2007
 355.009598'09045—dc22
                              2006028178

Cover photo: TEMPO/Photographer Rini Prapti W. Ismail

Printed in Singapore

I dedicate this book to

my mother and father,
Leora and Gordon McGregor

Contents

List of Illustrations

Preface

The Indonesian military has always claimed to be unique. Their claims rest, firstly, on the idea that the Indonesian people created the military in the 1945–49 independence struggle against the Dutch and, secondly, on the idea that during this struggle the military assumed the mantle of national leadership after the capture of the civilian leaders of the Republic in 1948. It is on the basis of these two claims that the Indonesian military has long justified its right to play a dual role (*dwifungsi*) in defence and politics. Clearly history has been of central significance to the Indonesian military, especially for defending its rights to political power and influence in Indonesia.

When I began my research for this book in 1996, I was not aware of how influential the Indonesian military had been in producing and shaping New Order historical orthodoxy. My initial aim had been to unpack the key features of this orthodoxy and to examine how it was created and for what purposes. After surveying several official history publications and sites such as the National History textbook, the National Monument History Museum and the Satriamandala Armed Forces Museum, I repeatedly encountered one name — that of Nugroho Notosusanto. I also discovered that Nugroho was the author of the first published version of the 1965 coup attempt. The coup attempt, in which six Army generals and a lieutenant were kidnapped and killed by armed members of the presidential guard, marked a major turning point in Indonesian history because it allowed the largely anti-communist Army to move against the Communist Party by blaming them for the coup. Nugroho's role in New Order history-making was monumental and extended to far more projects than these — including other museums, films and history materials for educating both soldiers and civilians.

In addition to analysing New Order representations of the past, *History in Uniform* tells the story of how and why Nugroho came to work for the Indonesian military in his capacity as Head of the Armed Forces History Centre. It offers a biography of a central propagandist of the New Order regime. In order to compile this biography, I interviewed many friends, associates and foes of Nugroho. This was not always an easy task, as his friends and family were well aware of the criticisms of

Nugroho's work and expected that I might already hold similar views. In presenting a picture of Nugroho, I have tried to present a fair representation of this man and to grapple with the forces that shaped him, while also forming judgments on the impact of his works.

One scholar asked me to reflect on my own position in this project as an historian examining the motivations and life story of another historian. What were my motivations for writing about military representations of the Indonesian past? For me, the fascination lay in discovering how a regime used history for legitimation and the degree to which history can indeed be manipulated to suit the interests of different parties. It seemed to me that in the case of the 1965 coup attempt, military representations of the alleged barbarity of communists were particularly powerful and they also had an impact on the families of victims of the post-coup killings or imprisonments. A sense of compassion for these victims of New Order historical orthodoxy, who until 1998 were unable to openly challenge these narratives, informs this work.

History in Uniform includes analyses of a wide range of history projects directed at both civilians and soldiers, but there is an emphasis on military-created museums and monuments. After surveying a range of military history sites, I found that the diorama (or picture model) museums, such as the National Monument History Museum and the Satriamandala Armed Forces Museum, captured my imagination. One reason for this was the dramatic appeal of the dioramas; they are "a theatrical way of presenting the past".[1] It occurred to me that for visitors to these museums, the dioramas functioned as consumable snapshots of the Indonesian past. This was something that resonated with me. Unlike photographs or historical relics, which are remains of the past that a curator selects from and then frames in a museum, dioramas are composed and narrated at the time of a museum's making.[2] In this sense, they are frozen records of how the museum-makers constructed the past for public consumption. For this reason, I believed that these dioramas would be a valuable source for analysing how the military represented the past at different points in time.

I became fascinated as to how museum-makers put together a visual trajectory of the nation's past. Walter Grasskamp claims that since the 1970s, there have been more and more investigations into how history is constituted, and how the writing of history has changed. Writing in 1996, he expressed surprise that the history of the writing of history had not yet included an examination of the museum as a historical text. It was the museum, he claimed, that defended historical consciousness as its domain, by ordering "its chambers with historical lucidity" and moulding "a sense of historicism".[3] By setting out the past in a progression of images, museums offer a valuable means for examining constructions of national history. Because of the military's intention to create one narrative of the Indonesian past, the constructions of history put forward in these museums match those in many other official sources of New Order history and they are thus an important source of New Order historical ideas.

Researching the Indonesian military and its image-making efforts whilst the New Order regime was still intact presented me with considerable challenges. I began this project in 1996, a year in which the destruction of Megawati Sukarnoputri's rebel PDI (Partai Demokrasi Indonesia, Indonesian Democratic Party) headquarters by security troops reinforced the authoritarian character of the regime. In Indonesia, the general opinion was that only Suharto's death would bring the regime to an end. In this political climate I began the process of applying for permission to research in Indonesia through the research body LIPI (Lembaga Ilmu Pengetahuan Indonesia, The Indonesian Institute of Sciences). I knew from my enquiries that the LIPI research approval committee included representatives of the BIA (Badan Intelijen ABRI, ABRI Intelligence Agency) and that I would subsequently be under some scrutiny merely for the fact that my research included the word "military" in its title.

After seven months of waiting, I received news that my visa had been granted. I was greatly relieved but also anxious as to how much access the research permit would allow me to military-controlled sites. Although most museums and monuments are open to the general public for viewing, I needed to gain access to military historians and to more detailed documentation such as museum and monument plans in order to draw conclusions about how these representations of the past were compiled.

On arrival at my designated primary research site Satriamandala Armed Forces Museum, which is located on the same site as the Armed Forces History Centre on Jl. Gatot Subroto in Jakarta, I introduced myself and presented my letters of permission from LIPI. I was then requested to present myself for an interview at the "liaison unit" situated within the heavily-guarded Army headquarters on Jl. Merdeka Utara in the city centre near the presidential palace. As a result of the interview, which involved detailed questioning by three military officers, I was given permission to go ahead with my research. I consequently found myself, however, under close guidance and scrutiny. In addition to receiving a daily phone call from the Army liaison officer to check where

I had been each day, every research site that I listed on my research proposal was notified by internal communication that I would be visiting and seeking information. The benefit of this was that I was able to interview museum staff and staff at the Armed Forces History Centre headquarters. On the other hand, the staff were particularly guarded and careful in their responses and I no longer enjoyed the anonymity of being merely another foreign tourist visiting these locations. At the site of the Sacred Pancasila Monument, for example, which contains highly sensitive representations of the 1965 coup attempt, a guide closely followed me around the museum. When I stopped to look at a diorama, the guide would look at the diorama and then back at me, as if to try to read my thoughts. Perhaps the greatest surprise for me was when I arrived at the Army museum in Yogyakarta, where I was immediately acknowledged as "the Australian researcher" and directed to meet the Head of the Sudirman Museum in the same city. This man, who on my final visit to Yogyakarta revealed he was a BIA agent, insisted on accompanying me dressed in full military uniform and by means of military jeep to all the historical sites of Yogyakarta listed in my research plan. Although this kind of close attention did not contribute to a stress-free research environment, the caution that the military took with my research topic provided me with further information on how guarded the military was about their role as history-makers.

As a result of going through formal channels, I also had unique opportunities. I was granted permission to attend a number of state ceremonies including a ceremony of *renungan* (reflection) at the Kalibata Heroes Cemetery on the eve of Independence Day commemorations, the Sacred Pancasila Day ceremony at Lubang Buaya in Jakarta and the General Attack celebrations in Yogyakarta. In addition, I was granted permission, with the encouragement and assistance of my Yogyakarta guide, to follow the General Sudirman Walking Pilgrimage. Each time I took up these offers, I did so with some trepidation as my presence on these occasions as a foreign civilian woman amongst masses of mostly male officers often provoked extensive questioning and deliberate intimidation. On the occasion of the midnight *renungan*, for example, I was even temporarily abandoned (perhaps deliberately) by my guide whilst one of Suharto's intelligence agents searched my bag and questioned me just prior to Suharto's arrival at the cemetery.

My conviction is that the military allowed, and at times assisted me to conduct my field research in 1997–98 because at the time the military were experiencing an image crisis. The position of the Indonesian military varied over the course of the long New Order regime.

By the mid-1990s, the military was increasingly being marginalised by Suharto, yet Suharto continued to call on the military to suppress regime opposition. As a consequence, the military's popularity amongst the people was waning. This was particularly so after the tragic 27 July affair of 1996, involving a violent government-led attack on Megawati Sukarnoputri's banned PDI-Struggle Party headquarters, which received widespread media coverage and prompted widespread rioting.[4] The Indonesian military was consequently rethinking its position in anticipation of the post-Suharto era, and how they could best secure their dual role in politics and defence. Evidence of this is provided by their efforts in 1996 to once again turn to the historical record for legitimacy. On Armed Forces Day 1996, for example, the usual celebrations of military might were replaced by a colossal musical performance by members of the Armed Forces and the Armed Forces wives' organisations. The musical told the story of the Indonesian struggle from the time of Diponegoro and highlighted the Japanese occupation, the 1945 proclamation of independence, the return of the Dutch, the General Attack of 1949 then moving on to the Free Irian campaign, the coup of 1965 and the 1972 election as the last scene.[5]

The military may have been interested in what the results of my research would tell them about their efforts at building their historical image. It is more likely, however, that they saw this as an opportunity to promote their image to the outside world through me, either by the gesture of granting me permission or taking the chance that my research findings would promote their historical image.

In May 1998, less than a month after I returned from Indonesia, Suharto resigned as President, thus finally drawing to a close the end of a long regime. Amidst a major backlash against abuses of power and human rights, the Indonesian military also agreed to rescind its political role. This had several implications for my research. The great majority of my observations of military representations of the Indonesian past were recorded during the New Order period. In the post-Suharto era, official history inside Indonesia has been openly challenged. In the first year after his passing, history was at the forefront of public commentary. The catharsis of historical information that the fall of Suharto triggered provided evidence of the extent of private contestation of New Order historical orthodoxy. It also demonstrated that, despite years of manipulation, Indonesians still considered interpretations of the past to be important.

Despite challenges to New Order historical orthodoxy and some curtailment of military influence, in the post-Suharto years the military has largely continued to defend and uphold many of the representations of the past considered here. It has done so with considerably less vigour, yet representations of the independence struggle in particular remain central to the military's claim for continuing political influence, rather than a political role. Since the fall of Suharto, the Indonesian military has retreated from politics, but it is still jostling for some influence, particularly through retention of the territorial command system. Until the military has completed the process of professionalisation, if indeed it does, we can expect a lag in adjustments to the constructions of the past that it has long defended.

Future political change means that some of the sites and sources of history I have examined might be revised. For these reasons, *History in Uniform* provides a valuable record of how the authoritarian New Order regime recorded and celebrated the Indonesian past in official history sources. It also offers an important comparative record against which to measure future narratives of the Indonesian past and indeed other narratives of the national past or history-making processes in comparable regimes.

Acknowledgements

Throughout the time I have been working on this project, I have received support, inspiration and guidance from many people. My sincere thanks go to Charles Coppel, the principal supervisor of the thesis from which this book stemmed. It was Charles who, on noticing my enthusiasm for Indonesia, encouraged me to pursue this project many years ago. Charles' detailed knowledge of Indonesian history has greatly enriched this work. Other people who have expertly guided me on the pathway to this book are the associate supervisors of my thesis, Antonia Finnane and Tim Lindsey, and the Southeast Asia Publications Series editor for the Asian Studies Association of Australia, Howard Dick.

In both Indonesia and Australia, many academics and people working at my sites of research were extremely generous in suggesting leads, introducing me to contacts and helping me during my stay in Indonesia. I would particularly like to thank Herb Feith, who passed away in 2001, for his boundless encouragement, for his efforts to help me foster further contacts in Indonesia and for the many ideas he shared with me. Ian MacFarling and the Military Attaché at the Australian Embassy in Jakarta, Brigadier Ernie Chamberlain, also deserve a special mention for their assistance in helping me get permission from the military to do this project. Indria Samego of LIPI was supportive during my year of field research in Indonesia and Hilman Adil, as Head of the Centre for Social and Cultural Research at LIPI, was most generous to agree to act as my research counterpart for a research visa.

I thank the staff of the Armed Forces History Centre who, following formal permission from the Army Military Attache, consented to be interviewed and helped explain the history of this institution to me, in particular Rochmani Santoso, Colonel Sus Sri Hartani, Amrin Imran and A.D. Saleh. I also extend my appreciation to the heads and staff of all the museums I visited in Indonesia. Major Herkusdianto kindly arranged for me to join the Sudirman Walking Pilgrimage in addition to permitting me to attend the General Attack annual celebrations. Sokiman of the Armed Forces History Centre library, was very patient with my extensive photocopying orders. Irma Nugroho Notosusanto was extremely kind to allow me to interview her about her husband who played a controversial part in history-making. I would also like to thank the artists Saptoto and Edhi Soenarso for their interviews and patient explanations of the artistic process of making museum dioramas and monuments. Uka Tjandrasasmita and Sumartini provided me with a wealth of material on National Monument History Museum. The staffs at the National Archives, Kalyanamitra, LIPI library, the history section of the Department of Education and Nation Council of 1945 library were also very patient and helpful. George Miller at the Menzies Library at the Australian National University and Helen Soemardjo at the Monash University Asian Studies library also helped me locate relevant materials.

I am extremely grateful to those people who at various times have read drafts of chapters and related publications. Apart from my supervisors listed above, these include Herb Feith, Angus McIntyre, William Frederick, Helen Pausacker, Robert Cribb, Anthony Reid, Michele Ford, Richard Tanter, Hugh O'Neill, Steven Drakeley, Mary Zurbuchen, Henk Maier, Ros Lethbridge, Ellen Warne, Katya Johanson, Nicki Tarulevicz, Robert Horvath, Jo Cruickshank, Vannessa Hearman and my father, Gordon McGregor. The Series Editor of the Asian Studies Association of Australia Series, Howard Dick, has been extremely generous with his time and provided invaluable advice on the content of this book. Carolyn Leslie has also contributed significantly to editing the final drafts of this book.

Other people who have assisted me with materials and inspiration for different parts of this work are Harold Crouch, Onghokham, Hardoyo, Taufik Abdullah, A. Made Toni Supriatma, Bob Elson, David Reeves, Y.B. Mangunwijaya, Salim Said, Bob Lowry, Barbara Hatley, Arief Budiman, David Bourchier, Gerry van Klinken, Adrian Vickers, Harry Aveling, Sita Aripurnama, Yuyud, Jai Singh, Simon Tiranda, David Jenkins, Dwi Marianto, Jim Supangkat, Curtis Levy, Hans Antlöv, Lance Castles, Robert Goodfellow, Klaus Schreiner, Ulf Sundhaussen, Sander Adelaar and Cindy Salim.

I am very grateful to Asialink for the Weary Dunlop Asia Fellowship I was awarded in 1997–98, which enabled me to carry out my field research and acquire a healthy collection of primary and secondary sources. Antonia Finnane and Patricia Grimshaw of the University of Melbourne History Department were very kind to recommend my appointment to several teaching positions throughout my candidature, all of which broadened my knowledge of both world and Asian history and provided rewarding student interaction. Charles Coppel was also generous in giving me some research assistant work and some teaching during his absence on leave. Publication of this work was assisted by a Publication Grant from the University of Melbourne and a grant from the Research and Graduate Studies Committee, Faculty of Arts, The University of Melbourne.

Many more people have shown kindness and understanding and assisted me in more practical ways throughout this long journey. These people include friends in Indonesia who helped relieve the stress of what was sometimes a difficult and sensitive topic. During my field research, Chatarina Purnamdari, Ari, Mohamad, Sari Sitalaksmi, Dani, Irin, Soenarsono, Maretha, Irma, Sue Cattermole, Julienne Baron, Liza Kappelle, Kayoko Tsumori and Ewan Ward were great friends. In the Department of History, Ellen Warne, Katya Johanson, Jon Ritchie, Catherine Nolan, Daniel Mandel, Nicki Tarulevicz, Jemma Purdey, Richard Trembath, Kalissa Alexeyeff, Tracey Banivanua Mar and Juliet Flesch were all very supportive fellow travellers. In addition, my sister Sarah McGregor and friends provided invaluable support.

As teachers, my parents fostered a love for learning in me at an early age and I want to thank them both for that and for their unwavering love and support throughout this period of my life. During the course of this journey, I met my husband Kelana Jaya. I also want to thank Kelana for encouraging me to extend myself and for his constant belief in me, and also my young daughters Zahra and Khalila for the laughter and relief they have brought me.

All translations of Indonesian material appearing in this work are my own unless otherwise indicated. I have used modern Indonesian spelling throughout (except in cases where the title of a historical representation or the name of a person, place or publisher is provided in old spelling in the original source). Some material from Chapters 1, 2, 3, 5 and 6 has been incorporated into prior publications.[1] I wish to thank the publishers of these works for permission to reproduce some material in this book and the publishers of the visual material from whom I have also gained permission to reprint the illustrations.

The Indonesian military was referred to as ABRI (Angkatan Bersenjata Republik Indonesia, The Armed Forces of the Republic of Indonesia) for the duration of the New Order regime. ABRI included the four forces of the army, navy, air force and police. In 1998 the military's name was changed to the TNI (Tentara Nasional Indonesia, Indonesian National Army, Airforce and Navy) to reflect the separation of the police force from the military as the first step in military reform. For this reason the term military is generally used to refer to both the four forces in the New Order period and the army, navy and airforce after 1998.

Introduction

Analysing Constructions of Indonesia's Past

In February 2006, the House of Representatives approved Air Marshall Djoko Suyanto's appointment to the position of military commander. Suyanto's appointment was a milestone for several reasons. Firstly, Suyanto was the first Air Force officer to be appointed head of the Indonesian military largely due to the history of army dominance and the stigma associated with the Air Force for the involvement of some Air Force officers in the 1965 coup attempt. Secondly, Suyanto has been recognised as a reformist within the military and a man concerned with public perceptions of the military. In his 1999 chapter in the publication *New Indonesia and the TNI's Challenges — Thoughts for the Future* (*Indonesia Baru dan Tantangan TNI — Pemikiran Masa Depan*), he stated the need for the armed forces to remain neutral in politics and to prioritise the needs of the people. He also reflected openly on the reasons why the military (TNI) was now regarded so lowly, when it had once been valued by the people (according to Suyanto).[1]

The House of Representatives subjected Suyanto to a mandatory fit and proper test prior to his confirmation to the position of Commander. During this test, he faced questions about his commitment to reform and civilian supremacy, to ending military involvement in business and politics, and to resolution of human rights abuse cases involving the military.[2] Suyanto answered most questions to the satisfaction of the House of Representatives commission — with the exception of the issue of abolishing the territorial command system, which has military personnel mirroring the civilian government right down to the village level. Suyanto argued that it was necessary to maintain the territorial command, because of the early warning mechanism this system allows for future possible

1

non-conventional threats.[3] He argued that because the military's capacity
to defend the archipelago was not ideal they needed officers in the
regions to monitor security. He suggested that the newly named
kewilayahan (areal) system was a break from the past territorial system,
where the military was used to back up the government's political
manoeuvres, and that military officers could now no longer arrest people
at the request of the administration or political groups.[4] Critics in the
Anti Militarism Alliance (Aliansi Anti Militerisme) argued that this
system could be used to continue the military's political role and that
is should only be operational in a war situation.[5] Despite Air Marshal
Suyanto's reputation as a reformist, some Indonesians remain sceptical
about the commitment of the military to winding back its political roles
in the post-Suharto era (1998 onwards). In particular, they see the continuing operation of military businesses as incentive for the military to
continue intervention in political affairs.

The degree of scrutiny Suyanto was subjected to in the press and
the confirmation session in House of Representatives reflects a new level
of civilian monitoring of the military that has characterised the post-
Suharto years. The public, for example, viewed Suyanto as a good choice,
because he did not have a record of human rights abuses. This is a
consideration that had no bearing on New Order appointments to the
position of Armed Forces Commander that were made solely by President
Suharto. The concern to guard against a return to military dominance
is part of a major backlash against the Suharto regime and Suharto's use
of the military to repress dissent. Yet it is interesting that in 2004, just
six years after the fall of Suharto, Indonesians voted in a democratic
presidential election for Susilo Bambang Yudhoyono, a retired military
officer. It seems that despite the will to see an end to the militarism of
the New Order years, for many Indonesians the perception that military
men make the best leaders for the nation is entrenched.

This was an idea the Indonesian military worked hard to instil in
the New Order period (1966–98), largely by means of constructions of
the Indonesian past. One man who contributed significantly to this
perception of military men as natural leaders of the nation was the New
Order historian Nugroho Notosusanto. Nugroho had been deeply
influenced by his early exposure to military life as a *pejuang* (independence
fighter) in the 1945–49 independence struggle. Through this experience,
Nugroho became a deep admirer of military values. He was largely
responsible for the militarisation of Indonesian official history in the
New Order period. Dating from his appointment as unofficial Head of

the Armed Forces History Centre in 1964 to his death in the position of Education Minister in 1985, Nugroho worked tirelessly to promote and defend the Indonesian military and its political roles through a wide range of history projects.

History in Uniform tells the story behind these history projects. It examines military representations of the Indonesian past found in a variety of media including museums, monuments, commemorative days, films and written texts including the *National History Textbook* (Sejarah Nasional Indonesia, SNI). I am interested in how history is constructed in these media and what choices are made about these representations and why. In this way, I look at official histories as texts in an attempt to scrutinise the dynamics of history-making. This book therefore responds to a call made by Heather Sutherland in 1997 for research into

> ... how the Indonesian "national myth" has been created, revised, contested and recast over the past sixty or seventy years, with conflicting assertions and denials, deletions and much heavy editing, until a core narrative has been hammered out, defining generally accepted parameters.[6]

In contrast to earlier studies, which focus solely on New Order historiography, this book traces shifts in historical representation from the Guided Democracy era (1959–65) to the New Order (1966–98), illuminating both new and recycled trends in historical representation. One dominant pattern is the continuing use of history to bolster contemporary ideologies ranging from President Sukarno's on-going revolution to President Suharto's obsession with the Pancasila. The Pancasila is Indonesia's national philosophy, consisting of the five principles of belief in one God, humanitarianism, nationalism, democracy, and social justice. The name Pancasila and the original five principles were first drafted by Sukarno on 1 June 1945 and later amended to the five principles listed above.

Military representations of the past are significant because of the military's elevated position in Indonesian society due to their dual defence and socio-political roles. The military, especially the Army, has enjoyed a privileged position in national politics from the mid-1950s onwards, and is thus one of the most significant forces in recent Indonesian history. The operation of martial law between 1957 and 1963 increased military control over local administration. In 1958, the Army's Chief of Staff, Major General Abdul Haris Nasution, a Dutch-educated officer who had remained prominent in the military from the independence struggle onwards, formulated a concept known as the "middle way", in which the military was to be represented in the government, legislature and administration.[7] At the first Seskoad (Sekolah Staf dan Komando Angkatan Darat, Army Staff and Command School) Seminar, held in April 1965 for the purpose of developing a military doctrine, the Army put forward the concept of a combined socio-political and defence role or dual function. After the 1965 coup attempt, which triggered a military takeover, the military's dual function was ratified and more military men were moved into key positions of government. At the second Army seminar of 1966, the Army also began to position itself as playing a key role in nation- and character-building.

One consequence of the military's political dominance was that the Armed Forces History Centre's projects were not directed only at soldiers. Civilians were also subject to an aggrandised version of the military's role in history, especially in the *National History Textbook*, for which Nugroho Notosusanto was partly responsible.

Through an analysis of military history projects, I reveal how the Indonesian military used its own interpretations of its historical roles, particularly during the New Order regime, to motivate military cadets, promote internal military unity, bolster its legitimacy and create a sense of ever-present enemies within Indonesian society. *History in Uniform* illustrates the politics behind representations of some of the most influential periods of Indonesian history including the independence struggle of 1945–49, the Darul Islam revolts of the 1950s and 1960s, the radical years of late Guided Democracy, the coup attempt of 1965, the associated transition to the Suharto regime (including the anti-communist massacres) and, finally, the struggle between Islamic and secular forces in the 1980s.

In this introductory chapter, I introduce the theoretical scope of the book; the approach taken to analysing representations of the past; and the question of a potential gap between the intention of authors of these representations of the past and how such representations are interpreted by various audiences. Finally, I outline the scope and nature of this inquiry by signalling the key findings and significance of the study of official history-making.

CONCEPTUAL FRAMEWORK AND SOURCES

A central concept in this book is that of representation. A useful definition of what a representation constitutes is:

... a discursive mediation which occurs between the event and the culture which contributes to the construction of national ideologies. Its importance is not finally as a reflection, or as a refraction of the past, but as a construction of the present.[8]

The concept of representation attempts to emphasise the influence of the present on re-presenting the past. According to Pierre Nora, increasing scrutiny of the history-making process from the 1970s onwards resulted in a new distinction between the terms "history" and "memory". He implies that while "history is a representation of the past", memory represents all the possibilities of the past — including the possibilities of remembering, forgetting or even reviving lost parts of the past. Whereas memory was once subsumed by history, the emergence of a history of histories enabled history "to highlight many kinds of memory, even turn itself into a laboratory of past mentalities".[9] In *History in Uniform*, the context in which histories are produced is examined closely. The concept of representation also draws attention to the question of who performs the representing.

Sociologist Maurice Halbwachs emphasised the influence of social context over the way in which social groups remember and was largely responsible for stimulating broader interest in what is termed "collective memory".[10] Some authors, including Natalie Zemon Davis and Randolph Starn, have described museums and other forms of official history as a form of institutionalised "collective memory". Although they emphasise that when "collective memory" is invoked it is important to ask the questions "by whom, when, in which context, against what?"[11] I have avoided using the term "collective memory" because I believe this term disguises "the processes of intense contest, struggle and, in some cases annihilation"[12] of memories presented as history in the sources I examine. Because of the military's use of history to justify their political role, Indonesian military sources are more appropriately described as engaging in the institutionalisation of "official memory".[13] While suggesting that the term "collective memory" is useful in reminding us that "all remembering occurs within social contexts of environment and discourse", Amos Funkenstein cautions that a limitation of this term is that "only individuals are capable of remembering".[14]

The central focus of most studies of the Indonesian military is the military's combined political and defence roles. Most studies are chronological accounts of the evolution of the Indonesian military in politics and focus on a set time span. There are also several studies that consider military ideology. *History in Uniform* differs from previous studies of the military in that it looks closely at one specific institution of the military, the Armed Forces History Centre and its projects. It provides a record and analysis of the military's efforts at image-building aimed at both members of the military and at the wider community.

A significant shortcoming of most literature on the Indonesian military — and a great deal of literature on Indonesian history and politics — is that it largely ignores gender.[15] Recent feminist theory has introduced important information about gender and the military. Cynthia Enloe argues that the military as an institution is inherently masculinist because of the centrality of the notion of "combat" to notions of "manhood".[16] Combat is upheld as the ultimate test of manhood. This does not, however, mean that military ideology is concerned solely with men. Indeed, Cynthia Enloe suggests the concept of "masculinity" espoused by the military "only makes sense if supported by the complementary concept of 'femininity'".[17] This is because:

> Without assurance that women will play their "proper" roles, the military cannot provide men with the incentives to enlist, obey orders, give orders, fight, kill, re-enlist, and convince their sons to enlist.[18]

The fact that a highly masculinist institution controlled representations of the Indonesian past during the New Order is important, especially given the military's efforts to uphold these versions of the past as models or lessons for the young generation. If Cynthia Enloe's assertions apply to the case of Indonesia, it could be expected that when women do appear in military representations of history, they will appear in a manner consistent with tightly-constrained constructions of gender in which male and female roles are demarcated. *History in Uniform* is not a gender-centred history, but it seeks to incorporate an awareness of the fact that it concentrates mainly on male elite producers of and actors within history. I consequently reflect on military models of femininity espoused in representations of women in the two key periods of the 1945–49 revolution (Chapter 5) and the 1965 transition to the New Order (Chapter 3) and on some models of masculinity espoused by the military (Chapter 4).

Previous research on the military has largely drawn on interviews, speeches, newspapers, military doctrines and occasionally on military history in order to establish an argument about the military. This book, in contrast, begins with Indonesian military history sources as the primary focus of the research. The principal sources used are museum diorama images and captions, as observed in museums and recorded in museum guidebooks. Other sources used are museum planning reports (where available); history publications of the Armed Forces History Centre; commemorative histories of the Armed Forces History Centre; textbooks on which Nugroho worked; articles from the Armed Forces History Centre magazine (*Senakatha*); military seminar records; military doctrines and interviews with staff of the Centre. Observations of monuments, monument guidebooks, interviews with artists and other written materials produced by the military for commemoration are also used.

Previous studies of official historiography[19] have tended to focus on one specific medium, whether school history texts, museums or film. I will refer to parallels between representations in all of these sources. I work on the assumption that the Indonesian public is simultaneously exposed to many sources of representations of the Indonesian past, and that these representations, as intended by the military, work in concert to mould the historical consciousness of Indonesians. The uniformity in historical representations between these mediums is also significant, because it points to the singular versions of the national past that were circulated during the New Order period. This is not, however, to suggest that these hegemonic representations of the past were simply absorbed by Indonesians. Audiences to these mediums are, as discussed later, capable of making their own readings of these texts.

The Armed Forces History Centre actively expanded the number of military history projects throughout the regime. As well as encouraging further development of museums of the four forces and territorial divisions (Chapter 4), the Armed Forces History Centre founded a series of ABRI museums; that is, museums related to the history of the Armed Forces as a whole. This book focuses on these museums, products of this one centralised military organisation. The military museums for which the Armed Forces History Centre was directly responsible are Satriamandala Armed Forces Museum (opened in 1972); Museum of the Sacred Pancasila Monument (1982); the Museum of Eternal Vigilance (1987); the Soldiership Museum (1987); and the Museum of Communist Treachery (1993).

The collections of these museums feature relics, replica relics, photographs and weapons. The most extensive display of weapons is found in Satriamandala Armed Forces Museum, which has a separate hall devoted to weaponry used by the Indonesian military from the independence struggle through to the present.[20] It is striking that many of the weapons on display have been used against other Indonesians (internal enemies), and that they are labelled as such. This provides evidence of the extent to which internal state enemies have been "othered" by the military (Chapter 6). These representations seek to remind Indonesians that national unity, which is emphasised in Indonesia's regional museums, will be imposed when necessary by the threat or use of force.

The use of dioramas in museums of the Armed Forces History Centre is prolific. Satriamandala Armed Forces Museum has no less than 74 dioramas. They are also the most dominant feature of the four other museums of the Centre. The choice of this method of display may have been influenced by the absence of active collecting policies during the Indonesian military's campaigns, whether because of a general lack of perceived value in historical objects in Indonesia or because of the lack of funds at the disposal of the Republic. One consequence of this was that military museums founded in the New Order period competed for surviving objects from the independence struggle and had to rely on donations from private collections.[21] As a result, their collections were often incomplete. The humid tropical climate of Indonesia, which causes rapid deterioration of material objects and the cost of conservation also discouraged reliance on historical objects, even in cases where the objects were indeed valued. A further reason for the use of dioramas in the museum of the Centre was probably the personal preference of Nugroho Notosusanto himself. As noted earlier, he had worked on the National Monument History Museum, the first museum in Indonesia to use a series of dioramas to represent an historical narrative.

Monuments and commemorative days and activities are two other important means by which the Indonesian military has attempted to communicate its versions of the Indonesian past to the public for valorising the military and promoting acceptance of its political role and the people's need to be protected. Benedict Anderson first noted the significance of monuments as a form of political communication in Indonesia. He suggests that monuments "are really ways of mediating between particular types of pasts and futures". He has also focused on the use of monuments as a way of claiming "tradition".[22]

Unlike colonial museums, which Indonesians chose to continue to use,[23] Dutch monuments were torn down as vestiges of Indonesia's colonial past. Scattered around the colonial capital of Batavia was an array of monuments commemorating colonial wars, Dutch military heroes and Governor Generals. These included the Aceh Monument; the

Jan Pieterszoon Coen Monument; the Battle of Waterloo Memorial; the Michiels Monument; and the van Heutsz Monument. More so than Dutch museums, these monuments celebrated Dutch superiority and conquest, and many were pulled down in the period of the Japanese occupation and the early years of the Republic.[24]

Within a few years of the transfer of sovereignty, the Indonesian government set about creating Indonesia's own monuments. This was a project to which President Sukarno, himself an architect, was particularly devoted. Visitors to the city of Jakarta today frequently notice the proliferation of monuments across the city — including the Welcome Monument on Thamrin; the Space (*Dirgantara*) Monument on Gatot Subroto; the Free Irian Monument at Banteng Square; and the Revolution Monument on Menteng Raya.[25] Although most of the monuments in Jakarta were projects inspired by Sukarno, and do not celebrate the military, there are many other monuments throughout Indonesia that are dedicated to the Indonesian military and, in particular, to the military's role in the 1945–49 independence struggle. A directory of Army monuments, published in 1977, lists over 130 military monuments in Indonesia, most of which were devoted to the theme of the struggle.[26]

Sacred Pancasila Monument located on the outskirts of Jakarta, was the most important New Order monument for justifying the Army's ascension to power. Shortly after the 1965 coup attempt, in which six Army generals and a lieutenant were kidnapped and killed, work began on preserving the site, Lubang Buaya in Jakarta, at which the bodies of the seven Army "martyrs" were found. Over time, an elaborate monument and museum complex was built. *History in Uniform* considers the representations of history made in the monument complex, which is now controlled by the Armed Forces History Centre, and the theme of the sacredness of the Pancasila developed in this monument complex and in the annual commemorative day of 1 October.

Commemoration is an integral part of forging a national memory. Despite the plethora of commemorative days in Indonesia, including National Awakening Day (20 May); Kartini Day (21 April); Independence Day (17 August); Sacredness of Pancasila Day (1 October); Armed Forces Day (5 October); and Heroes' Day (10 November) — to name just a few — to date there have been few investigations into the politics and history of historical commemoration in Indonesia.[27] The significance of commemoration is that it "lifts from an ordinary historical sequence those extraordinary events which embody [according to official memories at least] our deepest and most fundamental values".[28] For this reason, the choice of which days to commemorate and why can be extremely political. This is eloquently demonstrated by the protest raised by nationalist Suwardi Surjaningrat (Ki Hadjar Dewantoro) in 1913 at Dutch festivities in the colony organised to celebrate the centennial of the Dutch "national liberation" from the French. In an article entitled "If I were a Dutchman", Suwardi claimed "if I were a Dutchman, I would not organise an independence celebration in a country where the independence of the people has been stolen."[29] Commemoration of 1 October in the post-1965 period similarly isolated relatives of victims of the anti-communist post-coup mass killings or those who had escaped the violence but continued to live in fear of retribution. After the crushing of the coup attempt, up to 500,000 people were killed and many others imprisoned, for membership of or affiliation with the PKI (Partai Komunis Indonesia, The Indonesian Communist Party).[30] The military's promotion of Supreme Commander General Sudirman, the first Commander of the Indonesian military, as an historical figure in monuments and the annual commemorative pilgrimage for cadets is another example of the attempted use of commemoration to instil values in Indonesians through the medium of history.

ANALYSING REPRESENTATIONS OF THE PAST

Analysis of representations of the past requires simultaneous consideration of the actual historical event represented and of the social context in which these representations are made. Barry Schwartz has criticised Maurice Halbwach's explanation of collective memory on the basis that Halbwach's preoccupation with the social context in which memories are expressed implies "there is no objectivity in events, nothing in history that transcends the peculiarities of the present".[31] This criticism could equally be applied to studies of representations. As an alternative to excessively emphasising the present, Barry Schwartz suggests we should study representations of the past on the basis that "the past cannot be literally constructed, it can only be selectively exploited".[32] *History in Uniform* concentrates on the exploitation and in some cases fabrication (*rekayasa*) of the past. One scholar who has emphasised *rekayasa* in Indonesian history is Asvi Warman Adam.[33]

    History in Uniform makes extensive use of literature that has covered the post-proclamation history of Indonesia in order to establish both the context of a museum, monument, film or textbook's production and the history of a particular event. In terms of information about the events represented, this book does not attempt to break new ground. The aim is rather to examine the history-making process. One limitation of this approach, however, is that in order to make comments about representations of the past and how it is portrayed, my own analysis relies on other representations of the past, those found in scholarship on Indonesia. Given that my aim is to expose the many selections made by museum, monument and textbook-makers, it is also necessary to acknowledge the many selections I have made from documents, images, interviews and secondary sources in order to present my own story of military representations of the Indonesian past.

Because of the military's emphasis on visual history as a resource for communicating history, this book examines a number of visual media. In the guidebook resulting from the 1973 seminar on ABRI museums, Nugroho Notosusanto reasoned:

> In a society like Indonesia which is still in the process of developing, where the habit of reading is still developing, we [presumably the military leadership] believe historical visualisation remains an effective way to express the identity of ABRI.[34]

The assumption behind what may be construed as a highly patronising comment on Nugroho's part was that, given the limitations posed by illiteracy and a lack of intellectualism (Nugroho's words), historical visualisation would reach the largest and broadest audience in Indonesia. In 1971, according to UNESCO statistics, 41 per cent of all Indonesians aged over ten had no schooling (defined as less than one year of schooling) and were thus presumably illiterate. Of the urban populations however, the figure was only 22 per cent.[35] Because museums are mostly located in cities, and those living in urban areas would be those most likely to visit them, illiteracy was not in fact so significant.

Another reason for my focus on museums, monuments, textbooks, commemorative ceremonies and activities is the authority that these sources of history invoke. They imply authority by virtue of their endorsement by the government and the fact that they were intended for mass audiences. In addition, museums and monuments, unlike written histories, do not generally emphasise their authors. An impression is consequently conveyed that they are unauthored texts. In a similar way to the artifice of commemoration, the act whereby a government selects particular events for annual commemoration is similarly disguised, thus enhancing the perceived authority of these historical activities and their messages.

The role of artists in the process of visualising the images dictated to them by historians is of considerable significance in the case of monument reliefs, museum dioramas or cinematic images. The most commonly used diorama artist and monument-maker in Indonesia is sculptor Edhi Soenarso from Yogyakarta, who generally works together with a team of artists from his company PT Tiga Hasta Kreatifa. Soenarso was the head artist for diorama images in all five museums of the Armed Forces History Centre, in addition to those in National Monument History Museum, the Vredeberg Fort Museum and other projects. On the process of compiling dioramas, Soenarso says that he obtained information about such things as the width of streets, what buildings there were and their style from photos and interviews with those who had witnessed events.[36] He claims, however, that until his most recent projects in the 1990s, he was "not allowed freedom of expression in his work and that those who commissioned him usually wanted the dioramas made to their own tastes".[37] He suggested that the Armed Forces History Centre and Nugroho (who lived to 1985), in particular, played a close role in supervising and approving diorama images.

One of the most interesting observations I made from discussions with people involved in making the dioramas was an insistence on their accuracy as representations of the past. In order to reinforce the audience perception that the dioramas represented access to the past "as it was", the Head of Satriamandala Armed Forces Museum suggested that historical souvenirs (including weapons) were often displayed alongside the dioramas to convince the visitor of the reality of this event.[38] Sound recordings were also used in Museum of the Sacred Pancasila Monument and the Museum of Communist Treachery to recreate the atmosphere of the period and location or to evoke feelings.[39] Emphasis on the "authenticity" of these representations is part of an attempt "to represent curatorial knowledge as legitimate and authoritative".[40] In a fascinating article examining the social hierarchies in museums and the processes behind museum displays, Georgina Born exposes the artifice of dioramas by means of an image of a museum worker installing a giant caterpillar in a natural history diorama exhibit.[41] This image reveals what museum audiences rarely, if ever see: human agency behind these images and the fact that, like a written text, these representations are also made by someone.

Dioramas, as pictorial representations of the past, go further than objects towards interpreting the past. Klaus Schreiner claims that the prolific use of dioramas in Indonesian museums may be motivated by the desire to provide "a definitive and authoritative interpretation of historical facts".[42] This is consistent with trends in New Order historiography. One means by which historians or museum curators gain further control over the way in which audiences interpret dioramas is by means of captions. Captions attempt to dictate the story that dioramas tell. As Eilean Hooper-Greenhill notes, museum labelling is a means of controlling the meaning of a visual image because "we see things according to what is said about them".[43] All dioramas in museums of the Armed Forces History Centre are, consistent with the requirements of the International Community of Museums (ICOM), accompanied by captions in both Indonesian and English.[44] The fact that captions also appear in English reminds us that these military museums were also intended for international audiences.

AUTHORS AND AUDIENCES OF REPRESENTATIONS

It should be noted from the outset that *History in Uniform* focuses primarily on the military as producers of representations of the Indonesian past rather than the audiences of these representations. Museums, monuments, textbooks and commemorative ceremonies are some of the most public images of the Indonesian past that the Indonesian military have authored. More than anything else, these forms of commemoration are records of the Indonesian military's self-made image. As Susan Douglas notes in her work on media audiences:

> We will always know more about the motives and assumptions of the producers of media images — including their assumptions about the audience — than we will about the audience itself.[45]

Sources on audiences are far more limited because their opinions are harder to access and analyse.

How audiences respond to military representations of the past in museums and other forms of commemoration or history is difficult to measure without surveying museum visitors, participants in commemoration or students. Because of the military's sensitivity to my topic, I was not permitted to conduct surveys amongst visitors or to access the comments in museum visitor books. I acknowledge the potential gap between the messages the military attempts to communicate in representations of the past and the messages audiences take away from them. Curator Gurian suggests:

> The public continually thwarts our attempts to teach incrementally
> in our exhibition. They come when they want, leave when they
> want, and look at what they want while they are there.[46]

Whilst visiting the museums and interviewing staff, including asking
questions about audience responses, I did occasionally come across
information that suggested that the messages absorbed were different
from the intended messages. Wherever possible I have tried to incorporate this information into my discussion to emphasise the autonomy
of audiences to make their own meanings of military representations of
the past. Another aspect of audience response is that "viewers do not
come to museums as cultural blanks".[47] Audience responses to mass
media are conditioned by their exposure to similar messages in other
mediums such as films, newspapers or school history texts. In some cases,
the audience's over-exposure to hegemonic histories may have encouraged
their dismissal of the history presented in these museums as fiction.

One important factor in the receptivity of audiences to these
military-produced representations of the past is public attitudes towards
the military. Because the Indonesian military came to life at the beginning
of an independence struggle, there is undeniably a sense of romance
about their origins. This is a fact about which the Indonesian military
is not naïve and which has been repeatedly emphasised in their histories
and doctrines. Some key military slogans are, for example, "ABRI was
born from the people" (*ABRI lahir dari rakyat*) and "ABRI is the child
of the independence struggle" (*ABRI adalah anak kandung perjuangan
kemerdekaan*). The involvement of the military in the independence
struggle may have instilled a sense of respect for the military, yet much
of this respect has been eroded by years of military dominance, not
only in politics, but also in business.[48] While some students protested
against military dominance, there were also some Indonesians, young
men in particular, to whom a culture of militarism appealed. One
example of this is the popularity of the university military regiments
(Regimen Mahasiswa, Menwa). There were also some Indonesians, who
— at least until the suppression of the Malari riots of 1974 — held
the military in high regard due to their role in crushing the communists
after the 1965 coup attempt.

The Indonesian military of the New Order is often portrayed as
uncompromising and imposing its will on citizens by means of force.[49]
In the ideological realm, however, the activities of the Armed Forces
History Centre provide evidence of military concern for their image and
on-going attempts to promote their image to the people. The curators

of museums of the Centre were aware that some Indonesians feared the military. They took steps to overcome this fear by suggesting their museums be friendlier places. The 1973 guidebook for planning military museums recommended two ways in which military museums could overcome the intimidation associated with the military so as to reach broader publics. It is, for example, specifically stated in the guidebook that museum security staff should not wear their uniforms to avoid the psychological effect of the military uniform on visitors. The guidebook explains that if a person intends to visit an armed forces museum and then sees a guard in military uniform, they may be frightened and lose their desire to come to the museum.[50] The guidebook further elaborates that, although military museums display war collections, in reality the purpose of displays is to instil the attribute of "knighthood" and to communicate that the armed forces are the "protectors of the people". The guidebook also claims that military museums, including some already in existence, would be more effective at reaching the public if they were located at places other than military headquarters to remove the possible negative psychological effect.[51] Given the claim that the Indonesian military is the protector of the people and the common expression that "ABRI is born from the people", these are curious acknowledgments of the military's own awareness about the gap between military-produced ideology and reality.

OUTLINE OF *HISTORY IN UNIFORM*

History in Uniform does not cover every museum, monument, commemorative activity, textbook or history sponsored by the Indonesian military. There are too many such projects. Instead, this is a selective analysis of projects under the auspices of the Armed Forces History Centre and/or the military historian, Nugroho Notosusanto. One large museum and monument complex not examined here, for example, is the Return of Yogya Museum (Museum Yogya Kembali) located in the city of Yogyakarta, which is run by a private foundation. In addition, there are many other so-called "struggle museums" located around Indonesia that are not covered for reasons of space.[52] The military projects I examine were produced between 1964, when the Armed Forces History Centre produced its first written history and 1993, which marked the last museum project of the New Order period, the Museum of Communist Treachery. The museums, monuments and commemorative celebrations listed as the central focus of this study are all located in Java, especially

Jakarta. This is a product of the concentration of power and wealth in Jakarta and the fact that the Armed Forces History Centre is itself located in Jakarta. This does not mean that military history projects in other islands of Indonesia are not significant, but limitations of time and resources precluded a wider investigation.

This book focuses primarily on representations of history made in the New Order period, with some comparisons to Guided Democracy and earlier histories. In May 1998, less than a month after I returned from my field research in Indonesia, Suharto resigned as President of Indonesia, thereby marking the end of the New Order regime. This had several implications for my research. The great majority of my observations of military representations of the past in museums, monuments and ceremonies were recorded during the New Order period. My own work consequently became a frozen record of how the military recorded the past during this period.

In the post-New Order period, a climate of greater openness has ensured that official history is being openly challenged in Indonesia. These challenges provide evidence of the extent to which history was tightly guarded in the New Order period. They also highlight private contestation of official versions of the past, which had previously been muted due to press censorship. These challenges to official history also demonstrate that, despite the accumulated cynicism towards history during the New Order period, history is still important to many people.

Chapter 1 discusses the history of history-writing in Indonesia. I highlight the extent of military control over historical representation during the New Order regime and the extent to which the military consciously turned to history as a source of legitimacy for their dominance by examining their takeover of the National Monument History Museum. After reflecting on the defining features of the New Order regime, I look more broadly at the role of history, education and thought control in authoritarian regimes, thus placing the regime in comparative perspective.

Chapter 2 introduces the central historian of the New Order regime, Nugroho Notosusanto, and traces the origins of the Armed Forces History Centre through which Nugroho became the voice of official historiography. Drawing on extensive interviews with people who knew Nugroho, I provide unique insights into the key historian behind most of the history projects discussed in this book. I examine Nugroho's early life, charting the impact of his participation in the 1945–49 independence struggle on his thinking as evidenced in his short stories and his own commentary. I point to his genuine belief, shared by his contemporaries, in the Indonesian military as leaders of the nation. I also reflect on the significance of his thwarted desire to pursue a military career to his history projects.

The second part of Chapter 2 looks at General Nasution's initiative to found the Armed Forces History Centre in 1964 to defend the military's version of the 1948 Madiun rebellion as a communist plot. The first history project the Centre worked on was a response to the proposed issuance of a communist history project, in which the Madiun rebellion was to be omitted, and thus an important part of the power struggle between the military and communists in the late Guided Democracy period. This history project also marked the beginnings of Nugroho's career as military historian.

Representations of the 1965 coup attempt were of critical importance to the legitimacy of the New Order regime because of the perceived political necessity of public belief in the coup being a communist and not an Army plot. Chapter 3 outlines the initial production and continuing embellishment of the official version of the 1965 coup attempt in a series of history projects. Public acceptance of this version of the coup, combined with the Army's successful suppression of the rebellion, spelled the end for the Communist Party. This version of the coup was thus crucial to the legitimacy of the new regime. It was also used to justify the 1966–68 anti-communist massacres and to promote the New Order's commitment to the national philosophy Pancasila, especially the first principle of "Belief in One God".

Drawing on interviews with key employees of the Armed Forces History Centre, I first trace the role of the Centre in promptly providing an official military interpretation of the 1965 coup attempt, in which six top-ranking generals and one lieutenant were kidnapped and killed, as a communist plot. I also uncover Nugroho's part in the political transition from the Sukarno to Suharto presidencies in his capacity as the key historian for the Armed Forces History Centre and as Assistant Rector in Charge of Student Affairs at the University of Indonesia.

Secondly, I trace the progressive memorialisation of the official version of the coup as a communist plot under the direction of both President Suharto and Nugroho Notosusanto. This included the production of a four-hour docu-drama, the creation of a monument and museum complex built around the disused well at Lubang Buaya, into which the bodies of the Army victims of the 1965 coup had been dumped, and annual commemoration of Sacred Pancasila Day at this site. The chapter examines the emergence of a consolidated story about the origins of the New Order regime encapsulated by the key themes of the Army as the guardians of the people and the national philosophy Pancasila; the Communist Party as a national traitor; and the New Order regime as the restorer of societal order. Drawing on commentary from the artists behind these projects and a history of art in Indonesia, it also considers the symbolism of this story of the coup attempt and the consequences of these potent representations for surviving Communist Party members and their families.

Chapter 4 examines the use of history by the Indonesian military to both consolidate military unity and to instil belief in the legitimacy of the dual function (*dwifungsi*), especially among the younger generation. Central to these aims were representations of the military's roles in the 1945–49 independence struggle.

The Armed Forces History Centre attempted to use the history of the independence struggle in the early years of the New Order regime as a means of consolidating unity amongst the four military services. The Communist Party and President Sukarno had successfully exploited divisions between and within the Army, Navy, Air and Police Forces. To achieve this aim of building internal unity, the Centre founded the first combined museum of the four forces of the military, Satrimandala Armed Forces Museum. Instilled with visions of rivalling other great military museums that he had visited such as England's Imperial War Museum, Nugroho Notosusanto intended this museum to be a place of reverence for the Indonesian military. Representations of the 1945–49 revolution, or independence struggle, were central to military efforts to justify a continuing political role (dual function) and to promote military values more widely amongst the population. The 1972 Army seminar on the transfer of the so-called 1945 values marked the beginning of a concerted effort to align the military exclusively with the legendary 1945 generation and the spirit of the revolution. I examine how seminar participants defined the 1945 values and the plan to promote military values not only within the military, but also to school and university students by means of new history projects. In Chapter 4, I also reveal new insights into military ideology and the place of the hero General Sudirman within it, based on my observations of the 1997 Sudirman Walking Pilgrimage, which military cadets complete as a final component of their training at the Military Academy in Magelang.

Chapter 5 considers two other projects inspired by the 1972 seminar on the transfer of values: the *National History Textbook* released in the late 1970s, and the school subject the *History of the National*

Struggle (Pendidikan Sejarah Perjuangan Bangsa, PSPB), which Nugroho implemented in his capacity as Education Minister in the early 1980s. In both the textbook and the curriculum subject, Nugroho turned to representations of the independence struggle to promote reverence for the military and military values. I examine representations of history in these texts and criticisms of these projects and broader New Order debates about history writing.

Chapter 6 examines the direction of the Armed Forces History Centre after Nugroho's death in 1985. It identifies new and recycled themes in three major museum projects. In the context of the emergence of a new generation of soldiers, the National Soldiership Museum focuses on establishing a long tradition of soldiership in Indonesia. The Centre's two final projects the Museum of Eternal Vigilance and the Museum of Communist Treachery focused on continuing threats to the national philosophy and hence the nation from "extreme Islam" and communism respectively. Each project reveals significant shifts in military ideology and continuing efforts on the military's part to claim legitimacy in the closing decade of the New Order regime.

In the concluding chapter, I reflect on the production and content of New Order ideology and the implications this has for understanding the regime and the Indonesian military. I compare the efforts of the Indonesian military to uphold its legitimacy through history with those of similar military regimes. I question how authoritarian the regime was in enforcing its versions of the past and the part of other historians in supporting or resisting these hegemonic representations. Finally, I trace the impact of the military's promised retreat to the barracks since the fall of Suharto on military constructions of Indonesia's past and reflect on the history as a tool of authoritarianism.

1

History in the Service of an Authoritarian Regime

Debates over the roles and function of history have become more intense in recent decades, particularly in the domain of textbooks. In Japan and Australia, these debates have centred on how to deal, or indeed whether to deal with past violence. Conservatives in Japan, led by the Orthodox History Group, have rejected versions of Japanese colonialism and of Japan's crimes in World War II which portray the Japanese in a negative light, arguing that history should instead foster national pride.[1] In Australia, conservatives have argued for the teaching of national history that does not overemphasise settler violence or crimes against indigenous Australians, instead presenting a version of the past designed to instil pride in white Australians.[2] In both Japan and Australia, historians and other concerned members of the public have contested these conservative views in debates and protests. In Indonesia, by contrast, the past has only recently become a topic Indonesians can freely debate. For the duration of the New Order regime, history was used to defend the military's political role and to promote nationalism and conformity. Despite the end to restrictions on freedom of expression in 1999, many Indonesian historians have been reluctant to abandon the idea of history as a source for nation-building.

In this chapter, I examine the long-established trend in Indonesia of using history to foster nationalism, along with muted resistance to this trend. The New Order regime was not the only regime to use history for regime legitimation. This trend was also prevalent in the period of Guided Democracy. During the New Order period, however, the Indonesian military took centre-stage in producing and monitoring representations of Indonesia's past.

One of the clearest examples of the military's foray into the production and control of nationalist history was President Suharto's appointment of Nugroho Notosusanto to take over the National Monument
History Museum in 1968. Through an analysis of the ways in which
Nugroho revised the original Guided Democracy version of scenes for
this museum, some of the dominant themes of New Order historiography
become apparent — including the promotion of military supremacy, a
commitment to the Pancasila and the need for a strong military role in
safeguarding the nation.

The New Order regime is often described as authoritarian. Certainly
in the realm of ideology and hence official history this holds true, but
the constellation of power throughout this regime between Suharto
and the military was not constant. In this chapter, I also examine the
shifting dimensions of military power and those key ideological tenets
of the New Order regime identified by David Bourchier (such as familism
and organicism). In doing so, I point to some key parallels between New
Order Indonesia and pre-war Japan. These parallels also extend to the
ways in which both regimes used history for legitimacy. There are
similarities, for example, with the case of militarised pre-World War II
Japan and the associated Imperial Rescript on Education to instil military
values in young Japanese students with the Pancasila-based education
system in New Order Indonesia.

A HISTORY OF HISTORY IN INDONESIA

On 17 August 1966, as President Sukarno was being slowly eased out
of office by Major General Suharto and the military, he delivered his last
Independence Day speech entitled "Never Ever Leave History". In this
address, Sukarno criticised the recent decision taken by the Provisional
People's Consultative Assembly (MPRS, Majelis Permusyawaratan Rakyat
Sementara) to ratify the Instruction of 11 March 1966, an instruction
issued under pressure by President Sukarno to Major General Suharto
directing him to take all necessary measures to ensure security and
stability (a move Sukarno described as a coup); he continued to refer to
Malaysia as a neo-colonialist project (despite his knowledge that Foreign
Minister Malik had just negotiated a secret deal to end hostilities);[3] and
he insisted that the Conference of the New Emerging Forces (a sequel
to the 1963 Games of the New Emerging Forces GANEFO[4]) should go
ahead soon. He described the period that Indonesia was passing through
as a critical period in history, one in which the direction of the nation

would be decided. His central message was that Indonesian history —
especially the last 20 years — had been about the struggle to rid
Indonesia and the world of imperialist influence and warned that those
who sought to ignore this history would fail. He referred back to the
Indonesian Declaration of Independence as a manifesto to abolish
colonialism everywhere.[5] While Sukarno's message about the direction
that history had set for Indonesia was largely ignored, the leaders of
the newly emerging New Order regime heeded his message about the
importance of the past. From the 1965 coup attempt onwards, the new
military leaders turned to producing their own representations of history
for the purpose of presenting a new historical model appropriate to the
direction in which they sought to move Indonesia.

There is a well-established precedent in Indonesia of recording the
past. In the territory now known as Indonesia, past rulers documented
their glory in written records. The court chronicler Prapañca, for example,
from the Majapahit kingdom, recorded the glorious features of that
kingdom in his fourteenth-century poem *De'sawarnana.*[6] Aristocratic
families also frequently compiled genealogies as a means of recording
persons and events for posterity and aligning themselves with their most
prestigious ancestors.[7] The Indonesian word for "history", "*sejarah*",
derives from the Arabic word "*syajarah*", which means "genealogy".[8]

In the early twentieth century, in the era of nationalist awakening,
the idea of a former golden age in Indonesian history which encompassed the former kingdoms of Majapahit and Sriwijaya, and the shared
experience of "three hundred and fifty years" of Dutch colonialism,
formed an integral part of Indonesian nationalist thought. This is clearly
articulated in Sukarno's famous speech delivered in his defence before
the colonial court in 1930.[9] From its beginnings, representations of
history were therefore an important part of Indonesian nationalism.

One important issue discussed at the first conference on history
in Indonesia, held in 1957 at Gadjah Mada University in Yogyakarta,
was whether history should be used to create and bolster support for
nationalism, or if it should be protected from the immediate demands
of nationalism and instead be used to promote a "general deepening of
social understanding".[10] Although many new nations were turning to
nationalist history as a means of consolidating a sense of being one
nation, others had lost enthusiasm for nationalism and nationalist histories.
This was largely a result of their experience of two world wars and a
perception that the nationalist histories of Germany and Japan, which
respectively exalted the nations of Nazi Germany and military expansionist

Japan, had in part been responsible for the catastrophes of these wars.[11] In post-war Japan, Minister of State Shidehara Kijuro indeed pointed to the "misbegotten educational system as a root cause of the war because of this imperialist ultra-patriotic formalism".[12] Some Indonesians, such as the historian Soedjatmoko, shared these concerns about the dangers of too much emphasis on nationalist history,[13] yet for various reasons, including the youth of the Indonesian nation and the need for forging an identity, nationalist historiography continued to be prioritised. In the early 1960s, as Indonesia embarked upon the mission of the "return" of West Irian and the Malaysia confrontation, the tendency towards prioritising nationalist history, this time with anti-imperialist, socialist undercurrents, continued. In the New Order period, nationalist historiography, now with a militarist slant, remained a priority.

There is very little material that deals with official historiography or elite representations of history in the period of Guided Democracy. Some exceptions are Ruth McVey, who has examined communist histories in the Guided Democracy period;[14] Klaus Schreiner, who has written about state-endorsed veneration of Indonesian heroes dating from the late 1950s onwards;[15] and H.A.J. Klooster, who has provided the most comprehensive survey of official (including military) histories.[16] *History in Uniform* aims to fill this gap by looking at several history projects that eventuated in the late Guided Democracy period, including the National Monument History Museum, the National Front publication *Sedjarah Pergerakan Nasional* (History of the National Movement); and several military specific works, including *Sedjarah Singkat Perdjuangan Bersendjata Bangsa Indonesia* (A Concise History of the Armed Struggle of the Indonesian Nation) and the contributions of each of the Armed Forces to *20 Tahun Indonesia Merdeka* (20 Years of Indonesian Freedom). These history texts variously promoted nationalism; the idea of a progression towards socialism; the idea of history of and for the people; the role of each of the Armed Forces in the revolution; and military accounts of the past.

Official historiography produced in New Order Indonesia has received more scholarly scrutiny than histories produced in the Guided Democracy period, perhaps because of the duration of the New Order regime. In many instances, New Order historiography has been considered in a vacuum. Themes, such as the characterisation of the 1950s as a period of chaos and the suppression of regional difference,[17] which authors have pointed to as features of New Order official historiography, also appear in Guided Democracy histories. Although the main focus of *History in Uniform* is New Order official histories, it is therefore also necessary to examine Guided Democracy histories in order to make observations about the continuities and breaks between these sets of histories, and the extent of military influence over each. Although comparisons with works produced in the 1950s are also useful, a further reason for comparing official history in both the Guided Democracy and New Order periods is that, during both regimes, it was expected to conform to the ideological priorities of the national leadership.

In the period of Guided Democracy, historians and all other public figures were under pressure to toe the Sukarnoist line by inserting references to President Sukarno's Political Manifesto (Manipol-Usdek)[18] ideology about the on-going revolution towards socialism, into their work. The trend towards ideological conformity is perhaps best illustrated by the response to the Manikebu (Manifesto Kebudayaan, Cultural Manifesto). In 1964, a group of artists issued this manifesto, which rejected the idea of "Politics is the Commander" espoused by the communist-affiliated cultural organisation LEKRA (Lembaga Kebudayaan Rakyat, Institute of People's Culture), and defended the right to freedom of expression in literature and art, based on the cultural philosophy of the Pancasila.[19] The signatories to this manifesto were subsequently attacked by LEKRA in the press and in demonstrations on the basis of the manifesto's failure to mention Manipol (Manifesto Politik, Political Manifesto). In April 1964, President Sukarno banned the Manikebu and purges followed of Manikebuists or "reactionary elements" especially in the area of education.[20] The historian Taufik Abdullah suggests that history also underwent Manipol-isasi in this period, such that historical thinking was constrained by power holders for the purposes of "the revolution".[21]

While Abdullah implies historians felt greater freedom to express their views free of ideological language at the beginning of the New Order,[22] history was not released from the shackles of the state's ideological needs. Official historians were, as we shall see, also required to project the regime's preoccupation with the Pancasila and the 1945 Constitution and to provide justification for the military's political role. Although historians were able to put forward some criticisms of parts of official history when they felt "the truth" had been stretched too far, such as Nugroho's efforts to downplay Sukarno's role in conceptualising the Pancasila (Chapter 5), some aspects of official New Order history were tightly guarded and effectively deemed off-limits for academic analysis. Most historians knew the permissible limits of investigations into the past. Until 1996, with the publication of *Shadows of the PKI* (Bayang Bayang PKI)[23] for example, no Indonesian had attempted publicly to launch a book that challenged the official version of the 1965 coup attempt, according to which the coup was a communist plot. This publication, as with foreign publications that made their way to Indonesia and mentioned other versions of the coup, was quickly banned. The most common official reason provided for the banning of books was that the facts and representation of historical truth (*fakta dan kebenaran sejarah*) presented in these works were not acceptable. Oei Tjoe Tat's memoir *Oei Tjoe Tat, Assistant to President Sukarno* (Oei Tjoe Tat, Pembantu Presiden Sukarno) a book which included an alternative view of politics in the period of Guided Democracy and the transition to the New Order was banned on the ground that it gave the "wrong view" about the 1965 coup and about communism.[24] The government endorsed hegemonic, tightly controlled interpretations of some parts of the Indonesian past. Obstacles were furthermore created to prevent research into sensitive topics, such as the period of Guided Democracy and the 1965–68 transition period. Materials such as newspapers from the 1965–67 transition years were removed from public libraries. In addition, historians and students had first to get permission from intelligence agencies Bakorstanas (Badan Koordinasi Pemantapan Stabilitas Nasional, Co-ordinating Agency for the Maintenance of National Stability) and Bakin (Badan Koordinasi Intelijen Negara, National Intelligence Co-ordinating Agency) and the Head of the National Library to use materials that were banned to the public.[25] Several studies of the highly sensitive post-coup killings were, however, completed by Indonesian historians whilst studying abroad.[26]

Professional historians such as Taufik Abdullah, Sartono Kartodirdjo, Onghokham and Anhar Gonggong were frustrated by the restrictions placed on history during the New Order period. Although they all protested the effects such history would have on young minds, an important question is the impact of these histories on students or museum audiences. On the basis of a study of a single classroom in Solo, James Siegel suggests that school students were well aware that the history they were taught was simply part of a knowledge store they were required to learn and repeat.[27] Yet the fact that students felt angry towards their history teachers when alternative versions of the coup attempt of 1965 were published, in the climate of press openness after Suharto's resignation in May 1998, indicates many were unaware of how censored were the versions of the past they had been taught.[28] Gerry Van

Klinken argues that New Order historiography was anti-intellectual and responsible for the appalling historical ignorance even among liberal arts university students in Indonesia.[29]

THE MILITARISATION OF HISTORY UNDER THE NEW ORDER

A clear example of the military's new-found role as both dictator and guardian of official history is Suharto's appointment of Nugroho Notosusanto, then Head of the Armed Forces History Centre, to oversee representations of the national past in the National Monument History Museum. The museum, located in the base of the famous National Monument (Monumen Nasional or Monas) (Illustration 1.1), was a project first initiated by President Sukarno in the late Guided Democracy era. By the time of the coup attempt of 1965, the Guided Democracy committee, headed by the then-Minister of Education Priyono, a supporter of the nationalist-communist Murba party,[30] had completed their written descriptions of the scenes to be installed and sketches prepared by a team of artists for the planned dioramas were awaiting approval from Sukarno. During the period of violence, turmoil, and rapid change following the coup, the museum project lay dormant. Four years later, in 1969, the now-established Suharto regime turned its attention to this museum.[31]

A comparison between the overarching themes of the two versions of this museum highlights the emergence of what were to become dominant themes in the New Order version of the national past. Although the version of the national past compiled by the Guided Democracy museum committee was never installed in the National Monument History Museum, from surviving records it is clear that the key themes that shaped Sukarno's vision of the Indonesian past were progression towards a brighter future, characterised by Indonesian socialism and appreciation of Indonesia's greatness as a nation.[32] Nugroho's version of the national past as put forward in the new diorama scenes, by contrast, emphasised the Indonesian military and the Pancasila, erased all mention of socialism and severely curtailed Sukarno's historical profile. This was consistent with President Suharto's instruction that the museum committee reflect in their displays the changes in national direction mandated by politicians in the parliamentary sessions held during the transition years from 1966 to 1968.[33] Decisions made in these sessions included, among many other things, to enhance the military's political role, to abandon socialism as a national goal, to ban the Communist Party, and

Illustration 1.1 The National Monument.
Source: Image reproduced from a postcard. In the foreground, beside the National Monument, is a statue of the hero Diponegoro.

to strip Sukarno of his titles. These decisions were also a product of the important 1966 Second Army Seminar held at Seskoad (the Army Staff and Command School) in Bandung, in which the military confirmed its role in national leadership. The Provisional People's Consultative Assembly also decided to increase emphasis on religion, to ratify the Instruction of 11 March (Supersemar), in which President Sukarno handed power over to Major General Suharto, and to appoint Suharto as the new President. The new vision of the past put forward in this museum also reflected an important theme promoted by the central New Order ideologue, Lieutenant General Ali Moertopo: that the New Order itself constituted "a negation of the Old Order, a renovation along new lines and patterns, especially of values".[34]

One dilemma for the New Order committee was that the museum displays were required to cover more than four centuries of history and also to project and legitimate the military's increased role in society, yet the Indonesian military had only been created in 1945. In Section B of the museum, dealing with anti-colonial resistance, the New Order committee had planned to include depictions of virtually the same heroes as the Guided Democracy committee. They chose, however, to emphasise the military deeds of these men rather than their status as individual heroes who resisted colonialism. The scene labelled "The hero Diponegoro" (Pahlawan Diponegoro) in the 1964 outline, for example, was changed to "The Diponegoro War" (Perang Diponegoro). The word *perang* (war) similarly replaced the word *pahlawan* (hero) in scenes concerning Iman Bonjol and Si Singamangaradja, who also fought against the Dutch. By shifting the emphasis in these scenes Nugroho as the museum committee head attempted to highlight a tradition of knighthood or soldiery to justify the New Order military's increasing role in domestic politics. An interesting adjustment to the scene titled "The Birth of the Indonesian Military" was the addition of a backdrop showing Borobudur (Illustration 1.2). Borobudur is a symbol for the ancient past, for the golden age, the time at which Indonesia was great.[35] The resulting diorama image replicated a photograph of General Sudirman and his troops in front of the temple. One possible motive of both the person who took or requested the original photograph and of Nugroho who chose this image to become a museum scene was to associate this ancient temple with Indonesia's military, thereby suggesting that the nation's military tradition was equally old. This theme was later reinforced in Nugroho's project, the National Soldiership Museum. In choosing this image, Nugroho also associated the military with a non-Islamic

Illustration 1.2   The Birth of the Armed Forces.
Source: Image from Badan Pengelola Monumen Nasional di Jakarta, *Monumen Nasional Dengan Museum Sejarah Nasionalnya*, Badan Pengelola Monumen Nasional di Jakarta, Jakarta, 1989, p. 47.

national symbol at a time at which Islam posed the greatest political challenge to the military.

Projecting Pancasila values back on to the distant past was equally difficult as was the task of representing the abstract principles of the Pancasila, including belief in one God, humanitarianism, nationalism, democracy, and social justice. Some of these themes are nonetheless discernible in the new 1969 museum scenes. The committee, for example, added four scenes representing the role of religions in promoting national unity. The four new religious scenes included: (1) "The Blend of Sivaism and Buddhism in Temples", (2) "The *Pesantren* (Islamic boarding school) as a Unifier of the Indonesian Nation in the Fourteenth Century", (3) "The Activities of the Protestant Church in the Process of Uniting the Indonesian Nation" and (4) "The Role of the Roman Catholic Church in Unifying the Nation". This was clearly an attempt to include references to the first principle of Pancasila, belief in one God, and to reflect the new regime's commitment to religion. Religious organisations were key participants in the military-led, anti-Communist alliance that worked to overthrow President Sukarno and destroy the Indonesian Communist Party. Many who joined this alliance believed that religion had been under-emphasised during the Guided Democracy period. The New Order government, by contrast, made religion a priority both to appease religious forces and as a bulwark against communism.

Apart from the new trends of accentuating the role of the Indonesian military and the Pancasila in the Indonesian past, the New Order version of the national past embodied in this museum also established the trend of writing former President Sukarno out of history. The New Order committee had to decide how to deal not only with Sukarno's ideological influence on the original museum plan, but also how to represent him as an historical figure. During the period between the 1965 coup and 1969, Sukarno had gradually been eased out of office. However, the military leadership still feared Sukarno's ability to rally the people. Nugroho, as the museum head, was particularly concerned with controlling what he described as a cult of personality focused on Sukarno.[36]

One way in which the New Order committee diminished Sukarno's profile was through reducing the emphasis on the connection between Sukarno and the Pancasila in the scene concerning the creation of the Pancasila. The version of this scene planned by the 1964 committee was entitled the birth of the Pancasila (Lahirnya Pancasila). This scene was to depict Sukarno's first articulation of the five principles of the Pancasila on 1 June 1945.[37] In the revised scenes planned for the 1969 museum, the title and focus of this diorama are subtly changed to fit Nugroho Notosusanto's own theory of the origins of the Pancasila. According to that theory, Sukarno was only one of three of the excavators (*penggali*) of the Pancasila, and in fact the real birth date of Pancasila was 18 August 1945, the date on which the Pancasila was legally confirmed, together with the 1945 Constitution.[38] The title of the revised scene was The Ratification of the Pancasila and the 1945 Constitution (Pengesahan Pancasila dan UUD 1945). Although the order and exact wording of the principles of the Pancasila changed slightly between 1 June and 18 August, Nugroho's revision was based on a pedantic distinction to disassociate the Pancasila from Sukarno so that the New Order regime could claim the five principles as its own.[39]

The revised Pancasila scene, in which Sukarno still appeared, constituted a more subtle form of censoring Sukarno out of the national past. Three other scenes proposed by the 1964 committee in which Sukarno was featured as the principal actor were also erased in the 1969 plans. These included the scenes showing Sukarno in front of the

Colonial Court and in the act of issuing the Presidential Decree of 5 July 1959, as well as a diorama about the 1964 Games of the New Emerging Forces (GANEFO).

Ironically, after Nugroho had reduced the number of scenes glorifying Sukarno, he attempted to promote a similar cult of personality featuring Suharto. He inserted Suharto, together with other military men, into new scenes. Suharto appeared in exactly three scenes in the 1969 museum plan, including the "Liberation of West Irian" (Pembebasan Irian Jaya), "Sacred Pancasila Day" (Hari Kesaktian Pancasila) and the "Instruction of 11 March" (Surat Perintah 11 Maret Supersemar): the General had figured in no scenes in the first museum plan. General Sudirman was also awarded one scene focusing exclusively on his role as the first Commander during the 1945–49 Revolution.

The most important scenes in this museum from the new regime's perspective were those that represented the transition to the New Order. The version of the transition set down in this museum encapsulated in three scenes of "Sacred Pancasila Day", "Three Demands of the People" (Aksi Aksi Tri Tuntutan Rakyat, Tritura), and the "Instruction of 11 March" would become a familiar trilogy in official representations of the transition period for the next 30 years.[40] These were the most important scenes in this museum because they attempted to establish the legitimacy of the new regime.

The first transition scene entitled "Sacred Pancasila Day" represents the military's suppression of the coup attempt on 1 October 1965 as the salvation of the Pancasila. This scene was meant to depict a significant break with the past and, once again, to associate the Pancasila closely with the New Order regime. By the time this museum scene was designed, representations of events on 1 October had already become familiar icons in the regime's portrayals of its own origins. Each year since 1967, 1 October had been commemorated at the site where the bodies of the victims of the coup attempt had been dumped.[41] Most Indonesians would recognise the scene chosen as the subject of the diorama image (Illustration 1.3) due to the repeated publication of photographs taken at the site of Lubang Buaya on the day the bodies were recovered from the well. Major General Suharto is depicted in his camouflage uniform and sunglasses standing over the well at Lubang Buaya, overseeing the recovery of the bodies of the murdered Army officers who fell victims to the coup. This scene and the accompanying text replicate the official version of the 1965 coup attempt (Chapter 3), according to which the communists are held responsible for the coup

Illustration 1.3   Sacred Pancasila Day.
Source: Image from Badan Pengelola Monumen Nasional di Jakarta, *Monumen Nasional dengan Museum Sejarah Nasionalnya*, Badan Pengelola Monumen Nasional di Jakarta, Jakarta, 1989, p. 60.

and the military are positioned as the saviours. It also positions the communists as an anti-Pancasila force.

The second scene entitled the "Three Demands of the People" focuses on the 1966 student protests resulting from President Sukarno's lack of response to the three student demands to lower prices, ban the Communist Party, and purge the Cabinet of Sukarnoists and Communists (Illustration 1.4).[42] The diorama features a group of students and other members of society assembled in front of the National Monument. Members of the crowd are holding up placards detailing each of the demands. A group of students, wearing the yellow jackets of the University of Indonesia, stand at the forefront of the crowd, facing a soldier of the Cakrabirawa Presidential Guard holding a rifle, who appears at the front of the scene with his back to the diorama lens. A bloodied yellow student shirt, presumably that of student martyr Arief Rahman Hakim, is visible on the ground between the students and the soldier. It appears as if the students are demanding an explanation. In modern Indonesian history,

Illustration 1.4   Three Demands of the People.
Source: Image from Badan Pengelola Monumen Nasional di Jakarta, *Monumen Nasional dengan Museum Sejarah Nasionalnya*, Badan Pengelola Monumen Nasional di Jakarta, Jakarta, 1989, p. 61.

students have a reputation for acting as a moral force.[43] The committee's inclusion of this scene is meant to suggest that the military, working with the students to crush the Communists, also constituted a moral force. The caption to the scene notes that this student action was supported (*disokong*) by all the Pancasila forces in the military, in political parties, and in defiant mass organisations.[44] The scene attempts to highlight popular support for the new regime in the form of a Pancasila alliance.

While the scenes of the "Three Demands of the People" and the "Sacred Pancasila Day" highlight opposing forces within Indonesia, the last scene devised by the 1969 committee, the "Instruction of 11 March", signalled an end to this conflict. These three scenes introduce the New Order by highlighting a background of heightened conflict within Indonesia between pro- and anti-Pancasila forces and the resolution of this conflict by means of the Instruction of 11 March, which was subsequently used to ban the Communist Party. These scenes accentuate the potential fragility of Indonesia's unity, especially if the Pancasila were not correctly implemented.

The New Order version of the Indonesian past in this museum thus attempts to highlight the existence throughout Indonesian history of Pancasila values; the threat to these values posed by the communists; and the New Order regime's restoration of these values. While the Guided Democracy committee and President Sukarno gave priority to scenes depicting nationalism and a united Indonesia citizenry, Nugroho was prepared to expose divisions within the Indonesian nation. He did so in order to legitimise the new regime, and also to suggest to his audience that Indonesian unity was fragile. Nugroho featured the Communists as national traitors. The existence of internal enemies throughout Indonesian history became a dominant theme in official New Order historiography, as did the new emphasis on the centrality of the Pancasila and the Indonesian military to the story of the Indonesian past.

NEW ORDER OFFICIAL HISTORY-MAKING IN COMPARATIVE CONTEXT

The tightly guarded nature of some versions of the past in the New Order era was largely a product of the military, President Suharto and the central bureaucrats' combined power. By means of censorship and control of official history, they were able to dictate public versions of history. What other comparable regimes are there to Indonesia's New Order regime in respect to efforts to control national narratives of the past and to use history to promote ideological conformity and inculcation of set values? To answer this question, we need to first consider the nature of the New Order regime.

Although the New Order has been described as a military regime, this is not an altogether satisfactory definition for it fails to reflect the complexity of changing dynamics of power throughout this 30-year period. Jamie Mackie and Andrew MacIntyre describe three phases and four key players in the evolution of New Order power including the military, Suharto, the bureaucracy and technocrats. During the 1965–74 period, the armed forces were central in the power structure. In this period Suharto held office because of the armed forces' support and the bureaucracy was weak. In the next period (1974–83), the bureaucracy and state enterprises were more powerful. The military was still a decisive force. President Suharto's most vulnerable point came during the 1975 Pertamina oil company scandal. From 1983 onwards, Suharto was at his most powerful. The armed forces' power declined while the influence of the bureaucracy and technocrats increased.[45]

The division into four key players however, is complicated further by the fact that these are not discrete categories. Many retired military men, for example, took up positions within the bureaucracy and in business. Throughout the New Order period, many military men held key positions in the bureaucracy, as members of the government election vehicle Golkar, as cabinet members and as governors. In addition to the personal involvement of military men in the bureaucracy, every regional capital has a military command as a kind of mirror government. Some military men also served President Suharto personally as personal assistants (Aspri, Asisten Pribadi) or through institutions such as Opsus (Operasi Khusus, Special Operations).[46]

The New Order regime has also been characterised as authoritarian because of tight state control of the media and education, manipulation of elections, a lack of freedom of speech and a tradition of using the military to handle so-called "threats to national security" or regime opposition. In ideological terms the regime also fitted the definition of "authoritarian" because of its strict insistence on the unity between the state and society. In one of the most perceptive analyses of New Order ideology, David Bourchier argues that the regime's ideological basis is best described as organicist or integralist, whereby "state and society are viewed as part of the same organic unity often symbolised by a family or harmonious village community".[47] This claim rests on the idea of the state replicating a system of unique indigenous tradition.

David Bourchier claims the real source of these ideas is a stream of European anti-Enlightenment philosophy adopted by Indonesians in the 1920s and 1930s. He traces sources of organicism in Indonesia to Dutch legal scholars in Leiden, arguing that it is best understood as "part of the structural legacy of colonialism which was developed and used as a political-ideological formula by sections of the elite which felt threatened by popular pressures".[48] In the New Order period, officials began to revive organicist ideas put forward by legally trained nationalist Supomo in the 1940s as a new source of justification for the regime. In particular, they promoted the ideas of state familism (*negara kekeluargaan*) and the idea that members of a society are responsible to others.[49] Within this discourse, the Indonesian military positioned itself as guardians of the family and role models for society. On this basis Nugroho Notosusanto, with the support of retired General Suharto, represented the military's historical roles as models for emulation for young Indonesians. During the course of the New Order regime, the national philosophy Pancasila was transformed into a key element of organicist ideology and increasingly upheld as representing the "essential and eternal character of the Indonesian *bangsa* (nation)".[50]

One of the most striking comparisons to New Order Indonesia is pre-World War II Japan, a period in which history, and more generally education, increasingly became a vehicle for the transmission of ultra-nationalist and militarist ideology. From the beginnings of modern Japan, as in the case of Indonesia, Japanese statesmen advocated education and history as a means of imparting nationalism. In 1890 the Emperor issued the highly influential Imperial Rescript on Education in response to social confusion over the direction of modernisation and how the line between Japanese spirit and western learning (*wakon yosai*) was to be determined. Teruhisa Horio aptly describes this document as constituting a masterful formulation of the moral base created to dictate a switch in people's loyalties from family and clan to Emperor and nation.[51] The Rescript's aim was to make people feel a sense of being Japanese by prescribing particular national values such as Confucian-inspired filial piety, loyalty to the Emperor, obedience to the state and laws and the promotion of the common good.

The Rescript became a cornerstone of Japanese nationalism. Paul Brooker describes the Rescript as "the ethical social dimension of Japanese nationalism", as one of two pillars of state fraternalism, the other being state Shinto.[52] By means of the Rescript, Japanese elites sought to impart lasting bonds of familism amongst its citizens. To do this, the Rescript focused on the idea of a unique Japanese spirit or *kokutai* (national essence). David Bourchier has noted the parallel here with the function of the Pancasila in New Order Indonesia.[53] As Japan became increasingly militarised, particularly after the introduction of the 1925 Peace Preservation Law aimed at stemming socialism in Japan, emphasis on the national spirit increased. Martial spirit was emphasised in teachers' ethics textbooks from 1937 onwards, described as a characteristic of Japanese morality, "the way of loyalty".[54] As in the case of New Order Indonesia, history was used in pre-war Japan as a means of imparting prescribed values to citizens. In both cases, an authoritarian approach was taken to education in the sense that educational authority lay in the hands of the state rather than the people.[55]

Another parallel between pre-war Japan and New Order Indonesia was the use of the Rescript and the Pancasila respectively as codes of values to be followed by citizens. Compulsory Pancasila moral education courses started in state universities in the early 1970s and schools by the mid-1970s. From 1978 Pancasila indoctrination courses expanded to include all civil servants. The courses were largely aimed at associating the New Order with the Pancasila and creating bonds of loyalty between the people and the Pancasila, and hence between the people and the regime. Emphasis in these courses was on concepts of hierarchy, order, the family, respect for leadership, harmony and subordination of the individual to the group.[56]

Other idealised values promoted by the New Order regime were the more military-specific 1945 values. Emphasis on history as a mode of imparting these values began after the 1972 Army seminar on the necessity of a transfer of values between Indonesian generations. This represented a consolidation of the long-running Indonesian mission of using history for utilitarian purposes.

In communist states such as the People's Republic of China or the former USSR, educational content has also been overtly political, although the Communist Party rather than the military determined this content. During the Chinese Cultural Revolution, members of the People's Liberation Army were upheld in history textbooks as models of virtue for people to emulate. The deeds of heroes (including martial ones) were outlined in history books to portray ideal values to Chinese citizens. The textbooks promoted examples of people who had successfully implemented Chairman Mao's thought.[57] Communist ideology dictated that the people were to be positioned as the actors of history, but the focus was their deeds rather than the elevation of particular individuals — with the exception of Mao (in the case of China) and Stalin (in the case of the USSR), around whom hero cults were developed. In the USSR history's "didactic potential" was also stressed and history was similarly viewed by the Communist Party and educators as a means of inculcating prescribed values through lessons of the past.[58]

As in the case of Japan, foreign military challenges resulted in a strong emphasis on martial patriotic themes in textbooks produced by the militaristic regimes of the Soviet Union and South Korea.[59] This contrasts with the case of New Order Indonesia, where martial patriotic themes in official histories are instead the result of the constantly promoted need to defend the nation from internal and ideological threats rather than an external enemy. Most Indonesian military confrontations after the independence struggle of 1945–49 have involved internal rather than external enemies, resulting in a preoccupation with military efforts to crush state enemies. This preoccupation with internal enemies is, however, common to politicised militaries and hence to the ideology of military dominated regimes such as those of Burma (see Afterword).

While historical representation of the idea of the Japanese *kokutai* focused on a long lineage from the Sun Goddess Amaratesu to the Emperor, New Order military histories focused on the more recent past. Some mention of the pre-independence pasts, especially the former kingdoms of Majapahit and Sriwijaya and a pantheon of martial heroes who fought against the Dutch, was made in New Order histories, but greater emphasis was placed on post-1945 history. Having no indigenous army before 1945, the Indonesian military could only be legitimately accentuated in this recent past. The New Order focus on the relatively recent past as a resource for national lessons is comparable to uses of the post-independence history in Singapore, a country with an even shorter independent history.

CONCLUSION

History is still a new discipline in Indonesia and a tradition of critical historiography is as yet underdeveloped. From the inception of independence, history has been used to foster national pride. In the Guided Democracy and New Order periods it was also used to promote ideological conformity and a shared vision of the national past. A comparison of the Guided Democracy and New Order versions of the past presented in the National Monument History Museum suggests that the theme of a glorious past remained constant. The New Order regime, however, moved towards greater emphasis on a long tradition of military leaders and of the existence of threats to the nation, in addition to downplaying former President Sukarno's historical contributions.

The New Order regime shared similarities in its history-making efforts not only with the regime that preceded it but also with other authoritarian regimes across the globe. Some striking comparisons can be drawn, for example, with pre-war Japan and the emphasis in history courses then on promoting militarism. Indonesian historians have on the whole remained committed to the use of history for nation-building. One of the firmest supporters of their cause was Nugroho Notosusanto.

2

Nugroho Notosusanto and the Beginnings of the Armed Forces History Centre

Nugroho Notosusanto was one of the most important propagandists of the New Order regime. He not only produced and consolidated the official published version of the 1965 coup attempt, upon which the legitimacy of the regime rested, but in his capacity as Head of the Armed Forces History Centre (1965–85) and as Education Minister (1983–85) he also tirelessly promoted the heroism of the Indonesian military in museums, docu-dramas and school textbooks. This chapter firstly focuses on Nugroho's life experiences up until the era of late Guided Democracy, at which point he was appointed by General Nasution to a military history project. I consider key influences on Nugroho, including his elite background, his experience of the 1945–49 independence struggle, his short career as a short-story writer and his days as a student leader and history lecturer on the campus of the University of Indonesia. I also highlight Nugroho's commitment to Indonesian nationalism, his ambitions to be a person of influence and his belief in the unique leadership qualities of members of the 1945 generation, all of which led him to a career as historian for the military.[1]

The chapter then examines the first military history project on which Nugroho worked: *A Concise History of the Armed Struggle of the Indonesian Nation* (Sedjarah Singkat Perdjuangan Bersendjata Bangsa Indonesia). This book aimed to defend the Army's interpretation of the 1948 Madiun Affair as a communist revolt. The publication highlights the battle over history in the early 1960s between the Communist Party and the Army. The participation of Nugroho and other staff from the

University of Indonesia in the history project was part of a wider
developing alliance between the Army and the university. This project
is an important part of the story of the transition between the Guided
Democracy and New Order eras. By contrasting this history project to
leftist versions of the past from the same era, this chapter also highlights
important shifts in historical representation of Indonesia's past.

NUGROHO'S SOCIAL POSITION AND EARLY LIFE

Nugroho Notosusanto was born on 15 June 1931 in Rembang, central
Java, with the title Raden Panji (meaning prince or descendant of
royalty).[2] Nugroho's grandfather, Raden Panji Notomidjojo, was the
Patih (Chief Minister of the Regent) in the regency of Rembang.[3] His
grandfather's position in the colonial civil service illuminates the
background of Nugroho's family. In general, high officials had greater
social and professional contact with Europeans than most indigenous
Indonesians.[4] This was especially so in Rembang, because it was a coastal
city and a point of trade with the outside world.[5] Consistent with the
norms of *priyayi* (elite Javanese) families of this time, the Dutch language
was spoken in Nugroho's household.[6] In consequence, Nugroho's family
was most likely cosmopolitan in outlook. Some who knew Nugroho
described him as a Javanese courtier, suggesting that his aristocratic
origin was also apparent in his character. He was often described as
composed and controlled, idealised Javanese attributes expected in the
behaviour of the *priyayi* class.

The sons of high-ranking officials in the indigenous civil service
were amongst some of the few Indonesians to receive a Dutch higher
education.[7] Although Nugroho's father, Notosusanto, did not study
abroad, he did receive a Dutch education in Jakarta at an elite law
school, the Rechtskundige Hogeschool.[8] He studied in the late 1920s
and early 1930s, a period of heightened nationalism in the Netherlands
Indies, and was exposed to important nationalist leaders such as Sukarno
and Muhammad Hatta. As a result, Nugroho's father became sympathetic
to the nationalist movement a significant break from family tradition.
Despite his nationalist sympathies, however, he does not appear to have
been active in the nationalist movement itself. Before the proclamation
of independence he worked for both the Dutch and then Japanese
civil services.[9]

Nugroho showed early signs of devoted patriotism. As a child
he enjoyed playing *wayang* (Indonesian shadow puppets) with paper

cut-outs. He and his relative, Budi Darma, would act out stories. Nugroho's stories usually included fighting and were bursting with nationalist sentiment. This was before 1942, at the time the Netherlands Indies was occupied by the Dutch.[10] Budi Darma comments that when Nugroho heard the national anthem Indonesia Raya on the radio "he would stand up like a soldier and show his respect".[11]

NUGROHO'S EXPERIENCE OF THE INDEPENDENCE STRUGGLE

Nugroho grew up in the four cities of Rembang, Malang, Yogyakarta and Jakarta. Early in the independence struggle, Nugroho's family moved to Yogyakarta in order for his father to take up a position in the Justice Department in the newly formed government of the Republic of Indonesia. Both his parents were Republicans, and the young Nugroho was also firmly committed to Indonesia's independence. It was for this reason and peer pressure, in 1945 at age fourteen Nugroho joined the independence struggle. Nugroho suggests that many youths such as himself felt compelled to join the struggle: "In those heroic times one was not considered 'in' when one had not been to the front, even if one was only in his teens!"[12]

Nugroho served as a member of the Seventeenth Brigade of the National Army, often referred to as the Student Army (Tentara Pelajar), which was made up entirely of secondary school and university students.[13] Many members of the Student Army originated from youth militias trained in the period of the Japanese occupation. Although Nugroho was probably too young to have joined these Japanese youth groups, he seems to have shared with them an acceptance of "authoritarian mentalities with a positive respect for force and emotional anti-Westernism".[14] In his work on the Japanese-created military organisation PETA (Pembela Tanah Air, Defenders of the Fatherland), he demonstrated considerable respect for war-time Japanese ideas, such as the emphasis on the *bushido* (fighting spirit).[15] Unlike other armed units, members of the Student Army were characteristically young, non-political nationalists. They maintained their own identity during the struggle and were typically neutral in terms of political party factions. They were loyal to the government of the Republic of Indonesia and co-operated with the Indonesian National Army (Tentara Nasional Indonesia, TNI).

The enthusiasm and spirit of the Student Army contributed psychologically to the struggle. The Student Army taught courses for

prominent villagers with the hope of instilling "a sense of purpose in
the people for the success of the struggle [*perjuangan*]".[16] Nugroho's
unit was responsible for guarding against Dutch approaches. In a
description of the kinds of activities which the Student Army were
engaged in, Nugroho notes:

> Our patrols were only reconnaissance patrols, they were never combat
> patrols which was the task of the mobile troops. But sometimes we
> ran into an enemy patrol or even walked into an ambush where an
> engagement was unavoidable. Luckily we never lost any men. Some
> were wounded occasionally.[17]

The Student Army also participated in intelligence operations, carried
messages, laid traps for the Dutch and occasionally (when they could
come by them) carried arms. Like Nugroho, many members were from
the elite *priyayi* class.

During the independence struggle, Indonesian villagers fed and
sheltered Nugroho as they did for all *pejuang* (independence fighters).
As a privileged youth, he noticed the difficulties that most Indonesians
endured, including the lack of education for village children. The effect
of his contact with the *rakyat* (people) was later reflected in his humanistic
style short stories about this period. Living away from home, sleeping
in the jungle and sometimes not even sleeping at all would have been
new and challenging experiences for the young Nugroho.

In 1973, when writing a paper on this guerrilla period and the
effects on the Armed Forces Nugroho drew significantly on his experience.
His observations on the interaction between the guerrillas and villagers
who hosted them were a telling insight into his own awakening from
the confines of the elite world.

> We almost never talked to our hostesses and if we did we addressed
> her as "*bu*" (from "*ibu*") [meaning "mother" or polite form of
> address for an older or respected woman] and not "*embok*" [the
> Javanese lower term for older woman]. They would address our
> Commander"— who is a lieutenant — as "*pak*" [the polite form for
> older respected man] but they would call us "*mas*" [the egalitarian
> term for a man] or even "*dik*" [the close term for younger brother
> or sister], if the person in question had lived for considerable time
> in the city. In another social context they would have called us "*den*"
> (from "*raden*") [meaning "Javanese nobility"] or even "*ndoro*" (from
> "*bendoro*") [for young male nobility]. In our experience our hosts
> would treat us respectfully but in a relaxed manner.[18]

Despite having lived with villagers, Nugroho indicates that he felt a sense of difference and distance from them. William Frederick suggests that this sentiment was common amongst freedom fighters. They felt superior yet they were dependent on the villagers.[19] Nugroho seems to have experienced tension between the aristocratic culture of his family and the values inherent in his *pejuang* experience.

THE BREDA OFFER

After the transfer of sovereignty in December 1949, the government of the Republic of Indonesia offered a military education at Breda in the Netherlands to all former members of the Student Army. Fresh from the independence struggle and brimming with enthusiasm for the future of his country, Nugroho was faced with a choice between continuing a career or following in his father's footsteps by pursuing a higher education. On his appointment as Rector of University of Indonesia, Nugroho, revealed that at the time the offer was made he had indeed wanted to join the military and go to Breda.

> My father delicately instructed that I follow the second path (that of academia). I have made an effort to carry out that instruction as best I could, although I have not ignored my first inclination.[20]

Nugroho possibly felt a sense of loss at missing out on the military career, for those members of the Student Army who went to Breda and survived the Permesta/PRRI rebellions of the 1950s, the Irian Jaya campaign (1958–62) and the Malaysian Confrontation, went on to achieve high ranks in the military. One well-known member of the Student Army who studied at Breda was Major General Soebijakto Prawirasoebrata, who became Governor of the National Resilience Institute (Lembaga Ketahanan Nasional, Lemhanas).

The most likely reason Nugroho's father discouraged him from joining the military related to a general attitude shared by elite members of that generation. Many older members of the nationalist movement, such as Sukarno and Muhammad Hatta (the first Vice President of Indonesia), were wary of the military. The first Republican Cabinet did not include a Minister for Defence and there were no plans to create an armed force for the Republic.[21] Even when an armed force was formed, it was initially given tentative names such as Body for the Protection of People's Security (Badan Keamanan Rakyat, BKR), reflecting the political will to peacefully negotiate independence. Nugroho characterised members of his father's generation, whom he referred to as "the generation of the 1920s", as conservative, as not revolutionary, as rejecting violence and instead envisaging the struggle to end colonialism through political means alone.[22] Both his father's actions and the anti-military attitude of the nationalist generation forged Nugroho's own theory on the distinction of his own generation and the special role it was to play in the newly-born nation.

NUGROHO'S THOUGHTS ON THE 1945 GENERATION

In the 1950s, Nugroho published a letter in the ex-Student Army newspaper *Kompas*.[23] In the letter, which is addressed to a Dutch writer, Jef Last, he firmly expresses his views on the distinguishing characteristics of his generation.[24] Nugroho wrote:

> Your introduction to me is at the same time an introduction to a still newer generation of Indonesian young people, which has already gained its position in the community, even though it has not yet completely voiced its ideas. Three or four years ago we were known as the Student Army. That was the name which our society came to give to all the secondary school and university students who freely left their desks for interests greater than personal ones to join in a life-and-death struggle to save our people from drowning in the mud of history.[25]

Nugroho believed that members of his generation, who had made the sacrifice of suspending their studies to fight for their country, represented the beginning of a promising future for Indonesia.

In this letter, Nugroho demonstrates considerable resentment, if not a patronising attitude, towards civilian leaders, particularly those involved in diplomatic negotiations. Nugroho clearly distinguishes between those who fought for independence with arms and those who played important roles in influencing world opinion:

> As a matter of fact, our *bapaks* [fathers or male elders] who are now giving themselves to so much theorising, were trembling in fear and were counselling us on the need to start negotiations. We had better negotiate and keep on negotiating, without building up as much support as we could. They were full of deference to the "international standard", whereas we were struggling against mountains of diffi-culties. And when these mountains had been dug away, it was easy for them to pat their *pemudas* [youths] on the back and give them fulsome praise, which stuck like syrup ....[26]

As we shall see in Chapter 4, Nugroho's sentiments mirrored those of many members of the Student Army who blamed the lack of direction of politics in the 1950s on the failures of the older generation and their abandonment of the *semangat* or "spirit" of the struggle. This extract suggests that Nugroho concurred with the Japanese war-time promotion of respect for force and glorification of armed struggle and fighting spirit (*seishin*) amongst Indonesian youths. However, in true nationalistic fashion, his own thesis on the origins of the Indonesian military firmly dismisses the role of the Japanese period in moulding the TNI's ethos, arguing that this ethos was instead born "from the womb of the revolution".[27] Nugroho's reference to *bapak* is ostensibly directed at nationalist leaders who became involved in diplomatic negotiations during the struggle. But his criticism can also be read as referring to his own *bapak* (father), who was a member of the negotiating team for the Republic of Indonesia at the Round Table Conference of 1949. Such language to describe one's father is particularly impolite when emanating from a Javanese son.

The idea that the 1945 Generation had made a central contribution to the achievement of independence became a dominant theme in the ideology of the early New Order period as Army officers of this generation took their seats in power. Nugroho was to make a significant contribution to this ideology. He significantly expanded on this theory of the uniqueness of the 1945 Generation through his contributions to the history projects resulting from the 1972 Army seminar on the transfer of 1945 values (Chapter 5).

Nugroho's experience of the independence struggle thus had a lasting impact on his attitude and beliefs. Although he obeyed his father's wishes and pursued an education, he was never completely to lose sight of his military ambitions and he continued strongly to identify with this institution throughout his life.

STUDENT LIFE AT THE UNIVERSITY OF INDONESIA AND NUGROHO'S SHORT LITERARY CAREER

In between his experience of the 1945–49 struggle and his 1964 reunification with the military world, Nugroho channelled his energies into student life and writing short stories. In 1951, he enrolled in the Faculty of Letters at the University of Indonesia, Jakarta, quickly emerging as a student leader. In 1952, a year after entering campus, he was elected Chairman of the Student Senate of the Faculty of Letters. A friend of

Nugroho's from his student days, Muharyo, recalled early signs of Nugroho's ambition:

> He always wanted to lead and he was difficult to lead. I supported his opinion, that to become a student leader was the best training to become a state leader.[28]

Having experienced responsibility during the struggle, Nugroho had come to believe that his generation had a particular mandate to contribute to and guide the future nation of Indonesia. As a student, he sought to live out this mandate by immersing himself in student activities in Jakarta.

Nugroho was Head of the Indonesian Student Co-operative Agency for the Arts, which organised several student arts activities. He was also heavily involved with the student press.[29] Nugroho was one of the leaders of pro-independence demonstrations to the British Embassy on behalf of Egypt in the early 1950s and to the French Embassy on behalf of Algeria in 1958. Nugroho also represented his university on many occasions, both in Indonesia and abroad. In 1954, Nugroho went to Malaysia and Singapore as a participant in the Language Congress Goodwill Visit. In 1956, he was a delegate to an Asia–African Student Conference in Indonesia. In 1957, he was Head of the Indonesian Delegation to the Asian Student Press Conference in Manila. In 1959, he attended a Harvard International Seminar at which Henry Kissinger was present and in 1962 he went on a US, Japan and Malaya study tour (Illustration 2.1).[30]

Illustration 2.1   The young Nugroho.
Source: Image from H.B. Jassin, *Kesusastraan Indonesia Modern Dalam Kritik dan Esai,* Gunung Agung, Djakarta, 1967.

Despite his temporary departure from the military world, Nugroho's romantic view of the independence struggle endured in the short stories he wrote in his twenties. At this time, the 1950s, the independence struggle was a dominant theme in literature.[31] Nugroho represented the struggle as one very much worth fighting and dying for. He was drawn to the romanticism of sacrifice for one's nation and his stories were concerned primarily with the common experience of soldiers of comradeship, loyalty, masculinity and the battle front, which oddly had little application in a guerrilla-style war. The style of his short stories was sympathetic and humanist, reflective of a particular genre of the 1950s sometimes referred to as the 1945 Generation (Angkatan 45).[32] Amongst Nugroho's best known short stories are the collections *Morning Rain* (Hujan Kepagian), *Three Cities* (Tiga Kota), *Green is my Land, Green are my Clothes* (Hijau Tanahku, Hijau Bajuku), *The Feeling of Love* (Rasa Sayang).

During his time as a short-story writer, Nugroho fostered acquaintances with several other writers. In particular, he was close to the literary critic H.B. Jassin, who lectured in literature at the University of Indonesia. Although Nugroho spent time with artists and writers, he himself was not a typical artist, being formal in terms of style, dress and behaviour. He evidently left the world of creative writing behind, writing his last short story at the age of 26.

THE MOVE TO HISTORY

After enrolling in the Faculty of Letters in 1951, Nugroho eventually chose to specialise in history. Nugroho took a keen interest in world figures and the history of developed nations and hoped to learn lessons from this in order to benefit Indonesia. He was increasingly obsessive about history in later life for he was aware that it was in history that national identity was located.[33] Because of his writing and his student activism, Nugroho did not complete his undergraduate education until 1958. He then took up a teaching position in the History Department, a rather small department and not very popular among students.

As outlined in Chapter 1, a debate about the direction of historical studies was under way in the late 1950s. Nugroho was amongst those who firmly agreed with the project of producing history for the sake of nationalism. He claimed that history should answer the question "Who are we as a nation?" and in this way provide a resource for national identity.[34] Nugroho argued, in an essentialist manner, that one of the most important factors in the production of nationalist historiography was that "national history should only be written, or can only be written by historians with national spirit".[35] He then suggested that national spirit means "faith in the Indonesian nation as a synthesis of all ethnic groups" and "believing and having faith in the establishment of an independent nation-state as the embodiment of nationality".[36] Nugroho was therefore amongst those committed to history for the purposes of nationalism. He did not appear to share the concerns raised by historian Soedjatmoko in the first National History Congress of 1957 about the excesses of nationalism. This is not, however, to suggest that Nugroho was unaware of the subjectivity of nationalist history. On several occasions, including this "Kompas" article, Nugroho elaborated on the theme of objectivity and subjectivity, concluding that objectivity was not possible and that as a consequence historians should be "up front" about subjectivity.[37]

In 1960, Nugroho received a scholarship from the Rockefeller Foundation to take a Masters programme in Historical Method in the School of Oriental and African Studies at the University of London. At that time, it was common for Indonesian students to choose an American education, but, Nugroho chose to go to England. His decision was based on the advice of his friend Priyono, then-Minister of Education and a leftist who later became a target of the 1966 student demonstrations, who forbade him to go to the US, but also his own perception that the English had been able to maintain their history as the basis of the identity of their nation.[38]

For Nugroho, this time overseas was not a fulfilling experience. Unlike many of those who went to the US in those years, he was unhappy in England.[39] He did not complete the Masters degree for which his scholarship provided funding and actually studied in England for only one year. In 1961, when Indonesia was going to war with the Netherlands over West Irian, he returned to Indonesia at Priyono's request to resume teaching history at the University of Indonesia and take up the position of Head of the History Department.[40]

When Nugroho returned to Indonesia in 1962, the political atmosphere had altered considerably. The Indonesian Communist Party was gaining strength and competing strongly with the Army for power in the triumvirate of President Sukarno, the Communist Party and the Army.[41] This conflict also had repercussions in the field of history. As a result of this growing conflict, Nugroho was eventually recruited by General Nasution to help defend the Army's version of history in light of a new communist history project that would omit the Madiun Affair of 1948.

THE MADIUN AFFAIR: A BATTLE OVER HISTORY

Looking back on the period of late Guided Democracy, the Armed Forces History Centre suggests that "the PKI's efforts to dominate all areas of state and society from the 1960s onwards finally led them to the field of history".[42] By this time, the Indonesian Communist Party had significantly increased its influence over national politics, largely because of the President's increasing support for communist platforms. By 1964, President Sukarno sided with the Communist Party on all major domestic issues — including a decision against a merger of all political parties into one (which would have severely hurt the Communist Party); support for the accelerated enforcement of the land reform programmes; and the outlawing of Manikebu, the Body to Support Sukarnoism (Badan Pendukung Sukarno, BPS) and the Murba Party; and the suspension of journalists of BPS papers.[43] The Communist Party had also gained ideological ground through Sukarno's increasing emphasis on the accomodationist ideology of Nasakom (Nasionalisme Agama Komunisme – Nationalism, Religion and Communism) and through his new foreign policy vision *Nefos*, or the Newly Emerging Forces which (in Sukarno's words) encompassed "the forces for freedom, the forces for justice, the forces against imperialism, the forces against exploitation, the forces against capitalism".[44] The Nefos foreign policy vision moved Indonesia from the position of non-alignment to de facto alliance with the communist states and other progressive world forces pitted against colonialists, neo-colonialists and international capitalists. According to Herbert Feith, the Nefos policy stance was a virtual declaration that Indonesia's principal enemy was the West.[45] By contrast, by 1964 the influence of the Army in national politics had suffered a setback, due to the abolition of martial law in 1963 and the accumulated effects of the replacement of the independent-minded General Nasution with the more amenable General Yani as Army Chief of Staff.

The Communist Party history project that originally caught the attention of Nasution was to be co-ordinated by Amir Anwar Sanusi, a member of the Communist Party politburo and Vice-Secretary General of the National Front. The National Front was an organisation involved in conducting indoctrination courses on Nasakom, Manipol, Pancasila and the 1945 Constitution, Guided Economy and Guided Democracy.

All parties were, in fact, involved in the indoctrination, but the National Front is often remembered as being a communist-dominated institution. Looking back on this project, the Armed Forces History Centre claims that, "by wrongly using the National Front, Anwar Sanusi formed a team to write a history book containing a communist version of the national struggle". The Centre claims, also that the Communist Party planned to request President Sukarno's permission for this to become the official history of the national struggle. The most important characteristic of this project, however, was that the Madiun Affair, commonly represented by the Army as a Communist Party revolt against the government, was to be left out. Because these statements are issued by the Armed Forces History Centre, there is cause for caution in treating them as factual. While I could not establish whether the assertion that the Communist Party intended this to be an official history of the national struggle or not, the omission of the Madiun Affair from Sanusi's contribution to *History of the National Struggle* (see below) suggests the assertion to be plausible.

HISTORY OF THE NATIONAL MOVEMENT

It is unclear whether the Communist Party history referred to was ever completed.[46] In February 1965, a notice was placed in the communist paper "Harian Rakjat" announcing that a team of historians had commenced work on the *History of the National Movement* (Sedjarah Pergerakan Nasional). The head of this project was recorded as being the Vice-Secretary General of the National Front. It was noted that a seminar on writing, the *History of the National Movement* was to be held shortly by the Institute of History and Anthropology (Lembaga Sedjarah dan Antropologi). The notice specifically stated that the seminar would be attended only by history experts and students who were Manipolis and agreed with President Sukarno's ideas on history.[47]

There is circumstantial evidence that this history project was related to, or perhaps inspired by, a series of history seminars delivered in 1964 by the National Front to the Revolutionary Cadres of the Dwikora Forces (Pendidikan Kader Revolusi Angkatan "Dwikora") who had been mobilised for the Sukarno-led Confrontation with Malaysia. The history papers used in the 1964 training courses were published under the same title — the History of the National Movement — which, in this case, included the history of Indonesia since the creation of modern organisations at the beginning of the twentieth century until the present.[48]

Although A. Anwar Sanusi was not the sole author of this volu..., was a major contributor.[49] Whether or not this is the publication refer... to by the Centre as part of the Communist Party's "offensive strategy in the area of history", it is likely that Sanusi's contribution was at least representative of the kind of national history the Army, and General Nasution in particular, feared might be presented as Indonesian national history. Nasution, who was also a contributor to this volume, would have been fully aware of Sanusi's approach to national history.

Because the Indonesian military expressed opposition to Sanusi's history project, it is useful to examine his contribution to the *History of the National Movement.* His analysis draws on a Marxist framework to interpret Indonesian history and is couched within Sukarno's idea that the Indonesian struggle was "part of an international struggle between Nefos and *Oldefos*".[50] Sanusi takes up Sukarno's reference to the existence of *kaum sini* ("us") and *kaum sana* ("them") throughout the course of the Indonesian revolution. The "us" indicated those on the correct side of the revolution and the "them" indicated those less committed to the true revolution.[51] This categorisation of historical forces into revolutionaries and counter-revolutionaries is typical of Marxist histories that attempt to suggest movement towards a brighter future led by the revolutionaries against bourgeois elements.[52] Sanusi highlights the threat of counter-revolutionaries, especially capitalist bureaucrats, and "those who were not fully against Malaysia" in the recent phase of the revolution.[53] No doubt the reference to those "not fully against Malaysia" would have angered the Army leadership, who despite publicly backing the Malaysia campaign were secretly negotiating with the Malaysian leaders behind Sukarno's back.[54] Sanusi is also more directly antagonistic towards the Army, criticising both the take-over of foreign assets and the internal revolts of the 1950s, and suggesting that during this period there were those amongst the liberals who wanted to impose a military dictatorship.[55] Julie Southwood and Patrick Flanagan note that from 1960, the Indonesian Communist Party had increased their criticisms of military dominance in the economy, labelling those who had taken over nationalised assets of being "bureaucratic capitalists".[56]

In his contribution, Sanusi attacks those who are "communist-phobic", an accusation frequently made against the Army at this time, and suggests the need for "re-tooling" the Army leadership.[57] The aggressiveness of Sanusi's contribution reflects the renewed confidence of the Indonesian Communist Party in directing the revolution.

Marxist theory to problematise which events
...luded in a national history and who should
...s of history, the people (*rakyat*) or only promi-
...e states that, for the purposes of this course, it
role of the people would be considered as being
...ders. Then, quoting President Sukarno's expression
...ple I am nothing, I am only an 'extension of the
peo... (*penyambung lidah rakyat*)", Sanusi proposes that
particula. ...viduals are only made great by the people.[58] Sanusi
emphasises the role of farmers (*kaum tani*) and workers (*kaum buruh*)
in Indonesian history. This is consistent with contemporary communist
rhetoric which emphasised the role of the masses. In the period of late
Guided Democracy, President Sukarno implemented a Maoist programme
called *turun kebawah* ("to go down a level"), whereby Indonesian leaders
were encouraged to leave their offices and learn from the masses, so as
to become "true" revolutionary forces.[59]

One of the aims of Sanusi's representation of national history, like
other communist histories of this period, is to provide "a model for the
future not simply in terms of recommended action but in categories of
perception, presenting certain ways of looking at things and excluding
others".[60] Sanusi in particular points to the role of the people in blowing
up rail bridges, in seizing Japanese weapons and radios and in placarding
all foreign companies with the signs *milik Indonesia* (Indonesian property)
in the revolt against the Japanese and then the Dutch.[61] He notes that
in this struggle the village was the fighting unit where food, manpower
and a base were provided. Sanusi reminded the cadres of the debt still
owed from this period to the people (more specifically the farmers).[62]
This is quite a different message to that put forward in New Order
representations of the struggle which privileged the Indonesian military
(Chapter 4).

Consistent with General Nasution's accusation that Sanusi would
have left out the Madiun rebellion in his proposed Indonesian Communist
Party version of history, it is indeed left out in Sanusi's contribution to
the History of the National Movement, which deals with the years
1945–64 (labelled the "Manipol Period").[63] The Madiun Affair involved
a revolt on 18 September 1948, in which lower-echelon Communist
Party leaders, who were aggravated by Muhammad Hatta's rationalisation
of leftist troops from the military, took over the local government and
set up a revolutionary government. Ann Swift puts forward the theory
that the Madiun Affair was the product of mutual suspicion and

anticipation from each side that the other would soon move against it. She notes that since the Madiun Affair, interpretations of this episode have often been influenced by Cold War politics and fall into two extreme interpretations of the episode. One, with little weight, was that it was an American provocation aimed at getting the government of the Republic to suppress leftist opposition in return for diplomatic support.[64] The second was that it was a Soviet plot, according to which the Russians sent the leader of the Indonesian Communist Party, Musso, back from Moscow to radicalise the party in line with Stalinism and to overthrow the government.[65] The weakness of the second theory, according to Benedict Anderson, is that Musso was taken by surprise by the revolt led by Indonesian Communist Party subordinates. Anderson suggests that Musso was duped into supporting the movement, originally instigated by a middle-ranking Indonesian Socialist Youth (Pemuda Sosialis Indonesia, Pesindo) leader from Surabaya, after the central government (including Sukarno, Muhammad Hatta and Nasution) seized this opportunity to "denounce this local affair on national radio as the beginning of a national-level uprising by the communists".[66] Orders came from Yogyakarta, then the Republic's capital, to crush the party and its allies. As a result, many communists were executed and communist-influenced units of the Army were destroyed or disbanded.[67]

Swift notes that after the Madiun revolt, the government made an attempt to prove the coup was an established communist plot by drawing on fabricated evidence and publicising the discovery of documents that were never released to the public.[68] Because this version of the revolt was repeatedly circulated, the nationalist credentials, which the communists had earned in the 1926–27 revolts against the Dutch, were temporarily lost.[69]

For the Indonesian Communist Party, the Madiun Affair represented an inconvenient slur on its name. By 1964 however, the Communist Party had restored its credibility amongst many Indonesians. The Communist Party Chairman, D.N. Aidit, had even began to re-circulate the theory that the Madiun Affair was a provocation rather than a Communist Party revolt, that is, that Communist Party leaders had been duped by the Republic into supporting a local movement. In 1955, 1958 and 1964, Aidit published a defence of the Madiun Affair.[70] It is likely that the increasing circulation of the Communist Party's version of the Madiun Affair aggravated the Army and provided the trigger for Nasution's response to the planned national front history volume. The Army leadership continued to regard the Communist Party with an abiding suspicion as a result of Madiun, and Nasution in particular, was determined that the Army version of the Affair as a Communist revolt would not be forgotten.[71] The omission of the Affair from Sanusi's planned national history was therefore the central stimulus for the Army counter-history.

The initiative for writing a counter-version to the Communist Party's proposed history came from General Nasution, whom President Sukarno had recently sidelined by limiting his role as Chief of Staff of the Armed Forces to administrative tasks. This position was less powerful than Nasution's previous post as Chief of Staff of the Army, because at the same time he appointed Nasution to the new position, Sukarno also promoted the Chiefs of Staff of each of the forces to Commanders. Lieutenant General Ahmad Yani was appointed as the Army Commander.[72] H.A.J. Klooster refers to Nasution as the father of military history-writing in Indonesia.[73] Apart from General Nasution's strong personal interest in military history, this initiative was also a defensive effort to enhance the unity of the Armed Forces against President Sukarno's moves to encourage separate development of the forces (Chapter 3). The counter-history was to be written on behalf of the Armed Forces as a whole.

The contrast between the ideas of Sanusi and General Nasution on how the national past should be written is clear from Nasution's own contribution to the collection of indoctrination materials, the *History of the National Movement*. Nasution provides a detailed account of military events of the struggle for independence. Despite Sanusi's suggestion that it had been agreed that the people should be seen as the principal historical actors, Nasution clearly positions military men as the historical actors. In the New Order period, during which the military had no comparable competitor to the Communist Party, Nasution's interpretation of history became dominant.

In his contribution, General Nasution also makes a point of including the Madiun Affair. Wary, however, of accusations directed at the Army of being "communist-phobic", he provides a cautious justification of its inclusion. He writes:

> I myself am not that happy about including this event, because what we faced was us against us [Indonesians against Indonesians or an internal dispute], but, although this was the case, for the purposes of recording all military events I must reveal all military operations.[74]

Although Musso and his affiliation to the Soviet Union is mentioned, Nasution does not directly label the revolt of 18 September 1948 in Madiun a Communist Party revolt.[75] Instead, he refers to the event as the Madiun Affair (Peristiwa Madiun). Despite this caution, Nasution does provide a subtle critique directed at those not so convinced of the desirability of the Communist Party's revival, by stating "I think we must always learn from historical experiences that nothing is always constant and correct."[76] This message suggests that perhaps the Communist Party were not as righteous as they presented themselves to be and that there was cause for scepticism based on their historical record. Following the attempted coup of 1965 in which General Nasution narrowly escaped death, he laboured this point, stating that the Indonesian Communist Party had once again stabbed the Republic in the back. He called for the elimination of the Communist Party "down to its very roots so there will be no third Madiun".[77]

THE BEGINNINGS OF THE ARMED FORCES HISTORY CENTRE[78]

In response to rumours about Sanusi's forthcoming history project, General Nasution appointed a team of researchers to research and to write an Army version of the history of the armed struggle of the Indonesian nation.[79] This team constituted the beginnings of the Armed Forces History Centre. In order to gather a team of researchers together, Nasution requested assistance from the Faculty of Letters at the University of Indonesia. Nugroho Notosusanto, from the Department of History, and several other faculty teaching staff were subsequently appointed to work in the newly created Armed Forces History Centre.[80] It was easy for Nasution to co-opt staff of the University of Indonesia to join this project because by this time the Army and the University of Indonesia had already established several links. Under the teaching scheme set up by Brigadier General Suwarto of Seskoad, the Army Staff and Command School in Bandung, sympathetic (anti-communist) lecturers from the University of Indonesia were invited to teach academic subjects, particularly economics to improve the educational level of officers.[81] Those recruited from the University of Indonesia came especially from the Economics Faculty. David Ransom argues that this strategy of recruiting university elites to teach at Seskoad was part of an American-backed scheme to create a new "modernising elite" that would be ready to replace Sukarno when the time came. Several of these recruits, including Muhammad Sadli and Widjojo Nitisastro, became known as the "Berkeley Mafia" due to their American training. These two men went on to become key advisers to President Suharto in the early New Order period.[82] Nugroho, who was related to Brigadier General Suwarto by marriage, was amongst those recruited to lecture at Seskoad.[83]

In the context of late Guided Democracy, Nugroho's decision to join the project possibly represented a commitment to challenging the communists. This was certainly the intention of General Nasution, the instigator of this project, yet it was also a decision fuelled by Nugroho's belief in the military. It is difficult to determine the strength of Nugroho's commitment to anti-communism in the Guided Democracy period and all too easy to project the sentiments he displayed in his history projects after the coup back onto this period. Nugroho had not openly emerged as anti-communist, but he did have several links to anti-communist groups. He also had acquaintances with sympathisers and members of the PSI (Partai Sosialis Indonesia, Indonesian Socialist Party), several of whom taught with Nugroho at Seskoad as part of the Army's professional training scheme. The platforms of the PSI included economic planning, modernisation, social welfare and acceptance of foreign capital. Nugroho's closest link to the PSI was Brigadier General Suwarto, who sympathised with the PSI.[84] Despite the label "socialist", members of this party were fittingly described as salon socialists (*kaum sosialis salon*) and only paid lip-service to the term "socialism". They were firmly anti-communist.[85] Nugroho was also a friend of H.B. Jassin — a key signatory to the Manikebu, which was vehemently attacked by the leftist cultural organisation LEKRA on the grounds that it failed to mention Manipol. Goenawan Mohamad, however, claims that Nugroho agreed to the banning of Manikebu. According to him, Nugroho's reasoning was that he did not support the kind of freedom of expression advocated in the manifesto and instead believed that the arts should also be geared towards the project of the revolution.[86] What this suggests is that unlike the narratives of his latter-day history projects in which he deplored the failings of Guided Democracy, Nugroho did not oppose all aspects of this regime.

One further reason for suspecting that Nugroho might have been wary of communism was his religious background. Nugroho's father, who became professor of Islamic law at the University of Gadjah Mada, was known as a pious Muslim. This influence on Nugroho might have fostered a wariness that many other Muslims shared of the link between

Communism and atheism. His recruitment to Nasution's history team no doubt drew him closer to anti-communist elements in the Army, including Nasution.

From General Nasution's perspective, the recruitment of Nugroho served to strengthen ties between students of the University of Indonesia and the Army. At the time he was appointed to the history project, Nugroho was working at the University of Indonesia as Head of the Department of History and Assistant Rector in Charge of Student Affairs. The campus of the University of Indonesia was dominated by HMI (Himpunan Mahasiswa Indonesia, The Muslim Student Organisation) and to a lesser extent by the Catholic University Students' Association of the Republic of Indonesia (Perhimpuan Mahasiswa Katolik Republik Indonesia). Both these organisations were anti-communist. Ruth McVey notes students at established universities, such as the University of Indonesia, generally came from elite backgrounds. She claims, the student's "class attitudes and anti-establishment ideals combined among them to produce a virulent anti-Communism".[87] Nugroho's position as Assistant Rector therefore put him in a position of influence amongst anti-communist forces. The alliance between students of the University of Indonesia and the Army was to become central to the downfall of the Indonesian Communist Party and of Sukarno. As the left gained support at the national level in 1964–65,[88] tensions heightened on campus. The Muslim student organisation HMI came under attack with accusations that it was anti-Manipol and "counter-revolutionary".[89] At the height of this drive on 28 September 1965, Communist Party Chairman Aidit had challenged all members of the leftist student organisation, CGMI (Consentrasi Gerakan Mahasiswa Indonesia, Indonesian Student Movement Centre) in a statement at Senayan stadium, suggesting that if they were not capable of breaking up HMI it was better for them not to wear their pants any more, but to exchange them for sarongs.[90]

Despite his careful positioning, Nugroho who worked on this HMI-dominated campus, also became a target for leftist resentment. Nugroho's position became increasingly uncomfortable when in 1965 he became the centre of a scandal for screening "imperialist" American and English films for a fund-raising activity for the fifteenth anniversary of the University of Indonesia, held at the State Palace. Some students from the university protested against Nugroho's actions on the basis that Indonesia was then engaged in confrontation against the British.[91]

Although Nugroho seems to have positioned himself close to anti-communist elements, a student activist of the 1966 Generation notes that resentment from leftist groups stemmed perhaps from their inability to convert Nugroho to their views, rather than from his own actions or the sentiments he displayed.[92] At all times, Nugroho acted with caution and balance.[93]

Another likely reason why Nugroho joined the Armed Forces History Centre was his admiration for Nasution as a successful military leader and one who believed in the value of history. Nugroho praises Nasution's efforts to record history and he was particularly impressed by Nasution's formulation of the concept of a "total people's defence" or the guerrilla tactics employed in the 1945–49 revolution.[94]

THE CENTRE'S FIRST PROJECT: A CONCISE HISTORY OF THE ARMED STRUGGLE OF THE INDONESIAN NATION

Nasution encouraged the research team for the Army history project to work as quickly as possible, so that the counter-history would be released before the Communist Party history. In the space of three months, the Army's version of the struggle, *A Concise History of the Armed Struggle of the Indonesian Nation* (Sedjarah Singkat Perdjuangan Bersendjata Bangsa Indonesia) was published.[95] Although the principal author of this book is listed as Major General A.J. Mokoginta, Nugroho Notosusanto was given responsibility for writing most of this book. Because it was an internal publication of the Department of Defence, and Nugroho as yet had no formal ties, it was not appropriate for him to be named as the sole author.[96] This was the first of many books he wrote on behalf of the Indonesian forces and represented the beginning of his career as official military historian. The content of the publication was representative of what was to become a common New Order history format. *A Concise History of the Armed Struggle of the Indonesian Nation* is divided into five periods: (1) the "Greatness of the Golden Age", including Sriwidjaja (a symbol of the maritime greatness) and the war to found Majapahit; (2) "the Prelude to Independence", which focuses on armed resistance with no mention of the nationalist movement or anti-Dutch communist revolts of 1926–27; (3) "the Independence War", which highlights the creation of the military, Heroes' Day, the first and second Dutch aggressions and Sudirman's contributions; (4) "saving the Revolution", which highlights military contributions to national unity by suppressing rebellions of the 1950s; and (5) "Improving the Defence of the Revolution", the period since 1959, including the struggle to free West Irian. The general themes are moderate in comparison to rhetoric in other history volumes of this era, such as Sanusi's contribution to *The History of the National Movement*, and the two last themes in particular of "saving and defending" the revolution implied, contrary to Sukarno's rhetoric, that the revolution was complete.[97]

Consistent with the stated aim to counter Sanusi's version of history, *A Concise History of the Armed Struggle of the Indonesian Nation* emphasises the Madiun Affair. The book stresses that at the time of the Madiun Affair, the military was facing the greatest threat from the Dutch and as a result the Communist Party revolt was a major setback for the Republic. It suggests that the lesson of Madiun was that Indonesians should always defend and uphold unity in the face of external threats despite differences in understanding or opinion among themselves.[98] This was a theme later developed by the regime (Chapter 3).

In keeping with the politically defensive position the Army found itself in by 1964, the targeted audience of General Nasution's publication was internal military circles to ensure that members of the Indonesian military were not swayed by communist versions of the past. This fact in itself points to Nasution's awareness that his ranks were not impenetrable and that some members of the Armed Forces were already attracted to Communist Party ideology. Another initiative Nasution took to prevent the spread of communist influence in the Army was to promote increased religiosity in officers.[99] Indeed, throughout 1963 the Communist Party had been granted permission to conduct indoctrination courses at each of the staff and command training schools.[100] That the publication was intended for internal circulation explains the relatively bold position taken on Madiun. Wider publication of this volume in the political climate of 1964 would have been likely to arouse protest because it was insufficiently couched in terms of the on-going "revolution".[101] The emphasis on Madiun as a communist plot would no doubt also have angered Aidit, the Chairman of the PKI. Within internal military circles, the publication of *A Concise History of the Armed Struggle of the Indonesian Nation* therefore represented a small victory in this battle over history.

CONCLUSION

The Armed Forces History Centre was founded for the political purpose of defending its own version of history, according to which the Madiun Affair was a communist revolt. The Army's principal objection to the proposed Communist Party history publication was that it was an attempt "to misuse history as an instrument of political struggle".[102]

By the early 1960s, because of both his short stories and his student activities, Nugroho was a well-known figure, both inside Indonesia and abroad. He was larger-than-life and many people had hopes for him to become a great intellectual. By this time, Nugroho had fostered friendships with several Western Indonesianists, such as Herbert Feith and Benedict Anderson, and he had a wide circle of friends within Indonesian intellectual circles, including his key mentor, Priyono, a Murba-leaning leftist. Nugroho had also begun to mentor promising young intellectuals, such as Soe Hok Gie and Onghokham, at the University of Indonesia.

While Nugroho Notosusanto's life story is unique, many important New Order figures, such as President Suharto and General Nasution, were also members of the 1945 Generation who had grown up in the Japanese occupation and fought with arms in the independence struggle of 1945–49. Nugroho shared a similar mindset to these men and it was for this reason that he was so valuable to the regime. In the person of Nugroho, General Nasution found a trained historian, devoted to both the Indonesian military and Indonesian nationalism. Nugroho was the perfect recruit. In 1964, General Nasution appointed Nugroho as Head of the Armed Forces History Centre, and it was from this position that he went on to produce some of the most important history projects for the New Order regime, the first of which was the Army version of the 1965 coup.

3

History in Defence of the New Order Regime

The events of the coup attempt are still shrouded in mystery and it is unclear to what extent elements of the Indonesian military or the Communist Party were involved. There are numerous interpretations of the events of 1 October 1965. Some theories suggest the movement was an internal military affair in which some communist leaders were co-opted,[1] or the result of a split in the Communist Party between Second Deputy Chairperson Njoto and Chairperson Aidit.[2] Others suggest President Sukarno[3] or Major General Suharto[4] were key plotters in the events. What is important for our purposes is that, in the wake of the 30 September Movement (the name the rebels assigned to their actions) the Army officially declared the movement a coup attempt by the Communist Party against the government and took immediate steps to control the version that reached the public. Communist and other leftist publications were quickly shut down, and pro-Army papers emerged. The aim of the propaganda campaign was to direct public opinion against the Communist Party and in favour of the Army, thereby leaving President Sukarno without a major ally. Much to Sukarno's consternation, the Army successfully ignited already existing tensions by spreading stories about the ill-treatment of the officers prior to their deaths. Oei Tjoe Tat, for example, recalled Sukarno as having said, "I order all concerned not to inflame the situation.... Don't join in inflaming the situation by saying that their penises were cut into 100 pieces!"[5] The press was, however, only one site in which the military attempted to control, replicate and defend its own version of the coup attempt.

This chapter examines the role of Nugroho and the Armed Forces History Centre in producing the first published version of the coup attempt. Nugroho produced the book identifying the coup as a communist plot in just 40 days. Three years later, following the appearance of the Cornell Paper which described the coup as an internal military affair, Nugroho again rose to the challenge of defending the regime, this time to the outside world with the help of US officials. This chapter also maps the subsequent contributions of Nugroho and the Armed Forces History Centre to the foundation and defence of the New Order regime by replicating and memorialising this version of the coup attempt. President Suharto personally intervened to ensure that the official version of the coup attempt was memorialised and commemorated. Suharto called for the creation of a monument and commemorative space on the site at which the corpses of the victims of the coup attempt were retrieved. Nugroho and the Armed Forces History Centre fulfilled these wishes.

In this chapter I also analyse the contents and purpose of the military master narrative about the coup attempt. The story of the coup attempt can be seen not only as a means of defending the regime's legitimacy, but also as a means by which the regime defined its core values, including defence of the Pancasila and a restoration of moral order to society. This narrative, although rejected by some Indonesians, had long-term consequences for the political prisoners of 1965–66, who were demonised as former communists.

THE FIRST PUBLISHED VERSION OF THE COUP ATTEMPT

As we have seen in Chapter 2, the Armed Forces History Centre was already operational by the time of the coup attempt. Under Nugroho's direction, the Centre swung into action with the immediate goal of publishing the Army's version of the coup attempt. The result was *The Forty Day Failure of the 30 September Movement* (40 Hari Kegagalan "G-30-S" 1 Oktober–10 November),[6] which was largely a consolidated version of Army propaganda setting out "proof" that the coup attempt was a communist plot. The foreword begins with a quotation from Sukarno to the effect that "We must learn lessons from history". Nugroho then suggests that the coup attempt might have been prevented if a complete account of the origins of the Madiun Affair had been published before the coup occurred. He argues that in both cases, the Republic had been stabbed in the back, while it was focused on external enemies. Of course, at the time of the independence struggle, the external enemy was the Dutch, whilst in the early 1960s, according to the Confrontation campaign and Sukarno's ideas in general, it was the British and other "imperialist" forces.[7] The purpose of this publication, according to Nugroho, was therefore to prevent such an affair as Madiun occurring ever again.

Publication of the book must be seen in context. There was much confusion in the days following the coup attempt. Major General Suharto, in his capacity as Commander of Kostrad (Komando Cadangan Strategis Angkatan Darat, Army Strategic Reserve Command) had moved quickly to crush the coup attempt, yet the direction events were to take was still unpredictable. Although President Sukarno honoured the Army victims of the coup attempt with the title "Heroes of the Revolution" (Pahlawan Revolusi), his refusal to blame the Communist Party for the events of the coup also posed a challenge to the military. The legitimacy of the Army take-over rested on the general public's belief that the coup attempt was a Communist Party plot and not an internal military affair. This version of events was problematic because the coup plotters themselves had declared, in their initial broadcast on 1 October, that the 30 September Movement was an internal military action carried out to safeguard Sukarno from a coup plotted by a council of corrupt, high-living Jakarta generals who were tools of the American Central Intelligence Agency.[8] The Army also had to consolidate its version of events in order to justify the mass killing of communists that it had set in train in the months following the coup.

The priority accorded to *The Forty Day Failure of the 30 September Movement* is also made clear by the fact that Nugroho and his team of assistants worked day and night to complete it for publication in December 1965. Representatives of the Armed Forces History Centre were sent to Central Java soon after the coup in order to find materials on the movement in this area for the publication. In November staff from the Centre, together with a team from the Armed Forces Staff, was given the task of interviewing the families of the Heroes of the Revolution. The research team also made use of many of the propaganda-based newspaper reports.[9]

Because an attempt had been made on the life of General Nasution in the course of the coup attempt, Nasution considered himself and his aides to be in potential danger. Nugroho and other staff were temporarily relocated from their homes to a private residence in Kemang, where they completed this project.[10] Nugroho and his research team thus worked on this project in a highly-charged political atmosphere, in which the fate of the Communist Party had not yet been sealed. They took considerable risks to complete this work by siding with the Indonesian

Army in its power struggle with the Communist Party and President
Sukarno.

This was not, however, the only contribution Nugroho made to
this struggle. Once the atmosphere of uncertainty after the coup attempt
had passed, Nugroho re-emerged from temporary hiding to use his
influence on the campus of the University of Indonesia as Assistant
Rector to help establish a new political order. The University of Indonesia
was a key campus in organising the mass student demonstrations of
1966. These demonstrations contributed to the subsequent banning of
the Indonesian Communist Party.

In October 1965, Rector Brigadier General Sjarief Thayeb held
discussions with student leaders who were agitating for retribution for
the deaths of the murdered generals. These discussions resulted in the
formation of KAMI (Kesatuan Aksi Mahasiswa Indonesia, The Indonesian University Student Action Front).[11] After the formation of KAMI,
Nugroho became the students' military contact and assisted in building
and co-ordinating a student–military alliance. Nugroho consulted mainly
with two people prior to and during the student demonstrations. He
conferred with Soe Hok Gie, one of his history students, in order to
monitor student activities; and with Lieutenant General Suwarto (then
the Commandant of Seskoad, the Army Staff and Command School,
and Nugroho's wife's uncle), to ensure the military's support and protection for student demonstrations.[12]

On the seventeenth anniversary of the student actions, Nugroho
reflected on his own part in the 1966 demonstrations, hinting at his own
involvement:

> In fact I, as an historian, witnessed the Tritura [Three Demands of
> the People] actions from close quarters and often it is also not clear
> to several groups including myself, if I also wasn't also a participant.
> As Assistant Rector in student affairs and alumni at that time I
> certainly had a close relationship with the students and because of
> that we were together most of the time, in classrooms, in the field
> or in the streets.[13]

Soe Hok Gie's brother, Arief Budiman, claims that although Nugroho
played an important role in facilitating military and university links
during this time, he was very discreet about this role.[14] The Army under
Suharto's leadership sought to appear loyal to President Sukarno and to
be responding to the people's will rather than imposing their own
agenda. Nugroho was generally very clever at positioning himself. Behind

the scenes, however, Nugroho made a significant contribution to the campaign to oust Sukarno both on the campus of the University of Indonesia and in his role as author of the first version of the coup attempt.

The Forty Day Failure of the 30 September Movement was the first book on the coup to be released in Indonesia. It marked the beginning of a narrative that was consolidated repeatedly throughout the regime. The Armed Forces History Centre claims that the book convinced society as a whole that the Indonesian Communist Party was behind the coup, rather than the coup being an internal military affair.[15] It is more likely that in the frightening atmosphere after the coup attempt, most Indonesians were too scared to question this version of the coup. Yet the regime remained forever wary of challenges to this narrative.

THE OFFICIAL ENGLISH VERSION OF THE COUP ATTEMPT

In 1967, Guy Pauker of the Rand Corporation in California alerted Major General Suwarto of Seskoad to the existence of an alternative version of the coup attempt compiled by scholars at Cornell University. The three researchers — Ruth McVey, Frederick Bunnell and Benedict Anderson — had originally intended the contents of the paper to remain confidential. The contents of the paper became known after publication of an article by Joseph Kraft in the *Washington Post*, in which a summary of the findings in this paper were referred to as coming from a paper prepared by Cornell staff.[16] The Cornell Paper, as it became known, concluded that the coup attempt was more likely the result of severe intra-Army conflicts. Of course, this presented a major challenge to the newly established New Order regime and it was something that concerned not only the new Indonesian government but also its Cold War ally, the United States.

There have been numerous theories about the involvement of the United States of America in the coup attempt in Indonesia and the mass killings that followed, with much less evidence of this role.[17] However, in the case of the Cornell Paper, the US government clearly acted to help the New Order regime defend its version of the coup and hence its legitimacy. A list of the government-sponsored Rand Corporation publications in the years 1963–72 indicates that it carried out an extensive range of research on communism in the Soviet Union, China, Vietnam, Latin America (especially Cuba) and Indonesia. This suggests that the

Rand Corporation, which was set up by the American Air Force at the conclusion of World War II to monitor international affairs, was acting as a Cold War watch-dog for the American government. The Rand Corporation's preference for military regimes over civilian governance in developing countries is also evidenced by its publications.[18]

A key analyst of Indonesian affairs in the Rand Corporation in the 1960s was Guy Pauker. Pauker had cultivated close ties with anti-communist elements of the Indonesian military from the early 1960s onwards by encouraging US funding for training of military officers.[19] Between the years 1963–69, he wrote a series of articles on Indonesia for the Rand Corporation in which he examined the possibility of Indonesia falling to communism and several positive assessments of the New Order regime.[20] Having observed the increasingly leftist direction Indonesia took during the late Guided Democracy period and having welcomed and encouraged the military takeover after the coup, he was determined to prevent any challenges to the legitimacy of this newly installed anti-communist regime.

In response to the discovery of the Cornell Paper, Pauker invited Major General Suwarto, who by 1966 was the Commandant of Seskoad and a close adviser to General Suharto, to visit the Rand Corporation in Santa Monica. Suwarto was Pauker's strongest link with the Indonesian military. Suwarto had spent time in the US at Fort Benning (1954–55) and at the US Command and General Staff College at Fort Leavenworth (1958–59) and had also served as military attaché to America from 1965 to 1966.[21] During Suwarto's visit to the Rand Corporation, Pauker suggested that the military had to counter the "Cornell Paper", not only by denouncing this version of events, but by producing their own official version in English. In response to Pauker's suggestion, Suwarto sent Nugroho Notosusanto and Lieutenant Colonel Ismail Saleh, a prominent prosecutor involved in the military show trials of early 1966 (known as the Mahmillub — Mahkamah Militer Luar Biasa, Extraordinary Military Tribunal), to visit the Rand Corporation. Nugroho and Ismail were requested to gather opinions and arm themselves with responses to the Cornell Paper before producing an official book in English about the coup attempt.[22]

Nugroho and Ismail went to California in 1967 where they worked together with Pauker to produce the publication entitled "The Coup Attempt of the '30 September Movement' in Indonesia".[23] Benedict Anderson claims that Pauker had initially contributed his own section to this book, but prior to publication a decision was made to leave it out.[24] The preface gives thanks to persons "in Indonesia as well as abroad who expressly wish not to be mentioned by name". It was therefore not only the Indonesian military who sought to defend the military's takeover by means of this version of the coup attempt.

The foreword to the English version of the coup attempt notes that it was written as a response to a "campaign waged by certain circles in Western countries against the New Order government". Further evidence that it is a rebuttal of the Cornell Paper is provided by the dedication of one section of the book to the issue of why the coup attempt was not an internal military affair. Nugroho and Ismail's English publication included "evidence" from the Extraordinary Military Tribunal, which began two months after the "coup attempt". This material was not available when *The Forty Day Failure of the 30 September Movement* was written. Ismail's contribution to this book concentrates on defending the legitimacy of the trials, which outside observers described as being "show trials". He alludes to the fairness and neutrality of the trials, the openness of the court and the right of the defendants to legal representation.[25] Nugroho's contribution focuses on the background to the coup, an explanation of the events and principal actors. It attempts to make the case for Communist Party complicity in the coup plot. The key points made by Nugroho and Ismail are: (1) that in order to co-opt others to follow the 30 September Movement, Aidit proposed the existence of a Council of Generals who were planning to move against the President on 5 October 1965; (2) that the trials revealed the issue of the Council of Generals to be a fictitious creation of the PKI; that the coup was staged to look like an internal Army affair; (3) that, in fact, the coup attempt was the plot of a special Communist Party bureau in co-operation with progressive officers described as "PKI sympathisers in the Army"; and (4) that trial evidence suggests "that all those involved in the 30 September Movement were either members of the Communist Party or were managed by them".[26]

Nugroho and Ismail insist that the Indonesian Communist Party and its mass organisations, particularly the Indonesian Women's Movement (Gerwani, Gerakan Wanita Indonesia) and the People's Youth (Pemuda Rakyat), were involved in the plot to assist in the military operations of the coup. It is expressly stated in the second half of the book, covering the tribunal, that the involvement of these organisations proves the coup attempt was not an internal military affair. The evidence provided for this is that the People's Youth and other Communist Party "volunteers" were amongst the Cakrabirawa, presidential guard, or other military units involved in the missions to kidnap Nasution and Yani.[27] Anderson and Ruth McVey, who argue that the coup was an internal military plot, conversely suggest that members of the People's Youth (who had been training at Halim Air Force Base, a site which included the Lubang Buaya area) were deliberately co-opted by the Army coup plotters to assist with the kidnappings and to compel the Communist Party to support the movement if anything went wrong.[28] The primary preoccupation in both the first Indonesian and the English version of the coup attempt was therefore to dismiss the claim the event was an internal military affair. Although it is not the aim of this book to assess the merit of this theory, some authors have pointed to weakness in this official account.[29] Robert Elson concludes that the most plausible explanation of the coup attempt is that it was instigated by some PKI leaders and some junior officers connected with the Diponegoro Central Java Division of the Army and the Air Force, based on the belief that the generals were planning to move against the President or the PKI or both.[30]

The successful completion of an English version of the coup attempt earned Nugroho and the Armed Forces History Centre considerable kudos. Previously, there had been "those within the armed forces who asked the question why does the armed forces need history?"[31] The Centre had proved its worth and in 1968, as a sign of recognition, the Centre received new offices on Jakarta's main square at Medan Merdeka Barat No. 2, close to the National Monument. The Centre had started as a small operation, located in a building behind the main building of the Armed Forces Staff Headquarters on Medan Merdeka Barat.

The Indonesian and English publications on the coup were only the first steps for the military in a long process of propagating the official version of the coup attempt to Indonesians and outsiders. The regime also preserved the site at which the corpses of the army victims of the coup attempt were located and then built an expansive memorial complex that was progressively added to over the next thirty years. Every year on the anniversary of the coup attempt President Suharto would also preside over a state authorised commemorative ceremony to remind Indonesians of this tragic day.

PRESERVING AND MEMORIALISING THE WELL AT LUBANG BUAYA (CROCODILE HOLE)

As Michael van Langenberg has argued, the state in which the bodies of the Army victims of the coup were found formed an important part of the initial propaganda about the coup.[32] The corpses of the Jakarta coup victims, comprising six of the most senior Army generals and one lieutenant, were located on 3 October 1965. They were covered by rubbish in a disused well at Halim Air Force Base, in the region of Lubang Buaya, East Jakarta. Upon the retrieval of the bodies on 4 October 1965, Suharto made a speech in which he claimed the corpses provided evidence of the barbaric (*biadab*) acts of the coup instigators, who called themselves the 30 September Movement.[33] By using the word *biadab*, Suharto was presumably referring both to the state of the decomposed bodies, which was presented as "evidence" that some of the officers had been tortured prior to death, and also to the manner in which the bodies had been dumped. Although not all the coup victims were Muslim, the way in which the bodies of the victims had been dumped in a well and covered by rubbish was particularly offensive to followers of Islam, the majority religion in Indonesia. Islam requires that the bodies of the deceased be ceremonially bathed by ritual ablution (*wudhu*) with clean water by family members and buried as soon as possible in white cloth, with their heads positioned to face Mecca. In addition to the association of communism with atheism, the manner in which the Army martyrs were allegedly killed and then discarded prompted a rationalisation that the coup plotters must have been non-religious. In his recollections of the post-coup period, Pipit Rochiat claims that the comment that "such brutal murders could only be the work of *kafirs* [non-believers] namely, the Communists", was frequently heard.[34]

The site of the well became famous not only because of the press coverage of the exhumation of the corpses but also because of the subsequent mythology that developed. At first the images were captured by film crews and cameramen. Harold Crouch notes the exhumation of the corpses was in fact delayed "until a full battery of journalists, photographers and camera men had been assembled".[35] These photographs were printed in contemporary newspapers and in the first official published version of the coup attempt. They were then replicated in history textbooks and annually in newspapers and television clips on the commemorative date of 1 October. Rumours circulated in the coup period suggesting that thousands of other "Lubang Buayas" or holes had been prepared around the country, for the burial of anti-communists once they had been executed.[36] The well was therefore also a reminder of the idea that if the communists had not been killed, they would have killed others. This was an important justification used by members of religious vigilantes both during and after the post-coup killings.[37]

For these reasons, the well at Lubang Buaya became a potent symbol of the fate that might have befallen others had the communists not been stopped. The well was thus preserved as physical "evidence" of the necessity of the killings of communists.

Aware of the significance of the well as a site of memory, General Suharto, in his capacity as then-Minister of Defence and Commander of the Army, recommended preservation and memorialisation of the disused well shortly after the coup attempt.[38] The entrance to the disused well was preserved with clay moulding (Illustration 3.1) and covered with red glass, a reminder of both the colour of the blood the heroes shed and the colour of communism. To satisfy visitors' curiosity, a mirror is affixed to the centre of the ceiling of the structure covering the well such that they can look down into the well, thereby imagining the plight of the "Heroes of the Revolution", the name Sukarno awarded the Army martyrs (Illustration 3.2). A lamp shines down into the well past the grille, positioned one metre below the well's entrance. According to official commentary, the purpose of the lamp is to convey the fact that, by allowing the corpses of the "Heroes of the Revolution" to be found, "God Almighty indicated the truth".[39] The choice of the symbol of light is related to the Islamic concept of *wahyu* (from the Arabic for "light") according to which light can be a sign of religious merit.[40] The use of this motif also reinforces the religious framework within which the coup attempt was framed. In the first published Army version of the coup attempt, it is noted that the reason the coup failed in spite of the impressive prologue was, first and foremost, because of "the hands of God".[41]

The way in which the well is memorialised also highlights the deaths of the martyrs in other ways. A four-pillared pavilion structure, called a *cungkup*, is positioned over the top of the well (Illustration 3.3). The *cungkup* is a smaller form of *pendopo*, an audience hall, a classical Javanese architectural structure that appears in royal courts, temples and royal graves. It has also been used in modern times to denote the graves of famous people, such as Commander Sudirman (Chapter 4). Visitors are directed to show respect and adopt a certain mood of solemnity when they reach the *cungkup* itself. Signs indicate that visitors should remove their shoes, as when visiting a home or mosque, before ascending the white marble steps leading to the well's entrance.[42] The deaths of the "heroes" are also denoted by the presence of two bronze *makara*, mythological beasts with "an elephant's trunk, parrot's beak and fish's tail",[43] on either side of the *cungkup* (Illustration 3.4). According to

Illustration 3.1 The preserved well at Lubang Buaya.

The inscription on the plaque above the well reads "It is not possible that the ideals of our struggle to uphold the purity of the Pancasila will be destroyed merely by burying us in this well."

Source: Image from Pusat Sejarah dan Tradisi ABRI, *Buku Panduan Monumen Pancasila Sakti Lubang Buaya Jakarta*, Pusat Sejarah dan Tradisi ABRI, Jakarta, 1997, p. 34.

Illustration 3.2 Visitors to the Sacred Pancasila Monument leaning over the barrier to peer into the well.
Source: Photograph by the author.

Illustration 3.3 The *cungkup* covering the preserved well at Lubang Buaya.
Source: Image from Pusat Sejarah dan Tradisi ABRI, *Buku Panduan Monumen Pancasila Sakti Lubang Buaya Jakarta*, Pusat Sejarah dan Tradisi ABRI, Jakarta, 1997, p. 34.

Illustration 3.4   *Makara* beasts positioned at either side of the *cungkup*.
Source: Photograph by Chatarina Purnamdari.

Indian mythology, the *makara* beast dwells in the *Amrita* or the "ocean of Elixir of Immortality", which is the ocean into which the initiate enters when he walks through the gate of the afterworld.[44] The monument sculptor Saptoto, a Yogyakartan artist and former assistant to the famous Indonesian painter Affandi, possibly used the *makaras* to indicate the deaths of the Army heroes.

The choice to include these beasts as part of the *cungkup* complex might also have been intended to bestow a temple-like property upon the structure. *Makaras* are usually positioned in pairs at either side of the entrance to Buddhist temples or monuments and function as gateways in temples like Borobudur and Candi Mendut.[45] Apart from these features, both the inner side of the *cungkup*, which consists of finely carved wood, and the roof and many other features of the monument complex include extensive use of symbols and motifs.[46] It is likely that this symbolism goes unnoticed by many visitors. Yet if they do recognise the use of even one motif, they are likely to be able to place it as belonging to the ancient past. In his observations of the use of motifs from the Javanese past in New Order architecture and monuments,

Timothy Lindsey notes that the most important feature of this imagery is not that it is familiar to most, but rather that "it is unusual and evocative and saturated with the significance the absent past so easily conjures up, especially in the hand of skilled conjurers".[47] I would suggest that, although the artist Saptoto probably researched or was already familiar with the meaning of such motifs, he most likely used them to suggest that this story, like those told in ancient temples, was also part of a preserved story of the past or a legend.

Over time, an extensive monument and museum complex was constructed around the preserved well. The second stage of development of the Sacred Pancasila Monument was the erection of a large monument. The monument features the backdrop of a large bronze *garuda* bird (the state emblem for the Pancasila) attached to a white marble wall, and is foregrounded by life-sized and life-like bronze statues of the seven Army heroes and an historical relief at the base of the monument (Illustration 3.5). The Armed Forces History Centre suggested that the Sacred Pancasila Monument represents an historical site that can continue to tell the story as objectively as possible so as "to prevent or deter the possibility of efforts to falsify or manipulate historical facts".[48] The monument, as a solid object fixed in stone, was to function as unchallengeable proof of

Illustration 3.5   The Sacred Pancasila Monument.
Source: Photograph by the author.

the military's versions of events and as defence against other representations. It is possible that the regime also saw the continued development
of the monument as a means of eternalising the Army version of the past.

THE MONUMENT BASE RELIEF

The relief found beneath the statues of the Heroes of the Revolution
was one of the first visual representations of the official version of the
coup attempt. Reliefs have a long history in Indonesian art and can be
traced back to ancient Javanese Hindu and Buddhist temples, the best-
known example being the famous Borobudur. They have also been used
in large post-independence monuments as a way of providing an historical
narrative to a monument's central message, or attempting to control
interpretations of a monument's message. The General Attack Monument
in Yogyakarta, for example, features a relief detailing the second Dutch
aggression, Suharto's role in the General Attack and the return of Sukarno
to Yogyakarta. Contemporary use of reliefs, a form of ancient motif, may
also be part of an attempt to "claim tradition".[49]

The dominant theme of the communists as an evil social force
is elaborated in the relief by means of reference to wayang imagery.
Wayang stories often contain moral messages.[50] It is highly significant,
for example, that within the relief Suharto and other recognisable military
figures, such as independence fighter Colonel Gatot Subroto who crushed
the Madiun Affair, Lieutenant General Ahmad Yani (former Army
Commander and victim of the 1965 coup), and General Sarwo Edhie,
the Commander of the Army Parachute Commando Regiment (Resimen
Para Komando Angkatan Darat, RPKAD) who co-ordinated many of
the initial "sweeps" against communists in Java and rallied students
against Sukarno, appear on the right side of each scene, whilst the
communists appear on the left. At the end of every *lakon* (story) in a
shadow puppet performance the *Pandhawa*, or good characters, appear
on the right, whereas the *Korawa* and *Raksasa*, or evil characters appear,
on the left.[51] In the relief, Gatot Subroto and Suharto feature delicate
noses and eyes, an indicator of ascetic power, a property traditionally
highly valued in Java.[52] Meanwhile, the communists in the relief feature
"fleshy noses and wide-open eyes"[53] and often appear without shirts
to display rippling muscles, both of which are an indication that they
are *kasar* (coarse).[54] The communist figures beside Suharto also appear
with upturned heads. In wayang posture, this indicates impatience
and aggression.[55]

Illustration 3.6   The Madiun Affair as visualised in the relief beneath the Sacred Pancasila Monument.
Source: Photograph by the author.

Like the first published version of the coup attempt, the monument relief, whose narrative was specified by Major General Sudjono from the ABRI Institute for the Traditions and Mental Upbuilding (Lembaga Pembinaan Mental dan Tradisi ABRI), tells the story of the prologue and epilogue of the coup attempt, in addition to the events of the coup attempt itself. The bronze relief beneath the Sacred Pancasila Monument consists of two small panels on either side of the base and one long panel across the front. Within these panels, six primary scenes can be discerned. Again signalling the importance of Madiun in Army histories the first scene in the relief is of the Madiun Affair (Illustration 3.6). In this scene, the people are pictured suffering and frightened on the left of the panel. Also on the left, angry men armed with weapons (the communists) are seen attacking others. On the far right of the scene stands the looming figure of Colonel Gatot Subroto, the celebrated military hero in the crushing of the Madiun Affair who went on to become a supporter of Suharto's military career. He stands with a straight outstretched arm pointing backwards at the communists whilst his head is turned towards the next scene, as if in anticipation of suppressing the next "communist coup".

The second scene features Sukarno on the far left of the front panel holding a *Nasakom* booklet. In front of him, Aidit, Communist Party

Illustration 3.7 The height of Guided Democracy: Sukarno, Nasakom and the fifth force as visualised in the relief beneath the Sacred Pancasila Monument. *Source:* Photograph by the author.

chairperson, is featured talking to a farmer holding a sickle (Illustration 3.7). As we shall see later, the anti-communist faction of the military interpreted Sukarno's Nasakom ideology as a great mistake. Lieutenant General Yani is to the right of Sukarno, Aidit and the farmer, with his hand up as if to say "stop!" in opposition to the idea of a fifth armed civilian force. In 1965, leaders of the Indonesian Communist Party proposed that peasants and workers be armed and given military training. President Sukarno responded by suggesting they could form a fifth force in addition to the four existing forces of the military. Under General Yani's leadership, the military attempted to cautiously block this proposal so as to maintain their monopoly on weapons in Indonesia.[56] In the background of the relief, farmers are seen training with weapons. The second scene fades into an image of people pointing back towards the generals, perhaps a reference to the alleged existence of a Council of Generals. Members of the 30 September Movement alleged that their movement was directed against the Council of Generals, senior members of the military who they alleged had been planning a coup against Sukarno on 5 October, Armed Forces Day 1965. Official accounts of the coup, which lean on the military trials for proof, claim that the Council of Generals was a fiction invented by the Indonesian Communist Party to justify their coup attempt. They claim that witnesses involved

Illustration 3.8   A scene of chaos: The 1965 coup attempt as visualised in the relief beneath the Sacred Pancasila Monument.
Source: Photograph by the author.

in the coup were unable to prove the existence of a Council of Generals and that there was no politically-based council amongst the leadership of the Armed Forces.[57] The pointing hands and the positions of the figures in the relief indicate tension.

The third scene, in the centre of the front panel, is the climax of the conflict between the Army and the Indonesian Communist Party: the scene at Lubang Buaya (Illustration 3.8). In the background, communists are pulling down the Garuda emblem, reinforcing the concept that the communists intended to discard the Pancasila (see p. 85). The kidnapped generals are shown suffering at the hands of "communists" and, in the foreground, the Army martyrs are being tied up, killed and thrown into the well. A crocodile appears beside the well, confirming the site as Lubang Buaya (Crocodile Hole). Sickles are being wildly waved around.

The front panel of this scene of chaos features women salaciously dancing beside the well. One of the dancing women wears a chain of flowers around her neck. This is a direct reference to the fabricated story of the dance of fragrant flowers. This story appeared in *Angkatan Bersenjata* on 11 October 1965 as a "testimony" of a woman who reported having participated in a naked "dirty, indecent dance", followed by an orgy at the site of Lubang Buaya.[58] This was just one part of a

Illustration 3.9 The dancing women in the scene of chaos.
Source: Photograph by the author.

larger propaganda campaign targeted at members of Gerwani, a women's organisation aligned with the Communist Party. Other rumours suggested these women sexually fondled and then mutilated the genitals of the Army victims prior to their deaths.

The images of women depicted on the monument are striking for several reasons. First, the women's *aurat* (the parts of the body that Islam recommends should be covered —including the neck and arms) are clearly visible (Illustration 3.9). In general, Indonesian sculptors do not carve "broadly curving hips" or "swelling, high-set breasts" sometimes found in Indian artistic depictions of women.[59] Second, men and women appear dancing together. Traditional Indonesian dances are usually single sex — when they are mixed, there is little or no contact between the sexes.[60] The women in the relief are not shown torturing the Army victims as initial post-coup propaganda alleged. In fact, they project an image of dreamy serenity with their half-closed eyes and floating bodies. This may constitute censoring on the part of the artist, given the allegation that the women had fondled and mutilated the victims' genitals. The eroticism of the women is clearly communicated, yet it is from other sources that Indonesians had to learn of their alleged acts of torture.

The scene at the front of the relief is a scene of chaos. The sculptor signals complete disorder in the cosmos in his representations of the

Illustration 3.10   Military suppression of the 1965 coup attempt.
Source: Photograph by the author.

attempt to pull down the Garuda Pancasila emblem; of the sexually
unrestrained women; and of the torture and killing at Lubang Buaya.

The fourth scene in the relief depicts the beginning of the military
suppression of the "coup attempt" (Illustration 3.10). A large figure,
General Sarwo Edhie, appears with a microphone. The image recalls
his role in working with the students to oppose the communists and
President Sukarno. The Army proper confront the communists. Suharto
appears on the far right, another larger looming figure. Several communists
holding sickles look up at him with awe. The appearance of Suharto in
the relief is marked by a distinct break in the narrative. Representation
of the Old and New Orders as a contrast of disorder and order is a theme
that has frequently been noted.[61] In this monument relief, the theme of
disorder contrasted to order is extremely clear. The scene of the funerals
of the Heroes of the Revolution features people standing in neat lines
(Illustration 3.11). In the monument relief, we also find a very clear
projection of how the New Order sought to define itself by means of
the story of the coup attempt.

Jacques Leclerc has commented on the dancing women in this
relief.[62] What he failed to observe was their mirror-image, the appearance
of two very pious women placed on the right-hand side of Suharto in
the relief (Illustration 3.12). These two women have their heads bowed

Illustration 3.11 Enter Suharto: The restoration of "order" as visualised in the relief beneath the Sacred Pancasila Monument.
Source: Photograph by the author.

Illustration 3.12 Two modest women: A sign of order restored as visualised in the relief beneath the Sacred Pancasila Monument.
Source: Photograph by the author.

and arms held modestly across their chests, covering their breasts. In Indonesian dance, bowed heads denote patience, dedication and the highest virtues.[63] One woman is shown nursing a baby, linking her to motherhood. This is in direct contrast to the image of the immoral communist-linked women in the Lubang Buaya scene. These contrasting images suggest that women were used as symbols to represent how the New Order wished to distinguish itself from the Old Order.

The representation of the two moral women alongside the debauched women provides further evidence for Saskia Wieringa's assertion that these representations of Gerwani women were a metaphor for the disorder of society in the period of Guided Democracy, symbolised by the women's sexually perverse behaviour and the need for new, more "moral", models of womanhood in which women were subordinated to men.[64] As Wieringa notes, the new regime used these symbolic representations as justification for depoliticising the Indonesian women's movement and for putting forward appropriate roles for women. Founded in 1970, the Family Welfare Guidance Organisation (Pembinaan Kesejahteraan Keluarga, PKK) designated five roles for women including: (1) a woman's duty as a wife; (2) a woman's duty as a mother; (3) a woman's duty as a procreator; (4) a woman's duty as a financial manager; and (5) a woman's duty as a member of society. Each of these five roles were subsequently incorporated into government five-year development plans.[65] The immediate consequences for Gerwani members of these binary representations included death or imprisonment, often accompanied by rape.[66] In addition, these representations provided the justification for reforms that had less direct consequences for all Indonesian women.

The scene of "the return to order" in the relief culminates with the image of Sukarno holding Supersemar [the Instruction of 11 March (Illustration 3.11)]. The actual document, which has been supposedly lost, instructed Suharto to "take all measures considered necessary to ensure peace and *order* and stability of the Revolution".[67] In the relief, Sukarno is positioned near the top of the relief to give the appearance of taking a step back. The final scene appearing on the right panel is that of the Extraordinary Military Tribunal on the left with the swearing in of President Suharto on the right (Illustration 3.13). The Garuda Pancasila emblem of legitimacy appears on the wall in the background, another sign of order being restored.

By means of the story of the coup attempt, the new regime sought to define itself. A close study of the monument relief, for example,

Illustration 3.13 The final scene visualised in the relief beneath the Sacred Pancasila Monument, detailing the Extraordinary Military Tribunal and the election of Suharto as President.
Source: Photograph by the author.

indicates that the image projected of communists (including Gerwani) represented everything the New Order rejected. The New Order was, for example, to be a government that abided by the rules of religion and morality, in contrast to those who had "abandoned" religion and were consequently equated with barbarity and immorality. In Islam, the dominant religion in Indonesia, pre-Islamic societies (the *jahiliya*), are often described in such terms as "barbarous" and "immoral", implying the New Order government wished to associate itself with the introduction of a new system of morality. This mirrors the religious representation within the Islamic holy book, the Koran, of the beginnings of a purified society after the introduction of Islam in seventh-century Arabia.[68]

When the monument complex at Lubang Buaya was opened to the public in 1973, it included the preserved well, the monument and relief and a large fence around the 14-hectare enclosure. At the opening of the complex, President Suharto declared the purpose of the monument to be to present the facts about the treason and terror carried about by the Indonesian Communist Party, to remember and honour the deeds and sacrifices of the Heroes of the Revolution, to increase alertness to protect the Pancasila from enemies who seek to undermine or destroy the Pancasila and to instil awareness of the sacredness of the Pancasila.[69] The government, therefore, also intended the monument complex to represent the failure of the coup attempt as proof of the sacredness of Pancasila. It also intended to convey the message that the New Order regime was the protector of the national philosophy.

THE SACREDNESS OF THE PANCASILA

The idea of the sacredness of the national philosophy, Pancasila, is central to the monument at Lubang Buaya and the annual commemorative day held on this site. With the exception of Susan Selden Purdy's work,[70] the theme of the sacredness of Pancasila has received little attention to date. In his 1967 Presidential Decision, regarding the commemorative date of 1 October, Suharto declared that commemoration of Sacred Pancasila Day (*Hari Kesaktian Pancasila*) was premised on:

> ... the special character and features of 1 October as a day on which
> people's certainty in the truth and *kesaktian* of Pancasila, as the only
> life view which can unite the entire state, nation and Indonesian
> people, was strengthened and instilled.[71]

Suharto implied that from 1 October 1965 onwards, the people — presumably under the direction of Suharto and the Army — embraced the Pancasila and rejected all other ideologies, notably communism, which Suharto quickly banned in 1966.

Although *kesaktian* can generally be interpreted as meaning "sacred", it has a number of meanings, some of which have implications for the intended messages of both the monument and the commemorative day. Generally, *kesaktian* implies sacred, supernatural, divine or magical qualities.[72] Mark Woodward traces the origin of the concept of *kesaktian* or magical power in Saiva Hinduism, according to which *sakti* refers to the creative and destructive power of the Gods.[73] After the arrival of Islam in the fourteenth century, the Hindu-Javanese concept of *kesaktian* was incorporated into a compatible strain of Islam which reached Java, that of Sufi Islam, in which there is strong emphasis on the mystical components of Islam, including the use of magical objects such as amulets and emulation of the Prophet in order to attain power. According to Woodward, it was by this route that the concept of *kesaktian* became an important element of syncretic *kejawen* (mysticism associated with the Javanese world) culture. Michael Van Langenberg also notes *kejawen* culture is dominated by mystical religiosity and identification with ancient imperial traditions and was frequently drawn upon by the New Order state.[74] There is cause for caution in referring to Javanese concepts for explanations for twentieth-century Indonesian politics. In this case, however, where the government chose a particular term loaded with Javanese-derived connotations, it is reasonable to at least explore this concept within the framework from which it derives.

Benedict Anderson describes the *kejawen* as:

> ... that intangible, mysterious and divine energy which animates the universe. It is manifested in every aspect of the natural world, in stones, trees, clouds, and fire.[75]

In related aspects of *kejawen* culture, such as the *wayang* world, texts and magic formulas can also be sacred. In the Javanese court, sacred *pusaka*, or heirlooms, are also considered to be objects endowed with magical properties.

A famous legend that illustrates the concept of *kesaktian* is the story of Ken Arok, who overthrew the Kediri dynasty in 1222 and then founded the new palace of Singhasari. Ken Arok is believed to have had magical powers by means of a sacred kris, a specially crafted Javanese dagger considered to be one of the most potent sources of *pusaka* endowed with magical power.[76] One of the central motifs of this story is that the kris, because it had not been completed, was impure and that its sacred properties meant that the kris was both potentially beneficial and harmful to its owner. The Ken Arok story thus indicates that sacred or *sakti* objects are powerful and must be guarded and treated with care.

As 1 October 1965 was the day on which the coup attempt was both carried out and suppressed, the name given to the commemorative day, Sacred Pancasila Day, suggests that it was on this day that the Pancasila was tested or threatened. Although anti-communists clearly believed communists were incapable of accepting the Pancasila, the most likely basis for the assertion that the communists would abandon Pancasila if they took power was a rumour circulated in the late Guided Democracy period about the alleged content of one of Aidit's speeches. In 1964, Aidit was accused of saying that once Indonesian socialism had been implemented, the Pancasila would no longer be needed as a unifying philosophy.[77] It appears that this rumour was re-circulated after the October coup.[78] What is interesting about this assertion is that the 30 September Movement declared in a statement issued on 1 October that the movement had been carried out in the interests of:

... safeguarding the implementation of the Pancasila and the *Panca Azimat Revolusi* ("Five Magical Charms of the Revolution") in addition to the interests and safety of the Army and Armed Forces in general.[79]

In the official New Order version of the coup attempt, however, it is Suharto, together with Kostrad troops, who are associated with the salvation of the Pancasila.

The name of both the monument and the commemorative day were also clear attempts to align the new regime with the Pancasila. In addition to highlighting the significance of Sacred Pancasila Day, the Suharto government also sought to phase out commemoration of the Birth of the Pancasila, celebrated on 1 June, the day most strongly associated with Sukarno's first pronouncement of the Pancasila in 1945. Although the Birth of the Pancasila was not a major celebration in the Old Order, 1 June was certainly widely recognised as the birth date of Pancasila and it was commemorated on a large scale in 1964. The slogan for commemoration in 1964, "Pancasila forever!" (*Panca Sila sepanjang masa*) reinforces the importance of the Pancasila, as a political symbol at least, in the leftist period of late Guided Democracy.[80]

On the first anniversary of the Birth of the Pancasila in 1967, during which Suharto was acting president, he made a speech in which he stated:

> We are proud of the exaltation of the Pancasila, not because it was rediscovered and formulated by someone [read: Sukarno] from the womb, identity and ideals of the Indonesian nation which were hidden away for centuries, but rather because the Pancasila has already proven its truth, after having stood the test of the history of the nation's struggle.[81]

In his speech, Suharto attempted to shift emphasis from Sukarno's discovery of the Pancasila to the defence of the Pancasila, including his own role in the salvation of the Pancasila from the "communists". Although this was clearly part of a broader scheme of de-Sukarnoisation, it also constituted an attempt by the New Order regime to present itself as the protector of Pancasila.

At the same time, the New Order attempted to claim ownership of the Pancasila through the official version of the coup attempt, Nugroho Notosusanto began working on an investigation of the origins of Pancasila, another history project designed to disassociate Sukarno from the Pancasila. In the 1970s, Nugroho began to circulate his theory that

Sukarno was only one of three *penggali* (excavators) of the Pancasila and that the real birth of Pancasila was on 18 August 1945, the date on which Pancasila was legally confirmed together with the 1945 Constitution rather than 1 June 1945, the date on which Sukarno first pronounced this idea.[82] Nugroho based this theory on an allegedly altered version of Yamin's 29 May 1945 speech to the Preparatory Committee for Independence appearing in Yamin's publication *Documents for the Preparation of the 1945 Constitution* (Naskah Persiapan Undang-Undang Dasar 1945),[83] which Nugroho claimed contained Pancasila-like concepts. In 1975 a five-person investigative committee headed by Muhammad Hatta, the first Vice-President, found the transcript provided in Yamin's book to be a significantly altered version of Yamin's 1945 speech.[84] Although the order and exact wording of the principles of Pancasila did change slightly between 1 June and 18 August, this pedantic distinction was designed purely for the political purpose of disassociating Sukarno from the Pancasila.[85]

Nugroho's work on the origins of the Pancasila was perhaps the most blatant case of historical manipulation for the New Order regime. In the early 1980s, his theory prompted a polemic in the mass media and a national seminar entitled "Who really discovered Pancasila?"[86] The most likely reason for the timing of this polemic is the introduction from 1978 onwards of Pancasila courses into which Nugroho's theory was incorporated (Chapter 5). Criticisms directed at Nugroho's work attacked his distortion of available evidence and his reliance on suspect sources. Some historians branded Nugroho's book a "pamphlet", implying that it was not sufficiently researched or neutral for the work of a scholar. Nugroho responded that if what was meant by the term "pamphlet" was that the material was in accordance with the opinion of the present government, then "that was only a coincidence".[87] Nugroho was also accused of attempting to tarnish Sukarno's historical image and to deny his role as the "discoverer" of Pancasila, which the New Order regime hoped to take on as its own.[88] Despite the controversy over Nugroho's work, his theory remained part of the government Pancasila indoctrination courses — P4 (Penataran Pedoman Penghayatan dan Pengamalan Pancasila-Upgrading Course on the Directives for the Realisation of Pancasila) — and continued to be included in volume six of the *National History Textbook*. The Department of Education also made Nugroho's book on the Pancasila theory compulsory reading for schoolteachers who taught the Pancasila moral education course and as a reference book to accompany the National History Series.

The claim that Pancasila was sacred initially received some criticism from liberals. In the early years of the New Order, there was some freedom publicly to express criticisms of the government. In a 1970 editorial piece, Jakob Oetama of "Kompas" newspaper suggested, for example, that the term "Pancasila sakti" implied the government took the view that the Pancasila was in fact a *pusaka* (an heirloom) or something which was to be respected and valued, but put away.[89] Oetama's response reflected a growing sense of frustration with the New Order regime. Oetama had particular cause for cynicism at the government's claims to upholding the Pancasila, as in 1969 he had been pressured by the military not to report on the most "un-Pancasila like" behaviour of the military in the mass killings of prisoners by the Army in areas around the town of Purwodadi in late 1968 to early 1969.[90]

The hypocrisy of the new regime's attempt to associate itself with the pure implementation of the Pancasila, a philosophy that includes the principle of "a just and civilised humanity" and "social justice", can only be fully grasped by considering the actions taken in this period against enemies of the regime, primarily communists — in the name of upholding the Pancasila. Perhaps as many as 500,000 people were killed and many more were imprisoned without trial. As Robert Cribb has suggested, "one looks in vain in the Pancasila ... for reasons why communists should be exterminated rather than, say, gently re-educated".[91] The politics behind commemoration of 1 October, like that of preserving the site of suffering of the Army heroes, are highly charged. Commemoration of 1 October demands a focus on the events of this day in 1965, particularly on the deaths of the Army martyrs. What this commemoration obscures is the far greater violence that took place in the wake of the coup attempt against communist supporters. This is evidenced by the fact that frequent comment was made in annual commemoration of Sacred Pancasila Day, that 1 October 1965 was "the most traumatic day in modern Indonesian history".[92]

The message of the "sacredness" of the Pancasila is communicated in the Sacred Pancasila Monument by means of specific details and by the overall layout of the monument. A careful study of the extensive monument complex reveals a layout similar to that found in a Javanese *kraton* (palace). The monument consists of a large *gapura* (archway) at the entrance (Illustration 3.14) followed by a long driveway with lush gardens to one side. The driveway ends in a large open space similar to an *alun-alun* (a town square — Illustration 3.15). To one side of the *alun-alun* is a large pavilion labelled a *paseban* (usually a waiting room

Illustration 3.14 The gateway to the Sacred Pancasila Monument.
Source: Photograph by Chatarina Purnamdari.

Illustration 3.15 The square in the middle of the Sacred Pancasila Monument complex.
Source: Photograph by Chatarina Purnamdari.

in a Javanese palace). On the other side is the entrance to the first museum of the complex, which then leads visitors by stairwell to the second museum. On the west side of the *alun-alun* is a gateway entrance to the inner domain of the monument. The inner domain includes a ceremonial field, another gateway and a *cungkup* that covers the well and the main monument. The palace of Yogyakarta similarly has a large gateway leading onto a square, then an audience hall and a series of gateways and pavilions leading to the inner quarters of the palace.[93] The significance of this replicated layout is that it provides cues — to those familiar with the palace structure at least, including many members of the Javanese political elite — of a sense of movement towards an inner core. It is within the very core of the kraton that the so-called *sakti* objects (including ancient heirlooms) are stored under close guard. In the case of the monument, the mimicking of the layout of a kraton implies that the epicentre of the monument complex, the preserved well and monument, are also sites or sources of *kesaktian*.

The message of the "sacredness" of the Pancasila is communicated more explicitly in the details of the monument. The seven Army heroes featured in the monument that faces the *cungkup* stand in strong accusing poses, with clenched fists reflecting confidence, strength and alertness (Illustration 3.16). These statues send out a warning to those who

Illustration 3.16 The figures of the Army martyrs in the Sacred Pancasila Monument.
Source: Photograph by the author.

challenge the Pancasila, as indicated by the presence of a looming Garuda Pancasila emblem affixed to a seventeen metre-high white wall behind the military statues. The statue of General Yani, the Commander of the Army in 1965, holds out a pointing finger directly towards the well in an accusing and threatening pose. The plaque on top of the well records the message Yani is delivering: "It is not possible that the ideals of our struggle to uphold the essence of the Pancasila will be destroyed merely by burying us in this well". Together, the monument and preserved well are therefore meant to function as affirmations of the enduring power of the Pancasila.

In 1980 management of Sacred Pancasila Monument complex was transferred from the State Secretariat to the Armed Forces History Centre. Shortly afterwards the Centre added a museum detailing the events of the coup attempt and a relics room. At around the same time he was working on the new museum, Nugroho Notosusanto, also helped create the epic propaganda film *The Treachery of the 30 September Movement* (Pengkhianatan Gerakan 30 September), which also repeated the official version of the coup attempt. Despite the mass killings of communists that followed the 1965 coup and the banning of communism in 1966, the government had kept the spectre of a communist threat alive by means of periodic warnings about the return of communism as well as annual commemoration 1 October. Because of the length of time that had passed since the coup attempt, the government decided in the early 1980s that anti-communism should be reinvigorated. For members of the older generation, memories of the killing of communists were perhaps sufficient to warrant fear of being associated with anything branded communist, yet for the younger generation, who did not share these memories of communist treachery, it was more difficult to make such associations. The anti-communist revival was therefore targeted at them. At around the same time as the museum and film projects were being implemented, the Operations Command to Restore Order and Security, together with the National Resilience Institute (Lemhannas, Lembaga Ketahanan Nasional), began to plan Tarpadnas (anti-communist indoctrination) courses to be directed at civil servants and youth in particular.[94] In continuing to espouse the existence of a communist threat, the regime sought to provide on-going justification for the killings, but also to maintain a convenient and potent label for political dissent. Ariel Heryanto has aptly described the regime's use of the threat of communism as "an instrument of authoritarianism".[95]

THE SACRED PANCASILA MONUMENT MUSEUM

The Sacred Pancasila Monument Museum consists of diorama images, a relics room and a small theatre for viewing documentaries about the events of 1965. The museum features six small dioramas and three life-sized dioramas. Like the relief, these scenes also play out the script of transition from disorder to order. The disorder is represented by a communist meeting for the preparation of the coup, volunteers training at Lubang Buaya, the kidnapping of Lieutenant General Yani, culminating in the cruel treatment (*penganiayaan*) at Lubang Buaya. The first two scenes — which cover the prelude to the coup attempt — seek to establish the complicity of the Indonesian Communist Party. The first scene of the communist meeting emphasises the role of Syam Kamaruzaman as Head of the Special Bureau in recruiting *oknum* (suspicious elements) of the armed forces on behalf of the Chairperson of the Indonesian Communist Party, Aidit. The second scene on the volunteers, like earlier accounts of the coup attempt, focuses on the presence of members of Gerwani and the People's Youth at Lubang Buaya, suggesting they were being trained in preparation for the coup attempt.[96] The scene of Lieutenant General Yani's shooting is highly graphic (Illustration 3.17).

Illustration 3.17   The Kidnapping of the Chief of the Armed Forces, Lieutenant General A. Yani (1 October 1965).
Source: Image from Pusat Sejarah dan Tradisi ABRI, *Buku Panduan Monumen Pancasila Sakti Lubang Buaya Jakarta*, Pusat Sejarah dan Tradisi ABRI, Jakarta, 1997, p. 25.

It closely replicates both the film scene of his death and the preserved evidence on display in the Army-run Ahmad Yani memorial museum. In that museum, the door through which Yani was shot is preserved as it was on the day of his death, complete with bullet-holes. A gold plate marks the place on the floor where he fell.[97] The caption to the museum scene entitled "The Cruel Treatment at Lubang Buaya" directly replicates the newspaper propaganda surrounding the deaths of the heroes, noting that "those still alive were tortured one by one, then shot in the head".[98]

The scenes representing the restoration of order feature the securing of the Air Force Base by Kostrad troops under Suharto's command; the retrieval of the corpses from the disused well; Supersemar; the appointment of Suharto as president and a scene covering the banning of communism in 1966 and further measures to prevent the return of communism in Indonesia.[99]

The dioramas in this museum are accompanied by sound recordings to which visitors can listen by inserting special tokens into small boxes beside each diorama. Zainuddin, the sound expert for the museum, notes that the purpose of the sound recordings was not to provide information, but rather to help recreate the atmosphere of the period and location or to evoke feelings. This, he suggested, could be achieved by means of the use of excerpts from music and language.[100] The sound recordings therefore feature eerie music or dramatic audio re-enactments of events which, in a similar mode to the film (see pp. 96–100), appear to be geared towards creating an atmosphere of fear and trepidation.

The museum also includes a small gallery of portraits of the seven Army victims of the coup attempt: Lieutenant General Ahmad Yani, Major General Suprapto, Major General M.T. Haryono, Major General S. Parman, Brigadier D.I. Pandjaitan, Brigadier Sutoyo Siswomihardjo and Lieutenant Pierre Andreas Tendean (Illustration 3.18). These portraits remind museum visitors of the heroic victims of "communist" violence and have also been repeatedly replicated in history texts[101] and in giant billboards displayed on the ceremonial field at Lubang Buaya for commemoration of Sacred Pancasila Day (Illustration 3.19).

The relics room, which adjoins the diorama displays, further personalises the suffering of the Army martyrs by displaying the personal possessions of the heroes at the time they were kidnapped (Illustration 3.20). A commemorative history of the Armed Forces History Centre notes that these relics are:

> ... silent testimonies of the cruelty of G30S/PKI which can still be witnessed for example from the work clothes of Major General TNI

Illustration 3.18 Portraits of the Heroes of the Revolution displayed in the Sacred Pancasila Monument Museum.
Source: Images from Pusat Sejarah dan Tradisi ABRI, *Buku Panduan Monumen Pancasila Sakti Lubang Buaya Jakarta,* Pusat Sejarah dan Tradisi ABRI, Jakarta, 1997, p. 30.

Illustration 3.19 Schoolchildren lined up in the Sapta Marga field at the Sacred Pancasila Monument for the commemoration of the 1997 Sacred Pancasila Day.
Source: Photograph by the author.

S. Parman, which contain holes in the stomach region as a result of bullet wounds. The cruelty can also be witnessed by means of the bloodspots on the sarong and shirt of Major General Suprapto and in the remaining tatters of the jacket of Lieutenant Pierre Tendean as a result of stab wounds from a sharp object in the stomach region.[102]

These objects are not only on display, they are also carefully and meticulously preserved. Conservation is carried out on the heroes' clothes on a monthly basis, including dust suction of displays and control of corrosion.[103] This attention to the preservation of objects is uncharacteristic of Indonesian museums. Many relics of ancient temples, for example, sit uncased in the humid open air conditions in, for example, the National Museum. The level of care of the hero's clothes indicates the enormous priority awarded to preserving "evidence" of the suffering of the Army heroes.

The small theatre, which is housed in the same building as the dioramas and relics room, enables small groups to view a number of different audio-visual presentations about the "crushing" of the "G30S/PKI", the official acronym used to associate the 30 September Movement

Illustration 3.20 A display of the jacket and pants of Lieutenant P.A. Tendean in the relics room in the Sacred Pancasila Monument Museum. *Source:* Image from Pusat Sejarah dan Tradisi ABRI, *Buku Panduan Monumen Pancasila Sakti Lubang Buaya Jakarta*, Pusat Sejarah dan Tradisi ABRI, Jakarta, 1997, p. 31.

with the PKI. These films include the television interview conducted
between the national television broadcaster, TVRI and the former
Commander of the Army Parachute Commando Regiment (Resimen
Para Komando Angkatan Darat, RPKAD) TNI Lieutenant General
Sarwo Edhie Wibowo; film footage of the recovery of the bodies of the
"Heroes of the Revolution" from the well on 4 October 1965 and the
film *Pengkhianatan Gerakan 30 September.*

THE FILM: *THE TREACHERY OF THE 30 SEPTEMBER MOVEMENT*

The film *The Treachery of the 30 September Movement* (Pengkhianatan
Gerakan 30 September) was perhaps the best-known official representation of the 1965 coup attempt, because after its release in 1983 it
was screened on national television on every 30 September during the
New Order period. Because the government intended the film for broad
circulation, great care was taken with the representation of events within
the film. The key persons involved in making the film were Nugroho,
who edited the film and whose version of the coup formed the primary
basis for the script, Brigadier-General Dwipayana, a trusted member of
the presidential staff who was then director of the State Film Corporation,
and director Arifin C. Noor.[104] The filmmakers describe the film as a
"docu-drama". The film makers paid acute attention to detail, particularly
in the reconstruction of the kidnappings. Because of the sensitivity of
the topic the film was checked before it was screened by persons involved,
such as President Suharto and General Sarwo Edhie, and by other senior
military figures.[105]

Although scholars have frequently mentioned this film, the details
of its content are not often discussed. Because of the length of the four-
hour "docu-drama", representations of Indonesian "communists" are
more developed in this film source than in the official written versions
of the coup attempt and those in the museum. The narrative emphasises
the themes of evil, scheming, corrupt communists. Members of the
Communist Party are shown sitting smoking in secret meetings in clouds
of smoke, reminiscent of popular images of gangsters (Illustration 3.21).
The narrative builds towards the climax of the events at Lubang Buaya,
with a progression of excerpts indicating mounting communist terror.
The film includes motifs of fire and frightened animals such as running
deer at Sukarno's Bogor palace to portray a sense of uneasiness. A scene
of an attack on an Islamic school reminds the audience of the religious

Illustration 3.21   The gangster image of the Indonesian Communist Party in the film *The Treachery of the 30 September Movement*.
Source: Image from the film *Pengkhianatan Gerakan 30 September* as reproduced in the novel based on the film Arswendo Atmowiloto, *Pengkhianatan G 30 S/PKI*, Pustaka Sinar Harapan, Jakarta, 1994, p. 41.

framework of this story. In a scene preceding the coup attempt, an impoverished looking boy asks his weeping mother, "Who killed Daddy, Mum?" (*"Siapa membunuh bapak, ibu?"*). The mother replies, "The communists, they are evil" (*Orang komunis mereka biadab*).

A significant part of the film is taken up with individual re-enactments of each of the kidnappings and deaths of the "Heroes of the Revolution". While an account of each of the kidnappings was outlined in Nugroho's book *The Forty Day Failure of the 30 September Movement*, the film medium allows the kidnappings to be more intensely dramatised. In an attempt to add to the authenticity of the film, scenes were shot in the original homes of the generals. Each kidnapping scene in the film begins with frames of each of the general's families panning over photos with wives, and then a tranquil scene of the homes at night-time. The children of the generals are shown sleeping in their beds. From these

Illustration 3.22   S. Parman's omen in the film *The Treachery of the 30 September Movement.*
Source: Image from the film *Pengkhianatan Gerakan 30 September* as reproduced in the novel based on the film Arswendo Atmowiloto, *Pengkhianatan G 30 S/PKI*, Pustaka Sinar Harapan, Jakarta, 1994, p. 97.

scenes of the sanctity of the home, the film switches to a shot of flaming fire and a communist meeting at Lubang Buaya. Those present seem wild and spirited. They are shouting "Long live the People, Long live Nasakom, Long live Bung Karno, Long Live Bung Aidit" (*Hidup Rakyat, Hidup Nasakom, Hidup Bung Karno, Hidup Bung Aidit*). We return to General Parman, who has an omen (Illustration 3.22). Hearing the sound of a bird cry in his dream, he gets up from bed, but his wife tells him it was just a dream. Yet the bird's cry was so clear! To obscure the passivity of the military men in their deaths, the generals are portrayed as having an acute sense of a looming threat. The film then switches back to chanting at Lubang Buaya.

Shots of campfires at Lubang Buaya are shown while discordant piano music indicates impending doom. Communists are shown marching

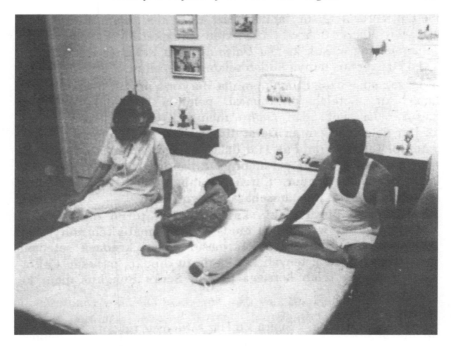

Illustration 3.23   The 1965 coup attempt depicted as disrupting the family in the film *The Treachery of the 30 September Movement*.
Source: Image from the film *Pengkhianatan Gerakan 30 September* as reproduced in the novel based on the film Arswendo Atmowiloto, *Pengkhianatan G 30 S/PKI*, Pustaka Sinar Harapan, Jakarta, 1994, p. 110.

with red scarves. Over and over we see the violent disruption of the tranquil family home (Illustration 3.23). The audience relives the scenes at the house of Nasution, where adjutant Lieutenant Tendean instead was taken alive; General Yani, who was shot opposing his summons to the palace; General Soetojo, who is taken alive and doesn't have time to get dressed; General S. Parman, who is taken alive; General Suprapto, who is taken alive; and General Pandjaitan and General Harjono, who are shot dead in front of their families. The film emphasises the invasion of the home by communists "disguised" as soldiers (see p. 105). The death of Nasution's daughter Ade, who was caught in cross-fire during the attempted kidnapping of Nasution, was also fully exploited in this film in the context of the "destruction" of the family. Shiraishi suggests the disruptions to the family unit in this film are also part of an image contrasting with the New Order's emphasis on the family.[106] It is again possible to see this scene as a representation of chaos before order, which Krishna Sen notes is a dominant feature of most New Order period films.[107]

The film *The Treachery of the 30 September Movement* provides a vivid depiction of the torture of the generals. In the film, the wild scenes at Lubang Buaya begin with dancing, fire and chanting. We see the bloodied face of a general and the bodies being dragged around. Music accompanies these gory scenes of torture, including eye-gouging and genital mutilation performed by women. Some generals are shot to the chant of "kill, kill" (*bunuh, bunuh*). The bodies are then forced into the well. Women are also shown dancing around the well.

REPRESENTATIONS OF TORTURE

Both the official film and the Museum of the Sacred Pancasila Monument feature explicit representations of torture. This contrasts with earlier official representations of the coup including *The Forty Day Failure of the 30 September Movement*, the military's English version of the coup attempt and the monument relief in which torture is only subtly implied. Neither of the two publications directly reproduce the most gruesome accounts of torture of the Army heroes prior to their deaths, including lurid statements that the victims' eyes were gouged out and their genitals cut off prior to death.[108] Although these wounds are consistent with the autopsy report, what Nugroho fails to mention is that the doctors suggested such wounds were the possible result of either clubbing with the butts of guns that fired the bullets or injuries caused to the corpses by the 36-foot drop into the well (which would mean the injuries occurred after death).[109] Theses sources do, however, imply torture, which may be the result of the later date at which these representations were created, by which time the regime perhaps felt safer that it would not be challenged, at least from inside Indonesia, on these issues.

In 1987 Anderson published a translated version of the autopsy report ordered by Suharto following the retrieval of the corpses of the military heroes from the well. The report found that none of the victims' eyes had been gouged out and that their penises remained intact.[110] This did not deter the Armed Forces History Centre, however, from adding a more blatant representation of the torture of the Army heroes to the monument complex in 1991. The Centre installed a large scale diorama (Illustration 3.24) just beside the preserved well in an original building.

Illustration 3.24   The large-scale diorama display of the alleged torture of one of the Heroes of the Revolution.
Source: Image from Pusat Sejarah dan Tradisi ABRI, *Buku Panduan Monumen Pancasila Sakti Lubang Buaya Jakarta*, Pusat Sejarah dan Tradisi ABRI, Jakarta, 1997, p. 36.

The diorama features life-size figures of the generals tied up with gaping wounds. Communist men and women in green uniforms, red berets and with red kerchiefs round their necks are shown taunting their victims. General S. Parman is shown being forced to sign a document admitting the existence of a Council of Generals.[111] One figure holds up a sickle, the symbol of communism, suggesting that the sickle was used as an instrument of torture. Representations of the torture allegedly carried out at Lubang Buaya were also replicated in school texts at a later date. A unit of the *History of the National Struggle* (Pelajaraan Sejarah Perjuangan Bangsa, PSPB) for primary school, for example, included a script of the events at Lubang Buaya for a class play. One of the designated scenes for students to act out was entitled, "The Cruelty at Lubang Buaya". The dialogue consisted of simplified phrases such as "Kill him, kill him", "Cut up his flesh", "crush his head", "Cut off his tongue and his hands" (Illustration 3.25).[112] Accompanying instructions suggested those in the role of the PKI should have replica weapons and mime the beating of the "good" generals. This whole "socio-drama" directed at primary school

Illustration 3.25   The torture of the generals as represented in a school text.
Source: From Poedhyarto Trisaksono, *Sosiodrama Pelengkap PSPB untuk Sekolah Dasar*, Tiga Serangkai, Solo, 1985, p. 44.

children is alarmingly violent. It also reinforces the fact that the New Order regime was determined to instil anti-communism into the young generations in Indonesia.

A curious omission in the national monument complex at Lubang Buaya is reference to the actions of the 30 September Movement in other cities in Indonesia, such as the significant events in Yogyakarta in which two further military heroes, Colonel Katamso Dharmakusumo and Lieutenant Colonel Sugijono Mangunwijoto, were killed. I would suggest that one reason for this was to distract attention away from the fact that in Central Java the military involvement in the 30 September Movement was much clearer. While in Jakarta it was the troops of the Presidential Guard who carried out the kidnappings, in Yogyakarta five out of the seven infantry battalions in that area were dominated by supporters of the 30 September Movement.[113] It may be that the events in Central Java were ignored in the national monument to put forward more convincing evidence that the coup was a communist plot, pure and simple. A monument similar in layout and symbolism to the Sacred

Illustration 3.26   The Kentungan Monument, Yogyakarta.
Source: Photograph by the author.

Pancasila Monument was, however, erected at a later date at the site at which the two Yogyakarta military heroes were found — the battalion 403 military site known as Kentungan (Illustration 3.26).[114]

REPEATED MESSAGES, MIXED RECEPTIONS

As a result of repeatedly replicated images of the evil communists, a tendency developed of seeing the PKI as:

> ... part of a new demonology; something that is very evil yet very strong, something that is dark and secret, something that from time to time can pounce on us again at the time we are careless.[115]

Referring to the Madiun rebellion and the 1965 coup attempt, the military warned of the cyclical nature of communism (Chapter 6). Continued circulation of the official version of the coup attempt in the monument, museum, film, history books and in commemoration of 1 October had a lasting impact for survivors of this period and their families. Stereotypes about communists, and Gerwani in particular, contributed to social stigmatisation for the children of these families who were taught to feel shame for the alleged actions committed by their parents.[116] Many families with relatives who were political prisoners were, for example, stunned by the film and wept with grief at these representations of communists each time the film was replayed every year.[117] For released former political prisoners, the repeated circulation of these images, combined with the social restrictions placed on them (including limitations on job choice and freedom of movement) also contributed to prejudice and isolation.[118]

Because of strict censorship controls during the New Order period, most Indonesians only received the black-and-white simplified versions of the past, which dealt purely in these kinds of stereotypes. Some children who had previously viewed *The Treachery of the 30 September Movement* or learned about "communists" at school would arrive at the Sacred Pancasila Monument holding up their arms as if to hold a weapon, demanding "Where are the PKI?" as if ready to shoot.[119] In the post-Suharto period, historian Taufik Abdullah has strongly criticised this style of history writing, which he characterises as history for exacting revenge.[120]

Yet the fact that students had to ask the question "Where are the PKI?" suggests that there was some ambiguity involved in identifying the communists in representations at Lubang Buaya. The troops who kidnapped the generals were members of the Presidential Guard and wore green military uniforms. In the film and the diorama images at Lubang Buaya, the "communists" disguised as guards also appear in green uniforms. An observer noted that in 1996, due to viewers' confusion, a caption reading "a group of the military infiltrated by the PKI" was added to the kidnapping scenes to clarify this issue to viewers of the film.[121] The necessity of adding this caption indicates the ambiguity of representations between the representor and the audience, and the potential for audiences to read these images as they like. Some viewers gained the impression that the military and communist were indistinguishable. Despite all their efforts to guard the official version of the coup attempt, the military was not therefore able to control how this version was interpreted.

One consequence of the repetition of homogeneous versions of the coup attempt was a fascination with alternative versions demonstrated by some Indonesians, especially those who travelled abroad. Adrian Vickers recounts one Javanese as having described the writings of Western scholars about the coup as being like a kind of political "pornography" during the New Order period.[122] Because this version was so closely guarded, it most likely led to scepticism as to its truth.

CHALLENGES TO THE OFFICIAL VERSION OF THE COUP ATTEMPT IN POST-SUHARTO INDONESIA

Accumulated cynicism at official representations of the coup attempt was also demonstrated by the backlash against this version after Suharto's resignation, when press freedom permitted the expression of such views. Days after the fall of Suharto, Lieutenant-Colonel Latief, a political prisoner convicted of involvement in the events of the coup attempt of 1965, claimed in a press interview that the night before the coup attempt, he had forewarned Suharto that the generals would be kidnapped. He also reported that Suharto had chosen not to act until the coup was completed.[123] In response to this scepticism, the new President, Habibie, axed the annual screening of *The Treachery of the 30 September Movement.* By the time of the 1998 anniversary of the coup attempt, a flood of special feature articles questioning the official version of this episode appeared.[124] This sparked confusion in school classrooms on the part of teachers. Students felt considerable anger towards both history-writers and their teachers that the history they been taught for years was suddenly exposed to open questioning. The release of all remaining political prisoners from 1965 also raised the question for students: why, if they had indeed done something wrong, were they suddenly released?[125]

Most articles immediately after Suharto's downfall focused on the question of his culpability in the coup attempt, focusing in particular on Latief's version of the coup attempt, rather than that of the military as an institution. In some articles, Ruth McVey and Benedict Anderson's theory that the coup attempt was an internal military affair was also outlined.[126]

The apparent focus on Suharto's culpability and associated attempts to discredit his historical role as the hero of 1965 share similarities with the New Order regime's early efforts to erase Sukarno's historical achievements from the record.

The Air Force, which had been disgraced because of the alleged involvement of Air Force officers in training volunteers for the coup attempt, also used this opportunity of a freer press and cynicism towards the Army as a result of widespread exposure of human rights abuses during the New Order to release their own version of the coup attempt, in which they denied their involvement.[127]

Some newspaper reports also featured rebuttals of the official version that the Army heroes were tortured prior to their deaths, making reference to the autopsy reports from 1965.[128] In the post-Suharto period, a significant challenge to the gender mythology surrounding the 1965 coup attempt was also posed by the release of a translated version of Saskia Wieringa's comprehensive study of Gerwani, in which she rebuts the myths about them, and by the publication of Sulami's memoirs which present a personal story of a Gerwani woman who was imprisoned for 20 years.[129] Kuntowijoyo notes that the publication of Wieringa's book "shocked many with the revelation that all the dioramas at various historical monuments ... are in fact based on fabricated facts".[130] The significance of these reports was that they cast suspicion on the endlessly repeated propaganda about the coup attempt.

The Sacred Pancasila monument and commemorative day have also been subject to some criticism in the post-Suharto era. Historian Taufik Abdullah put forward the strongest critique of Sacred Pancasila Day. He stated, although the tragedy of the 30 September Movement is undeniable:

> Everyone remembers that this tragedy was followed by an equally
> horrible tragedy. But what did the government do? They made this

day Sacred Pancasila Day. Where is the sacredness of the Pancasila? That sacredness hurt some members of the Indonesian population. Many died because of this and then came the clean environment concept.[131]

Prior to this criticism, surprisingly few people had drawn a parallel between the deaths that followed the coup and the hypocrisy in the name of this day. Most attention was in fact directed towards the regime's failure to uphold the Pancasila.[132] In 2000, the Gus Dur-Megawati Sukarnoputri government changed the name of this commemorative day to the Commemorative Day for the Betrayal of Pancasila [Peringatan Hari Pengkhianatan (terhadap) Pancasila]. The official reason provided for this name change was "to change the misrepresentation that Pancasila, the national philosophy, was sacred".[133] It seems this name change, like President Habibie's decision to scrap the Pancasila indoctrination courses, was a response to accumulated cynicism at the New Order regime's sacralisation of the Pancasila.

In October 2000, one of the most direct challenges to Sacred Pancasila Monument was put forward. Political psychologist Hamdi Muluk, from the University of Indonesia, after noting that this monument featuring the statues of the seven Heroes of the Revolution was still standing, asked whether they were in fact the only victims? He then went on to mention that, in fact, hundreds of thousands of people — possibly a million — were killed in the name of revenge for what "they" did to the heroes of the revolution. Although it was not just the propaganda that incited people to kill,[134] Muluk's suggestion that the fact that the monument was still standing was evidence that there was still some kind of "allergy" to the Indonesian Communist Party well-founded.[135]

Sacred Pancasila Monument incorporates many of the features of the initial coup propaganda. The preserved well and the elaborate symbolism that accompanies its presentation highlights the theme of the barbarity and a-religiosity of the communists. The monument relief details the New Order myth of origin: the progression from disorder under Sukarno to order under Suharto.

In the monument, the museum and the official film about the coup, the regime used representations of communists as a symbolic space to represent everything the New Order was allegedly not. Communist women were, for example, portrayed as symbols of a debauched and immoral society, while the New Order represented itself as the return to a "moral" society. The communists were also portrayed as being opposed to the Pancasila, which as we have seen, was such an important rallying point for the new regime. The theme of the sacredness of Pancasila was also given progressively more emphasis in the monument and the annual commemorative ceremony.

The official version of the coup attempt also promoted a simplistic view of history directed towards highlighting an enemy. During the New Order, some Indonesians privately questioned the official version of the coup attempt. Other signs of scepticism became apparent after the fall of Suharto.

Although some of the key elements of the official story of the coup attempt have been debunked, the monument at Lubang Buaya remains standing and open to visitors. In his observations of monuments Andreus Huyssen suggests:

> The promise of permanence of a monument in stone will suggest it is always built on quicksand. Some monuments are joyously toppled at times of social upheaval; others preserve memory in its most ossified form, either as myth or as cliché. Yet others stand simply as figures of forgetting, their meaning and original purpose eroded by the passage of time.[136]

The fact that the Sacred Pancasila Monument remains intact, several years after the fall of Suharto and that it is still highlighted on the Armed Forces History Centre website, indicates that there has not been the kind of radical social change that incited the removal of Dutch monuments during both the Japanese period and thereafter. The reason for this is that to date there has not yet been a thorough re-examination of anti-communism in Indonesia. This may in part be due to the success of New Order propaganda and continuing emphasis on the communists as barbaric and inhuman, but it is also related to psychological consequences of re-evaluating the idea that the post-coup killings were not justified (see Chapter 6 for more on this theme). Signs in the immediate post-Suharto era therefore suggest that this monument will probably remain standing in its current form. Whether it will become a myth or cliché will depend on the extent to which firmly entrenched anti-communism is re-examined.

CONCLUSION

Establishment of the Armed Forces History Centre proved timely when, just over a year later, the coup attempt took place. Nugroho Notosusanto, as Head of the Centre, was the principal author of the first published version of coup attempt. *The Forty Day Failure of the 30 September Movement* was significant because it consolidated Army propaganda about the coup and provided a linear account detailing the Communist Party's complicity. It was to form the basis of the official New Order version of the coup for the next three decades.

Representations of the coup attempt were of central significance to the legitimacy of the regime and the banning and justification for the destruction of the communist party. It was for this reason that the military continued to defend and replicate this narrative in written and visual form for the duration of the regime. The 1968 English language version of the coup attempt, written by Nugroho Notosusanto and Ismail Saleh with the assistance of the US government in response to the appearance of the Cornell Paper, attempted to preserve the legitimacy of the regime in the eyes of the outside world. The extent to which the version of the coup attempt was memorialised at the site of Lubang Buaya also highlights the regime's concern to entrench this version of history. The fact that anti-communism has survived the New Order indicates some success in this project, but many Indonesians also questioned this version of the past because it was forced upon them. Although, in the post-Suharto era, questioning has arisen as to the official version of the coup attempt, some Indonesians remain committed to both this version and to anti-communism because of the various meanings they have invested in this past. For ex-political prisoners and the families of former communists, this was a damaging discourse that pushed them into the position of social outcasts.

Representations of the coup attempt tell us far more about the new regime than about the coup itself. The official version of the coup attempt was used to define Indonesian core values, including a commitment to religion and morality. The preserved well at Lubang Buaya attempts to remind Indonesians of the allegedly barbaric deaths of the Army martyrs at communist hands and the *cungkup* above the well of God's guiding hand in allowing the corpses of the Army martyrs to be found. The relief beneath the Sacred Pancasila Monument details the pathway to national crisis under Sukarno and the influence of immoral communists through to the restoration of order and morality under Sukarno. The monument complex and the annual commemorative day also reinforce the theme of the sacredness of the Pancasila and the threat communism posed to the first principle of belief in one God. The museum located at this site, the film *The Treachery of the 30 September*

Movement and New Order commemorations of Sacred Pancasila Day similarly replicated the themes of communist treachery, the suffering of the Army martyrs and Suharto and the Army's roles in safe guarding the Pancasila.

The coup was the first historical episode to receive detailed attention from Nugroho and the Armed Forces History Centre. Within a short space of time, the Centre turned to other historical episodes to promote the military's role in Indonesian history and to consolidate military unity and military values.

4

Consolidating Military Unity

Factionalism is a significant threat to the power of political militaries, and it is consequently an important task for a political military to ensure sufficient unity across the forces and across military generations. By the early New Order period, the Indonesian military had already experienced internal division several times. Conflict between the older Dutch-trained KNIL (Koninklijk Nederlands Indisch Leger, Royal Netherlands Indies Army) and younger Japanese trained PETA (Pembela Tanah Air, Defenders of the Fatherland) officers was a central cause of military disunity in the post-revolutionary period. Japanese-trained officers, in particular, objected to the perceived favouring of Dutch-trained officers for promotion. This conflict triggered an inter-military and military-parliament disagreement, which culminated in the 17 October affair of 1952. By late Guided Democracy, factionalism (this time between the forces) was again weakening military power. Each of the four forces had developed separate identities and loyalties. Each force, for example, had its own history centre and its own museums. Divisions between and within the forces were further accentuated by the involvement of sections of the military in the 1965 coup attempt. Members of the Army (especially from the Central Java Diponegoro Division) and members of the Air Force (including the Air Force Commander Omar Dhani, who publicly declared his support for the actions of the 30 September Movement) were subsequently purged from the military.

At the outset of the New Order regime, the military was faced with a pressing problem of internal divisions. The military turned to history as a means of promoting shared values and a shared identity across the forces. The Armed Forces History Centre began to emphasise the history of the armed forces as a united story by means of a centralised military museum and a new series of history readers for soldiers.

As the regime progressed, the military also turned to history as a means for creating a common vision between the older and younger generations of members. Central to these efforts was the concept of the 1945 Generation and the 1945 spirit, both of which made reference to the legendary generation that had experienced the 1945–49 independence struggle. In this chapter, I highlight the attempt of the older military generation to claim ownership of the shifting meanings of the term. The 1972 Army staff and command school seminar on the transfer of the 1945 values was at the centre of these efforts to appropriate the 1945 values. The seminar stimulated a wide range of history projects, which promoted the military's role in the 1945–49 independence struggle.

In the last section of this chapter, I focus on how the military used representations of General Sudirman to promote the 1945 values. I examine one project resulting from the seminar that was directed at military cadets: the General Sudirman Walking Pilgrimage. Here I analyse how the dual function and the supposed unity between the people and the military were rationalised to young cadets and the reason why the guerrilla era of the struggle was highlighted in most representations of this era.

CONSOLIDATING AND BUILDING AN IMAGE OF UNITY IN ABRI

While the New Order regime is often represented as all-powerful, the regime in fact began as a loose alliance of Army strongmen and technocrats with outside support from the anti-communist Western world. It took considerable effort to build a united military, and this unification process only began in the early years of the new regime.

During the late Guided Democracy period, President Sukarno fostered divisions within the Army, particularly between those who supported him personally and those who stood behind Nasution. In 1962, for example, he manoeuvred to replace General Nasution as Chief of Staff of the Army by Lieutenant Ahmad Yani, a man with stronger loyalties to the President. There were similar divisions within the Navy. Sukarno had also played the four military forces against each other to limit the political power of the Army.[1] In this period, many of the same organisational functions were replicated in all of the forces. Each force had its own doctrine, its own intelligence units, an independent command structure and a separate commander. Consistent with this pattern, each force also had its own history centre.[2] These history centres contributed to the development of separate identities for each of the forces. For example, in the nine-volume commemorative publication, *20 Years of Indonesian Independence* (20 Tahun Indonesia Merdeka), in addition to contributions from a range of government departments, there were separate contributions for each of the Armed Forces. It was intended that "although each of the forces would reflect its own style and personality an integrated harmonious relationship would characterise their development".[3] Although antagonisms between the forces are not evident in this volume, there is equally no sense of the forces working together in harmony.

The contributions to *20 Years of Indonesian Independence* by the four Armed Forces each tell of their own triumphs and sources of pride. The Navy, for example, emphasises its role in operations after the independence struggle, including the rebellions of the 1950s, the Liberation of West Irian operations and the Malaysia Confrontation operations. The third section of the volume, endorsed by the then-Commander of the Navy, Vice Admiral R.E. Martadinata, is about the history of the Navy. Themes include the symbolism of the Navy and its various roles, including involvement in community projects such as emergency food deliveries. It also highlights the Navy's connection to Indonesia's former maritime glory in the age of Sriwijaya and Majapahit,[4] highlighting its own motto, "In the sea we are great" (Jalesveva Jayamahe). The Air Force emphasises its acquisition of personnel and equipment especially from the Soviet Union, highlighting its roles in suppressing the regional rebellions (the PRRI, Revolutionary Government of the Republic of Indonesia and Permesta, Total Struggle rebellions) and in the West Irian and Malaysia campaigns.[5] By 1965, the Air Force described itself as a well-equipped outfit and was particularly proud of the beginnings of an affiliated national aero-space project. Krishna Sen notes that during the 1960s, films funded by the different military divisions also began to appear suggesting that history was seen as a source of creating unique identities at the divisional as well as at force level.[6] The pattern of emphasising each force in its own right contrasts sharply with New Order ABRI commemorative publications such as *Thirty Years of ABRI* (30 Tahun ABRI),[7] *Forty Years of ABRI* (40 Tahun ABRI)[8] and *Fifty Years of ABRI* (50 Tahun ABRI),[9] in which the forces are referred to in a singular narrative with emphasis on the Army. The contributions of each of the history centres to volume three of *20 Years of Independence*, reflected President Sukarno's encouragement of the other forces to act in competition with the Army.

In the early stages of the New Order, consolidating unity within the Armed Forces was a high priority for the Army. This meant reducing inter-service rivalry and creating a more homogeneous officer corps with loyalties to the emerging regime. Consolidation was a priority because of the involvement of elements of some divisions and parts of the forces in the coup attempt and because of the enduring loyalty to Sukarno of many officers. The Air Force was thoroughly purged because of the involvement of prominent officers in the coup attempt, but the Navy and Police Force — which had no major involvement in the coup — could not so easily be purged of Sukarnoists.[10] In October 1969, once the Army had firmly consolidated its position and Suharto had finally replaced Sukarno as President, Major General Sumitro announced a reintegration programme for the Armed Forces in his capacity as Head of the Department of Defence and Security. Its aim was to put an end to the operational independence of the services. Full operational command of all forces was transferred to President Suharto as Supreme Commander of the Armed Forces.[11] The heads of each of the forces were downgraded from Commanders to Chiefs of Staff, responsible only for implementing the policies and orders of the Commander of the Armed Forces and his deputy.[12] The Commander of the Armed Forces now became the apex of the system. As a result, the Armed Forces History Centre became directly responsible to the Commander of the Armed Forces. It also received a boost in prestige as a result of this move. The specific function of the Centre was now "to assist the Head of Staff in carrying out the promotion of history in the Department of Defence in general and especially in the forces".[13]

Because of the contribution the individual history centres of the forces had made to the development of separate identities of the forces, these centres became a target of the reorganisation programme. During the first stage of re-integration, known as Co-ordination Integration and Synchronisation (Koordinasi Integrasi Sinkronisasi) the Armed Forces History Centre began co-ordinating meetings with the history divisions of the forces.[14] At the first meeting in 1968, it was agreed that the combined objectives of these centres were to popularise history, to organise a history curriculum and to make plans for the production of integrated histories.[15] Although the history centres of each of the forces initially worked together with the Armed Forces History Centre, their roles were reduced over time. Since 1984, only the Armed Forces History Centre held the status of a centre. The history centres of the other forces were subsumed into larger functioning units of each of the forces.[16]

Only the long-established Army History Centre in Bandung continued to operate unfettered.

The Army leadership called upon the Armed Forces History Centre to make a contribution to the reintegration process by using history as a tool of unification. Members of staff of the Centre suggest that the period of transition was the peak of activity for the Centre.[17] In a 1968 publication on the history of the armed forces, Nugroho stressed that in history teaching:

> The oneness and unity of ABRI should be emphasised especially because of the efforts of political movements, the remaining elements of G.30.S/PKI and other opponents to pit one force against another.[18]

At the first meeting of the history centres, it was decided that with "a unified historical language, a shared self image of ABRI could be established".[19] The Centre set about creating that vision of a united armed forces.

Two of the most important projects geared to the task of producing an integrated history were the texts which made up the *Reading Series for Soldiers* (Seri Bacaan Prajurit), and the first integrated museum of the Armed Forces, Museum ABRI Satriamandala (Satriamandala Armed Forces Museum). Both these ideas originated from the 1968 meeting of the history centres of all the forces. For the purposes of educating all officers, each volume in the 24-volume series *The Reading Series for Soldiers* was to detail one military operation with representation of the combined roles of each of the forces.[20] By the end of 1968, the team has completed 15 of these publications covering either security operations or biographies on behalf of the Armed Forces History Centre.[21] In fact Nugroho's history students from the University of Indonesia completed most of these publications. Amongst these recruits were Marie The, Onghokham, Jusmar Basri, Soe Hok Gie and Rochmani Santoso. The latter stayed on at the Armed Forces History Centre as a civilian employee for over 30 years. As of 1969, the history series, which was gradually expanded, was used in ABRI training schools from the Armed Forces Academy for officer recruits through to the National Resilience Institute for senior officers seeking higher promotions.[22]

Nugroho, who was convinced of the utility of museums, felt that it was necessary to have a central museum for the armed forces depicting their united struggle to encourage greater unity within the forces.[23] Because of the urgency placed on the goal of creating a united museum, the Satriamandala Armed Forces Museum was opened on Armed Forces Day 1972, with an initial collection of only 20 dioramas covering the independence struggle. This museum celebrates the military's united role and leadership in the national past in the tasks of both achieving and fulfilling Indonesian independence. The first 20 diorama scenes installed in the museum included representations of the initial formation of a military and several key battles (Surabaya, Ambarawa, Bandung Lautan Api, Bogor, Cibadak, Aceh, Palembang and the suppression of the communist three region affair).[24] They included events that related to the development of the Air Force (The Take Over of a Japanese Airbase in Malang); the Police Force (The Young Police Force Takes Action); and the Navy (The Sea Traffic Operation Banyuwangi to Bali and the Maluku Expedition).[25] During the struggle for independence, the Air Force and Navy lacked equipment and trained personnel. The deliberate inclusion of scenes relating to them reflects an effort on Nugroho's part to imply the existence of a single united developing force. At the time when the museum was established in the early 1970s, the forces were in reality divided, each with its own ethos and vision.

In order to consolidate the image of a united military, the Centre also moved to establish itself as a military-specific museums directorate. Existing museums of the individual forces, such as the Duty of the Heroic Soldier Army Museum in Yogyakarta, the Police Museum in Jakarta, the Sky Operations Air Force museum in Yogyakarta, the Cadet R.S. Hadi Winarso Naval Museum in Surabaya, and other divisional, territorial or personalia-based military museums thus came under the direction of the centralised Armed Forces History Centre.

The foundation of the Satriamandala Armed Forces Museum also reflected a new sense of pride on the part of the Indonesian military and a need to boost the military's public prestige. Prior to the founding, President Suharto, in his capacity as Minister of Defence and Commander of the Armed Forces, instructed Nugroho Notosusanto to research famous overseas military museums. The museums Nugroho visited included the Army, Air Force and Navy Museums in France; the Imperial War Museum in England; the Army Museum and the Royal Netherlands Indies Army Museum in the Netherlands; the Army Museum in Yugoslavia; and the Australian War Memorial.[26] After this tour, Nugroho requested the Cipanas Palace or the Bogor Palace as the location for the armed forces' central museum. This again indicates how important Nugroho felt the Indonesian military and its history was. His request was not granted, but President Suharto instead offered the former Japanese-style house of

Sukarno's Japanese-born wife, Dewi Sukarno, Wisma Yaso, on Jalan Gatot Subroto.[27] It is curious to note that Nugroho's proposed sites and Suharto's chosen site were all strongly associated with the former President Sukarno, providing a symbolic signal that the armed forces had replaced President Sukarno. Wisma Yaso is a large building surrounded by attractive and spacious gardens that were eventually to be filled with displays of Army tanks, small planes and other military vehicles (Illustrations 4.1 and 4.2). The name "satriamandala", chosen for this museum by President Suharto, means "sacred place for knights to gather" (*lingkungan keramat para satria*)[28] and also attempts to confer an aura of grandeur on the site. This indicates that the museum functioned not only as an educational site for young students in the region of greater Jakarta, for whom annual school visits were compulsory, but also as a monument to Indonesian soldiers.

THE 1945 VALUES

Another initiative aimed at consolidating military unity was the 1972 Army seminar, which focused on the necessity of a transfer of the "1945 values" to the younger generation of soldiers. The seminar's

Illustration 4.1   Entrance to the Satriamandala Armed Forces Museum.
Source: Photograph by Chatarina Purnamdari.

Illustration 4.2   Outdoor military aeroplane displays at the Satriamandala Armed Forces Museum.
Source: Image reproduced from a postcard issued by *Museum Pusat ABRI Satriamandala.*

purpose was for older military officers to evaluate whether the values of the younger generations of military officers matched those of the 1945 Generation.[29] The seminar was held at a time when more than 50 per cent of officers were from the young generation, defined as those who "did not physically assist in fighting for and maintaining independence". The older generation suggested that before leadership of the military passed over to the next generation, both generations should agree on the military's values and core concerns.

Members of the older generation were all too aware of the outcome of previous clashes in values between military generations such as that of the 17 October Affair. One of the principal arguments of Japanese trained officers in this dispute was that an officer's fighting spirit or demonstrated fighting record (*semangat*) should be the principal determinant for promotion, rather than the degree of formal training.[30] In the 1970s, by contrast, younger officers were disgruntled that those who had fought in the revolution would not retire. Pleas were made to President Suharto and the Army leadership to wind up the period of rule of the 1945 Generation and to hand over honourably to their successors in the next few years.[31] The seminar was therefore, in part an effort to ensure continuity in military values.

The military leadership deemed consistent values necessary, such that the young generation of the military could apply these values to the nation's new challenges. The military defined these challenges in the 1966 Tri Ubaya Cakti army doctrine as being:

> ... to achieve a new mental attitude with the aim of creating social, political, economic and cultural life which was based on the morals of Pancasila, and in particular the principle of Belief in One God.[32]

The military stated its role in this project of creating a Pancasila society as being "to modernise the state and people by playing a part in nation and character building".[33] The 1972 Army seminar therefore represented a paternalistic form of guidance for younger military officers as to how to face the challenges of the future and to lead the nation in doing so.

THE TERM "1945 GENERATION"

The term "1945 Generation" has generally been used to refer to the youth of the revolution. Exactly what this generation represents is, however, difficult to define. The youth of the revolution were involved in a wide range of activities and organisations. They were represented in both the Army and in more informal armed units such as militias (*lasykar*). Not all of these units supported the Republic. Some youth supported alternative states based on either a particular region or on different philosophical premises, such as Islam. There were other groups who refused to support the Republic on the grounds that they strongly opposed negotiations with the Dutch. One such group were those who followed Tan Malaka, the Dutch-educated communist and his People's Army. Likewise, not all youths were exclusively associated with *perjuangan* or armed struggle. Some youths were represented in the government and in political parties. Among the young women who joined the revolution, there were also some who participated in political activities and others who volunteered their labour for more physical chores such as working for the Red Cross, helping in public kitchens or conveying intelligence. The youth of the revolution were, consequently, a heterogeneous group of both men and women working within and outside of the military.

When the term "1945 Generation" is invoked either by scholars or popular historians in Indonesia, it does not seem to include all of the youth of the revolution. In both scholarly and popular histories, the

Battle of Surabaya has been highlighted as a demonstration of the fighting spirit of the youth (*pemuda*) in the revolution. The battle of Surabaya, which occurred on 10 November 1945, was the result of a refusal of Indonesians to give up their arms to the British. It was the heaviest of any Republican offensives, including those against the Dutch, and represented the climax of attacks upon allied British soldiers by both Republican soldiers and other *pemuda*.[34] Veteran Roeslan Abdulgani, who recorded his memories of the Battle of Surabaya, described the battle as "the cauldron in which Indonesian people were cooked … wherein the dynamic energy of our youth was welded with the calculated thinking of our elders".[35] Benedict Anderson has also emphasised the role of the youth *pemuda* in the lead up to and during the Battle of Surabaya, suggesting that it was in Surabaya that the character of the youth movement was at its "most memorable and startling form". His only reference to the actual battle, however, draws on a British source, one in which David Wehl suggests that if battles like this had occurred throughout Java, "millions would have died and the Republic of Indonesia and the Netherlands East Indies alike would have drowned in blood". Anderson also refers to the "fanaticism and fury of Surabaya".[36] According to William Frederick, being a *pemuda* during the revolution also had "everything to do with spirit".[37] One aspect of the youth that scholars have also highlighted is the attitude of freedom or death (*merdeka atau mati*).[38] At reunions of members of the 1945 Generation, also known as *pejuang* (independence fighters), they often chant the catch cry *merdeka* whilst punching their fists in the air.

So what exactly did this spirit refer to? Scholarship on the late colonial period through to the 1945–49 revolution confirms the emergence of different outlooks amongst some youth in this period of dramatic social change. The first to emphasise the importance of youth in this period was John R.W. Smail, followed by Anderson in 1974, who examined the emergence of a new outlook amongst *pemuda* originating particularly in the Japanese period.[39] Frederick has, however, suggested that these new outlooks had earlier origins in the pre-war nationalist movement.[40]

George Kahin claims youths who were recruited to Japanese paramilitary organisations, for example, gained new outlooks as a result of their inculcation into "authoritarian mentalities and anti-Westernism".[41] Reid suggests they were also expected to "imitate Japanese discipline, self-confidence and sacrificial patriotism".[42] Through participation in Japanese martial traditions, many also came to absorb the fighting spirit (*seishin*) upheld by the Japanese.[43] Exposure to Japanese training therefore set some youths apart from their elders, who had greater contact with the Dutch and especially with those who were Dutch-educated.[44] As discussed in Chapter 2, the spirit of the 1945 Generation was also frequently referred to as encompassing non-compromise, a refusal to negotiate with the Dutch. The actions of the youths who kidnapped President Sukarno and Vice President Muhammad Hatta in 1945 in order to pressure them to proclaim independence free of Japanese supervision are often highlighted as an example of this spirit of non-compromise (Chapter 5). For some youth, this spirit of non-compromise spawned from the discontent members of Japanese war-time organisations felt with Japanese rule.[45] Ruth McVey also notes that those youths who were recruited to the Japanese-sponsored PETA Army, many of whom later joined the Indonesian Army, were persuaded by their Japanese mentors of "the need for military independence from civilian control".[46] This also set them apart from Dutch-trained officers, who were more committed to military professionalism.

Although there are some vagaries in the definition, the term "1945 Generation" has therefore generally been used to refer to the dynamic youth of the revolution. They are described as possessing a particular spirit and outlook, which set them apart from the older generation. The values and meaning assigned to members of the 1945 Generation has, however, changed over time. Herbert Feith claims that by 1957, the term "1945 Generation" was already in use in Indonesia in a wider sense, but different political groups had also used it at different times.[47] Even during the revolution, attempts were made to distinguish the contributions of some over others to the revolution. In 1948, for example, Murba supporter Adam Malik published *A History of the August 1945 Proclamation* (Riwayat Proklamasi Agustus 1945), in which he highlighted the role of youth (who became the 1945 Generation) in insisting on non-compromise with the Japanese and providing the fire of the revolution. He also made clear distinctions between the views of youth and of Sukarno and Hatta, whom he represented as being overly cautious with the Japanese.[48]

In the 1950s, as we have seen in Chapter 2, Nugroho made similar assertions about the 1945 Generation. Radical nationalist groups such as the Murba party and former members of the Student Army blamed the lack of direction in the 1950s on the national leadership (or the failures of the older generation) and continued to emphasise the importance of spirit or *semangat 45*. By making his call for the "return to the rails of the revolution" in 1959, Sukarno sought to co-opt the leaders of these groups (Chaerul Saleh, Achmadi and Isman respectively) to rally support for "burying the parties". He tried to co-opt these youths by arguing that what had gone wrong since 1950 was that the nation had strayed from the ideals of 1945 and that it consequently needed to return to the spirit of 1945. These ideas were first expressed in Sukarno's 1957 concept and then articulated once more in the 5 July 1959 Decree, in which he declared Indonesia was returning to the 1945 Constitution.[49]

The central veterans' organisation, the National Council for the 1945 Generation (Dewan Harian Nasional Angkatan 1945, hereafter National Council) has also at different times provided varied definitions of the goals of the 1945 Generation. The National Council was founded in 1954 with the aim of upholding the spirit of 1945. Its membership has always included persons who did not serve in official military units or did not go on to pursue military careers after the revolution. In this sense, it is not a military-dominated body and provides a point of contrast for later military definitions of the 1945 Generation.

Although the National Council is an umbrella veterans' organisation, in the 1950s and 1960s it had links to a particular group of freedom fighters. Its headquarters are located at Menteng 31, a colonial period building in the prestigious Jakarta suburb of Menteng. This building is famous for its former status as a Japanese sponsored *asrama* (dormitory) which formed the base of the radical national youth group Young Generation (Angkatan Muda) who kidnapped Sukarno and Hatta in 1945. Membership of this *asrama* included Chaerul Saleh, Sukarni, A.M. Hanafi, Ismail Widjaja, Aidit, Lukman and Sjamsuddin Tjan.[50] During the revolution Chaerul Saleh and Sukarni joined Tan Malaka's People's Army, which led a coup attempt against the Republic in July 1946 in protest at continued government negotiation with the Dutch. Chaerul Saleh was one of the radical nationalists Sukarno courted in the late 1950s to gain support for Guided Democracy. Between 1960 and 1966, Chaerul Saleh served as chairman of the National Council. By this time, Saleh had become a Sukarno loyalist and an influential politician. He held the positions of Co-ordinating Minister for Development, Deputy Prime Minister, Head of the Provisional People's Consultative Assembly and Chairman of the National Front.[51] Saleh's leadership of the National Council during the early to mid-1960s reflected the increasingly leftist outlook of national politics of this period, although it should be noted Saleh, like other Murba supporters, was anti-PKI due to disagreements between the two parties.[52]

In 1960, the National Council provided the first definition of the mission of the 1945 Generation. At the organisation's first consultative meeting (*musyawarah besar*) held at the Ikada sports stadium in Jakarta, the members collectively defined themselves as:

> ... the *pelopor* (pioneers, vanguards) and *pelaksana* (implementers) of the August 1945 Revolution who in a revolutionary, devoted, active and consistent manner fought to oppose imperialism, colonialism, fascism and the remnants of feudalism to bring into reality the independence of the homeland in the form of a unitary state of the Republic of Indonesia based on the 1945 Constitution which is based on Pancasila with the aim of a democratic, just and prosperous society in the form of Indonesian Socialism.[53]

This definition upheld the notion of the 1945 Generation as revolutionary and, above all, anti-imperialist. This fitted closely with President Sukarno's emphasis on anti-imperialism at the time. It also tied this generation to two of the central ideological tenets of the Guided Democracy era — the 1945 Constitution and the Pancasila with the Sukarnoist qualification that socialism was the ultimate aim of the revolution. The rhetoric of this organisation matched that of Sukarno, yet the ideals promoted were also consistent with the people at the centre of the National Council (who had in turn been central to Sukarno's call for a return to the revolution).

At the second consultative meeting held in December 1963, consistent with the increasingly radical tone in Sukarnoist rhetoric, the definition of what the 1945 Generation represented was given more revolutionary bite. The words "defenders and continuers of the revolution of the generation of 1945" were added, along with the explanation that they had also "fought to oppose neo-colonialism" (mostly likely a reference to support for opposition to the formation of Malaysia). Later, the 1972 Army transfer of values seminar introduced a very different interpretation of the 1945 values.

THE 1972 ARMY SEMINAR ON THE TRANSFER OF VALUES

The "transfer of values" seminar was conducted over five days, 18–22 March 1972, at the Army Staff and Command School in Bandung. There were five hundred participants, including members of the 1945 Generation as well as members of the "younger generation".[54] The chairman of the seminar, General Umar Wirahadikusuma (the then-

Deputy Chief of Staff) and most of its key speakers were members of
the 1945 Generation who had pursued military careers after the revolution.
The principal representative of the young generation of officers was
Major Try Sutrisno, a 1959 graduate of the Army Technical Academy
and later Vice-President. Although this was an Army-sponsored seminar,
it was intended that the seminar be representative of all the forces.
Consistent with the 1966 Seskoad seminar held to revise the Tri Ubaya
Cakti doctrine, a number of technocrats, seen as key "strongmen" of the
new regime, also attended the 1972 seminar. These included the Harvard-
trained economics professor Dr Ir. Mohamad Sadli, the Yale-trained
lawyer Professor Mochtar Kusumaatmadja, the Cornell-trained sociologist
Professor Selo Sumardjan and scientist Professor Garnadi Prawirosudirjo.
Nugroho Notosusanto was another civilian included in the seminar
discussions. He was assigned the position of vice-chairman of the seminar
syndicate responsible for formulating ways by which the 1945 Values
could be passed on to the "younger generations".

The seminar participants attempted to define both the 1945 Values
and a more specific formulation, the Indonesian National Army 1945
Values (Nilai-Nilai 45 TNI). The definitions resulting from the seminar
were decidedly loose and, like the definitions put forward by the National
Council, were not as directly tied to the period of the struggle as one
might expect. The Army declared the key components of the 1945
Values to be the values contained in the Pancasila and in the 1945
Constitution. It was suggested that these were the values for which the
1945 Generation and those before them had fought.[55] It is debatable
how much those who fought in the struggle knew about either the
Pancasila or the 1945 Constitution, which were formulated by a small
elite of an older generation, before the outbreak of the revolution.

The Indonesian National Army 1945 Values were a more complex
formulation. These were defined as including obedience to the 1945
Values. In addition, they involved a duty to safeguard both the Pancasila
and the Constitution of 1945 and to uphold this as the politics of the
Army;[56] commitment to defence of honesty, truth, justice and self-
reliance; readiness to sacrifice for country and nation; the resolve never
to surrender; a commitment that the Indonesian National Army would
always remain national property; loyalty to the values of the Sapta Marga
as the code of ethics of the Indonesian military; and sworn obedience
to the eleven principles of leadership of the Armed Forces.[57] The Sapta
Marga or Seven-Fold ways are that soldiers are (1) citizens of the Republic
of Indonesia which is founded on Pancasila; (2) Indonesian patriots

who are the bearers and protectors of state ideology, who are responsible and will not countenance surrender; (3) Indonesian knights who are devoted to the One Almighty God and protect honesty, truth and justice; (4) soldiers of the Indonesian Armed Forces who are guardians of the Indonesian state and nation; (5) soldiers of the Indonesian Armed Forces who uphold discipline, who are obedient and loyal to their leaders and hold fast to attitudes and honour that characterise a soldier; (6) soldiers of the Indonesian Armed Forces who cherish gallantry and are always ready to devote themselves to the service of the state and nation; and (7) soldiers of the Indonesian Armed Forces who are loyal, retain their integrity and keep the Soldiers Oath (Sumpah Prajurit).[58] The eleven principles are (1) Devotion to God; (2) to give a good example to juniors; (3) to follow with energy and give inspiration to your juniors; (4) to influence and give encouragement to your juniors; (5) to be constantly vigilant and to be capable and brave in giving corrections to juniors; (6) to be able to prioritise correctly; (7) to behave in an unpretentious non-excessive manner; (8) to have a loyal attitude from top to bottom to those above and beside you; (9) simplicity and the capacity to limit usage and expenditure to essential requirements; (10) the will to sacrifice and the preparedness to be held accountable; (11) the will, sacrifice and sincerity at the appropriate time to pass on responsibility and positions to the next generation.[59] By this definition of the TNI 1945 Values, the military leadership therefore positioned themselves as the custodians of the 1945 Values and the defenders of these principles. The Indonesian National Army 1945 Values also included idealistic formulations of the martial roles of the military.

The results of the 1972 Army seminar were published as *The 1945 Sacred Duties* (Dharma Pusaka 45). This became a guidebook for the transfer of 1945 Values and TNI 1945 Values to the young generation of the armed forces. The name chosen for this book tells us something about the way it was intended that these values be received. The term *pusaka* refers to precious heirlooms. This implies that the 1945 Values were also something precious to be carefully guarded and bequeathed to new owners. Michael van Langenberg identifies the term *dharma* as being a key New Order concept emphasising contribution, duty and sacrifice, with an emphasis on duty to the ruler.[60] In this context, it was expected that those succeeding the 1945 Generation would also emphasise duty to their elders, most particularly the leaders of the regime.[61] This exemplifies the organicist stream to New Order military thinking whereby the military elite positioned themselves as the guardians of the family state.

The publication, *The 1945 Sacred Duties* makes several references to the "unique qualities" of the "1945 Generation". Consistent with scholarship on the revolution, the book suggests that members of this generation were "unique in spirit", because they developed in the atmosphere of a war of independence. Like Nugroho's earlier ideas, it contrasts members of the 1945 Generation to members of the 1928 Generation, generally identified as those who participated in the nationalist movement. The book also suggests that because members of the 1945 Generation came from all over the country and from all levels of education, rather than just from the elite campuses of Java like the 1928 Generation, they could more easily match the spirit of the Pancasila and the 1945 Constitution together.[62] The fact that it was largely members of the 1928 Generation who formulated both these concepts is passed over.

The seminar notes emphasise the armed struggle as being integral to the 1945 Values. It is noted, for example, that:

> Immediately after Indonesian independence was proclaimed on 17 August 1945, the sons of the Indonesian nation, members of the 1945 Generation, spontaneously acted on their patriotism and full of confidence in their own strength took up whatever arms they could find to defend the sovereignty of the state and nation, with unsurrendering spirit reflected in the motto *Merdeka atau Mati*! [Freedom or Death!][63]

It is thus the youth of the revolution who took up arms to whom the 1945 spirit is attributed. This emphasis on armed struggle represents a shift from Guided Democracy definitions of the 1945 Generation, which focused more on the spirit of this generation as a defining feature. Emphasis on those who carried arms as the real freedom fighters had the exclusionary effect of discounting the contributions of non-combatants to the independence struggle, whether they be women who were largely excluded from taking up arms or villagers who assisted in different ways in supporting the struggle (Chapter 5). The military-defined image of the freedom fighter was thus a model of martial masculinity.

PROMOTING GENERAL SUDIRMAN AND THE GUERRILLA STRUGGLE

Seminar participants proposed that histories of the revolution become a vehicle for the transfer of values to young soldiers and other Indonesian youths. They outlined a number of possible mediums for promoting the military's historical roles. One recommendation was to raise the profile of Indonesian military heroes. General Sudirman, the first Commander of the Army who was sick with tuberculosis throughout the revolution, became a key focus in this campaign. Sudirman was notably a military leader who was prepared to challenge the civilian government throughout the revolution.[64]

There is little doubt that General Sudirman was a popular hero. Soon after his death in 1950, for example, the Ministry of Information published his memoirs including romanticised versions of his role in the revolution.[65] It appears, however, that as the military accumulated more political power, the promotion of his image became increasingly important to the military as a symbol of military leadership. In 1964, President Sukarno proclaimed Sudirman a hero of the national revolution. Throughout the New Order regime, his image received continual emphasis. In 1968, for example, his portrait replaced that of former President Sukarno on the 1, 2.5, 1000 and 5000 rupiah notes.[66] In 1970, the Armed Forces History Centre published a textbook series on Sudirman's speeches.[67] There were also several museums and museum rooms dedicated to Sudirman. These include the Sudirman Museum in Magelang run by the Department of Education, the General for Life Sudirman Memorial Museum (Museum Sasmitaloka Panglima Besar Jenderal Sudirman) in Yogyakarta run by the Army history division and commemorative room displays on Sudirman at the Return of Yogyakarta Monument in Yogyakarta and the Satriamandala Armed Forces Museum in Jakarta. From the 1970s onwards, monuments of Sudirman also proliferated. The most elaborate of these monuments, the Monument to the Birth Place of Sudirman, is located in the village of Bantarbarang near Rembang in East Java and features a gateway (*gapura*), a relief, a mosque, a meeting hall and a bridge over a small stream.[68]

General Sudirman's image also came to dominate public landscape in the form of street names. Almost every major city now has one of its central roads named after Sudirman. Nas suggests that the new street names of both Sudirman and Ahmad Yani (the highest ranking Army victim of the 1965 coup) have replaced those of Sukarno and Hatta.[69] In addition, Sudirman's portrait appeared frequently on New Order historical billboards erected on national commemorative days and he has also featured as an important character in the big-budget films *Yellow Coconut Leaf* (Janur Kuning) (1979) and *Dawn Attack* (Serangan Fajar) (1983) and in a television series *Commander for Life General Sudirman* (Pangsar Soedirman, Panglima Besar Sudirman). In 1997, Sudirman's image received another boost when he was posthumously promoted, along with other retired Generals Suharto and A.H. Nasution, to the rank of five-star general.

Nugroho Notosusanto invested considerable energy into promoting General Sudirman as a military hero. He proclaimed Sudirman as his only idol because he displayed sacrifice, loyalty and a strong sense of nationalism.[70] One particular episode that Nugroho often highlighted to demonstrate Sudirman's leadership qualities was his decision to lead a guerrilla struggle outside Yogyakarta in response to the second Dutch military attack of 19 December 1948, after the capture of civilian leaders Sukarno and Hatta. The second Dutch military attack was a watershed in the revolution because it represented an attack on the then capital of the Republic and because it broke the cease-fire negotiated in the Renville agreement. Sudirman's guerrilla struggle is often emphasised by the military because during this period the military played a greater role in national politics.[71] This period was influential on the military's claim that the military should not be subordinate to the state.[72] Nugroho traces the origins of the Army's *esprit de corps* to the guerrilla period.[73] This explains why this period is accentuated in military-produced histories.

Prior to the second Dutch military attack preparations had been made for the leaders of the government to leave the city. Sukarno had promised to lead his people in armed struggle in the mountains if the Dutch attacked Yogyakarta.[74] When the Dutch did attack, Sukarno, Muhammad Hatta, H. Agus Salim and other members of the cabinet were faced with two options: to lead the struggle or to remain in Yogyakarta and be captured. As Anthony Reid notes, in essence their decision represented a choice between diplomacy or armed struggle, between "faith in international opinion and Indonesian strength".[75] Sukarno was, in fact, tempted by the romanticism of the role of leading the guerrilla resistance.[76] After careful but hasty consideration, the government chose the path of diplomacy and decided to remain in Yogyakarta. Prior to his arrest, Muhammad Hatta, then the Vice-President and Minister of Defence, issued an order to the Armed Forces and people to fight on no matter what happened to members of the government.[77] In addition, plans had been made prior to the capture of the leaders for an immediate transfer of power to an alternative civilian government in Sumatra under the leadership of Sjafruddin Prawiranegara.[78]

The decision was based on a calculated assessment of the outside world's combined condemnation of both the Dutch capture of the Republic's leaders and of the second Dutch military attack, which contravened a previous diplomatic agreement (Renville) of a cease-fire between the Republic and the Dutch. The leaders of state also took into account the fact that it would be easier for the Dutch to shoot them in battle than in captivity. There were insufficient soldiers left in the city to guard the leaders. The decision to stay was also based on the fact that the Good Offices Commission, the instrument of the UN, was nearby.[79] Some historians claim, based on the UN's subsequent action and America's decision to withhold aid to the Netherlands until further negotiation with the Republic had been resumed, that the calculations of the Republic's leaders were accurate.[80] The military, however, saw the choice of those favouring diplomacy as a betrayal.[81]

According to Reid, it was very clear that the military believed the politicians had betrayed the "total guerrilla struggle", both with their surrender to the Dutch and the Van Royen–Roem negotiations following the return of Yogyakarta to the Republic.[82] Armed Forces Commander Sudirman wanted his troops to fight on and did not trust the Dutch to negotiate. After Sukarno and Hatta's announcement of the cease-fire in August, Sudirman wrote a letter of resignation claiming the inconstancy of national leadership had brought on both the premature death of the Vice-Commander of the Military, Lieutenant General Oerip Soemohardjo, and his own illness. The letter was withdrawn after President Sukarno's threat also to resign. To demonstrate their displeasure with the resumption of diplomacy and the end of armed struggle, guerrilla troops did, however, mount their heaviest attack on 10 August 1949, before the cease-fire took effect, and they continued to clash with the Dutch in the last half of 1949. Nugroho's personal disregard for the civilian leaders of the revolution (as outlined in Chapter 2) obviously coloured the representations he made of this period.

THE COMMANDER FOR LIFE GENERAL SUDIRMAN PILGRIMAGE

Reflecting on why Filipino officers, despite having participated in a number of coups in the 1980s, had not successfully seized power, Alfred McCoy argues that the answers lie partly in the socialisation of the military officers in the 1940s at the Philippine Military Academy into the idea of military subordination to the government.[83] In Indonesia, military belief in the military's right to a political role has conversely been sustained since the 1970s by direct socialisation in cadet training into the idea of military supremacy over civilians. Central to this socialisation

PETA RUTE PANGLIMA BESAR JENDERAL SOEDIRMAN
YOGYAKARTA - BEDOYO

Magelang,   Oktober 1997
KEPALA DEPARTEMEN KEJUANGAN
Selaku
PENANGGUNG JAWAB MATERI LATIHAN

SOEGENG SOEGIRDJO ANANTO
KOLONEL INF NRP. 27235

Illustration 4.3   The guerrilla route of Commander for Life General Sudirman.
Source: Map reproduced from Akademi Militer, Departemen Kejuangan, *Buku Pedoman Tutor Napak Tilas Rute Gerilya Pangsar Jenderal Sudirman bagi Capratar Yogyakarta-Bedoyo 1997/98, 22–25 October 1997.*

is the Commander for Life General Sudirman Pilgrimage (Napak Tilas Panglima Besar General Sudirman, hereafter General Sudirman Pilgrimage), in which all military cadets participate prior to graduation. The walk retraces Sudirman's guerrilla route of 1948–49. It focuses on a re-enactment of the first commander's guerrilla route during the 1945–49 revolution. Instructors use examples of Sudirman's actions to instil military values, and values that represent justifications for the military's political role in the minds of the young cadets.

The walk was another of Nugroho's projects, this time inspired by Nugroho's belief in General Sudirman's devotion and sacrifice. In 1973, Nugroho together with a team of historians and Sudirman's former adjutants, retired Major General Tjokropranolo (the former Governor of Jakarta 1977–82) and Lieutenant General Widodo, departed for Central Java to research Sudirman's guerrilla route.[84] The Guerrilla Route of Sudirman was mapped out in the area south of Yogyakarta, beginning at Kretek near the seaside town of Parangtritis (Illustration 4.3). It then stretches for approximately 100 kilometres from Kretek to Bedoyo and is complemented along the way by billboards with historical

Illustration 4.4   The cadets marching over barren mountains in full camouflage gear, with weapons, on the 1997 General Sudirman Pilgrimage.
Source: Photograph by the author.

information. The route is sometimes referred to as a "monument". President Suharto officially opened it in 1974, and from the mid-1970s onwards all candidates training to become military cadets participated in the walking pilgrimage programme.[85] The walk is now the last stage of training and examination for qualifying as a military cadet and functions as an important introduction to the historical legacy of the Indonesian military.

In formal terms, the Armed Forces History Centre states that the pilgrimage is part of an effort to pass on the values of ABRI's struggle in a physical and visual way. Having followed the walk in October 1997 for two days, I was able to make some further observations of its functions. The trek itself is a challenge for most cadets as it requires walking for three consecutive days over barren mountains, unprotected from the sun, in camouflage gear, carrying full packs and weapons (Illustration 4.4). Although the walk has a physical side, the main purpose is clearly indoctrination into both military values and values specific to the dual function of the Indonesian military. Throughout the New Order period, the pilgrimage formed an integral part of the indoctrination component of the Armed Forces Academy (Akademi ABRI, AKABRI) curriculum.

The principal focus of the pilgrimage is to instil in cadets the values of *kejuangan* (the "state of struggle", a term used exclusively, it seems, by the military to refer to values of those who fought in the revolution) displayed by Sudirman.[86] As part of the preparation for the walk, instructors from the academy encourage cadets to hang banners of Sudirman's sayings around their quarters at the Magelang military academy. The cadets are also provided with lists of suitable quotes and extracts of Sudirman's speeches. One such quote is:

> Remember that Indonesian soldiers are not mercenaries, they are not soldiers who sell their manpower for want of gaining a handful of rice and they are also not soldiers who are easily swayed because of either trickery or the desire for material goods, rather an Indonesian soldier is one who joins the Army because of a realisation in his/her soul of the calling of the homeland, and a preparedness to dedicate his/her body and soul to the grandeur of nation and state.[87]

This extract from the 1949 radio speech of the first Commander of the Army, Sudirman, is presented to military cadets as a portrait of the ideal devoted and morally upstanding soldier who joined the 1945–49 revolution. Most of the quotes reflect generic military values such as "Never surrender", "Follow all orders", "Stay alert and cautious", and the more religiously-oriented quote *Lahir dan batin* ("Maintain discipline, both outer and inner").[88] Other quotes reflect nationalist spirit such as "Work together with all forces in the nation", "Once united forever united", "Once proclaimed forever defended", "Freedom!" and "Our Army will never surrender to anyone who wishes to colonise or oppress us". Quotes that suggest the unique character of the Indonesian Army are also used. One such quote, extracted from Sudirman's speech to the cadets of 1948, states that "The Army knows no compromise in defending the state and the basis of state politics"[89] — which of course by the time of New Order included dual function.

ACTIVITIES IN THE PILGRIMAGE

At several sites along the walk, the instructors describe to the cadets the conditions General Sudirman faced at that site. At Kretek, for example, the cadets are told it was here that Sudirman received news of Sukarno and Hatta's capture, which strengthened his resolve to lead the guerrilla struggle. The instructors highlight Sudirman's political and strategic skills. At other sites, the instructors emphasise the values of being ready

Illustration 4.5   Cadets praying at the grave of General Sudirman at the Yogyakarta Heroes' Cemetery before commencing the 1997 General Sudirman Pilgrimage. *Source:* Photograph by the author.

to sacrifice, being full of determination, being authoritative, committed and never capitulating to the enemy.[90]

Throughout the walking pilgrimage programme, the cadets are encouraged to revere Sudirman and to think of him as an ideal military leader.[91] On the first day of the walk, the cadets (usually numbering over one thousand) travel *en masse* into the city of Yogyakarta to visit the central Army museum, the Dharma Wiratama Museum and the Commander for Life General Sudirman Memorial Museum, where an instructor provides more historical information on the background of Sudirman's withdrawal to the mountains. They then make a *ziarah* (religious pilgrimage) to the National Heroes' Cemetery, where a small ceremony takes place. The cadets place wreaths of flowers on the stupa-shaped monument near Sudirman's grave and scatter petals around the cemetery as a sign of respect to the heroes buried therein. Sudirman's grave is covered by a *pendopo*, the same structure used above the well at Lubang Buaya. Most cadets remove their shoes and stop to pray in front of General Sudirman's grave (Illustration 4.5). Before leaving the cemetery, the cadets salute Sudirman's grave as a sign of respect. The last

activity in the city of Yogyakarta before the walk is the visit to the State
Building (Gedung Agung) where the instructors tell the cadets of the
historical circumstances surrounding General Sudirman's decision to
lead his forces in a guerrilla struggle. The instructors emphasise that if
Sudirman had not made this decision, history would have been different.
They continually stress the importance of Sudirman's actions in the past,
in order to convey the message of the necessity for independent military
leadership. They tell cadets that after the second Dutch military attack,
in response to President Sukarno's suggestion that Sudirman rest or go
to hospital, Sudirman refused. Instead he told Sukarno:

> That who is sick is Sudirman, the Commander is never sick, the
> best place for me is amongst my men, I will continue the guerrilla
> struggle until the last drop of my blood is finished.[92]

Sudirman's heroism is again emphasised alongside Sukarno's relative
passivity in order to reinforce the necessity of the military playing a part
in politics.

One of the highlights of the walk is the cadets' re-enactment of
the roles performed by Sudirman's aides during the guerrilla route for
their great leader. For one section of the walk, the cadets carry replica
sedan chairs (*tandu*) and pull horse carts (*dokar*), two forms of transport
used during the guerrilla period to carry the ailing Sudirman (Illustrations
4.6 and 4.7). By re-enacting this part of history, the cadets are encouraged
to imagine themselves back in the days of the revolution, accompanying
their martyr-like leader Sudirman. At the final resting point at Bedoyo,
the cadets are told that on his journey General Sudirman was mistaken
for Sultan Hamengkubuwono IX and that the villagers consequently
kissed his feet.[93] The reason Sudirman was mistaken for the Sultan is
most probably because he was either being carried in the sedan chair or
pulled along by men in a horse cart. The decision to re-enact this part
of Sudirman's journey, in which he was physically elevated above others
and carried by loyal soldiers, is also possibly intended to encourage
deference towards superiors.

The suggestion that General Sudirman had some form of mystical
power, a property also associated with kings, is made in one of the
first scenes of the film *Yellow Coconut Leaf,* in which the Dutch come
alarmingly close to Sudirman and his troops in the jungle. As the Dutch
approach them, Sudirman's lips move softly, perhaps reciting a prayer.
Within moments rain begins to fall and the Dutch are distracted and
pass by.[94] By re-enacting this historical episode the instructors hoped

Illustration 4.6 Cadets receiving a replica sedan chair to the one on which General Sudirman was carried during the revolution on display in the Sudirman Museum, Yogyakarta.
Source: Photograph by the author.

Illustration 4.7 A replica horse cart to the one on which General Sudirman was carried during the revolution on display in Museum Sasmitaloka Sudirman, Yogyakarta.
Source: Photograph by the author.

that the cadets would absorb the themes of the spirit of devotion, loyalty from below, unity between the armed forces and the people and the attitude of leadership.[95]

Before and during the walk, the cadets are usually addressed by members of the 1945 Generation. For many years, retired General Tjokopranolo, one of Sudirman's former adjutants, was invited to give the opening address on the first day of the walk.[96] Throughout the walk the cadets also met with several historical figures (*pelaku sejarah*) who were involved in Sudirman's guerrilla retreat. In the question time after an address by one witness on the 1997 guerrilla route, which I observed during my fieldwork, a cadet asked how a villager felt to carry Sudirman's sedan chair. The villager replied that in fact he did not know that it was Sudirman he was carrying. Only afterwards did he find out. There was no follow-up to this question because it touched on the sensitive issue of collaboration. The reason the villager did not know the identity of Sudirman at the time was that Sudirman was in fact travelling *incognito*. Tjokropranolo implies that General Sudirman had to be secretive in his movements, because there were spies amongst the Indonesian population. A similar account of the prevalent atmosphere of suspicion, even between military troops, is given in Captain Supardjo's account of a spy seeking Sudirman's whereabouts.[97] The historical fact of Indonesian collaboration with the Dutch was left unexplained to the cadets. Instead, to perpetuate the myth of unity in the revolution, stories were told of how the people welcomed Sudirman as a hero and gave him food.

THE GUERRILLA PERIOD AS MODEL FOR MILITARY-CIVILIAN RELATIONS

The guerrilla period was only a short phase of the four-year independence struggle against the Dutch, lasting from 1948–49, yet for the military this period is crucial to their claims to enduring close ties with the Indonesian people and to their claims to political roles. During the guerrilla period, the military followed Nasution's concept of *hankamrata* (Total People's Defence), meaning that soldiers and civilians were both mobilised together for the war effort. The military were also more closely united with the people in the guerrilla period because the military depended on the people for food, shelter and assistance in defence. Despite their dependence on civilians, the military generally thought of themselves as being in charge of civilians. An indication of the belief in military superiority is provided in the comments of former Armed Forces

Chief of Staff retired Lieutenant General T.B. Simatupang, second Deputy to Sudirman, on the duties of a *lurah* (village head) in the guerrilla effort and the necessity that a military man supervises the village head.[98] It is for these reasons that the guerrilla period became "a model for military-civilian relations".[99] Retracing the guerrilla route served to emphasise the guerrilla period, or this ideal model, in the minds of both the cadets and the local community of the Kretek–Bedoyo area.

The relations between the local community and military cadets during the walk, the time at which military values are supposed to be implanted, gives insight into the broader ethos of the military itself. The intention is that during the walk the cadets will appreciate the historical partnership between the military and the people. From my observations, however, commitment to this ideal seemed very shallow with little scope for genuine mixing between the people and the cadets. Most interactions were in front of large cadet audiences on makeshift stages and were characterised by excessive military formality and precision. The cadets were continually distinguished from villagers by their camouflage uniforms and the fact that they carried weapons. Based on research in the 1970s, Peter Britton observed that, during their training, cadets (who as of 1970 were usually from privileged backgrounds) were encouraged more fully to develop their class consciousness. They were taught to be selective, for example, about the transport they used and the venues they chose to eat at, in order to consolidate the impression that they were the chosen elite.[100] During the walk there was a definite sense that the cadets, although respectful of the villagers — particularly those who were historical actors — felt they should be at arms length from them. The cadets are, however, required to participate in civic action (*karya bhakti*) on behalf of the local community. On the 1997 Sudirman pilgrimage, the civic action programme consisted of clearing drains of debris in the village of Kretek. This kind of activity is often performed as part of the broader programme, the Civic Action Operation (Operasi Karya Bhakti), including the "ABRI goes to the village" (*ABRI masuk desa*) programmes. Sundhaussen dates Army civic action programmes to the 1950s as a form of follow up operation and social weapon in areas recently liberated from the Darul Islam (House of Islam) rebellions (Chapter 6). As of 1962, these programmes were implemented at the central and regional level.[101] Apart from contributing towards development, these programmes form an important part of the military's image-building project. One of the purposes of this exercise is to promote the theme of the total integration of the armed forces and the people (*kemanunggalan ABRI dan rakyat*), another organicist theme that positions the military as familial guardians.

Another reason for these targeted development projects was to monitor and control local populations. Britton suggested in the 1970s that many road-building projects, represented as part of ABRI's civic action on behalf of the people, were concentrated in areas which had been Communist Party strongholds.[102] Areas near to the walk, including Gunung Kidul, have traditionally been very poor areas. During the era of Guided Democracy, Gunung Kidul suffered severe economic hardship and communist ideas consequently gained popularity. A communist-affiliated university, Kiageng Giring People's University (Universitas Rakjat Kiageng Giring), was opened in this area in 1963.[103] In the early years of the New Order, a highway and two new schools were built near the Sudirman route. In addition, a local youth had also been elected to the parliament in Jakarta and the President had paid a visit and introduced new crops.[104] While he was mapping out the Sudirman route, an old timer (unidentified by name) reportedly said to Nugroho:

> We were lucky that Pak Dirman [Sudirman] had lived here during the *gerilya* [guerrilla period] , otherwise we would not have all [this] attention from the Pusat [central government].[105]

This villager was partly right to see the attention given to this area as part of a military tribute to Sudirman, yet there were other reasons for the specific development of this area and possibly also for the appeal of Nugroho's idea for the pilgrimage in this particular region. The purpose of the armed forces projects in this area is more likely to have been to ensure that the armed forces maintained close contact with the villagers in this region to prevent a revival of communist (or at least anti-New Order) ideals.

Another irony of the military's emphasis on General Sudirman's guerrilla struggle is that most of the cadets would find themselves fighting against guerrillas who were in a similar position to that of Sudirman during the revolution. When Sudirman fled to the mountains and took the guerrilla route, the Dutch army were in close pursuit. By killing or capturing Sudirman, the Dutch hoped to break the morale of the Republicans.[106] Sudirman's guerrilla struggle has romantic appeal because, despite the inferior weapons and resources of the Republican Army, Sudirman refused to surrender to the colonial power. During the New Order period, most graduates of the military academy would gain their field experience fighting against poorly equipped, but equally devoted guerrillas in the disputed territories of East Timor, West Papua and Aceh. Resistance movements in these regions relied on guerrilla-style warfare, depending heavily on local populations for support and supplies, because of the shortage of both weapons and resistance fighters. In these cases, the resistance leaders bore greater similarities to Sudirman as a guerrilla fighter, while the cadets could be compared to the better-armed colonialists. For many, however, this irony was not apparent. In fact, one officer revealed to me that during his experience as Field Commander in East Timor he would often recite stories of Sudirman in order to lift the morale of his troops. It is also possible that the guerrilla route serves as a means of familiarising the cadets with the type of warfare in which their future enemies are engaged. The cadets are told why Sudirman chose guerrilla-style warfare at this point in time, highlighting the advantages and features of this style of war.[107]

CONCLUSION

As in the case of representations of the military suppression of the communists as an effort to uphold the Pancasila, there is also a profound disjunction between historical legitimacy and reality in this case of military representations of the past. Aware of the impact of past divisions between territorial commands and the services, the Indonesian military worked hard in the first decade of the New Order to foster a sense of a united military with consistent values. The history divisions of the forces were amalgamated and the profile of the Armed Forces History Centre was raised. To promote a sense of shared identity amongst soldiers, the Centre turned to representations of the 1945–49 independence struggle, a period central to notions of Indonesian identity. The Centre focused firstly on the promotion of the struggle in military history textbooks and a centralised museum of the Armed Forces.

By the early 1970s, the military leadership was also concerned about the impact of handing over power to a younger generation of the military that had not experienced the independence struggle. The military wanted to ensure that the ethos formed in this era was passed on to the younger generation. The 1972 seminar on the transfer of values promoted a new interpretation of the 1945 values. The seminar participants highlighted the values of the Pancasila and the 1945 Constitution as representing the core "1945 Values". The "TNI 1945 Values" meanwhile comprised the more specific values of defence, military ethics, sacrifice and obedience. A noticeable difference between the Guided

Democracy definitions of the 1945 Values and those advocated in the 1972 seminar was that in the latter set armed struggle was given significantly more emphasis.

The 1972 seminar stimulated a range of history projects aimed at promoting the 1945 values. Each year, new cadets at the Magelang Military Academy would re-enact Sudirman's guerrilla journey so as to absorb a specific military ethos tightly bound to a romanticised version of the guerrilla period. The walk is therefore an important means of internalising the military's visions of its unique role in society in the young cadets and ensuring a continued expectation among young soldiers of a right to political roles. Emphasis on the guerrilla period also highlights an ideal model of civilian-military relations and introduces cadets to the mode of warfare they are most likely to encounter in the field.

Other history projects inspired by the seminar were directed more broadly at the Indonesian public for the purposes of promoting militarism and the acceptance of dual function. These projects, analysed in the next chapter, demonstrate the centrality of the military to official history-making in the New Order era.

5

Promoting the Military and Dual Function to Civilians

History textbooks are integral to the creation of shared notions of identity. By charting the most important aspects of the national past, their authors seek to dictate core values and beliefs to citizens. For authoritarian regimes, history textbooks are a valuable means for legitimating state ideology and authoritarian mechanisms. For militarised regimes such as Indonesia's New Order, textbooks are also a means for promoting the necessity of the military's political roles.

One directive of the 1972 Army seminar was for the military to circulate their own versions of history to the Indonesian public through military memoirs, films, museums, monuments and history textbooks. These projects targeted the younger generation to ensure that they appreciated the credentials of the 1945 Generation, who then dominated the most senior positions in the regime. In the new history projects, the military focused on promoting their roles as heroes and leaders of the 1945–49 independence struggle and promoting militaristic values more broadly. To set up these themes, some of the major history projects, like the *National History Textbook* (Sejarah Nasional Indonesia), sought not only to elevate the profiles of military men such as General Sudirman and President Suharto, but also to erase or diminish the profiles of nationalist leaders, especially former President Sukarno.

Nugroho Notosusanto was responsible for many of these projects, especially the national history curriculum which he revised during his 1983–85 term as Education Minister. In the mid-1980s one of the most significant historical controversies of the New Order period erupted over his new initiative of the *History of the National Struggle* course (Pendidikan Sejarah Perjuangan Bangsa, PSPB) and representations of history made in both this course and the *National History Textbook*. This polemic was part of a restrained, but audible backlash against Nugroho's influence in official history writing in Indonesia, the first being the Pancasila controversy of the early 1980s. Both Nugroho's appointment as Education Minister and his untimely death two years later in June 1985 triggered historians to express long-repressed resentment towards military intervention in history writing. This chapter examines the questions of how Nugroho, as a trained historian, justified military intervention in history writing, how he balanced his life in the academic and military worlds and why he remained so devoted to the Indonesian military.

TRANSFERRING THE 1945 VALUES TO ALL YOUNG INDONESIANS

At the opening of a meeting for military history in 1968, Lieutenant General M.M. Rachmat Kartakusuma, Chief of Staff for Defence and Security asked:

> How can we mentally develop our soldiers, introduce them to the sacred traditions or the unity of the forces in all of ABRI without using history? And how can we give society as a whole understanding *especially the young generation who did not experience the struggle of 1945*, about the reality of *dwifungsi* [dual function] [my italics], if we have not told them of the birth of ABRI and their maturation in the national struggle itself? They will certainly think that ABRI is the same as any other Armed Forces in another country, such that *kekaryaan* ABRI [the assignment of military officers to civilian posts] will be understood as militarism, because the role of ABRI stands out so much.[1]

Kartakusuma's comments highlight the importance of representations of the revolution, especially to the young generation who had no experience of the revolution, for justifying the military's dual political and defence roles. He claims that it is only by knowing this history that both soldiers and members of the wider public will understand, and by implication accept, the military's pervasive role in society.

Although the "transfer of values" concept outlined in the 1972 Army seminar was ostensibly directed at the younger generation of the military, it was also to have application to wider society. President Suharto had, in fact, requested that the seminar be upgraded not only from a Seskoad (Army Staff and Command School) to an Army seminar, but to a National Seminar, on the basis that the transfer of values was an issue that applied to the entire nation. For reasons of time, the scale of the seminar was not upgraded, but the seminar participants suggested ideas of how the 1945 Values could be transferred more broadly into society.[2]

The idea that the Indonesian military needed to pass on values to broader society is consistent with the mandate of character-building that the Indonesian Army designated for itself in the early years of the New Order. Ari Dwipayana *et al.*, suggest that indoctrination of broader society through schools, work places, associations and through the media into the values, ideology and organisational models of the military played a role in defending military domination in Indonesia.[3] I would agree with this suggestion, but I believe that the military perception that it was necessary to transfer the so-called 1945 Values to the population also reflects the military leadership's belief that they had a responsibility to instruct and guide Indonesian citizens. In his address to the seminar participants, for example, President Suharto elaborated further on what the 1945 Values were, suggesting they also encompassed a commitment to continuing dual function and to guarding the armed forces' capacity as a stabilising and dynamising force in Indonesian society.[4] At the core of the military's formulations of the 1945 Values were the promotion of dual function and the need for the military to continue to play a role in guiding society.

The older generation of the military was also alarmed by an increasing gap between the priorities of their generation and those of the youth. The New Order government's policy of re-establishing economic and cultural ties with the wider world resulted in profound changes in the first decade of the regime, including rapid growth and urban expansion. Along with this growth, which was partly buoyed along by foreign investment, came Western cultural influences including nightclubs, alcohol and increasingly permissive lifestyles.[5] Benedict Anderson, who has also commented on the 1972 seminar, points to an incident in 1972 as an example of why there was fear that there was a gap in "ideals" or loss of respect for elders at this time. On New Year's Eve of that year, a contest for the King and Queen of Freaks (*orang eksentrik*) was held in Surabaya at a stadium memorialising the legendary 1945 battle of Surabaya. The contest, held on this historic site devoted to the memory of the independence fighters, included nudity and sexual simulation regarded by many as scandalous and offensive.[6] Changing social norms no doubt promoted the feeling that there had been a loss of respect for older people, including the 1945 Generation.

Emphasis by officials on the existence of a "generation gap" also functioned to conveniently label more general discontent as being inter-generational.[7] The most significant generational challenge to members of the 1945 Generation in the government came from student protesters. Their criticism of the government centred on the government's own moral shortcomings. Between 1967 and 1972, many students became disillusioned with the direction the new government was taking, in particular with the re-emergence of trends that student activists had criticised in the period of Guided Democracy such as corruption and undemocratic, dictatorial rule.[8] In 1971 students and intellectuals joined together as a moral force to protest against both official mismanagement of funds and the coercive methods used by the military in the 1971 elections. Political leaders, therefore, had good reasons to legitimate themselves, particularly to the young generation. By means of the 1972 seminar, contemporary leaders from the 1945 Generation attempted to re-make their image by focusing more on their roles in the past than those in the present. Emphasis was placed on the respect owed to the 1945 Generation, and to the role of youth in making contributions to the nation, this time in the framework of a commitment to development and national stability. The seminar and the projects resulting from it can therefore be seen in part as a defensive effort by the military to remind the younger generation why the military was justified in playing a political role. As detailed in Chapter 4, the military's role in the revolution was central to this justification.

HISTORY PROJECTS RESULTING FROM THE 1972 SEMINAR

The 1972 seminar resulted in a broad range of history projects designed to promote the military's role in the revolution and, in turn, acceptance of their dominance in the New Order. Nugroho and the Armed Forces History Centre, were responsible for implementing many of these initiatives. As we have seen in Chapters 2 and 3, by 1974 Nugroho had already proved his ability to produce histories that legitimated military leadership both within and outside Indonesia. Nugroho also sought to publicise the concept of the 1945 Values and to promote to the outside world the idea that the fighting generation of 1945 was unique by presenting a paper on this topic to an international audience and then publishing a version in a brief pamphlet in English. The timing of this paper (August 1974), suggests that this was perhaps a reassertion of the good qualities of the leadership of the New Order regime, following the violent Malari riots of January the same year, in which the regime made its first serious crackdown on dissent.[9] By establishing the uniqueness of his generation, Nugroho perhaps hoped to provide further justification for the military's political role in Indonesia.

Some of the principal media identified as a means for enacting a transfer of values were memoirs of independence fighters, military and school history curricula, the print media, films, commemorative activities, commemoration of heroes and monuments and museums. An examination of some of the media through which the 1945 values were to be transferred tells us more about the actual values the military leadership were attempting to promote.[10]

Several recommendations for implanting the 1945 values were to improve the graveyards of Heroes of the Revolution; to preserve places of historical interest related to the struggle; and to build monuments to the revolution. In 1973, plans were made in conjunction with the Armed Forces History Centre for improving the National Heroes' Cemetery at Kalibata, including the installation of a monument dedicated to the unknown heroes of the revolution and enhancing the ceremonial space at this site.[11]

In addition to marking out the General Sudirman Walking Pilgrimage, efforts were also made to increase the number of other historical monuments relating to the Army's role in national revolution. By 1977, there were at least 60 monuments in Java commemorating the Army's role in the struggle, many of which were built after 1972.[12]

Seminar participants also recommended memoirs as appropriate for a transfer of values. Nugroho strongly endorsed the idea that members of the 1945 Generation record their own memoirs. He felt that both active and retired independence fighters (*pejuang*) should write histories and short stories about events of the revolution, because it was they who had experienced these values.[13] Under Nugroho's direction, the Armed Forces History Centre also commenced a project for recording the stories of independence fighters in the 1970s. In the 1980s, as members of this generation who had taken up military careers gradually retired, some began to publish their memoirs. Retired General A.H. Nasution, who had always taken an interest in history, was one of the first to produce his memoirs.[14] By the 1990s, biographies of the members, many who had by then retired, were proliferating.[15] Most military memoirs follow a standard formula, with at least one chapter devoted to their experience of the revolution and the rest to career and family.

In line with the original aims of the "transfer of values" initiatives, Susanto and Supriatma have suggested that, during the New Order period, these autobiographies functioned as advertisements and legitimisers for the military. In telling the story of the lives of elite members, these works are primarily concerned with the promotion and justification of the military's role.[16] There were, however, military members of the 1945 Generation who, once retired, also chose to criticise the political role of the military. In the 1980s these criticisms reached a peak, culminating in the Petition of Fifty.[17] Adam Malik, former Vice-President of Indonesia and a member of the Chaerul-Saleh Sukarni group who kidnapped President Sukarno in 1945, also challenged the military's exclusive claim to the 1945 values by demonstrating the diversity of the 1945 Generation.[18]

Among those to produce their own memoirs was President Suharto. The former President's autobiography provides a good example of the kind of stance taken by members of this generation who had progressed to elite positions. McIntyre suggests it was Suharto's intent that his autobiography be approached "in a mood of self-improvement".[19] In his autobiography, Suharto particularly promotes his own role in the general attack on the war-time capital of Yogyakarta in 1949, in order to promote his credentials as a member of the 1945 Generation.

Another recommendation of the 1972 seminar was that efforts be made to communicate the 1945 values to broader society in the form of print and audio media. Participants in the seminar recommended that there should be more books about the revolution available in school libraries and more bulletins produced with the theme of the spirit of the struggle of 1945. In addition, seminar participants recommended that writing competitions should be held on this theme. These competitions gained some popularity. A number of commemorative albums of the revolution dedicated to the young generation were also produced in the mid-1970s.[20] Nugroho also encouraged the young generation to read more history and short stories about the struggle.[21] On this front, the Armed Forces History Centre attempted to target the young generation, especially military cadets, with accessible history texts such as the *Reading Series for Soldiers*.

Participants in the 1972 Army seminar suggested that films should be made depicting the themes of the 1945 values. For the film industry, this was a clear statement to hitherto politically wary film-makers as to what kinds of historical films the new regime endorsed. Although the theme of the revolution had been popular in historical films since the revolution, during the period of Guided Democracy art, literature and film had become increasingly politicised, reflecting the aspirations of different political groups, including the then-influential Communist Party.[22] Krishna Sen notes a pause in historical film-making between 1965 and 1972, caused by the uncertainty surrounding the transition period and the importance of not being labelled "communist".[23] The resumption of historical film-making after this point is, at least in part, related to the directives issued at the 1972 seminar as to what were appropriate messages and topics for films about the past. Some post-1972 responses included the films *They Have Returned* (Mereka Kembali), 1975; *Bandung: A Sea of Fire* (Bandung Lautan Api), 1974; *Yellow Coconut Leaf* (Janur Kuning), 1979; and *The Dawn Attack* (Serangan Fajar), 1983. Consistent with the objectives of the 1972 seminar, Budi Irawanto suggests that films about the revolution increasingly became a medium for military ideology.[24]

The 1973 seminar on armed forces museums was a follow-up to the proposals of the 1972 seminar on implementing the 1945 values initiated by Nugroho. The seminar's purpose was to encourage the development of more military museums. It was attended by the heads of existing military museums in Indonesia and acted as a forum for sharing ideas and also to receive advice from museum experts. The seminar resulted in the publication of a booklet, *Guide for Planning ABRI Museums* (Pedoman Penyelenggaraan Museum ABRI), in which specific guidelines were set for the co-ordination, future design and running of military museums. In his foreword, Nugroho suggested that the purpose of the study of history was to express the identity of a social group and that armed forces museums provided a means of doing this in a visual form.[25] In this way, he argued, armed forces museums could serve as a means of introducing the Armed Forces to society. Following the UNESCO definition of a museum, the guide stated that museums were documentary and scientific research centres, charged with the task of interpreting the world of man and nature. It said that the aims of museums were to provide education for society as a source of information and as a guide for teachers in academic education — to act as a source of national pride — to function as national monuments by immortalising national heroes and, lastly, to function as recreational sites.

Although it was targeted towards armed forces museums, most Jakarta and regional museums sent representatives to the seminar.[26] This may have been a case of the museum world, like the film world, waiting

for safe directives about historical displays. In this seminar, the function
of military museums was stated as being:

> ... to develop the history of ABRI and to transfer the 1945 values
> to the younger generations by assisting in the gathering, research,
> preservation and display of historical artefacts or visual evidence of
> historical events concerning ABRI.[27]

The museum seminar booklet also called on museum-makers to attempt
to communicate and pass on the 1945 values in their displays. Nugroho
felt that building military museums was a way of raising the morale and
esprit de corps of members of the military and citizens and of improving
young people's knowledge about ABRI's role in the past.[28]

As noted in Chapter 4, the first Armed Forces history museum,
the Satriamandala Armed Forces Museum, focused on telling the story
of ABRI's role in the revolution. The stated aim of this museum was
also to transfer the 1945 values to the younger generations.[29] The scenes
in the museum make several attempts to characterise the spirit of the
youth of the struggle. Scenes clearly devoted to this theme include the
proclamation scene which emphasises the role of the youth in pressuring
President Sukarno and Vice-President Muhammad Hatta to make the
proclamation, the battle of Surabaya; the pulling down of the Dutch flag
from Hotel Yamato in Surabaya; and the role of the Student Army in
the struggle. Interestingly, however, none of these scenes are directly
connected to the military.

Commentaries on representations of the independence struggle in
this museum, like those in the 1972 seminar, focus largely on the roles
of male youths (*pemuda*). There are only two scenes in this museum that
feature women: one entitled communal kitchen (*dapur umum*) or a form
of temporary kitchen set up during the revolution and the other featuring
women's roles in the revolution. A brief analysis of these two scenes
suggests the kind of values young women were supposed to take away
from these museums as ideal for the female gender.

The communal kitchen scene serves largely, as the last line in
caption to the 1972 guidebook states, as a model of "the integration of
the people with the Armed Forces (my emphasis)".[30] The theme of
societal integration is similarly captured in the visual image that features
men and women farmers delivering their produce to the kitchen, male
soldiers arriving and eating under the awning of the kitchen and women
cooking in the kitchen (Illustration 5.1). In this scene, women are
primarily represented in one of the few roles military ideology recognises

Illustration 5.1   Communal kitchen.
Source: Image from postcard issued by *Museum Pusat ABRI Satriamandala.*

women as playing, that of either the provider or preparer of food and thus operating in a support role.[31]

In the second scene, however, some of the more diverse roles played by women in the revolution are recognised.[32] The caption to this diorama notes:

> Full of devotion Indonesian women made contributions to the areas of health, the public kitchens, intelligence, message carrying, community law and order and assisting the local government.[33]

The visual image for this scene is also markedly different. Whereas in the first scene, women are dressed almost exclusively in *kebaya* (a Javanese-style closely-fitted top) and sarongs, in this scene they are all dressed in Western-style uniforms (Illustration 5.2). Women in this scene are also featured holding arms. Consistent with Cynthia Enloe's idea that masculinity in the military centres around the notion that combat is an exclusive male domain, these women are only shown training with arms and not alongside men in direct combat. One frequently produced photo from the revolution shows women in a similar action of training with what appear to be *bambu runcing* (bamboo spears).[34] Thus, despite the reality

Illustration 5.2   The role of women in the revolutionary struggle.
Source: Image from postcard issued by *Museum Pusat ABRI Satriamandala.*

that some women fought with arms in the independence struggle, a choice has been made in this image not to show women in combat.

One likely reason for the inclusion of this specific image was to motivate women to spontaneously mobilise themselves, as they had during the revolution. Just as President Sukarno called upon women during the revolution to prioritise the nationalist struggle before their own concerns, the New Order regime called upon Indonesian women to prioritise the new Western influenced "struggle" of development first, this time with the harsher requirement that they abandon the women's movement. Rather than emphasising the relative freedom implied by the image of women training with arms and moving around the countryside as members of the Red Cross as ideal values, the museum-makers sought to emphasise the fact that women were involved in the challenges facing the nation. This representation of the revolution thus served as a model of ideal behaviour for women, ideal in the limited sense that women were involved and providing their services or contributions. It should be noted that although the names of women's militias (*lasykar*) are mentioned in the caption, no specific women are mentioned. This highlights the fact that women are viewed only as cadres serving a cause.

From the 1970s onwards, women were drafted to provide voluntary work for family welfare programmes, particularly through a system of civilian and military wives organisations.[35] Given the stated function of this museum to transfer the 1945 values, the words in the caption "Full of devotion Indonesian women made contributions" could also be seen as an example for Indonesian women. In this context, the apparent contrast between the women who appear in *kebaya* in the communal kitchen scene and those who appear in modern Western-style uniforms can also be explained. The modern Western uniforms could also be seen as a sign of the role women are expected to play in the "modern" project of development. Women serving in organisations such as the Family Welfare Guidance Organisation were required to own matching Western-style and *kebaya* uniforms for ceremonial and work-related tasks. The appearance of women in Western uniform could therefore be seen as a symbolic representation of women's duties both within and outside the home, in the kitchen or in charitable, development-oriented work.

In the context of the New Order period, the point of both dioramas in the Satriamandala Armed Forces Museum that include women is therefore to emphasise women's subordination to the armed state. For females who visit this museum, whether they are schoolchildren, members of the Armed Forces or members of the Armed Forces wives' associations, the message is that women have a duty to the nation and that they should commit themselves to that duty.

These representations of women's roles in the revolution were not, however, the sole responsibility of military men. The Head of Satriamandala Armed Forces Museum between 1978 and 1993 was a military woman.[36] As Robert Lowry has shown, women in the Armed Forces are strongly represented away from the "frontlines" in the history-making and indoctrination institutions and other administrative areas.[37] What this confirms is that women also participate in the production of conservative gender ideology. Throughout the New Order, there was, however, strong opposition to these gender models from some Indonesian women.[38]

Another recommendation of the 1972 seminar was for the inclusion of the military defined 1945 values into both military and general education curricula. Seminar participants recommended that the pre-school education curriculum should contain struggle songs and stories of heroes and that the primary school curriculum should contain national history, struggle songs and civics. For high school, the curriculum should include national history and instruction on dual function; and at the level of university it was suggested that a principal component of the study should be the 1945 values and subjects on defence matters and national strategy. For the broader society, they also suggested that integration of the military and the people should be promoted and that there should be courses on soldiership about military matters and military science in all institutions.[39] These suggestions make it clear that the "transfer of values" project was aimed at promoting broad acceptance of the military's political role and understanding of national defence. This is consistent with Kartakusuma's 1968 statement that in order to give the young generation understanding of dual function they needed to be taught the history of the armed forces.

Many of these ideas on how to transfer the 1945 values by means of indoctrination were implemented. The *Preliminary Education in National Defence* (Pendidikan Pendahuluan Membela Negara, PPBN) course was introduced at different levels of complexity from primary school to high school and was also used to indoctrinate employees in industry, farming and government.[40] It included instruction on the responsibilities of citizens to sacrifice for their nation, state and Pancasila, as well as providing an outline of national defence policy. A further study programme on military values made compulsory at university level were the soldiership courses, which were jointly developed by the Department of Education and the National Resilience Institute. Apart from being directed towards instilling nationalist spirit, the soldiership courses also included instruction on key military doctrines. Students were thus instructed in the Total People's Defence doctrine (Pertahanan Keamanan Rakyat Semesta – Hankamrata), a concept that General Nasution developed during the revolution to refer to the role of all Indonesians in national resilience; the Archipelagic Outlook concept (*wawasan nusantara*), which emphasises the geographic and social unity of Indonesia; and in Ideology, Politics, Economy and Social Cultural Issues (Ideologi, Politik, Ekonomi, Sosial Budaya – Ipoleksosbud), a concept that reflected the military's involvement in all these aspects of life.[41] The Pancasila indoctrination courses, introduced from 1978 onwards and intended for both school students and civil servants, also included promotion of the concept of the people's role in national resilience based on the doctrine of Total People's Defence and of the military's role in national development.[42]

As indicated in Chapter 1, political indoctrination was certainly not a phenomenon specific to the period of the New Order. During the Guided Democracy period, in which the continuation of the revolution was emphasised in ideology, students were also inculcated with the values allegedly displayed by Indonesian youth during the revolution. The *Seven Endeavours* (Sapta Usaha Tama, SUT) education programme, introduced as part of the eight-year development plan commencing in 1960, defined the values of the 1945 Generation as being discipline, patriotism, social awareness and creativity.[43] This definition of the 1945 values, provided by the then-Education Minister Priyono, shared the same commitment as the 1972 Army formulation to the promotion of patriotism and discipline. Emphasis on discipline was thus not specific to the military-dominated New Order period. Priyono's formulation of the 1945 values did not, however, emphasise that it was the military in particular that embodied the values of the 1945 Generation.

The Armed Forces History Centre was also able to promote the military-defined 1945 values in history because of its role in setting school history curricula from the early 1970s onwards. In 1974, the Minister of Education appointed Nugroho and another staff member as heads of a research team for history books for middle school.[44] Staff from the Centre also assisted in preparing the history textbooks for middle school and high school from 1975–76 and for tertiary education from 1970–74. The Centre also participated in evaluation of books for school libraries and in designing history curricula for schools.[45]

THE NATIONAL HISTORY TEXTBOOK

The *Indonesian National History Textbook* (Sejarah Nasional Indonesia) was also an initiative resulting from the 1972 transfer of values seminar. It was the first comprehensive Indonesian history series to be written by Indonesians.[46] Many well-known and respected historians from the most prestigious campuses in Indonesia were involved in the project. Thirty experts in various fields including archaeology, Islamic history, palaeontology, palaeography, the economy, anthropology and ethnology and history worked on the textbook. Along with Professor Sartono Kartodirdjo, Dean of Arts at Gadjah Mada University, and Marwati Djoened Poesponegoro, Nugroho was one of the editors for this project. He was responsible for Volume Six, which dealt with contemporary history from the Japanese occupation until the present.

Before this textbook was released to the public in 1976, Nugroho had already caused a scandal by prematurely submitting the manuscript for the series. When the government deadline for this project was approaching, some writers had finished their chapters and some had not.

Nugroho, who has been described as more disciplined than ordinary military personnel, had become accustomed to enforcing deadlines for his history projects at the Armed Forces History Centre. So as to meet the deadline for this project and in his capacity as an editor, Nugroho deviously instructed his assistant to procure a copy of the manuscript draft of Volume Six on the grounds of borrowing it for another purpose, and then immediately published it in its unfinished form.[47] Other members of the project were furious with Nugroho for publishing incomplete work without permission from the authors. They perceived this as a betrayal of the profession.[48] To many, Nugroho's actions seemed out of character, almost unbelievable.[49]

At the same time that he handed over the textbook to the Department of Education and President Suharto for approval, Nugroho sent a copy of the work for appraisal to Burhannudin Muhammad Diah, a well-known figure in the journalistic world and one of the youths who in 1945 pressured Sukarno to proclaim independence free of Japanese supervision. In an article published in the newspaper *Merdeka* on 8 April 1976, Diah provided a scathing critique of the textbook, outlining his disappointment with the partisan view adopted in presenting history in this volume. Quoting from the historian E.H. Carr, Diah began by noting that it is clear that historians will always be influenced by the time and society from which they write. He stressed the importance of this work as a standard history and the great responsibility that rested with its authors, given that it would be used for history in schools from primary school to tertiary institutions. First, he took issue with the tone in Volume Five written by Yusmar Basri because, for Diah, Basri described Indonesian nationalist leaders at the end of the nationalist movements as giving up hope, as not having faith in themselves. Diah suggests he should have been more specific about which nationalist groups were willing to co-operate with the Dutch.

Diah also claimed that historians need to evaluate why a person acted as they did from the person's own viewpoint. For example, when examining the history of the era in which Sukarno was President, historians should evaluate what the societal forces were at that time and why Sukarno did what he did, according to his own calculations. Diah accused the authors of Volume Five of representing the period of Sukarno's leadership as a backwards step for the nation on the basis of their disagreement with his actions. He claims the authors "cannot yet separate fact from values, reality from interpretation".[50] He also objected to the interpretation that President Sukarno took leadership into his own hands during the Guided Democracy era, arguing that there is no discussion of Sukarno's political rationale in the book. He also challenges the presentation of the idea that the 1945 Constitution was not carried out in a "pure way" during Guided Democracy as a fact, arguing that this is instead a matter of interpretation. He suggests that the authors' efforts to "present a thesis that Sukarno was a cruel person" constitute a kind of brainwashing. He also objects to the idea that President Sukarno fully supported the Indonesian Communist Party.

Diah urged all readers of history to find out about the writers of a work of history before they read it. Then, based on who the authors are, they could make an assessment of whether these works will stand up to examination. Diah claims that based on Nugroho's foreword to the *National History Textbook*, Nugroho gives the impression of being a sharp observer, like "a black hawk flying in the sky looking down with sharp eyes without [however] awareness of the hunters watching him". Diah suggests that perhaps Nugroho's position as an Army Brigadier General, who had already gained respect, gave him a sense of immunity to criticism.[51]

Highlighting the subjective interpretation of history in this volume, Diah calls for Nugroho and other authors of the volume to write letters of resignation to the Minister of Education.

> Prove to me, yes, confirm writers of the National History Textbook with your values, that President Sukarno fully supported the Communist Party, that president Sukarno did everything you said he did, formed an alliance or gave instructions to the Communist Party to arbitrarily rule the people, that he was dictatorial and not responsible at all to the people as you have outlined in this 'standard' history book.

Finally, Diah concludes, he was saddened to read this book because it is as if these historians have "discredited their own profession and become conformists of their era". Despite this scathing critique, which Diah notes Nugroho accepted but did not act upon, the *National History Textbook* went ahead as planned. Rather than becoming a source of shame for Nugroho, it seems his contribution to the project earned him extra kudos. In 1982, Nugroho was appointed to the position of Rector of the University of Indonesia and in 1983, he was appointed to the position of Minister of Education.

When Nugroho took up the position of Minister of Education, he took specific steps to further realise the goals of the 1972 seminar.

First, he put the staff of the Armed Forces History Centre to work on formulating the Pancasila Moral Education (Pendidikan Moral Pancasila) course, an important and long-lasting ideological component of the education system that accompanied the P4 courses.[52] He also devised a new school history course: *History of the National Struggle* (Pendidikan Sejarah Perjuangan Bangsa, PSPB). The purpose of the PSPB was to expand and develop the soul, spirit and values of 1945 for the younger generation.[53]

Diah's critique provides some indication of the content of the *National History Textbook* and of a pattern of playing down the roles of nationalists and discrediting President Sukarno. One of the places this is most evident is in the lack of mention in Volume Five of the textbook covering the nationalist movement, of Sukarno's 1930 trial in the Dutch colonial court in which he presented his famous speech, *Indonesia Accuses.* In Volume Six, Nugroho's controversial theory (outlined in Chapter 1) that Muhammad Yamin, rather than Sukarno, was the first to formulate the Pancasila is also replicated. Here it is stated that Yamin was the first to put forward the substance of the five principles, whereas three days later Sukarno gave the principles the name "Pancasila" and restated them.[54]

The *National History Textbook* project also received some criticism from Indonesian historians in the context of disquiet over the new *History of the National Struggle* course. Decree II of the government's 1983 Broad Outline of State Policy (Garis Besar Haluan Negara, GBHN), declared that the *History of the National Struggle* course covering history from the war of independence to the New Order was designed to perpetuate and develop the spirit and goals of the 1945 Values of the young generation by giving them "affective, inspirational and integrative materials to study".[55] According to Nugroho the purpose of the *History of the National Struggle* course was to raise the level of patriotism (*cinta Tanah Air*). To love their country, children needed to know in more depth about events and the situation of their homeland.[56] Consistent with his enthusiasm for projects inspired by the 1972 seminar, Nugroho explained he had attempted to get the *History of the National Struggle* course made part of the Broad Outline of State Policy for years and that it was only in 1983, after he became Education Minister, that he succeeded.[57]

Much of the press criticism of the proposed *History of the National Struggle* course related to the fact that insufficient time was left for the preparation of a textbook, such that teachers were required to start teaching the course in 1984 without a text. A temporary solution posed for this problem was for Nugroho's album, *30 Years of Indonesian Independence* (30 Tahun Indonesia Merdeka), produced for the 30th anniversary of independence, to be used as a supplement. One vocal commentator on this issue was historian Abdurrachman Surjomihardjo. He argued that *30 Years of Indonesian Independence* was unsuitable because it was not produced for this purpose. He also objected to inter-vention in the school curricula commenting that:

> In other countries the content of textbooks are not determined by people in positions of power, but based on creativity outside of the structure of power and then evaluated by the government on the basis of which parts need improvement and which parts are already acceptable.[58]

Given the *History of the National Struggle* course was Nugroho's initiative, this can be read as a criticism of Nugroho's own politics in history-writing. Surjomihardjo, along with several other historians, also protested the idea that this course should commence at 1945, on the basis that from an historical perspective the awareness of struggle began with the nationalist movement at the beginning of the twentieth century. The response of the then-Head of the Centre for Research and Develop-ment of the Department of Education and Culture, Professor Harsya Bachtiar, was that the *History of the National Struggle* course was not a chronological analysis of history, but intended to transfer the values or spirit of Pancasila and the 1945 Constitution to children, like the Pancasila Moral Education course.[59] Nugroho's own logic for commencing this course at 1945 no doubt stemmed from his theory on the origins of the Indonesian national spirit in his thesis on the Japanese created army PETA (Pembela Tanah Air, Defenders of the Fatherland). In this, he argued that 17 August 1945 represented the birth of a new spirit, a new beginning for Indonesians, and that it was incorrect to place too much influence on the role of preceding influences, such as the Japanese period, in moulding this new spirit.[60]

In 1985, shortly after Nugroho's death, a new polemic on the *History of the National Struggle* course and the *National History Textbook* erupted. On 9 September, the Institute for National History Research at the 17 August University held a seminar to discuss these matters. The Head of the Institute, Dr Soeroto, recommended that the Broad Outline of State Policy concerning the *History of the National Struggle* course be changed so that the chaos in the study of history in schools would not worsen. He also called for the start date for the subject to be changed to the date of the arrival of foreigners to Indonesia. The seminar participants also concluded that the lower secondary school adaptation of the *National History Textbook* (Sejarah Nasional Indonesia – SMP Volume 3, 1976) tried to destroy the good name of Sukarno. Participants recommended the book be withdrawn and banned from schools.[61] In a cutting critique of the treatment of Sukarno as an historical figure in these works, Soeroto suggested the writers of "national history" who were being attacked by society and the younger generation were nothing more than imitators of imperialist writers such as Cindy Adams, the biographer of Sukarno who "followed imperialist instructions to destroy the name of Bung Karno as the father of the nation and proclamator of Indonesian independence". At the centre of the scandal over the *History of the National Struggle* course was a statement, recorded on page 154, that claimed President Sukarno had received commissions from other countries. Soeroto asked why Indonesians would scorn and abuse their own national leaders without any feeling of shame as Indonesians. What would they gain from this? For whose benefit was this rotten version written and instilled in the spirit of our younger generations? He claimed that the Parliament and politicians had expressed regret that national history discredited national figures, and that they have asked the *History of the National Struggle* course to be revised.

> As a patriotic nation we should be aware that anti-Indonesian forces
> have already destroyed our nation and split us into parts by using
> our own history. We should be aware of efforts to divide us. We
> need an Indonesia-centric and authentic version of history.[62]

This is a very interesting critique, given that Nugroho considered himself the firm nationalist who argued for Indonesian-centric versions of history, written by Indonesians themselves.

Head of the Faculty of Letters of the Diponegoro University in Semarang, Dr Hamid Abdullah, also attacked these efforts to discredit Sukarno. He argued that the allegations that Sukarno received commissions from other countries should at least be supported by documentary evidence, so that the history text did not just become a traditional court chronicle (*babad*) in which anyone could throw an idea around.[63] Although staff of the Armed Forces History Centre claimed their assertions in the text were supported by records kept at the Centre, including decrees and decisions of the parliament,[64] Abdullah described the *History of the National Struggle* course as the biggest academic scandal

Illustration 5.3 A cartoon satirising the acronym "PSPB" (Pendidikan Sejarah Perjuangan Bangsa, History of the National Struggle).
Source: Rekaman Peristiwa, 1985, p. 138.

in Indonesian history (Illustration 5.3). He claimed that Sukarno's name was:

> ... equal to that of Nehru, Gandhi, Mao Tze Tung, Ho Chi Minh and other nationalists before World War II. His thinking greatly inspired national leaders of the world. Why then should it be us who tear him apart and destroy him?

Hamid Abdullah expressed his regret that this work had been compiled by a committee and suggested that this kind of historical manipulation

> ... usually only occurs in communist or totalitarian countries, so why have we [he asked], a country that follow the Pancasila philosophy and which is in fact anti-communist, made the same mistake as communist countries?

This clever critique again struck at the heart of the regime's ideological base and the regime's professed rejection of communism and all that was associated with it. Reflecting on how this might have happened, Abdullah suggested that Indonesian historians were also affected by the past. He claimed that if historians had posed the same critiques ten years ago with the intention of righting history, they would have been labelled Sukarnoist elements (*antek Soekarno*).[65] He thus implied that the trend of censoring Sukarno out of history was a residual effect of early New Order de-Sukarnoisation efforts and the necessity of rejecting Sukarno to prove one's loyalty to the new regime.

Historian Abdurrachman Surjomihardjo also offered some commentary on the *National History Textbook*. He suggested that several parts of the material in this book seemed:

> ... less than pure ... meaning history, what's more history for the young generation, must not contain messages or additions that prevent understanding. History must be pure. If you want to insert elements that are motivated to defeat political opposition or to corner a certain group, that is no longer history. This will be very dangerous for our young generation.[66]

This more direct criticism of political influence in this textbook mirrored Diah's original criticism of the work.

Professor Harsya Bachtiar, who had previously defended the history curriculum, also advanced some criticism of the *National History Textbook*. He claimed that "National History should describe the greatness of a nation and put forward the national values which people or leaders have struggled for." Pointing also to political influence in this text, he argued:

> ... the ideal and best form of national history is one which covers all groups and the aspirations of many groups in society. This means not writing the history of just one group ... if only the military or political groups are written about, then that is not national history.... That is only military or political history.[67]

In the context of New Order press censorship, this was one of the most direct attacks on military intervention in New Order history writing.

In 1985, Diah rejoined the debate, arguing that what was important was to critically examine the *National History Textbook* and its use in history teaching from primary school to universities. Diah claimed he had already put Nugroho on trial and questioned why other historians who had put their name to this work were not being held accountable. Diah called for Indonesians to "forget Nugroho's way of thinking", arguing that history should not just be produced for today or for political groups for there will always come a time when history will right itself. He stated:

I am sure that in the future when the people are aware that what they have read was not history, but rather the humiliation of one of the leaders in the history of the development of the independent nation and state of Indonesia, they will demand the same of Nugroho as I did.

For Diah, President Suharto's decision to support a revision of history texts was not the end of the matter. Diah asked "If we do not value our leaders and our heroes, whom will we respect?" He felt that *National History Textbook* was misleading and had acted to poison the thoughts of the young generation of Indonesians about Bung Karno (using an affectionate term for a respected older man).

Diah's original advice to Nugroho on his draft for the *National History Textbook* had been that the book not be printed, but be revised in accordance with the right kind of conscience for a historian and with a commitment to honesty and the purity of history, such that the book would not become the fuel for a campfire.[68] Diah's comments turned out to be prophetic: after the fall of Suharto, the *National History Textbooks* were indeed burned by some students in protest at the lies they felt hey had been forced to learn.[69]

While many commented on efforts to discredit Sukarno, most did not comment on who did make it into this history text. Emphasis on the military's role in post-independence history is made clear by the index to Volume Six, which lists only military aspects of the revolution such as the beginning of the armed struggle, responding to the first Dutch military action, crushing the 1948 PKI revolt, responding to the second Dutch military action and the guerrilla phase approaching the achievement of sovereignty.

A comparison of the roles played by President Sukarno and General Sudirman in response to the second Dutch attack highlights the emphasis on the military's reliability. In Nugroho's representations of this period, the two figures of Sukarno and Sudirman function as binary opposites of civilian inaction alongside military action:

> Several days after the (Renville) negotiations stalled, the Dutch carried out a military action on the Republic of Indonesia. Yogyakarta, the capital city of the Republic of Indonesia, was successfully taken back and occupied. The President and Vice-President and several other statesmen did not evacuate and were captured by the Dutch.... Although he was very ill, the Commander for Life, General Sudirman retreated from the city of Yogyakarta to

lead a total guerrilla struggle against the Dutch. For seven months, General Sudirman became the hope of all the people of Indonesia who carried out a dire struggle to keep the country of Republic of Indonesia alive.[70]

While this textbook makes mention of Sukarno and Hatta's transfer of power to an emergency government in Sumatra, it does not explain the rationale for the leaders' decision to allow themselves to be captured.

Other examples of aggrandisement of the military are the focus on the military's role in crushing the rebellions in the 1950s in the West Irian campaign and, of course, in suppressing the alleged communist rebels in the coup attempt of 1965. Here Nugroho's version of the coup attempt is replicated with emphasis on the barbarity of the communists. The rationale that the military were the saviours of Pancasila is also replicated with mention of Chairman of the Communist Party Aidit's much publicised statement of 16 October 1964 that "Pancasila is only an instrument of unity and when we have achieved unity, we will no longer need the Pancasila."[71] The textbook also replicates the famous photographs of the decomposing corpses of the seven Army victims of the coup attempt.

While coverage of the post-independence period is quite brief, it is notable that not one mention is made of women in this section. The values of militarism are also overtly promoted in Volume Six of the National History Textbook in the latter Section F on national defence and dual function.

NUGROHO'S DEVOTION TO THE INDONESIAN MILITARY

In the realm of education, Nugroho was committed to the idea that it was the role of the military to promote discipline in the "younger generations" of Indonesia in order to ensure continuing national development. Reflecting his own rather extreme view on what education should be, he noted in a speech as Minister for Education entitled *Regeneration and Motivation*:

> Since the New Order period began, education has never been a routine activity, rather it has been perceived as the formation of cadets to continue the nation's struggle or cadets for national development and the implementation of Pancasila.[72]

This commentary is consistent with the ideas of the 1972 seminar, in which it was suggested that both citizens and members of the Armed

Forces needed to be indoctrinated into the 1945 values, including the value of discipline and, by implication, dedication to the state. In 1996, Romo Mangunwijaya, a well-known priest and human rights activist, pointed to several features of the school system such as marching, the use of military style discipline and language and the system of memorising facts as indicative of the fact that schools were no longer schools, but organisations for "caderisation".[73] This is certainly consistent with Nugroho's vision, but how did students view Nugroho?

From 1964, Nugroho was Head of the Armed Forces History Centre and also an employee of the Department of History in the Faculty of Letters at the University of Indonesia. Neither Nugroho's appointment as Head of the Armed Forces History Centre, nor his recruitment of University of Indonesia history department students to the Centre in the early years of the regime, became an issue on campus because the military were, at that time, popularly viewed by many students as heroes.[74] Anti-communist students felt an alliance with the military, for by whom they had been carefully courted.[75] However, as the New Order regime consolidated itself and its authoritarian characteristics became clearer, student sentiment turned against the military.

On Nugroho's appointment as Rector of the University of Indonesia in 1982, he was met with belittling comments and a large poster reading "Don't stain our campus with military boots".[76] By this stage of his career, Nugroho had been lecturing in the Faculty of Letters at the same university for over 20 years, yet he was commonly perceived to be a military man. Because Nugroho was Head of the Armed Forces History Centre, he was accordingly awarded the titular rank of Brigadier General. He also chose to display his military status by wearing a military uniform and driving a military jeep. Students viewed his appointment to the position of Rector in 1982 (Illustration 5.4) as a military appointment, because the Rector usually came from a more prestigious faculty than Letters (such as Medicine or Law). History was one of the weakest departments at the time.[77] Nugroho was seen as a military man: "a government appointment put on campus to restrict the freedom of student life".[78] As Rector, Nugroho made his own contributions through the policy of Normalisation of Campus Life and the creation of the Body for the Co-ordination of Student Affairs, both of which were designed to restrict student political action to campus affairs. He also introduced the concept of "transpoliticisation, professionalisation and institutionalisation" in relation to university management. This encompassed the banning of political activities on campus.[79] The intention was that the University

Illustration 5.4 Nugroho as Rector of the University of Indonesia.
Source: Image from Nugroho Notosusanto, *Menegaskan Identitas Universitas Indonesia: Pesan Kepada Orangtua Mahasiswa Baru.* Universitas Indonesia, seri komunikari No. 4, Jakarta, 1982.

of Indonesia should never again become involved in opposing or toppling the government. Nugroho also abolished initiation activities on campus and instead introduced 100 hours of Pancasila indoctrination.[80] His appointment to Minister of Education in 1983 by President Suharto can be interpreted as a sign of approval for Nugroho's initiatives on campus and in the field of history.

Rising resentment against the New Order regime also made Nugroho's position in the academic world increasingly difficult. It should be said that Nugroho was not the only academic who chose to work for the military-dominated regime. Many of the technocrats, with whom the Army had fostered links in the Guided Democracy period by inviting them to teach at the Army Staff and Command School, were also academics. But as we have seen, as the New Order progressed and the continuance of authoritarianism persisted, many scholars became angered by the kind of histories Nugroho produced.

This sense of anger was also a product of the disappointment other intellectuals, both inside and outside Indonesia, felt at the path Nugroho had chosen. As mentioned in Chapter 2, in the early 1960s Nugroho had wide links in the intellectual world. By the mid-1970s, however, many had begun to distance themselves from him because of his closeness to the military, which was something they could not understand.

In 1978, Nugroho told a friend that he inhabited two worlds: that of the Army and that of the university. He said that in the world of the Army, people have a sense of honour and were not always competing with each other, whereas at university everyone was out for themselves.

This reaction was probably based on the sense of rejection from the academic world brought about by some of his controversial projects.[81] Yet, while Nugroho felt the military world was more honourable, nor was he completely accepted within the military world. A military man in the employment of the Army History Centre based in Bandung once posed the question about Nugroho and himself to historian Sartono Kartodirdjo:

> Tell me Sartono, what is worse: a military man who pretends to be
> an historian or an historian who pretends to be a military man?[82]

Nugroho would have received financial rewards for his work, yet it seems that for him promotions in both the military and educational worlds held more importance as a source of motivation. Nugroho was awarded titular rankings because of his position as head of an armed forces institution directly accountable to the Armed Forces Commander. In 1968 he was appointed titular Colonel and then in 1971 titular Brigadier General. Nugroho considered the award of these ranks as a sign of respect from the leaders of the armed forces, indicating their trust in his ability to head a military institution. One acquaintance of Nugroho's recalls him saying that he liked to travel overseas as it enabled him to wear his uniform and insignia.[83] This suggests that Nugroho's motivation was linked to status. But it also reflects Nugroho's nostalgia for the military career he might have had.

The primary mission of Nugroho's work was to bind people together by saturating his audiences in nationalistic meta-narratives about the past, including prescriptions of the ideal Indonesian nation. He said there were four functions of history: recreational, inspirational, instructive and educative.[84] He emphasised that inspiration was particularly important for a "third-world" country.

As a lecturer, Nugroho has been described as dry, but also encouraging and able to recognise potential.[85] A text he often referred to was the history method book *Understanding History* by the well-known historian Louis Gottschalk,[86] which Nugroho translated into Indonesian. He encouraged his students to write and to be published, and he even offered opportunities for some to contribute to the *Reading Series for Soldiers* for the Armed Forces History Centre. Nugroho himself subscribed to this philosophy of eternalising his name by producing a steady flow of written work.[87] An even stronger implementation of this idea was his creation of monumental museums.

Nugroho once suggested that criticisms of his work should be in academic terms, yet it was his own lack of academic scruple which was being attacked. Several commentators have suggested that Nugroho was not a great intellectual and his publications often earned derisive labels such as "pamphlets" or "quasi-academic".[88] Journalist and co-founder of *Tempo* magazine, Christianto Wibisono, claimed that from:

> Nugroho's writings on 1 June (the birth of Pancasila), dual function, and the salvation of Pancasila, it could be construed from many perspectives that this work was highly subjective and that he was an "advocate" or "legitimator" of the system of dual function in its present form.[89]

Nugroho's work was not balanced, because it was very much influenced by his reverence for the military and his conviction that history should be directed towards nation-building and regime preservation, two politically charged goals. As H.A.J. Klooster has noted,[90] in Nugroho's 1968 publication *History and Defense and Security* [91] and other works, Nugroho makes quite clear the ideological function of his military histories. It appears that Nugroho did not aspire to be a great intellectual. His forte was more in the realm of ideology.

Most countries have well-known official historians, yet Nugroho managed to incite more resentment and controversy than many others. Resentment towards Nugroho related partly to his position as official historian in an autocratic military regime. Nugroho legitimised and defended the Indonesian military in a way that many in university communities saw as betraying his integrity as an intellectual. In a repressive climate, he defended the military. He also attempted to project this history, filled with military glory, into school curricula.

Nugroho liked to think of himself as a specialist in contemporary Indonesian history. At times, he referred to the sensitivity of contemporary history when historical actors were still alive. After years of elite praise for his work, Nugroho enjoyed unusual freedom to express his views on contemporary history. He was trusted as the mouthpiece of the military. Yet for many historians and political scientists, the recent past was not an era on which they could speak or write freely. Many books were banned in the New Order period if they presented information or interpretations in a way contrary to Nugroho, that is, unfavourable to Suharto or the military.

Nugroho's continual dismissal of the role of diplomacy and the nationalist movement effectively discounted civilian contributions.

People's anger at this position no doubt related not only to a contested past, but also to a contested present in which the military continued to dominate what some saw as civilian posts and state assets. Nugroho's attacks on former President Sukarno as an historical figure and his attempts to write him out of history caused great offence. In the eyes of many, Sukarno, as proclamator of independence and founding President, remained an important figure. This feeling was reinforced by the growing discontent with the second President.

In response to the criticism he had endured since his controversial projects of the late 1970s and in his position as Rector, Nugroho for the most part retained his calm demeanour. It is hard to know how much he was personally affected. Nugroho was fond of shooting for the very reason that "this kind of sport teaches one composure".[92] Based on his observation of Nugroho's calm reaction in the face of attacks on him during a student press congress in the early 1960s, Satyagraha Hoerip, later a journalist for newspaper *Sinar Harapan*, once described Nugroho as sharing similar characteristics to the shadow puppet Arjuna (known as a refined and graceful figure who is nevertheless powerful and capable of attacking opponents).[93] In describing Nugroho as similar to Arjuna, he also implied that composure was one of Nugroho's greatest assets.

In terms of the continually shifting balance of power between the military and Suharto over the first twenty years of the New Order period, it appears that initially Nugroho could be classified as a military man. However, as time progressed he also became a Suharto loyalist. As Head of the Armed Forces History Centre, Nugroho received strong support from President Suharto for his museums and monuments. Almost every year, Nugroho's ideas to develop and organise history projects were approved by the President. All these ideas were implemented because of the financial support from the leadership of the Department of Defence. The President officially opened most of these sites and in some cases he formally named them (Illustration 5.5). Suharto was responsible for the Sanskrit names "satriamandala" for the first combined Armed Forces museum and also "Museum Waspada Purbawisesa" (the Museum of Eternal Vigilance) for the museum dedicated to the story of the theme of extremist Islam as a national threat.

Suharto would sometimes summon Nugroho for an audience at his home in Jalan Cendana to hear Suharto's memories of historical events. Nugroho was expected to make careful historical notes about key events in which Suharto had played a part, such as the General Attack on Yogyakarta on 1 March 1949, the crushing of the coup attempt in

Illustration 5.5   Nugroho giving Suharto a tour of Satriamandala Armed Forces Museum.
Source: Image from Pusat Sejarah dan Tradisi ABRI, *Seperempat Abad Pusjarah ABRI (5-10-1964 s.d 5-10-1989)*, Markas Besar Angkatan Bersenjata R. I., Pusat Sejarah dan Tradisi ABRI, Jakarta, 1994, p. 74.

1965, the Instruction of 11 March 1966 and the National Consensus of 1966.[94] The relationship between Nugroho and President Suharto recalls images of a traditional Javanese court chronicler recording a modern day *babad* (chronicle) of the glory and might of the court under the direction of its principal actor, the King.

Nugroho's public commentary suggested he continued to believe wholeheartedly in the New Order, yet it is difficult to discern how much of this was attributable to the value of military loyalty to which he firmly subscribed. In a 1981 interview Nugroho said that, of his literary works, his favourite short story was *River* (Sungai). In *River*, a man experiences a conflict of interest in his position as a father who loves his child and as a commander who must save his troops. While crossing a river in close proximity to the enemy, the father drowns his crying child so as not to alert the enemy to the presence of his troops. "This is the effect of big events on ordinary people", he suggested.[95] Nugroho's preference for this story reflects his own romanticised perception of military loyalty and the lengths to which he would go to defend it, despite the personal cost.

When Nugroho did criticise the military, he did so guardedly. In a 1970 piece on the dual function of the Indonesian military, Nugroho noted in a footnote the abandonment within the Indonesian military of what Janowitz termed the typically puritanical attitude of armies in new nations:

> Since the period of "Guided Democracy" dominated by the flam-boyant President Sukarno, there is a feeling that too many high-ranking officers have abandoned this "puritanical" attitude.[96]

It seems that Nugroho equated this puritanical attitude most closely with the 1945 generation. Nugroho follows this comment with a clarification that there remain many military men who do fit the puritanical mould.[97] In a 1974 paper on the transfer of values, he again notes in a passing comment that "(o)ne important obstruction to the smooth transfer of the values of 1945 is in fact that several members of the Generation of 1945 itself have deviated from those values".[98] Although Nugroho made these criticisms in the early years of the New Order, he seems to have resigned himself in later years to merely serving the regime. This is confirmed by his later promotions to Rector of the University of Indonesia and then Minister of Education and Culture.

One of the most important consequences of the history that Nugroho wrote for the New Order regime was the impact on the lives of those who were its victims. Initially, this applied to members of the Communist Party, many of whom had no knowledge of the attempted coup. While Nugroho never publicly reflected on his part in condemning all communists and members of affiliated organisations, he did on one occasion acknowledge that some persons were left out of his histories. This comment came out amidst Nugroho's reflections upon his experience of writing short stories in comparison to history writing. He noted:

> What used to motivate me to write fiction was its attraction as a way to express my feelings.... I cannot use history to express my sympathy for the ordinary people who are caught in the viciousness of big events that they do not control. Yes, ordinary people who are knocked over by big events. This wish I must fulfil through fiction, because history is the macro perspective, about big movements and mankind in collectivity.... Large historical events produce different emotions, colossal emotions.... History cannot capture subtle emotions.[99]

In this passage and in his short-story writing Nugroho demonstrated that he understood the effect of large events on ordinary individuals. This suggests that Nugroho was aware that the histories he wrote were necessarily exclusive meta-narratives, in the sense that they told singular big picture versions of the past without considering alternative voices or narratives. It is impossible to tell from this interview whether Nugroho extended his sympathy to victims of 1965 or if he was perhaps reflecting on unsung heroes of the independence struggle such as the commander or child in his story *River*.

Nugroho acted to protect some of his closest associates from the post-coup purges of those affiliated with the political left. In 1966, for example, he secured the release of his friend and student, Onghokham, from gaol.[100] Arief Budiman also recalls that Nugroho prevented Parsudi Suparlan, a respected anthropologist at the University of Indonesia, from being sacked for prior membership in the communist-affiliated student organisation, the Indonesian Student Movement Centre (CGMI). In his correspondence with Herb Feith in 1969, Nugroho referred to his disagreements with the "super-Orba" (the most hardline Orde Baru, New Order people) members of KASI (Kesatuan Aksi Sarjana Indonesia, Indonesian Graduates Action Front) who presumably favoured a more thorough cleansing of society.[101] In a further letter to Feith in 1970, Nugroho offered to pass on suggestions to the then-Chief Prosecutor, Sugih Arto, on how to improve the living conditions of political prisoners from 1965.[102] Although Nugroho may well have been posturing to his long-time friend who had begun to develop a deep concern for those imprisoned after the coup attempt, this correspondence reveals a greater sense of compassion in Nugroho than many would recognise. Nugroho was not so rigidly anti-communist to reject supervision of Soe Hok Gie's thesis at the University of Indonesia on the communist victims of the Madiun Affair.[103] Yet I found no trace in Nugroho's writings of sympathy for those outside the world of academia who were condemned to death, partly because of the version of the coup that Nugroho promoted.

Acquaintances of Nugroho describe him as softly spoken and very controlled. He was likeable, yet reserved. He was also guarded and gave the impression of knowing more than he would let on.[104] Many people who had known Nugroho as a student leader, an intellectual and as a writer of short stories were disappointed in his progression to what they saw as a defender of the New Order. Some acquaintances felt unable to reconcile the versions of this man that they felt they had known.[105] Yet this perception is based on an underestimation of the link that

Nugroho felt with the institution of the military as a result of his experience in the Student Army in the independence struggle and his existence thereafter in the dual worlds of academia and the military.

A good friend of Nugroho's from his student days noted that he was stubborn. It was difficult to change his opinion, elicit a compromise or concede on issues based on principle.[106] This observation seems consistent with Nugroho's continuing belief in the military and the state and his ideas about the uniqueness of his own generation, the 1945 Generation. Indeed as we have seen all these themes are taken up in his work, both in written form and visually in the museums he designed.

CONCLUSION

From the period of Guided Democracy to the early New Order, the Indonesian military moved from a highly defensive position, in which they produced history only for internal military purposes, to an offensive position, in which they sought to dictate the official version of the 1965 coup attempt to the Indonesian public. As the New Order regime progressed, the military moved to tighten control over official history.

The aim of the 1972 seminar was to bring about continuing reverence for the Indonesian military, especially through the concept of the transfer of 1945 Values. The Indonesian public who either read military memoirs, watched Indonesian films about the revolution or studied military sanctioned textbooks, became exposed to aggrandised versions of the military's role in the national past and to military values. The most influential media in which the 1945 Values were imparted is in Volumes Five and Six of the *National History Textbook* and the *History of the National Struggle* course, both of which were overseen by Nugroho Notosusanto. Despite press censorship, many academics and prominent figures protested against the versions of contemporary history provided in both these media, especially representations of President Sukarno. Some scholars pointed to the manipulation of historical facts of military bias in these works.

Nugroho defended his versions of history and the associated promotion of military values within them, affirming his belief that history should be used as a means of inspiring people to participate in national development. Despite some reservations about the direction some members of the 1945 generation had taken, Nugroho continued to glorify the Indonesian military until his death in 1985 because of his personal belief that military men could best guide the nation and perhaps also from his own ambitions to be a person of influence.

6

Establishing a Martial Tradition and On-going Threats to the Nation

Politicised militaries look both into the past and to the future for sources of legitimacy. If such militaries can point far back in time to ancient martial leaders, their own roles seem all the more natural. Demonstrating a long history of martial heroes also reduces the focus on one particular generation of military leaders. Political militaries also need to establish the need for continuing military roles in the future by reminding the public of on-going threats to the nation based on both past and contemporary evidence of such threats.

In the last decade of the Suharto regime the military experienced generational change and increasing marginalisation as a political force. As a result the Armed Forces History Centre moved both to consolidate existing historical sources of legitimacy and also looked for new sources. The Centre completed three major museums in this period. The first museum, the National Soldiership Museum (Museum Keprajuritan Indonesia) emphasised a long tradition of soldiership in an attempt to counter the impact of the retirement of members of the 1945 Generation. The two other museums, the Museum of Eternal Vigilance and the Museum of Communist Treachery, focused on continuing threats to the nation from "extreme Islam" and communism respectively. Each project reveals significant shifts in military ideology and continuing efforts on the military's part to grapple for legitimacy in the closing decade of the New Order regime.

This period of reassessment of the military's sources of historical and contemporary legitimacy coincided with the passing of the key New Order historian, Nugroho Notosusanto. Nugroho's influence was still, however, present in two of the museums discussed in this chapter.

NUGROHO'S PASSING

Many of Nugroho's former staff at the Armed Forces History Centre described him as being the driving force behind the Centre.[1] Nugroho's sudden death of a brain haemorrhage in June 1985 meant the Centre's initiatives for promoting the military through history lost some momentum. As we have seen, Nugroho had co-ordinated many written histories, written his own publications and worked on several very large and ambitious museum projects. The Centre struggled to find a replacement. All military candidates seemed insignificant by comparison.[2] Indeed, Nugroho was in many ways unique: he offered academic legitimacy combined with a sense of creativity, which he applied to a range of projects. Nugroho was also a member of the renowned 1945 Generation.

General Benny Murdani, then Commander of the Armed Forces, like General Nasution in an earlier era, took an interest in the production of military history. Murdani had begun his military career in the 1950s and participated in suppressing the Darul Islam (House of Islam) and Permesta rebellions. In 1962 he joined the campaign to reclaim West Papua from the Dutch and he played a significant role in the 1975 invasion of East Timor. During his term as Commander (1983–88), Murdani was considered the second most powerful person in Indonesia.[3] A major source of Murdani's power was his control of Indonesia's intelligence apparatus, resulting from many years of service in military institutions. As of 1974, he was Head of Intelligence for the Operational Command for the Restoration of Security and Order (Kopkamtib) and assistant to the Head of Staff for Intelligence in the Ministry of Defence. In 1977, Murdani was Deputy Head of the National Intelligence Co-ordinating Agency (Bakin) and Head of the Operational Command for the Restoration of Security and Order from 1978 to 1983.[4]

After Nugroho's death, General Murdani paid considerable attention to the activities of the Centre. This was possibly a response to the vacuum Nugroho's departure from the Centre created and the direct line of responsibility between the Head of the Armed Forces History Centre and the Commander of the Armed Forces. General Murdani made contributions to two museum projects of the History Centre in the mid-1980s, the first of which was the National Soldiership Museum.

THE NATIONAL SOLDIERSHIP MUSEUM: ESTABLISHING A LONG TRADITION OF SOLDIERSHIP

The initial idea for National Soldiership Museum came from Mrs Tien Suharto, the wife of President Suharto. In 1975 Mrs Tien had personally approached Nugroho and enlisted him in the task of designing a military museum highlighting the long history of Indonesian soldiership, including the story of many pre-independence heroes such as Diponegoro.[5] Mrs Tien intended the National Soldiership Museum to form an integral part of her controversial "Beautiful Indonesia in Miniature" project. The Beautiful Indonesia in Miniature theme park (otherwise known as Taman Mini) is an extensive tourist complex in East Jakarta containing replica regional houses from each of the provinces of Indonesia and a lake, over which tourists can ride in a gondola, looking down onto miniaturised replicas of the islands of Indonesia. The theme park was controversial because it was built at great cost and because hundreds of homes were razed to make way for the complex and their inhabitants inadequately compensated.[6]

A work committee for the National Soldiership Museum was formed in 1975 under the combined direction of Nugroho and retired Lieutenant General Susilo Sudarman, a member of the 1945 Generation and then Assistant for Personnel, Mental Upbuilding and Education in the Department of Defence. Although Nugroho contributed significantly to the design of the museum, he did not live to oversee the entire process of the museum's creation due to a long delay in the project. In 1985, when work on the project resumed, General Murdani took charge.

The stated purpose of the revised National Soldiership Museum project was to safeguard and preserve historical evidence of national soldiership, as a complement to the story of soldiership outlined in the Satriamandala Armed Forces Museum. As detailed in Chapter 5, the Satriamandala Armed Forces Museum covered the history of the military dating from its inception in 1945, without making reference to pre-1945 military heroes. It was thus intended that National Soldiership Museum would add to this established trajectory of military heroism in Indonesia by projecting backwards a longer tradition of martial history, similar to that established in National Monument History Museum. The museum covers episodes of resistance to the Dutch colonisers from the seventeenth to nineteenth centuries.[7] It consists of dioramas of famous battles, relief panels on the outside of the building and twenty-three bronze statues of national heroes and heroines. Consistent with Nugroho's initial inspiration, the National Soldiership Museum is built in the form of a fort (Illustration 6.1) replicating the Makassar Fort (formerly known as Fort Rotterdam) in which the Dutch held Diponegoro, one of Indonesia's most famous martial heroes. Nugroho visited the Makassar Fort for inspiration soon after Ibu Tien had approached him.[8]

Illustration 6.1   National Soldiership Museum.
Source: Photograph by the author.

The Armed Forces History Centre intended that the fort built to house the National Soldiership Museum would symbolise the military's role in defending the Indonesian nation. It has five sides, symbolising the solidity of the five principles of the national philosophy of the Pancasila.[9] In General Murdani's address, delivered at the opening of the museum in July 1987, he suggested:

> The spirit of soldiership had already proven itself as one part of national identity which motivated the Indonesian nation to expel the colonisers until the peak of the independence war in 1945.[10]

Invoking organicist ideas of an essentialised national identity, Murdani implied that soldiership was an integral part of Indonesia's enduring indigenous traditions. He also attempted to connect this tradition to the military's contemporary roles, claiming the spirit of soldiership also informed the armed forces' efforts to carry out development.

Commander General Murdani stressed the benefits of this museum to Indonesian soldiers at a time when the Indonesian nation, especially the armed forces, was undergoing regeneration. In the period 1985–88, leadership of the military was handed over to the post-revolutionary generation of officers. The new leadership comprised men born between 1935 and 1938, that is, men who were young boys during the revolution and in their early thirties at the time of the 1965 coup.[11] Although the idea for this museum was Mrs Tien's, the meaning Murdani ascribes to this museum is significant. Instead of the intense focus on the 1945 Generation, which characterised earlier history projects, this project focuses on a much longer trajectory of military tradition reaching far back into the past and extending into more contemporary military roles (such as promoting development). A primary reason for this seems to have been generational change within the military and the fact that many officers, including Murdani, were not members of the 1945 Generation.

It can be seen that by emphasising a longer soldierly tradition, this history project encouraged younger soldiers to see themselves as part of a more established tradition, while reducing emphasis on their lack of experience in the 1945–49 revolution. The military had promoted the martial exploits of pre-independence soldiers before, as in *A Concise History of the Armed Struggle of the Indonesian Nation* (Sedjarah Singkat Perdjuangan Bersendjata Bangsa Indonesia), which lists all the pre-independence wars as part of this struggle.[12] Creating an elaborate museum about these heroes, however, constituted a concerted effort to emphasise this connection and, implicitly, to provide alternative sources of military legitimacy to the revolution. The focus on the distant past in this museum represented a shift in emphasis in projects of the Armed Forces History Centre from the representations of the independence struggle and the coup attempt.

MILITARY DEFENCE AGAINST INTERNAL THREATS

Coinciding with the emergence of a new military generation, the Armed Forces History Centre also increasingly emphasised the on-going role of the military in protecting the country from internal threats. The perception that there are ever-present threats to the state is an integral part of military thinking. In Indonesia, this perception is exaggerated because the Indonesian military has primarily been concerned with defence against internal enemies.

The New Order version of military doctrine, *Tri Ubaya Sakti*, places strong emphasis on internal threats. The doctrine defines internal threats as:

... infiltration, subversion and revolts either mental or physical by forces within Indonesian society which disavow the Pancasila and the 1945 Constitution and challenge the process of renewal from the Old to New Order.[13]

The two most significant threats to the Pancasila which the military has continually emphasised are the threats of the extreme right or extreme Islam and of the extreme left or communism. The military perception that these are national threats dates back to the revolution, in which the Army viewed the proclamation of an Islamic state by the Darul Islam (House of Islam) movement and the 1948 communist Madiun uprising as equally treasonous.[14]

In the early New Order period, the regime ideologue and intelligence director Lieutenant General Ali Murtopo represented the military as "the guardians and defenders of the Pancasila from all kinds of deviation and attempts to undermine the Pancasila either by the extreme left or extreme right".[15] In his efforts to depoliticise Indonesian society, Murtopo argued that ideology had been at the root of all Indonesia's previous troubles and that ideology consequently needed to be removed from politics.[16] Lieutenant General Murtopo promoted the Pancasila as a kind of equilibrium ideology, which the military would defend in accordance with his aim of depoliticising Indonesian politics. The fear of extreme ideologies was not, however, a purely New Order phenomenon. President Sukarno had, for example, voiced fears in the early 1950s that national elections would lead to extremism of every sort.

During the New Order period, the perception of ever-present threats of the extreme right and the extreme left was institutionalised with the introduction in 1978 of a programme labelled the *National Vigilance Refresher* course (Penataran Kewaspadaan Nasional, Tarpadnas). Jun Honna notes that the introduction of this programme, which was initially undertaken in military circles only, was a reflection of the increasing dominance of men with intelligence backgrounds in the military. As Commander of the Armed Forces, General Benny Murdani expanded this programme to include lower-level government bodies such as the National Journalists Association (Persatuan Wartawan Indonesia, PWI) and the National Indonesian Youth Committee (Komite Nasional Pemuda Indonesia, KNPI). The effect of this programme was to spread the message amongst officers and citizens alike, that they should be on constant guard against threats of the extreme right and left.[17]

When General Murdani became Commander of the Armed Forces, in addition to expanding the scope of the *National Vigilance Refresher* course, he redefined the mission of the Armed Forces by placing even greater emphasis on internal security.[18] This was, in part, a reflection of Murdani's intelligence background and his sensitivity to internal subversion. Yet it seems this renewed emphasis on cyclical threats, which accompanied the generational changeover, might have also been an attempt to restate the need for continuing military dominance in light of fading memories of the revolution and the retirement of the 1945 generation from the military. General Murdani's revised military mission, combined with the regime's increased emphasis on threats to the Pancasila, had repercussions for the themes pursued in the projects of the Armed Forces History Centre. For its first eighteen years, the Centre's large scale projects had concentrated on the themes of the military's role in the revolution and in the transition to the New Order. Although the revolution remained an important reference point for the justification of a continuing military political role in the mid-1980s and early 1990s, the Centre presided over two new museum projects devoted to the military's ongoing role as the guardian of Pancasila from the threats of the extreme right (Islam) and the extreme left (communism) respectively, namely the Museum of Eternal Vigilance and the Museum of Communist Treachery.

MILITARY EMPHASIS ON THE THREAT OF EXTREME ISLAM

It is possible to trace increased military emphasis on the threat of extreme Islam to the late 1970s and early 1980s. In the lead up to the 1977 election, the United Development Party (Partai Persatuan Pembangunan, PPP), the product of a forced merger of all the Islamic parties, was emerging as a dangerous challenger to the government's electoral vehicle Golkar. From its inception in 1964 Golkar was a military-dominated "party" consisting of a wide range of functional groups including civil servants and occupational support groups, all of whom were co-opted to vote for and support the party. In response to this potential challenge by Islamic groups to Golkar, the Head of the intelligence agency, Kopkamtib (The Operational Command for the Restoration of Security and Order) conveniently "uncovered" plans for an Islamic holy war command (*komando jihad*) just before the 1977 elections.

Although Admiral Sudomo, Head of the Operational Command for the Restoration of Security and Order, stated there was no connection between the Islamic holy war command and the United Development Party, Muslim leaders saw the "uncovered plot" as a means of providing a ready excuse to arrest Islamic politicians.[19] Richard Tanter notes that, although the Islamic holy war command did exist in some form, Islamic leaders — especially former Prime Minister Muhammad Natsir — claimed that Ali Murtopo had instructed *agents provocateurs* to incite the group to acts of violence.[20] The persons involved in the Islamic holy war command were former members of the West Java Darul Islam, who had been temporarily released from jail and then encouraged by Lieutenant General Murtopo to work with him on the grounds of opposing communism.[21] This was part of a more complex pattern of infiltration and provocation of Islamic groups, instigated and then "uncovered" by security agents from Lieutenant General Murtopo's personalised intelligence agency Special Operations (Operasi Khusus, Opsus) and then later by other intelligence organisations.[22]

Another important episode of the "extreme right" that occurred in the early 1980s was the hijacking of a Garuda plane named "Woyla" on 28 March 1981, en route from Jakarta to Medan.[23] At the time of the Woyla incident, Admiral Sudomo categorised the terrorists as funda-mentalists of the "pure Islam current" who were not afraid to use violence against others and who aimed to establish an Islamic state. The military named as the key instigator of the hijacking, Imron, who had recently spent five years in Mecca. In the newspapers of the time, the movement behind the hijacking was variously described as the Holy War Command (*Komando Jihad*) or Mujahidin Command (*Komando Mujahidin*). There is also some suspicion as to the genuineness of this movement, especially given that the episode took place in the year before a national election.[24] Due to tight press censorship, there was no public discussion of these suspicions in the 1980s.[25] After the fall of Suharto, however, the magazine *Panji Masyarakat* reported that an intelligence agent, Najamuddin, had been instructed by Lieutenant General Murtopo to infiltrate Imron's group and make it active, so as to commit terrorist activities including the "Woyla" hijacking. The article also noted that two of the hijackers were intentionally executed, one by the Head of Operations, after they had been removed from the plane.[26] The hijackers were attacked in Thailand at Don Muang airport by Indonesian anti-terrorist troops under the direct leadership of General Murdani, then Head of the Operations Command to Restore Order and Security.[27] Murdani represented the military as the heroes of this event by awarding the anti-terrorist troops involved in this operation *Bintang Sakti* medals in recognition of their bravery.[28] He also made efforts to draw attention to his own heroic role in this event in his biography.[29]

Although a 2002 report by the Indonesian Crisis Group has revealed some genuine elements behind the "Woyla" and "holy war command" incidents, the Group also confirms that intelligence agents incited the people involved in these incidents.[30] The fact that there is a specific word in Indonesian, *rekayasa*, for an event created for propaganda indicates the frequency of such occurrences. This kind of provocation is listed as an activity in an Army training manual as a standard intelligence activity. The manual lists, amongst possible intelligence activities, the role of "creating and ripening an atmosphere or situation which furthers the interest and execution of defence and security in the political, economic and social fields, as well as in the psychological and other fields".[31]

Some of the most dominant images of "extremist" Islam in the Western press are of hijackings, hostages and of "Holy Wars" or "Armies of God".[32] Against the backdrop of the increasing use of terrorism by Islamic groups worldwide, the overall effect of the "Woyla" hijacking was to raise fears of the rise of Islamic fundamentalism in Indonesia, especially in the wake of the 1979 Iranian revolution. Indeed, in the case of the Woyla hijacking, Admiral Sudomo claimed links between Imron's group, referred to as the Indonesian Islamic Revolutionary Council (Dewan Revolusioner Islam Indonesia), and the Ayatollah Khomeni, who presided over the Iranian Islamic revolution.[33] Eposito notes the tactic of creating the perception of Islam as a threat in a predominately Muslim country is not peculiar to Indonesia.[34] The perception of Islam as a threat within Muslim countries is not, however, rooted in the same trajectory of a long history of Muslim–Christian antagonism as it is in the Western world. For this reason and because of the specific stipulation for Muslims to defend Islam if necessary by means of *jihad,* there is an inherent tension in the definition of extreme Islam in any majority Muslim country.

In Indonesia, the discrediting of politicised Islam reached its peak in the late 1970s to the mid-1980s. Because of increased government repression and rising discontent with the regime, Islam had proved an increasingly popular medium for the expression of moral concern at the direction the New Order regime and society was taking.[35] Increased government emphasis on Pancasila, dating from 1978 onwards, was a response to the perception that Islam was proving a potential source of opposition. Reflecting their increased assertiveness, members of the

Nahdlatul Ulama (NU) faction of the United Development Party walked out of parliament when the legislation for the Pancasila indoctrination courses was tabled. This faction, representing the largest Islamic organisation in Indonesia, protested in response to the impression that courses were an affront to Islam. This unprecedented act of defiance, combined with on-going resistance to these courses, prompted President Suharto to lash out in his 1980 Pekanbaru speech at "certain groups who displayed an anti-Pancasila attitude".[36] In that speech Suharto reminded his audience of the troubles different ideological leanings had brought Indonesia in the past, mentioning the Darul Islam rebellions of the 1950s and 1960s along with the 30 September/Indonesian Communist Party Movement.[37]

The peak of the regime's Pancasila campaign was the proposed sole foundation (*asas tunggal*) legislation, which required all organisations to make Pancasila their sole basis. Throughout 1984, this proposal sparked continuing discussion and protest, particularly from Muslim groups who saw it as an attempt to replace religion with the Pancasila.[38] On 18 September 1984, estimates of between 40 and 400 Muslim protesters in the area of Tanjung Priok were shot down by the military in an incident connected to heightened tensions over the sole philosophy legislation. After a clash between security forces and attendants at a local mosque, the military arrested four people. Amir Biki, a local religious figure and a known critic of the regime, led a procession to the police sub-area command to request the release of these people. On arrival the military dispersed the crowd by firing automatic weapons.[39] Prior to the incident, preachers in the area had been encouraged to speak out strongly against the ban on wearing of the female head scarf (*jilbab*) and the forced introduction of the sole philosophy, whilst in other areas of Jakarta this kind of seminar was banned.[40] The government covered up the details of the Tanjung Priok episode, particularly the manner and number of persons killed, with strict warnings to the press not to report non-official versions of the incident.[41] After Tanjung Priok, a series of bombs exploded throughout Java and in Jakarta. The military arrested well-known regime critics and prominent Muslim clerics and activists on charges of subversion in relation to these two incidents.[42] The bombings and the subsequent trials were vital to military efforts to demonstrate the continuing threat of extreme Islam. It was certainly in the military's interests to emphasise these so-called episodes of the "extreme right", whether or not they were genuine movements or military plots.

THE MUSEUM OF ETERNAL VIGILANCE

On Heroes' Day, 10 November 1987, President Suharto officially opened a new Armed Forces History Centre museum by symbolically striking a *kentongan* — a large elongated traditional bell used throughout the 1945–49 revolution to warn Indonesians soldiers of a Dutch approach.[43] The *kentongan* was used in the opening ceremony to highlight the mission of the new museum, which was to warn Indonesians, by means of historical representation, of the on-going threat of extreme Islam in Indonesia.

General Murdani had proposed the idea for this museum in August 1984, a month before the Tanjung Priok incident.[44] At the time Murdani made this proposal, he had been Commander of the Armed Forces for just one year. As noted above, General Murdani had personally fought against the Darul Islam movements and was also a key player in the suppression of the Woyla hijackers. In addition, he was a Catholic officer who had developed a reputation amongst devout (*santri*) Muslims, particularly modernists, as an anti-Islamic force in the Army, willing to repress devout groups.[45] Many Muslims suspect the complicity of Murdani and his intelligence network in the manufacture of the Islamic threat.[46]

The name Museum Waspada Purbawisesa (Museum of Eternal Vigilance) had particular resonance for Indonesians who, over the last decade, had learned by means of press releases of a wave of terrorist acts blamed on extreme Islam. The Head of the Museum noted in 1997 that the events of the 1980s convinced the military that it was necessary to build this museum in order to increase vigilance against this kind of threat.[47] Like the *National Vigilance Refresher* courses, the museum was an effort to increase public awareness or fear of this threat. The museum is housed on the same site as the Satriamandala Armed Forces Museum and the Armed Forces History Centre (Illustration 6.2). It includes two levels of diorama displays accompanied by relics of campaigns against the "extreme right", including weaponry and flags of rebel groups (Illustration 6.3).

The history of opposition of Muslim groups to the Pancasila is the principal theme of this museum. At the opening of the museum in 1987, President Suharto also stated that some groups had used the Pancasila "as a guise to introduce other ideologies that contradict the Pancasila". He went on to suggest that he hoped that from this museum, which shows:

Illustration 6.2   The Museum of Eternal Vigilance.
Source: Photograph by Chatarina Purnamdari.

Illustration 6.3   Darul Islam weaponry and flags on display in the Museum of Eternal Vigilance.
Source: Image from Pusat Sejarah dan Tradisi ABRI, *Museum Waspada Purbawisesa Buku Panduan,* Pusat Sejarah dan Tradisi ABRI, Jakarta, 1997, p. 39.

... the path of ABRI in defending this ideology, that the Indonesian nation could gain lessons from history of the threats to the Pancasila which have used the pretext of religion and made wrongful use of religion. As members of religious communities in a Pancasila state, Indonesians must be wise by holding respect for the holiness of religion and its teachings.... But the most important thing is that vigilance is implanted into our nation, such that thinking which deviates from the basis of the Pancasila state will not emerge ever again for eternity.[48]

Suharto's opening speech reflected the sentiment of his 1980 Pekanbaru speech. Part of Suharto's message is replicated on a plaque at the entrance to this museum.[49] As much as being a museum about the threat of the extreme right, the museum also attempts to reinforce that the Pancasila is the basis of the state. General Murdani, as Commander of the Armed Forces, delivered a similar message at the opening of the museum, stating that the museum dioramas would increase people's alertness towards efforts to endanger the Pancasila and educate the people as to some of the ways in which religion had been wrongly used.[50]

Representations in this museum begin with the decision made in 1945 that the Pancasila would be the basis of the Indonesian state. They then progress to representations of the Darul Islam rebellions of the 1950s and 1960s. The final scenes included in the museum portray incidents of the early 1980s, for which officials attributed blame to Muslim extremists.

THE JAKARTA CHARTER SCENE

The very first scene in the Museum of Eternal Vigilance is of the final formulation of the preamble to the 1945 Constitution made on 18 August 1945. This scene attempts to establish that Indonesia's founding fathers — there were no women on the deciding committee — decided that Indonesia would not be an Islamic state, but rather a state based on the Pancasila, which allows the adherents of several religions to follow their own faiths. The diorama features Muhammad Hatta, Sukarno and Ki Bagus Hadikusumo negotiating a revision to the 22 June agreement, which was known as the Jakarta Charter. The Jakarta Charter was adopted on 22 June 1945, between the first formulation of Pancasila and the final version of the preamble to the 1945 Constitution, after pressure from Islamic leaders for greater recognition of the Islamic majority in Indonesia. The Jakarta Charter attached the additional phrase — "with the obligation for adherents of Islam to carry out *syariah* [Islamic law]" to the first principle of Pancasila, belief in one God. In the museum diorama, the words of the Jakarta Charter, "with the obligation for adherents of Islam to carry out *syariah*", are shown flashing on a small screen inside the diorama with a red line through them.[51] The purpose of this scene is to remind Indonesians that these words, which were temporarily attached to the first principle of the Pancasila, were omitted from the preamble to the 1945 Constitution. The seven words of the Jakarta Charter were omitted in the final draft due to Muhammad Hatta's fear that Christian-dominated Eastern Indonesia would not support this formulation.

THE DARUL ISLAM SCENES

The majority of space in the Museum of Eternal Vigilance is taken up by representations of the Darul Islam (House of Islam) rebellions. Throughout the museum, the movement is referred to as "DI/TII" meaning Darul Islam and Tentara Islam Indonesia (Islamic Army of Indonesia). This was the name originally used by the movement. The preoccupation of the museum with the Darul Islam rebellions reflects the fact that these rebellions made the strongest contribution to the military's distrust of Islam as a political force.

The Museum of Eternal Vigilance was not the first form of commemoration of military efforts to suppress the Darul Islam rebellions. The Armed Forces History Centre's first publication, *A Concise History of the Armed Struggle of the Indonesian Nation*, devoted ten pages to descriptions of the military operations to suppress the movement in different areas under the theme of "the formation of a unitary state". Consistent with the political language of this period, the Darul Islam rebels were grouped with other rebels as counter-revolutionaries and the revolts were described as deviations from the goals of the August 1945 revolution.[52] In 1965, the History Centre released three publications covering the military suppression of the Darul Islam movement in three regions.[53] In the 1970s, there were also monuments and films produced dealing with a slightly different theme, the role of the people and the military in the suppression of the Darul Islam rebellions.[54] The Siliwangi Division, which was involved in the suppression of the most tenacious Darul Islam movement, that in West Java, also focused on this movement in the divisional history *Siliwangi From Then to Now*.[55] This museum project was, however, the largest history project to concentrate on this theme.

The Museum of Eternal Vigilance focuses on the Darul Islam rebellions as a lesson of the past. The rebellions, which included the establishment of an Islamic state as one of their aims, are represented as challenges to the Pancasila. The museum guidebook states:

> It is hoped that representations in the museum will not only provide insight to people's understanding about the ideology and movements of DI/TII but also become a source of inspiration in the framework of building and securing and placing national defence on a firm basis whilst preserving the Pancasila and the 1945 Constitution. [56]

Following on from the scene of the abolition of the seven words of the Jakarta Charter, the scenes of the Darul Islam movement seek to establish the deviance of these movements from the predetermined basis of the state, the Pancasila. Given the sacralisation of the Pancasila by the time this museum opened — the Pancasila indoctrination courses had by then been running for almost five years — this message would have had extra meaning.

ISLAMIC TERRORISM

Throughout the museum, attention is particularly directed at the leaders of the Darul Islam revolts and their "terrorist" methods. The scenes featuring the West Java revolt, for example, include the military caderisation (1942–49) of the followers of Sukarmaji Marijan Kartosuwiryo, the leader of the West Java revolt, Kartosuwiryo's proclamation of an Islamic state (1949) and several of the movement's acts of terror in West Java. Representations of the acts of terror include dioramas featuring the battle in Antralina (1949), the poisoning of a member of the Siliwangi division in Cijurey (1949), the sabotage of a train in Warung Bandrek (1953), the bus robbery at Tanjakan Emen (1954), terror in the kampung of Cikawung (1954), the brutality of the movement in Kampung Cigalontang (1954) and the Cibugel Incident (1959).[57] The final scene covering the movement in West Java is of the trial of Kartosuwiryo (1962). Scenes covering the Darul Islam movements in Central Java, South Sulawesi, South Kalimantan and Aceh similarly focus on the other leaders of these movements and the terror waged by them. The guidebook openly states that the Museum of Eternal Vigilance "attempts to present several historical facts about the cruelty of the 'terror' of DI/TII". Both the foreword and the museum captions emphasise that the Darul Islam movement created much suffering, sadness, and loss of both a material kind and of human lives and other disasters for innocent people.

In the Museum of Eternal Vigilance, the words terror (*teror*) and viciousness (*peganasan*) are used interchangeably to describe supporters of the Darul Islam. The terror of these movements is also highlighted by the display of "captured" and replica weapons of the Darul Islam rebels in display cases in front of each diorama. The theme of the terror of these movements seems to be a relatively new one. A similar representation of the Darul Islam movement is made in the film *They Have Returned* (Mereka Kembali), in which the Darul Islam followers are represented as crazed bandits devoid of religious feelings.[58] The 1964 publication, *A Concise History of the Armed Struggle of the Indonesian Nation*, for example, describes those following the movements as "rebels", rather than terrorists.[59]

In discussing shifting military interpretations of the Darul Islam movements and the trend of emphasising the terror of these movements, I am not attempting to deny that there was brutality in these movements. The West Java and South Sulawesi Darul Islam movements, for example, did become increasingly brutal in their last years of operation. Karl Jackson notes, in the case of the Darul Islam in West Java, that the Cibugel incident mentioned in this museum was particularly brutal because of the deliberate executions of 120 people, the majority of whom were women, children and infants.[60] There was certainly some truth to these representations. By branding Darul Islam supporters as terrorists, which implies inflicting harm on civilians, the Indonesian military sought to dismiss these movements as unsupported by the people. By focusing on both the terror of these movements and on their leaders, attention is shifted from the fact that all movements enjoyed some degree of support from the local population. Kartosuwiryo, for example, had a strong following in West Java in the areas of Garut-Tasikmalaya, Bandung, Sumedang and Ciamis in which some villages gave their full support to this movement.[61]

The last scenes in the museum deal with "terrorist" activities of the 1970s and 1980s, for which the government blamed Muslim extremists. The last scenes of the Darul Islam revolt features the end in 1962 of the Acehnese revolt, which was led by the former governor for Aceh province Muhammad Daud Beureueh (see p. 190). From here the museum jumps to a scene entitled "Operation Woyla, the suppression of the terrorist Imron". The caption to the Woyla scene describes Imron as "the leader of a fundamentalist Islamic group of an extreme orientation".[62]

The caption also highlights the roles of General Yoga Sugama, the Head of the National Intelligence Co-ordinating Agency (Bakin); General Benny Murdani, the Deputy Head of the National Intelligence Co-ordinating Agency who "quickly prepared anti-terror forces"; and Lieutenant Colonel L. Sintong Panjaitan, who led the anti-terrorist unit which seized the plane and "deactivated" the hijackers.

The next scene representing the threat of the extreme right in the New Order period is entitled "The Suppression of Warman's Terrorist Movement, 23 July 1981". This diorama features the capture of Warman, a prominent leader of the movement dubbed the Islamic holy war command (*komando jihad*). The diorama caption to this scene reports that since 1968, several ex-members of the House of Islam Movement in West Java attempted to reactivate their movement. The caption notes that a year later, this Islamic holy war command began to carry out acts of terror in several cities in Java and that Warman was caught in the subsequent military crack-down. After having escaped, Warman resumed terrorist activities until he was finally caught in July 1981.

INCLUSIONS AND EXCLUSIONS

In the context in which the museum was produced, the selection of scenes to be included had contemporary relevance. The Jakarta Charter scene was relevant because the debate over the Jakarta Charter had by no means ended in 1945. It resurfaced as an issue throughout the Darul Islam rebellions, in the debates of the Constituent Assembly in the 1950s, and again in the 1968 parliamentary debate concerning the ideological direction of the country. In the post-Suharto era, minor Islamic parties have also raised the issue of the Jakarta Charter in debates over the constitution.

Representations of the Darul Islam in this museum are highly selective. With the exception of the Aceh Darul Islam movement (see p. 190), a visitor to the Museum of Eternal Vigilance is provided with only one motive for the Darul Islam rebellions: the establishment of an Islamic state. Although this was a shared platform of all these movements, other common ideals were a rejection of Javanese (especially Central Javanese) dominance of the Republic's government. In particular, members of these movements shared an impression that the civil administration was being Javanised and that there was economic skewing in favour of Java. In some strongly Islamic areas such as Aceh, West Java, South Sulawesi, South Kalimantan and West Sumatra, the Javanese were accused of having replaced the Dutch.[63] Distrust of Javanese dominance also related to a rejection of syncretic Islam and a perception that this was a less pure form of Islam.[64] Reasons behind these movements therefore touched on the sensitive issues of regional autonomy, Javanese dominance and the perception of "impurities" within some strands of Islam practised in Java. Because these issues continued to have relevance in the New Order period, they were censored out of the record of this museum.

One of the most curious things about the inclusion of the 1980 Muslim terrorist scenes in this museum is that there is dispute as to whether these movements were spontaneous acts of Muslim rebels or intelligence fabrications (*rekayasa*). That representations of these incidents were presented in this museum, as part of the story of the threat of the extreme right in Indonesian history, makes the museum a tool of double propaganda. The Armed Forces History Centre indeed acknowledges that it worked together with BAIS (Badan Intelijen Strategis, The Strategic Intelligence Agency) on this project.[65] This prompts the question as to whether BAIS was providing the original scenarios for these plots from its own record, or evidence gathered after the events.

Although many incidents associated with Islam also occurred in the city of Jakarta in the 1980s, the Museum of Eternal Vigilance does not mention any. The final scenes in the museum, for example, feature the bombings of Central and East Java throughout 1984 and 1985. These scenes include representations of the bombing on Christmas Eve 1984 of both a Catholic church and the Southeast Asian Alkitab seminary in the city of Malang, and the bombings of Borobudur temple (21 January 1985) and of a Pemudi Express bus in Banyuwangi (5 March 1985). The most significant absence from this museum is a representation of the Tanjung Priok incident of 1984 and the bombings in Jakarta that followed. The omission of scenes covering these episodes was probably due to the location of this museum in Jakarta and an awareness of the possible sensitivity of those in the audience who may have either personally experienced these events, or had friends and relatives fall victims in these tragedies. The Tanjung Priok incident left a deep wound on sections of the Muslim community.[66] Armed Forces Commander General Murdani was only too aware of this wound. Realising how much damage had been done, Murdani organised to visit several Islamic boarding schools (*pesantren*) to make peace with Islamic groups after this tragic incident.[67] General Murdani also rejected what he called rumours that there was a religious background to this event and that security forces had attacked the Muslim community. He stated that this was not what was at issue; rather it was the misuse of a religious forum for another purpose.[68] Most Muslims remember this incident as one associated with Islam, even though Murdani refused to classify it this way.[69]

Another interesting omission from this museum is representation of the on-going struggle for Acehnese autonomy, in which Islam was also a motivating influence. There are six scenes devoted to the Darul Islam movement in Aceh, beginning with a scene featuring the proclamation of an Indonesian Islamic state in 1953 by Daud Beureueh, and ending with the 1962 agreement between Beureueh and the central government to end the revolt. The caption to the scene of the Acehnese proclamation of an Indonesian Islamic state notes that "a small group of Acehnese did not agree with the government's decision to make Aceh part of the province of North Sumatra and wanted Aceh to be given broad autonomy and the right to implement Islamic law".[70] This is the only hint of regionalist sentiment in representations in this museum. The museum excludes mention of both the 1959 government agreement to make Aceh a Special Region, with broad autonomy in areas such as religion, social customs and education and the New Order government's 1974 autonomy decree, neither of which were honoured for many years. The museum's representations of the struggle in Aceh suggest all was peacefully resolved in 1962, when, in fact, the struggle for Acehnese autonomy was continuing at the time the museum opened in 1987. It was not until August 2005, after regional autonomy was granted and following the devastating tsunami in which many key advocates of separatism lost their lives that the Free Aceh Movement (GAM) renounced independence agreeing instead to take part in local elections.

THE MUSEUM OF ETERNAL VIGILANCE AS A RELIC

Although plans for the museum began in September 1984, the museum was not opened until Heroes' Day, 10 November 1987. By this time, the sole foundation (*asas tunggal*) legislation had been passed and most organisations had complied with this requirement. The Nahdlatul Ulama faction had also left the United Development Party in 1984, thereby significantly reducing the political force of this Muslim party. Ironically, the sole foundation legislation eventually gave Islam a new political foothold in Indonesia, because the threat of Islam had temporarily lost its force.[71] As a consequence, the messages of the museum were out of date by the time of the museum's opening, making the museum a relic.

Curiously, President Suharto rejected Murdani's first choice of name for this museum, which was the Victorious Pancasila Museum (Museum Pancasila Jaya).[72] This name suggested that the Pancasila had triumphed on the issue of the Jakarta Charter. It also suggested that Pancasila had defeated all threats, in this case the threat of extreme Islam. President Suharto objected to the proposed name because of a reluctance to associate extreme Islam so directly with a contradiction of Pancasila.[73] The dispute over the museum's name reflected Suharto's re-evaluation of the Muslim vote after the implementation of the sole foundation legislation and his own move towards embracing Islam. This encompassed moves to create the Muslim Intellectual Organisation (Institut Cendekiawan Muslim Indonesia, ICMI) and personal pilgrimage to Mecca.[74]

Although Esposito establishes the common use of the threat of Islamic fundamentalism in Muslim countries to justify repressive state measures, this museum does include evidence of anticipated sensitivity from Muslim audiences to its messages. When asked whether there had been any negative reactions from Muslims to this museum, the Head of the Museum replied that such reactions only came from persons with limited historical awareness, from people who believed that Muslims were being pushed to one side in these events. She suggested these impressions were sometimes put forward by women who wore the *jilbab*, the Islamic head covering. In response, she would ask them why these people, if they were good Muslims, would kill women and children and challenge the legal government?[75] Although I cannot be sure this was intentional, on one of my scheduled appointments with the Museum Head, I was summoned into the room whilst the Museum Head was diligently reading the Koran. It seems she was concerned to demonstrate her Islamic credentials.

The message affixed to a plaque on the way out of the museum also indicates alertness on the part of the museum makers as to sensitivity of this museum's messages. The plaque reads:

> We record these events only to point out how this very country could be torn apart if the holiness of religious teachings is wrongly used.[76]

The original Head of this museum noted that the purpose of the visual display of this history is to make members of society aware that the Darul Islam movement has caused suffering and disaster and loss for people without sins. He insisted that it was not in any way intended "to discredit or besmirch one group or religion".[77] The sensitivity apparent in these statements made in the 1990s reflected the increasing Islamicisation of Indonesian society in the 1980s and 1990s. Although the government had acted strictly towards political Islam, it had also made gradual concessions to support the promotion and practice of Islam as a religion.[78]

In the last decade of the Suharto regime, the label "extreme Islam" became increasingly redundant as President Suharto demonstrated an increasingly warm embrace of Islam as a socio-political force. In 1990 he endorsed the creation of the Indonesian Muslim Intellectual Organisation headed by his close protégé, Habibie. At the same time, Suharto sought to Islamicise the once Army-dominated ruling party, Golkar. The Indonesian military's responses to Suharto's efforts to co-opt Islamic forces were divided. Some officers, known as "the red and white" or nationalist camp, which included Vice President (1993–98) and former Commander of the military (1988–93) retired General Try Sutrisno and other Murdani supporters, strongly objected to this move. Others, including German-trained General Feisal Tanjung, Commander of the military from 1993–98, were willing to mobilise the support of Muslim organisations for the benefit of the political elite.[79] The so-called red- and white-officers were, however, forced at least to make gestures to Islamic groups. For example, retired General Try Sutrisno, who was the Jakarta Regional Commander at the time of the Tanjung Priok incident, publicly stated that the depiction of Islam as a threat was "clearly wrong".[80]

In the late New Order period the military under the leadership of Suharto loyalist General Feisal Tanjung was again attempting to court Islam as a political force, with the hope of finding an ally in their opposition to democratisation.[81] General Tanjung published a collection of his speeches given between 1993 and 1997 on the similarities in visions and perceptions between the armed forces and Islam in a book entitled *ABRI and Islam: True Friends* (ABRI–Islam Mitra Sejati).[82] For the military itself, the Museum of Eternal Vigilance was clearly an increasingly uncomfortable relic. A decade after the opening of the Museum of Eternal Vigilance, which exposed the alleged deviations of Islam in Indonesia, President Suharto opened a new museum for Islamic art at the Indonesia in Miniature theme park. The new museum was largely a follow-up from the two Islamic arts festivals held at the national Istiqlal Mosque located in Merdeka Square, central Jakarta.[83] This was further symbolic evidence of reconciliation between the regime and Islamic forces.

In the post-Suharto period, victims of the repression of political Islam in the New Order period have come forward to demand recognition and justice. In 1998, relatives of victims of the Tanjung Priok riots, for example, founded the 18 September Foundation (Yayasan 18 September).[84] The more open political climate has meant that criticism of the New Order regime's repression of Islam has flourished, as have challenges to historical representations of the threat of the extreme right and new narratives of Islamic victimhood in Indonesia.[85] Despite this sea-change in the late New Order era and the military's attempts to court Islamic groups, support within the Indonesian military for the Western-led "War on Terror" may constitute sufficient grounds for keeping the Museum of Eternal Vigilance open. One interesting, and certainly unintentional, consequence of this museum — which is in essence a museum devoted to the military's enemies — is that it presents material or resources for latter-day Islamic movements to make martyrs out of the rebels portrayed there. Indeed, beyond the New Order period, the ghosts of both Kartosuwiryo and leader of the South Sulawesi Darul Islam revolt, Kahar Muzakar, enjoy renewed popularity.[86]

THE ARMED FORCES HISTORY CENTRE'S LAST MAJOR PROJECT: REVIVING THE COMMUNIST THREAT

The last museum project completed by the Armed Forces History Centre in the New Order returned to the long-standing theme of communism as a threat in Indonesia. Although the threat of the extreme left was, as discussed in Chapter 3, a well-established historical theme, in the context of the early 1990s it had renewed meaning because of newly defined threats to the regime.

Before the idea for this museum, the Murdani faction of the military had led a revival of the fear of communist threat. Initially the revival was aimed at discrediting Murdani rival (retired) General Sudharmono, then Chairman of Golkar, but in the late 1980s and early 1990s the label "communist" was also used as a means of controlling reform. The theme of this museum seemed like a rather desperate attempt to hold onto the threat of the "extreme left", particularly in response to the end of the Cold War. Believing that the political enemy of Islam was at this point largely discounted, the military was determined to keep the threat of communism alive to justify the continuing existence of societal threats and hence the need for military dominance. The museum itself was an attempt to "seal" the theme of communist treachery in the historical record once and for all by detailing repeated efforts of communist betrayal, especially in the 1948 Madiun Affair and the 1965 coup attempt. The museum is also replete with themes outlining "communist methods", which served as useful reinforcement for the labelling of groups demanding greater reform in the early 1990s.

Although the communist spectre evolved to a more complex formulation in the late New Order period, the persistent reinforcement of this theme seemed to reflect the impasse in which the military found itself in the early 1990s as it grew more isolated from Suharto. Throughout the New Order period, the military used the threat of a communist revival as a means of discrediting and demonising regime critics, of besmirching competitors for political power and as a bulwark against democratisation. The term "organisation without form" (*organisasi tanpa bentuk*), for example, was used to label almost any kind of regime opposition as communist, from those who appealed for human rights, environmental protection or democratisation, to those who discredited the government.[87] In February 1988, Suharto dismissed General Murdani as Commander, just prior to the appointment of (retired) General Sudharmono as Vice-President. In response, the Murdani faction of the military attempted to discredit Sudharmono by "uncovering" communist links in his past.[88] The goal of this campaign was to thwart Sudharmono's reappointment as Golkar Chairman and his appointment as Vice-President.[89] Although Sudharmono was ex-military, he had served as State Secretary for many years and during his time as Chairman of Golkar, the party had become increasingly independent of the military.[90] The campaign to discredit Sudharmono triggered a new wave of anti-communist purges known as the "clean self, clean environment" (*bersih diri, bersih lingkungan*) campaign, which was directed at individuals in the government and the press alleged to have communist sympathies or links to communist groups in the past.[91]

The failure of this effort to frustrate Sudharmono's election forced a realisation that, without Suharto's support, the military was relatively powerless.[92] In response to the military's anti-communist campaign, Suharto drew closer to Sudharmono and the bureaucracy.[93] He also took some punitive measures against the military by means of a new law that reinforced the constitutional supremacy of President Suharto as Supreme Commander of the Armed Forces.[94] In addition, he dissolved the Operations Command to Restore Order and Security, the intelligence agency long controlled by General Benny Murdani and which had played a part in spreading the rumours about Sudharmono.[95] This was the beginning of a slow process by which Suharto set about dismantling the pervasive influence of Murdani in the intelligence network. These developments, combined with the increasing generation gap between Suharto and other officers, signalled an increasing distance between the armed forces and Suharto. The impact of this rift was that, as of the late 1980s, Indonesia could no longer appropriately be described as being "ruled by a military regime".[96] Although the military remained influential, its institutional interests were now distinguishable from those of Suharto. This meant that the military was now occasionally pitting its interests against those of Suharto.

The year 1989 was marked by dramatic change both inside and outside Indonesia. The world witnessed the collapse of the Soviet Empire, precipitated by Gorbachev's policy of *glasnost* (openness), and the collapse of communist regimes in Eastern Europe. The climax of these changes was the end of 40 years of the Cold War. Within Indonesia, there was also mounting pressure for change from increasingly restless intellectuals, student groups and members of the press. In response to their increasingly marginalised position, the military spearheaded a campaign for greater openness in Indonesia in the hope of broadening its political base and simultaneously pressuring Suharto to implement reform. Between the years 1988 and 1992, the military faction of the parliament was quite vocal on issues of reform in an effort to gain broader support.[97] The short period of liberalisation was known as the period of openness (*keterbukaan*). It included a dramatic expansion in public discussion on political and economic issues and a general relaxation of controls. Students used this opportunity to demonstrate, often in the interests of other sections of society such as farmers and workers. As a concession to openness, the government also lifted a 27-year ban on industrial strikes in August 1990. As a result, there were 24 strikes in the Jakarta area between November 1989 and May 1990.[98]

At the same time the military and President Suharto made competing assertions of their commitment to openness, both continued to summon the communist ghost. They did so not as a means of attacking one another, but rather as a means of controlling the permissible limits of openness. As Edward Aspinall notes, the campaign for openness did not represent a "split between regime 'soft-liners' in the military and 'hard-liners' in the Suharto camp". Instead both sides were "fundamentally authoritarian (although both may [have contained] minority reformist elements)".[99] The label communist remained a convenient means for putting the brakes on openness. In 1990, the anti-communism campaign was reinvigorated by Suharto's April decree, which endorsed a renewed drive against "communism" using the term *keterpengaruhan* (a state of being influenced). This category of "communist" threat included "acting, speaking, writing or showing any attitude in a way which resembles or assists PKI strategy".[100] The *keterpengaruhan* campaign expanded the label "extreme left" to apply to persons using so-called "communist methods". This campaign was largely waged against student protesters and farmers who had been protesting against unfair compensation for land relocations.[101]

The continuing reassertion of the communist threat was also possibly related to nervousness that the climate of openness might produce information contradictory to the official version of the 1965 coup attempt. In August 1990, Indonesian newspapers took up the issue of CIA involvement in the anti-Communist purges, after the release of information in the United States of previously classified material. At around the same time, Suharto issued a Presidential Decree against former communists, which began with the assumption that 18 million former Communist Party members remained at large and possessed the potential for a comeback.[102] It is likely the military was also concerned that the events in the former Soviet Union would discredit the use of the label "communist", one of the regime's most popular "weapons of coercion".[103] Preserving the story of the 1965 coup attempt and the idea of a communist threat was important to both Suharto and the military, because the suppression of this threat justified their rise to power and continuing suppression of opposition.

The 1990 anniversary of the coup attempt was particularly significant because of the long established association between this day and the communist threat and because the Cold War had recently ended. Commentary on the commemoration of Sacred Pancasila Day in 1990 was characterised by reflections from the public and intellectuals as to what the end of the Cold War meant for the future of communism in Indonesia. An article in the *Jakarta Post* noted that Suharto's visit to the Soviet Union and the normalisation of relations with China in the last year "had mellowed the anti-element [sic] that this day had always implied".[104] The newspaper *Suara Pembaruan* also published a quote from Soedjati Djiwandono of the CSIS (Centre for Strategic and International Studies), a government think tank closely associated in the first decades of the New Order with the intelligence community, in which he stated that, keeping in mind the recent developments in the communist world, it was necessary to reassess the relevance of the latent threat of communism and the possibility of a communist comeback.[105]

Meanwhile the military made determined efforts to reinforce the idea that a communist revival was still a threat in Indonesia. An article in the military-sponsored newspaper, *Angkatan Bersenjata,* stated:

> The radical changes in Eastern Europe which have stamped out communism have proved the actions of the Indonesian government in 1965 to break up the G30S/PKI movement and ban communism and Marxist-Leninist and Maoist teachings were correct.[106]

The article also sought to establish that communism in Indonesia differs from that in Eastern Europe because there were still communist regimes in power in Asia. The author concluded that the mental attitude towards communism in Asia had not yet changed and that "if this applies to the PKI remnants in our country, then they still formed a threat".[107] The military was determined to rationalise the continuing relevance of this threat.

On the occasion of Sacred Pancasila Day 1990, the military made a concerted effort to remind the public of the gruesome death of the heroes of 1965. An article in *Angkatan Bersenjata* noted that, without displaying human emotions, members of the Indonesian Communist Party sadistically tortured the seven Heroes of the Revolution after kidnapping them from their homes. The stories about Gerwani dancing naked around the well, gouging out the eyes of the heroes and cutting off their genitals were also repeated.[108] To reinforce the cruel death of the military heroes, a colossal diorama torture scene (described in Chapter 3, Illustration 3.24 on p. 101) was added to the Sacred Pancasila Monument. This diorama, together with a photographic exhibition of the retrieval of the heroes' bodies, was opened at the monument on 1 October 1990. Armed Forces Commander, General Try Soetrisno, presented awards to members of the local population who had helped locate the bodies and to staff of the Gatot Subroto hospital who had nursed and bathed the bodies of the heroes.[109] He also delivered a speech in which he stated that "those who found the bodies had lifted the veil of deceit and exposed the inhumanity of the G30S/PKI group". General Soetrisno sought to emphasise the "brutality" of the communists by drawing attention to the appalling condition of the bodies of the Army heroes after exhumation.[110] By recycling the "terror" of the past, the military hoped to add weight to their claims that communism was still a threat.

Against this background of a concern to preserve both the record of the coup attempt and to perpetuate the idea of an on-going threat of communism, the idea for the Museum of Communist Treachery (Museum Pengkhianatan Komunis) was conceived. At the time of the museum's opening, on Sacred Pancasila Day 1992, General Try Soetrisno reported to Suharto that the purpose of the museum was to remind society, especially the young generation, that the latent danger of communism still existed.[111] Another purpose of the museum was to record the historic events of communist betrayal and the efforts of the military and the people to crush them.[112] The museum was also designed to expand the role of the monument so that it would become a centre of information and research about the deviations of the "extreme left" communists.[113] The Museum of Communist Treachery was a further attempt by the military to consolidate its power by again turning to the historical record. At the same time as this museum project got under way, the Armed Forces History Centre also began to compile a related four-volume series, entitled *The Latent Danger of Communism in Indonesia* (Bahaya Laten Komunisme di Indonesia). The first volume deals with the development of communism and the betrayal of the communists in Indonesian from 1913–48, the second deals with the suppression of the 1948 Madiun "PKI" revolt and the third volume deals with the consolidation and infiltration of the PKI (1950–59). The fourth volume, published in two parts in 1994 and 1995, deals with the revolt of G30S/PKI (Part A) plus a further volume on its suppression (Part B).[114]

A TOUR OF THE MUSEUM OF COMMUNIST TREACHERY

Consistent with the theme of Javanese court architecture in the rest of the monument (discussed in Chapter 3), the Museum of Communist Treachery is housed within a large building in the shape of a Javanese court audience hall (*joglo*). This museum was built adjacent to the main monument and is joined, by means of a stairwell, to the original museum completed in 1981, the Museum of the Sacred Pancasila Monument. This physical link (Illustration 6.4) means that, once visitors move through the Museum of Communist Treachery and into the Museum of the Sacred Pancasila Monument, they connect the earlier story of the Indonesian Communist Party with the story of the communists in the coup of 1965. The Museum of Communist Treachery consists of 37 dioramas, which are also the work of the Centre's preferred artist, Edhi Soenarso.

Illustration 6.4   The link between the Museum of Communist Treachery and the Sacred Pancasila Monument Museum.
Source: Photograph by Chatarina Purnamdari.

From a tour of the Museum of Communist Treachery it is possible to discern several themes in historical representations of the communists found in this museum. First, the museum attempts to establish both the Madiun Affair and the 1965 coup attempt as communist plots. Second, it highlights the theme of the communists continually waging terror on the people. Third, the museum attempts to represent the mass killings and imprisonment of communists as being both legal and necessary.

The first representation a visitor comes across in this museum is a photo mosaic featuring gory scenes of the victims of the Madiun Affair and the 1965 coup.[115] As discussed in Chapter 2, the military has often referred to the Madiun Affair and the 1965 coup attempt as a pair of events, both of which demonstrate the pattern of communist treachery. Most of the scenes found in this museum are representations of Madiun or the 1965 coup attempt. There are also some scenes dealing with the post-coup period.

The Museum of Communist Treachery establishes the lead-up to Madiun in a series of dioramas. These include a scene of a workers' strike in Delanggu (23 June 1948) and a scene entitled Disturbances in

Illustration 6.5   The Indonesian Communist Party Rebellion in Madiun.
Source: Image from Pusat Sejarah dan Tradisi ABRI, *Buku Panduan Monumen Pancasila Sakti Lubang Buaya Jakarta,* Pusat Sejarah dan Tradisi ABRI, Jakarta, 1997, p. 10.

Surakarta (19 August 1948). The first scene emphasises communist efforts to disrupt the economy by organising workers' strikes. The second scene focuses on a series of disturbances in the Surakarta area designed to distract the attention of the Army so that the Communist Party could safely carry out the Madiun revolt.[116]

The scene of the Madiun revolt focuses on people gathered outside a building waving communist flags (Illustration 6.5). This scene establishes the theme of communist betrayal or treachery. It focuses closely on the Indonesian Communist Party as a party, without distinguishing the acts of communist-influenced troops and the party. This gets around the embarrassing fact that military troops were involved in the 1948 communist revolt as well as the 1965 coup attempt. It was Indonesian Socialist Youth (Pemuda Sosialis Indonesia, Pesindo) troops who first took control of Madiun, unbeknown to Musso or other communist leaders. The Pesindo troops acted primarily in protest at Hatta's attempts to rationalise these troops from the Army.[117] The version of Madiun provided in the caption is consistent with the Cold War theory of Madiun as an international communist (Soviet) plot.[118]

The scene of the declaration of the Soviet Republic in Madiun is followed by scenes emphasising the cruelty of Indonesian Communist Party members in the months surrounding the Madiun Affair. One scene details the cruel deaths by means of strangulation by two bamboo poles of seven policemen at the hands of the communists in September 1948 in Ngawen district in Blora, East Java. Another scene reports on the military liberation of the prisoners of the communists at a sugar factory in Gorang-Gareng and the discovery of many other murdered prisoners. Two other scenes detail mass killings by communists of their hostages in Dungus district on 1 October 1948 and in Wonogiri district in the wake of the failed Madiun coup attempt. The visual image for the scene of the killings in Ngawen district (Illustration 6.6) features prisoners dressed in only loincloths, highlighting the "perverseness" of the killers and their "non-Muslim" rejection of the principles of "modesty" in dress. One prisoner is shown being tortured with bamboo poles, whilst another prisoner's body is being lowered into a latrine.[119] This scene closely replicates the frenzied diorama scene of events at Lubang Buaya in 1965 used in the adjoining museum, which focuses on the disposal of the bodies of the generals into the disused well. It therefore reinforces the association between the communists and sadistic acts. The caption to the Kanigoro scene, detailing an attack on an Islamic training session, claims that the communists tortured the Muslim worshippers; the Bandar Betsi plantation scene also represents the communists as an aggressive mob attacking an unarmed law enforcement officer. Like the representations of supporters of the "extreme Islam" movements found in the Museum of Eternal Vigilance, representations in the Museum of Communist Treachery attempt to dehumanise the communists.

Based on the official purpose of the Museum of Communist Treachery as a place of study, it is clear that the only message the museum creators intended visitors to take away were reinforced stereotypes of the communists as being evil and inhumane. There is no attempt made in the scenes to understand or reflect on the forces behind events. The tragedy of the Madiun Affair, for example, when Indonesians turned against each other, as supporters either of the Republic or of the communists, is considered irrelevant to the main story.[120]

The last scenes relating to the Madiun Affair are the shooting of Moscow-trained leader of the Indonesian Communist Party, Musso, on 31 October 1948 and the capture of Amir Syarifuddin, the disgruntled former Prime Minister of the Republic, on 29 November 1949, both of whom gave their support to the communist-aligned Pesindo revolt in

Illustration 6.6   The Killings in Kawedanan Ngawen (Blora) (20 September 1948).
Source: Image from Pusat Sejarah dan Tradisi ABRI, *Buku Panduan Monumen Pancasila Sakti Lubang Buaya Jakarta*, Pusat Sejarah dan Tradisi ABRI, Jakarta, 1997, p. 11.

Madiun. As in the Museum of Eternal Vigilance, the capture of rebel leaders is highlighted as a means of boosting the military's prestige, reinforcing the perception of their capacity to suppress enemies.

The next scenes in the Museum of Communist Treachery cover the activities of the Communist Party preceding the 1965 coup attempt. The key scenes are those of The PKI's Cultural Campaign; The PKI's Efforts to Undermine ABRI; The Kanigoro Episode; The Bandar Betsi Episode; The PKI's Revolutionary Offensive Parade in Jakarta; and The Intimidation of the Governor of East Java. Collectively, these scenes seek to establish that leftist cultural organisations are dangerous; that the communists attempted to divide and defeat the Armed Forces; and that the communist-affiliated youth organisation and farmers association were offensive to Islam. They also highlight the illegal land seizures carried out by communists and the growing assertiveness of the communists prior to the coup attempt. No attempt is made to communicate the context of this period of increased antagonisms, of the lags in government plans to implement land reform or of associated communist

Illustration 6.7 The Recapture of the Indonesian State Radio Headquarters (1 October 1965).
Source: Image from Pusat Sejarah dan Tradisi ABRI, *Buku Panduan Monumen Pancasila Sakti Lubang Buaya Jakarta*, Pusat Sejarah dan Tradisi ABRI, Jakarta, 1997, p. 18.

frustrations at attempts by rich Islamic landlords to conceal their land holdings. While there was certainly communist-instigated violence in the 1964–65 period, this violence was generally motivated not by the desire to inflict terror, as the museum displays suggests, but rather as a programme of achieving greater equality between landowners and peasants.[121] A primary reason for emphasising the terror of these groups is to inculcate in the museum audience a sense of ever-present threat and hence the need for military protection.

Because the scenes of the coup are covered in the adjoining the Sacred Pancasila Museum (discussed in Chapter 3), the Museum of Communist Treachery does not devote much space to the coup attempt. The coup in Jakarta is represented in one scene entitled "The Recapture of the Indonesian State Radio Headquarters". In the caption to this scene it is recorded that the communists took over this building to announce the formation of a Revolutionary Council. What is omitted from this explanation and from the visual image (Illustration 6.7) is the fact that troops from the Brawijaya Battalion had surrounded the Republic of

Indonesia Radio headquarters to protect members of the 30th September
Movement whilst they broadcast this statement. This museum also
includes one scene covering the coup attempt in Yogyakarta, focusing
on the kidnapping by "G30S/PKI" of Yogyakarta Resort Commander
Colonel Katamso and his deputy, Lieutenant Colonel Sugiyono.[122] The
remaining scenes in the museum are devoted to the post-coup period.

One of the stated aims of this museum is to represent the efforts
of all Indonesians and the armed forces to crush those who oppose
Pancasila, the basis of the state.[123] Two of the post-coup scenes include
representations of a partnership between the military and the people in
opposing the communists. They focus on the spontaneous formation of
several groups in society such as the Pancasila Front and support for
dissolving the Indonesian Communist Party.[124] Harold Crouch and
John Maxwell challenge the alleged spontaneity of support for these
public responses. Crouch notes that immediately after the coup attempt,
the Army leadership contacted and encouraged anti-communist organisations to form the Pancasila Action Front against the communists.[125]
Maxwell also suggests that as soon as President Sukarno fled to Bogor
on 11 March by helicopter, the military immediately set about organising a show of force for 12 March, including the preparation of trucks
and tanks to carry students in a "victory parade".[126] This victory parade
is replicated in the museum diorama entitled "The People of Jakarta
Welcome the Banning of the Indonesian Communist Party, 12 March
1965" (Illustration 6.8).

Another post-coup scene focuses on the Extraordinary Military
Tribunal, which commenced in 1966. The diorama scene features the
trial of Nyono, a member of the Communist Party Politburo and Head
of the Central Trade Union Organisation for Indonesian Workers (Sentral
Organisasi Buruh Seluruh Indonesia, SOBSI) in front of military judges
and an audience (Illustration 6.9). The Tribunal scene attempts to
demonstrate that, under the New Order, the rule of law was strictly
followed. This is a highly contestable representation. Persons who testified
in these trials were under great pressure to provide testimonies that fitted
with the military version of the coup attempt as a communist plot. In
most cases, defendants did not have access to lawyers or the right to
summon witnesses in their favour. They were also often required to make
confessions prior to the trial, which were frequently extracted by use of
torture.[127] Rather than being concerned to deliver justice, the ultimate
purpose of these trials was to prove that the Indonesian Communist
Party was complicit in the coup attempt.[128]

Illustration 6.8 The people of Jakarta welcome the banning of the Indonesian Communist Party, 12 March 1966.
Source: Image from Pusat Sejarah dan Tradisi ABRI, *Buku Panduan Monumen Pancasila Sakti Lubang Buaya Jakarta*, Pusat Sejarah dan Tradisi ABRI, Jakarta, 1997, p. 20.

Illustration 6.9 The Hearings of the Extraordinary Military Tribunal, 14 February 1966.
Source: Image from Pusat Sejarah dan Tradisi ABRI, *Buku Panduan Monumen Pancasila Sakti Lubang Buaya Jakarta*, Pusat Sejarah dan Tradisi ABRI, Jakarta, 1997, p. 20.

Both the caption and the diorama scene convey the impression that even highly ranked members of the Communist Party such as Nyono received a trial and "appropriate" punishment (in his case, the death sentence). Of those prisoners who did receive a trial, there were no acquittals and the minimum sentence awarded was 15 years.[129] In fact, however, the great majority of persons arrested in relation to the 1965 coup attempt did not receive a trial but were incarcerated, mostly for periods of between 1 and 14 years. Those who were imprisoned received extremely harsh treatment. Once released, ex-political prisoners faced further discrimination in the form of enforced abstinence from political activity, regular reporting to the authorities, compulsory marks on their identity cards, bar from employment in the civil service or the Armed Forces and requirement to seek permission for travel and publication of any material. From the mid-1970s onwards, Indonesia had received increased international criticism for the handling of its political prisoners. This may be one reason why the scene focuses on a case where legal process, however biased, was carried out.

The last three scenes in this museum deal with military operations directed towards crushing the Indonesian Communist Party. The word used in this museum to describe these operations is *penumpasan* (crushing), the most common term used to describe the suppression of communists.[130] The first of these three scenes covers the crushing of the communist resurgence movement in Blitar. The name of this scene is "The Trisula Operation in South Blitar (20 July 1968)". At the time of this revival, Major General Amir Machmud (of the Jakarta military command) suggested that the South Blitar uprising was evidence that the Communist Party was rehearsing for a major comeback in 1970.[131] To strengthen this representation, much was made of the similarity between the tunnels used by the communists in this area and those used by the pro-communist forces in Southern Vietnam.[132] The visual in this museum also focuses on the tunnels used by the South Blitar communists (Illustration 6.10).

The military also dedicated two museum scenes to the communist revivals in Purwodadi, Central Java and West Kalimantan. In the late 1960s, the military draw attention to a Communist Party resurgence in Purwodadi in response to calls for investigation of mass Army-directed executions of prisoners in areas around the town of Purwodadi. Haji J.C. Princen of the Human Rights Defence Foundation attempted to protest against these killings. He reported in an interview published in *Harian Kami* (26 February 1969) that between two to three thousand people had been killed in Purwodadi since November 1968 by members

Illustration 6.10   The Trisula Operation in South Blitar, 20 July 1968.
Source: Image from Pusat Sejarah dan Tradisi ABRI, *Buku Panduan Monumen Pancasila Sakti Lubang Buaya Jakarta,* Pusat Sejarah dan Tradisi ABRI, Jakarta, 1997, p. 21.

of the Diponegoro division. He claimed that the victims were struck on the back of the neck with iron bars before being buried in nearby teak forests.[133] The military tried to draw attention to the Purwodadi area as being a hotbed of underground communist activity.[134] This representation is repeated in the museum. The third episode of communist revival represented in a museum scene is the Sarawak People's Guerrilla Army (Pasukan Gerilya Rakyat Sarawak). This movement consisted of mostly ethnic Chinese from Borneo, who had originally been armed by the government to fight in the Malaysia Confrontation. In response to the military takeover of power in the capital, they refused to surrender their arms. This movement was also an important element of earlier anti-communist propaganda.[135]

The Armed Forces History Centre highlights all three of these episodes in the museums as evidence of a continuing communist threat and as justification for the mass killings of this period. The killing of perhaps 500,000 people, who were allegedly communists or sympathisers, in the post-coup period was never denied by the regime. Although the killings were sometimes recorded in official accounts, representations of the killings were understated and concentrated on incidents such as those described above, in which there was evidence of possible communist revivals. One possible reason for these selective representations of the killings is the difficulty of explaining the agency of so many people in a "coup" plot and hence justification for such large-scale revenge. Many members of the Communist Party had been taken by surprise by events of the coup. These people suddenly found that their past affiliations put them in a life-threatening situation.[136] The three scenes in this museum that cover the post-coup suppression of communists all represent movements in which there was an armed enemy at large. This image of communist resistance provides a far more threatening image than alternative accounts of the killings, in which victims were passively taken from their homes and killed.[137]

The caption accompanying the Trisula scene also helps establish why these three scenes are included in this museum. The caption notes that "after the PKI had been dissolved the party re-established itself in the form of a guerrilla base".[138] In these three cases, unlike earlier military "clean-up operations", the Communist Party had already been banned according to Decree 25 of the 1966 Provisional People's Consultative Assembly session, thereby providing legal weight to this military campaign.

The three scenes representing campaigns against the communists also skip over the most intense period of killing, 1965 to 1966. From the museum representations at Sacred Pancasila Monument, a visitor gains little sense of the extent of the post-coup killing. There is no hint of the frightening witch-hunt-like atmosphere of the period, of the nightly curfews and night raids.[139] Alongside the reported "brutality" of the communists in 1948 and 1965, the "brutality" used in the so-called crushing of the communists — which included torture, rape and the killing of many innocent persons — is not mentioned.[140] The outrage expressed in representations in this museum like those in the Sacred Pancasila Monument, framed as they are within the context of a story of the armed forces' defence of the Pancasila, is thus highly hypocritical.

COMMUNIST METHODS: LESSONS OF THE PAST

Several scenes in this museum were possibly chosen for inclusion as a means of presenting evidence of communist methods. It is possible, for example, that the museum-makers kept in mind popular targets of the

1990 *keterpengaruhan* (influenced by) movement when choosing the scenes suited to this museum. The caption to the scene "The PKI's Cultural Campaign" reflects a broadly held opinion of the New Order regime that there is no place for politics within art and literature. The scene could be seen as a warning about the potential danger of literature being penetrated by communist thought. The relevance of this message to a 1990s audience was that the works of ex-political prisoner and former LEKRA (Lembaga Kebudayaan Rakyat, Institute of People's Culture) member Pramoedya Ananta Toer, arrested in 1965 on the grounds of being influenced by communism, had recently been accused of being influenced by communism. This theme is developed further in the series *The Latent Danger of Communism in Indonesia*. An entire section of one of the four volumes of this series is devoted to "The commotion over the literature of Pramoedya Ananta Toer's writings" (*Heboh Sastra Karya Pramoedya Ananta Toer*).[141] Two of Pramoedya's books, *Earth of Mankind* (Bumi Manusia) and *Child of All Nations* (Anak Semua Bangsa), were banned in 1980 on the grounds that they were directed at encouraging the young generation to use communist tactics in art, the press and other media to challenge those in power.[142] In 1988 *House of Glass* (Rumah Kaca) — a later volume from this historical twentieth-century trilogy — was also banned on the grounds that it was "disguised communism". The seriousness with which the military took this ban was demonstrated by the arrest of students in Yogyakarta for selling and possessing this work, despite the new freedom of expression, which was supposed to be in place at this time.[143]

The museum-makers might have considered the Incident of Bandar Betsi plantation significant because in the 1980s land disputes between the people on one side and the bureaucracy and developers on the other had become increasingly common.[144] In the case of Kedung Ombo, one of the most controversial development projects of the 1980s, President Suharto made the suggestion that protestors, whom he labelled "PKI remnants", had distorted information about the case.[145] The label "extreme left" was thus applied to those who protested against land disputes. At the same time, inclusion of the scene on the Delanggu strikes was also useful for legitimating the labelling of workers' strikes as "communist-inspired" and therefore punishable. As noted earlier, the number of strikes had recently increased.

The caption scene entitled, "PKI Efforts to Undermine ABRI" seeks to identify attacks on the dual function as a communist tactic to weaken the armed forces. During the period of *keterbukaan* (openness)

there was some discussion about dual function and the future role of
the Armed Forces.[146] This claim makes it clear that use of the label
"PKI" was also a means of defending the military and its dual function.

Emphasis on the immediate post-coup alliance between the military and the people (students) in this museum may have been related to efforts of the military in the period of openness to once again court students in a new transitional alliance. At the time of the museum's creation, factions within the military — thought to be under (retired) General Murdani's influence — were trying to establish greater rapport with students. They occasionally gave their support for selected demonstrations.[147] This was an important part of the military effort to present, on the surface at least, receptivity to greater openness.

MUSEUMS DEVOTED TO STATE ENEMIES

The curious thing about this museum is that, like the Museum of Eternal Vigilance, it is devoted entirely to one enemy of the state. In this way, both these museums expose divisions within the Indonesian nation. A former Head of the Museum of Eternal Vigilance revealed that young visitors to the museum were often surprised to learn that there had also been civil wars amongst Indonesians.[148] Internal division within the Indonesian nation has generally been a topic deliberately avoided in official Indonesian histories. In her observations of censorship in Indonesian historical films, Krishna Sen has noted that Indonesian history has generally been made to conform to the story of Indonesians against outsiders and that film censors have worked hard to avoid public representation of conflict within the nation.[149] In this sense, these two museums are curious. Yet there is also a sense that extremists of both the left and right are represented as being outsiders to Indonesian society. They are, as Ariel Heryanto notes, "othered" along with other Indonesians, such as the ethnic Chinese.[150] This is accentuated by the display of weapons used against these "other" Indonesians in these museums.

The military chose to expose these divisions in these two museums to perpetuate the idea of Indonesia as "a fragile nation" in need of a strong military. An article about the Museum of Communist Treachery notes that "the truth of the scenes makes us aware that communism still forms a latent threat that can strike at any time".[151] The military intended that the display of repeated scenes of so-called communist rebellions throughout history would establish that the threat of communism was cyclical. It is interesting that, despite the continuance of the idea of communism as a latent threat for over 30 years, the most recent communist episode included in the museum is the capture in 1974 of S.A. Sofyan, accused of founding a new style of communist organisation supported by the People's Guerrilla Brigade of Sarawak and the North Kalimantan People's Brigade. The museum-makers, perhaps in response to public scepticism about the label "communist", chose not to include other historical movements, such as Fretilin in East Timor, which the regime also branded "communist".[152]

The two museums, the Museum of Eternal Vigilance and the Museum of Communist Treachery, in a sense formed a pair. Both laid out historical justification for two primary threats to the Pancasila, as defined by the military. Emphasis on on-going threats reflected the dominance of the intelligence thinking in the military in the 1980s and early 1990s.[153] Despite the continued dismantling of the old intelligence apparatus — BAIS (Strategic Intelligence Agency, Badan Intelijen Strategis) was dissolved in 1994 — the military continued to assert the existence of the threat of the extreme left throughout the 1990s. Both these threats were, however, subject to increasing popular scrutiny in the late New Order period and even more so after President Suharto's resignation in May 1998.

The military continued to summon the ghost of communism after the opening of the Museum of Communist Treachery. Public cynicism at the on-going "reds under the bed" campaign reached new heights after the 27 July Affair in 1996, but there was still firm commitment from some to this cause. Having already removed Megawati Sukarnoputri from the leadership of the increasingly popular opposition party PDI (Partai Demokrasi Indonesia, Indonesian Democratic Party), the government ordered a violent attack on her party headquarters on 27 July 1996 in response to the daily free-speech forums held there by her supporters. Over two hundred people were arrested in the riots following the attack, many of whom are still missing. The military blamed the riots on members of the illegal People's Democratic Party (Partai Rakyat Demokratik, PRD), which had been active in the free-speech forums and branded the party a "communist organisation" because of its so-called "communist methods". The PRD were involved in programmes to increase worker mobilisation and to further farmers' demands for land compensation in cases of forced evictions.[154] Krishna Sen and David Hill note that in the mid-1990s, around the time of renewed communist allegations directed at the PRD, heightened criticisms of the film *The Treachery of the 30 September Movement*, appeared in media such as the Internet.[155]

ANTI-COMMUNISM OUTLIVES THE NEW ORDER REGIME

It was noted in Chapter 3 that almost immediately after the fall of Suharto, alternative versions of the coup attempt of 1965 were published in the press. The appearance of these versions of the coup, including the Anderson and McVey theory that the coup was not a communist plot, challenged the idea of communists as national traitors. In the same period, there were also more direct challenges to the idea of communism as a latent threat in Indonesia. A number of surveys were printed in popular magazines on the question of whether communism was still a threat.[156] Perhaps the most significant challenges to the historical orthodoxy of communists as the dark knights of Indonesian history, however, were the appearance in 1999 of the Institute for the Investigation into the Victims of the 1965–66 Killings (Yayasan Penelitian Korban Pembunuhan 1965–66, YPKP) and President Abdurrahman Wahid (Gus Dur)'s 2001 proposal to lift the 1966 Special Consultative Assembly Decree (MPRS TAP 25) on the banning of communism and Marxist-Leninist teachings in Indonesia. He claimed that this proposal was based on humanitarian and constitutional considerations, especially the pre-amble to the 1945 Constitution.[157]

The Institute for the Investigation into the Victims of the 1965–66 Killings was founded by former political prisoners, including ex-Gerwani leader, Sulami. Its activities include investigating mass graves and collecting data on the killings from this period.[158] In investigating the killings, this organisation challenged the idea, promoted in the New Order, that the killings were justified, describing them as an abuse of human rights. The publication of Sulami's autobiographical account of her 20 years in imprisonment as a political detainee also constituted a challenge to New Order historical representations of communists.[159] Some media articles in the post-Suharto period have also attempted to reflect on the suffering of victims in the post-coup period.[160] This represents a dramatic break from the traditions of New Order anti-communism.

Unlike the case of emerging criticism of the New Order's suppression of Islam and the appearance of histories of associated anti-Islamic violence, which have met with little protest, efforts to re-examine the New Order's commitment to anti-communism have raised considerable ire. Gus Dur's proposal to lift the ban on communism provoked street protests.

Some Muslim organisations protested lifting the ban on the grounds of the association between communism and atheism,[161] while others suggested Abdurrahman's request for forgiveness from members of the Indonesian Communist Party for the killings was a sign he took the matter of communism too lightly.[162] Members of the Muslim-based PPP and the military also spoke out against this idea.[163] The Muslim Crescent and Star Party (Partai Bulan Bintang, PBB) went so far as to call for an emergency session of the People's Consultative Assembly to demand the accountability and possible impeachment of the President, based on the alleged contravention his suggestion posed of his oath to uphold the 1945 Constitution.[164] Although it is clear that some of the groups that protested this idea, most noticeably the Muslim Crescent and Star Party, may have been looking for a means to discredit Gus Dur and prompt a change in leadership, these protests also reflected a commitment to anti-communism.

The Institute for the Investigation into the Victims of the 1965–66 Killings has also experienced intimidation.[165] In March 2001 members of the Kaloran Islamic Fraternity Forum (Forum Ukuwah Islamiya Kaloran) forcibly obstructed an attempted reburial of 26 victims of the 1965 mass killings discovered in a mass grave in Kaloran, Central Java.[166] This act demonstrated strong resistance to revising the belief that the victims of the 1965–66 violence were sub-human and hence unworthy of proper burial.

One commentator, Ahmad Sahal, editor of *Kalam* magazine, questioned why Islamic groups of all derivations opposed the lifting of the ban on communism so strongly, asking the question whether this reflected the success of the New Order regime in spreading communist-phobia?[167] Not all Islamic organisations have objected to the opening of this past. The Yogyakarta Ansor youth movement (the youth wing of NU which was involved in the 1965–66 killings), for example, made an apology in November 2000 to the victims of the killings.[168] Nevertheless, it appears that in a climate of increased religiosity, consistent calls to rally anti-communism by emphasising the communist-atheist association have been successful amongst some sections of the population.[169]

Apart from Muslim participation in the 1965–66 killings, one reason for continuing commitment of some Muslims to anti-communism may be that the military was successful in its efforts to cast liberalisation as a Western tradition that was necessarily hostile to Islam and to associate liberalisation with leftist hence, communist tendencies.[170] What this means is that the anti-communist messages of the Sacred Pancasila

Monument and other museums within this complex still resonate with some Indonesians. It seems that many are unwilling to let go of this historical orthodoxy of viewing communism as a latent threat in Indonesia.

CONCLUSION

In the mid-1980s, coinciding with Nugroho's death, members of the 1945 Generation were retiring from the military. These changes altered the focus of the Armed Forces History Centre. In the 1960s and 1970s, the Centre concentrated on projects representing the military's role in suppressing the coup attempt and the revolution. In the mid-1980s, the Centre turned to different themes in an attempt to legitimise military men of different generations. The first museum project completed by the Centre in this period was the National Soldiership Museum, which concentrated on pre-independence heroes and anti-colonial resistance, thereby emphasising a long tradition of soldiership in Indonesia. This museum focused on an alternative source of justification for the military's continuing dominance in politics and the project of development.

Since the early New Order period, the military had emphasised its role as the defender of the Pancasila against threats of both the extreme left and the extreme right. Under the influence of intelligence expert Commander General Benny Murdani, emphasis on the threat of the extreme Islam increased. The Museum of Eternal Vigilance, which was devoted to this theme, stresses the terror of both the Darul Islam movements and the "Islamist" incidents in the 1970s and 1980s to reinforce the necessity of the military safeguarding the people from such threats. It was also an attempt to restate the need for continuing military dominance. More so than any other project of the Centre, this museum quickly lost relevance because of the acceptance of the sole foundation law, the falling out between President Suharto and General Murdani, and Suharto's subsequent rehabilitation of political Islam.

The story of the coup attempt remained the backdrop to the Museum of Communist Treachery, but greater emphasis was placed on the cyclical nature of communism and of its continuing existence as a threat. The museum expanded further on the theme of communist treachery by detailing scenes which established the "methods" of communists exhibited in the preludes to both the 1948 Madiun Affair and the 1965 coup attempt. This museum also highlights communist methods in the past as evidence for campaigns against contemporary societal "threats". A theme common to the last two museum projects of the Centre is emphasis on the "terror" imposed by both movements. The purpose of this theme is to dehumanise these "enemies" of the regime. Both museums serve as warnings to Indonesians of the existence of anti-Pancasila, and hence anti-regime, forces within society and the consequent need for on-going vigilance. They also provide material evidence for two very convenient labels for silencing regime dissent. In this way history was used as evidence of the need for the armed forces to wield control over society.

Afterword

The Militarisation of the Indonesian Past

By the end of the 32-year New Order regime, the military had become associated in the minds of Indonesians and non-Indonesians alike with violence, repression, corruption and an enduring authoritarianism. The public image of the military was of a powerful, cohesive institution exercising domination over the Indonesian people. This image was the product of people's experience, but also scholarly analyses of the military which to date have largely focused on military violence and military politics. Through an analysis of the military's history projects and military-produced ideology, *History in Uniform* has revealed the military's self-image as a self-sacrificing people's army, as the guardians of the spirit of independence and the protectors of the Pancasila. I have pointed to the hypocrisy of these historical representations in light of the violence members of the military inflicted on other Indonesians for the duration of the regime, but I have also demonstrated military awareness of the gaps between these historically located images and reality. This book has demonstrated the military's constant concern to build and guard their image in the eyes of both soldiers and citizens alike. The military's extraordinary attention to image-making challenges the idea of the Indonesian military as an all-powerful institution. Although the military was able to crush dissent by means of armed repression and continually propagate its versions of the past, controlling the minds of Indonesians was a far more difficult task.

History in Uniform has answered Heather Sutherland's call for analysis into how the Indonesian national myth has been transformed over time. It has revealed key shifts between Guided Democracy inter-pretations of the past and New Order historical orthodoxy produced largely by Nugroho Notosusanto and the Armed Forces History Centre. I have identified which parts of the past the military included or excluded from the "official" record in New Order histories. The main criteria for inclusion or exclusion were that representations should glorify the New Order regime and represent it as the apex of history; legitimise the military suppression of communists and promote anti-communism; enhance military unity; legitimise the military's political role; emphasise their support for, and defence of, a "Pancasila society" and justify the suppression of opposition to the regime.

In both the Guided Democracy and New Order periods, history served to reinforce the regime's ideological priorities. Although New Order histories were focused on divisions within the nation, they were also presented within the framework of nationalism through representing the sources of this division, including communists or extremist Muslims, as a kind of "other" within. All Indonesians were expected to be on guard against these national enemies and united in their opposition to them. Emphasis on the threat of communism remained constant throughout the regime as means of countering reform; on the other hand, the threat of extreme Islam was only emphasised for a short period in the 1980s. Ironically in the post-Suharto era, it is a small fringe of Islamist organisations that pose the greatest threat to peace in Indonesia. These organisations are in part a product of New Order repression, but some also have links to people involved in the Darul Islam revolts of the 1950s and 1960s, the core subjects of the Museum of Eternal Vigilance.[1]

A clear difference between New Order and Guided Democracy versions of the past is the place of ordinary Indonesians in these narratives. During the New Order, history was no longer a story of the Indonesian people united in opposition to imperialism as the Communist Party and Sukarno had both emphasised. Instead, history became a story of military triumphs culminating in the achievement of the New Order. For the Indonesian military, history was also primarily about a struggle between the Pancasila and anti-Pancasila forces in society and the military's continuing role as protector of the people from national threats and as guardians and heirs of the 1945 spirit.

The impact of New Order historical orthodoxy on the Indonesian public was varied. Representations of the 1965 coup attempt, and particularly of the "barbarity" of the communists, reinforced community prejudices towards former communists and made a contribution to strong anti-communist sentiment in Indonesia. At the same time, the extent to which Indonesians were saturated with such homogeneous representations of the coup attempt in film, school texts, commemoration, monuments and museums actually promoted the questioning of these narratives. While the Sacred Pancasila Monument enjoyed some popularity as a shrine to anti-Communism, the Museum of Eternal Vigilance did not attract large audiences and indeed its messages seemed increasingly offensive as Indonesian Muslims became more orthodox. Monument English Sacred Pancasila was the most frequently visited of the sites run by the Armed Forces History Centre, with average annual visitor numbers of 277,422 for the years 1981–94. The Museum of Eternal Vigilance, by contrast, had annual visitor numbers of just 148,469 for the years 1987–94.[2]

Military control of representations of the past also had gender implications. Military versions of the independence struggle, for example, promoted a masculinised version of the Indonesian citizen. It is only those independence fighters who fought with arms who find a place in the New Order definition of those granted membership to the legendary 1945 Generation. One product of military control of official representations of this period was that the contributions of both women and non-combatants to this pivotal anti-colonialist struggle were marginalised, and hence their own claims for rights of recognition were reduced. In representations of the 1965 coup attempt, communist women served as a metaphor for the immoral direction society was allegedly taking under the influence of communism. Military representations of women's roles in the 1945–49 revolution in the Satriamandala Armed Forces Museum also indicate that representations of women's roles were included for upholding models of women's sacrifices for greater national causes.

Glorification of the military's role in the revolution, however, also produced cynicism. Projects resulting from the 1972 seminar on the transfer of values did not, for example, stem the tide of student criticism of military dominance. Edward Aspinall notes that in the 1974 Malari protests, students called for reduced roles for the Army in government; by 1977–78 they were demanding a substantial or complete reduction in the military's role in politics and the abolition of the primary intelligence agency Kopkamtib. In the 1980s, anti-militarism was even more pronounced in student demonstrations, with students going so far as to symbolically burn military boots on campuses.[3] Anti-government student protestors also seized opportunities to criticise military leaders for their self-praise. On Heroes' Day 1977, for example, youths protested against Suharto's extravagant plans for a mausoleum for himself. Placards in the Jakarta protests read "Heroes, look at the result of your sacrifice" and in Bandung they read, "It is not the ideal of a hero to buy a mountain".[4] In the late 1970s, the military internally acknowledged that its image had suffered in recent years and it tried to rebuild its image by stressing the need to achieve greater integration of the people and the military.[5] For some Indonesians, however, such as those who joined the military or the university military regiments, military-produced histories contributed to the acceptance of military values.

By means of censorship and their monopoly on official history, the military ensured that many stories that might have been told about the Indonesian past were denied a public audience. This reinforces Lynn Hunt's observation that "history is better defined as the ongoing tension between stories that have been told and stories that might be told".[6] One of the most obvious exclusions from the military record of the past was of military violence against Indonesian citizens, which constituted a major breach of the Pancasila principle of humanitarianism. The aggrandisement of the military's role in the past also meant that the roles of other historical actors, including civilians (especially women), were excluded. When representations of civilians were included in military representations of the past, it was often as derogatory examples alongside instances of military supremacy. These representations of civilian incompetence may have contributed to the reluctance among some people — at least during the New Order — to see the military retreat to the barracks.

History in Uniform has also demonstrated the significance of history to politicised militaries for the purposes of both internal unity and wider legitimacy. Other politicised militaries created in the context of an independence struggle such as the Burmese and Algerian militaries have made similar attempts to draw legitimacy from the heroic circumstances of their origins. They similarly invoke the "birthright principle", arguing for continuing political roles because they were integral to the birth of the nation.[7] Drawing on their role in the independence struggle against the British, the Burmese military or *tatmadaw* also refers to itself as a people's army.[8]

In Indonesia this "birthright" ideology has been particularly well developed, especially during the 32 years of the military-dominated Suharto regime. The 1972 seminar on the transfer of 1945 Values was a calculated effort to ensure a continuation of the belief in the military as guardians of the 1945 spirit (including the function of leading the nation), even after the retirement of the 1945 Generation from the military. The history projects resulting from this seminar, including the militarised content in the *National History Textbook* and the *History of the National Struggle*, military memoirs and the establishment of more monuments and visual forms of commemoration of military heroes of the struggle, served to reinforce the military as legitimate political players because of their role in the 1945–49 independence struggle.

Under Nugroho's direction, the military also used representations of the independence struggle to reinforce the "birthright" idea to Indonesian soldiers. General Sudirman's 1948 guerrilla struggle, in particular, served as a model of the need for military leadership. By making young military cadets physically retrace Sudirman's guerrilla route and learn stories of his passage, military educators tried to convince cadets of the necessity for military intervention in the course of national history. It is important to recall that, at least until 1997, most soldiers were taught these views and that these ideas may thus persist for many years to come. Other politicised militaries have also valorised their founding fathers, such as Mustaffa Kemal Ataturk in Turkey who went on to become the President of Turkey. However, the Indonesian military has elevated General Sudirman to saint-like status, presenting him as the embodiment of a self-sacrificing soldier.

The Indonesian military's claims to a political role have also rested on a version of history in which it has repeatedly saved the nation from internal threats. Again, this is a theme common to other politicised militaries. The Burmese *tatmadaw* also extends its narrative of national salvation to the post-independence era by making claims to having held the nation, in this case the Union of Burma, together during times of national crisis such as the ethnic and communist "revolts" against the Rangoon government.[9] Like the narrative of the Satriamandala Armed Forces Museum in Jakarta, the organising narrative of the US$9 million Defence Services Museum in central Rangoon dictates that the *tatmadaw* has led the people on a pathway to progress in the face of "great odds".[10]

Because most politicised militaries of the twentieth century were anti-communist, the theme of communism as a significant national threat was not uncommon. The Brazilian military's anti-communist traditions parallel those of the Indonesian military. Until 1996, two central days in the Brazilian calendar commemorated the respective anniversaries of the military suppression of allegedly communist coups of 1935 and 1964. On November 27, the anniversary of the 1935 coup, and like the traditions of Sacred Pancasila Day, the Brazilian armed forces paid their respects to the victims of the revolt by visiting the mausoleum for the coup victims in the Sao Joao Batista cemetery (built in 1940). The Brazilian public was also encouraged to show their respect through larger scale commemorations at the monument erected at the site of the rebellion (built in 1968).[11] The military encouraged the Brazilian public to link these two coups together, just as the Indonesian military did for the 1948 and 1965 "communist" coups, as evidence of the treachery of communism and the ever-present potential of a communist revival. By 1996, however, in accordance with the end of the Cold War the Brazilian military declared the struggle against communism to be over and that the military heroes had died for the purposes of democracy.[12]

In the case of New Order Indonesia, anti-communist ideology outlived the end of the Cold War. One reason for this was that anti-communism had become so central to the legitimation of the New Order. Of all historical events, representations of the 1965 coup attempt as a communist plot were the most critical for the regime. The story behind the rush to produce the first published version of the coup in forty days, the determination to defend this version to the outside world in light of the Cornell Paper and the progressive and elaborate memorialisation of the well at Lubang Buaya all confirm this claim. The Sacred Pancasila Monument, with its accompanying museums, diorama installations and ceremonial and memorial spaces, together with the official film *The Treachery of the 30 September Movement* and the commemorative day, demonstrate the regime's careful and continual orchestration of a very specific national memory of this event.

Representations of the coup were also important because they telescoped memories of the transition from Sukarno to Suharto into a narrow focus on the coup attempt and the suffering of the army martyrs. In the context of strict censorship over this past, this created a climate in which the suffering of those who died or were imprisoned after the coup became unmentionable, at least in the public sphere.

The official version of the 1965 coup was also a means by which the new regime sought to define itself. The images projected of communists, and communist women in particular, were representations of everything the New Order regime presented itself as rejecting. The communists were portrayed, for example, as being "anti-Pancasila" and especially as having rejected the first principle of the Pancasila belief in one God. The names of the monument complex and commemorative day attempt to link the military suppression of the coup attempt with the putative salvation of the Pancasila. Communist women were portrayed in the monument relief and in the official film, *The Treachery of the*

30 September Movement, as symbols of a debauched and immoral society. The New Order, by contrast, claimed itself to be an upholder of moral society. By representing communism in this way, the new regime used history as a means of warning Indonesians of what they had been saved from, reinforcing the military's roles as heroes in the suppression of the coup attempt and in the elimination of communists. Through these constructions, the New Order was represented as the climax of history and its leaders credited with having set the nation on the right path.

Without the person of Nugroho Notosusanto, it is doubtful whether the Armed Forces History Centre would have been so prolific or influential. Nugroho was not only an enthusiast for history but also for the Indonesian military. A close analysis of the life stories of historians and ideologues helps us to understand why they write the kinds of histories they do and the sources of motivation for their actions and thinking. In the case of Nugroho Notosusanto, his formative years were spent in the throes of the Indonesian revolution as a member of the Student Army. This experience produced in Nugroho a romanticised idea of Indonesian soldiers as being self-sacrificing patriots with a mandate to guide Indonesians towards a brighter future. In this way, Nugroho seemed a convinced supporter of the ideas of famous military analyst Morris Janowitz on the puritanical attitude of the armies born out of independence struggles.[13] Nugroho's motivation for militarising Indonesian history and promoting and defending the military's political role to both soldiers and the wider Indonesian public was undoubtedly his genuine belief in the contribution of the 1945 Generation to the nation. At the same time there seems also to have been a desire for personal recognition within the institution he so admired.

In most cases, Nugroho's projects did not present new ideas. Instead they served to reinforce the regime's ideological bases of anti-communism, militarism and developmentalism. The first published version of the coup, for example, closely followed an interpretation of the event already provided by the military leadership and presented in the military-controlled newspaper *Angkatan Bersendjata*. The revised version of the National Monument History Museum also closely followed Suharto's directive that it mirror the changes in national direction mandated by the Parliament in the transition period of 1966 to 1968. In converting the regime's values into historical form, however, Nugroho made an important contribution to propagating New Order ideology. This was most evident in the ways he used history in the *National History Textbook* and the *History of the National Struggle* to support the military's claim to play a combined military and defence role. Nugroho focused on particular events, such as the military's commitment after the capture of the leaders of the Republic in 1948, to justify its claim to a role in leading the nation. As we have seen, in the case of the 1965 coup attempt, he also used history as a means of instilling the idea of societal threats into young Indonesians by circulating images of communists as depraved and demonic. In using history in this way, Nugroho attempted to popularise many of the ideas of leading New Order ideologues such as Lieutenant General Ali Murtopo (on the New Order as a form of puritanical renewal) and General Nugroho's mentor, Nasution (on the dual function).

The fact that other Indonesian historians, most of whom were employees of the New Order government and hence benefactors of the regime, were able to criticise some aspects of Nugroho's history projects points to the fact that military control of representations of the Indonesian past was not complete. This reinforces the need to look for instances of resistance within authoritarian systems. As Ariel Heryanto and Sumit Mandal have recently argued, authoritarianism is "a set of diffuse relationships both in the public and private spheres where the distribution of power is greatly unbalanced, but despite appearances, is never totally concentrated in a single person or group".[14]

Critiques of Nugroho's works launched during the New Order regime, especially in the mid-1980s, centred on the unpatriotic besmirching and belittlement of former President Sukarno in the *National History Textbook*; on Nugroho's politically driven thesis that Sukarno was not the sole author of the Pancasila; on Nugroho's reduction of Indonesian history to post-1945 history only in the *History of the National Struggle*; and on strong objections to government (including military) influence on these texts. Despite these critiques, it took President Suharto's resignation to prompt a major rethinking of the history curriculum and to this date there are still delays in agreeing on a new version of history.[15]

The end of press censorship after the resignation of President Suharto in May 1998, and the momentum of *reformasi* (the reform movement instigated by students from 1997 onwards), had a dramatic impact on the Indonesian military. Many cases of military abuses of human rights such as the mass killings of 1965–66, the Tanjung Priok tragedy of 1984, the 27 July affair of 1996, continuing violence in Aceh, West Papua and East Timor, the Trisakti shootings of 1998 and the kidnapping and disappearance of students prior to this, and the May 1998 riots were all exposed.[16] Public distrust and contempt for the military was at a peak. In September 1998, the Indonesian military felt compelled to hold a seminar on their role in the twenty-first century. At this seminar, a decision was made that the military had no choice but to listen to the people's demands that they "return to the barracks" and rescind their political role.[17] Since the fall of Suharto, the military's department of social affairs has been dissolved, the *kekaryaan* roles or assignment of retired military officers to civilian posts (such as governors) is being phased out and military seats in the House of Representatives and the People's Consultative Assembly were abolished in 2004. In 1998 the Police Force withdrew from the Indonesian military, which has now reverted to the name TNI (Tentara Nasional Indonesia, Indonesian National Army, Airforce and Navy), allowing the role of internal security to be handed over to the police. In addition, the military has agreed to phase out its dual socio-political role. Decree VII of the 2000 People's Consultative Assembly states that the TNI must play a defence role only.[18]

One of the clearest articulations of the military's new ethos in the post-Suharto era is provided in Law No. 34/2004 on the roles of the TNI and the police. This is the best guide so far to the military's revised historical image. Article 2 of this law attempts to define the *jati diri* or "true essence" of the TNI by the four appellations of a People's Army (Tentara Rakyat), a Struggle Army (Tentara Pejuang), a National Army (Tentara Nasional) and a Professional Army (Tentara Professional). The two descriptions of the TNI as a people's army and a struggle army nevertheless hold some resonance with pre-*reformasi* descriptions of the identity of the armed forces and point to the enduring significance of the independence struggle to the military's ethos.

The concept of a people's army draws on the idea that the Indonesian people spontaneously formed the army in the struggle against the Dutch. The expanded explanation of the term people's army in Article 2 states that the people's army is:

> … an army that originates from the people who took up arms to fight to oppose the colonisers and to take back and defend independence in the independence war of 1945–1949 with the motto of "merdeka atau mati" (freedom or death).[19]

The word *pejuang* (independence fighter) immediately conjures an association with the independence fighters of 1945–49. The concept also draws on the ideas of devotion to the nation embodied in earlier representations of the military's role in the independence struggle. The expanded explanation for this term in Article 2 states that as a struggle army, "the TNI, in carrying out its duties, struggles to uphold and defend the Unitary State of the Republic of Indonesia". It states that the word *pejuang* refers to the commitment of members of the military to "never surrendering in the face of each challenge or duty being carried out".

Emphasis on defence of the Unitary State of the Republic of Indonesia seems to have replaced the New Order obsession with defence of the first principle of the Pancasila or Belief in One God. In 2005, for example, President Susilo Bambang Yudhoyono used the anniversary of the 1965 coup attempt to reaffirm the country's commitment to the Unitary State of Indonesia.[20] In light of the separation of East Timor in 1999 and continuing support for separation in West Papua and Aceh (despite the peace deal of 2005), disintegration of the Unitary State has become central to military articulations of current threats to the nation. This concept resonates for many nationalist Indonesians who have little sympathy for victims of military repression in Aceh or West Papua and who lament the "loss" of East Timor in 1999 after the unanimous result of the ballot on independence.

Article 2 defines a national army as one "that works in the interests of the state and not in the interests of regions, ethnic groups, races or religious groups". This clearly endorses a commitment by the military to neutrality on issues of regionalism, ethnicity, race and religion. This concept may be a reaction to public awareness of the involvement of elements of the military in regional and religious conflicts in recent years such as the violence in Ambon and the anti-Chinese violence preceding and following the fall of Suharto.[21] Nico Schulte Nordholt describes these elements within the military as "dark forces" or non-official intelligence units within the military working to provoke and create violence.[22]

The last of the appellations in Law 34 is of the TNI is as "a professional army". The TNI is here defined as an army:

> ... which does not participate in practical politics or conduct business and which upholds state policies following the principles of democracy, civilian supremacy, human rights, national law and ratified international laws.

This is clearly the most radical change. If the military is serious about becoming professional, it will inevitably be forced to produce a new narrative about its past political roles and why these roles were abandoned.

The wording of the bill suggests that the military have not given up the cherished ideal of integration between the people and the military. Despite the inclusion of the final description of the TNI as a professional army, Marpuang *et al.* of the human rights group, Imparsial, suggest that the concept of the military's true essence as outlined in Article 2 allows scope for continuing political influence. They believe that the concept of *jati diri*, or true essence, outlined in Law No. 34 should be oriented towards the future and the future roles of the military. The concepts of a people's army and a struggle army are terms that refer directly to the military's role in the 1945–49 independence struggle, which not only looks backwards but also forms the basis of military claims to political roles. Aware of this association, Imparsial challenges the continuation of the idea of the military as a people's army. In the context of a democratic state, they argue, "the relationship between the people and the TNI is not one of integration and unity, because this relationship is limited by the existence of political authority".[23] Although the New Order slogan "the total integration of the TNI and the people" (*kemanunggalan TNI dengan rakyat*) is not used in this law, Article 1 refers to the system of defence as "a system which is all encompassing and involving every citizen, region and other national resources". There are thus efforts within the bill to uphold the idea of close integration between the people and the military.

Before passage of this law, human rights groups, women's groups, students and intellectuals criticised the draft law on the TNI for not going far enough in enforcing military professionalism.[24] Imparsial argued that the law still enabled some forms of military participation in politics by allowing retired military men to play significant roles in government, by continuing the territorial system (which includes a mirror government of military officials down to the village level), and for allowing the President the power to appoint and dismiss the Commander of the military.[25] Imparsial argues that the law still allows the military to act independently from political authority, particularly in the case of its territorial functions which are not covered by the law and which might be used as justification for political intervention.[26]

Law No. 34 includes greater emphasis on national defence than previous military doctrines, but the focus on internal threats to the nation has by no means been removed. These threats are listed in Article 1 as "threats considered to endanger the sovereignty of the state, the regional integrity of the state and the safety of the entire nation". These threats are detailed as including armed separatist move-ments, armed revolts and terrorist acts. Kees Koonings and Dirk Kruijt suggest that political armies believe strongly in their role in guiding the nation and for this reason they invite us to treat any proclaimed military retreat to the barracks with caution, arguing that military may simply remake claims for political influence by identifying new threats to national unity.[27] The military's revised ethos as articulated in Law No. 34 certainly points to new threats to national unity and this may be taken as further evidence that the military's retreat from the political stage is as yet reluctant.

Significantly Law No. 34 makes no mention of the 1965 coup attempt, once a central reference point for the need for military protection of the people. This may signal an attempt to disassociate the military from the New Order regime for which anti-communism was the cornerstone of state ideology. It may also reflect the fact that the new military leadership began their military careers after the coup attempt. Air Marshal Djoko Suyanto, the man appointed to the position of Commander of the TNI in February 2006, for example, graduated from the military academy in 1973 and is thus unlikely to have been involved in the Communist suppression. In fact Suyanto, as Air Force Marshal and Commander, felt able to state in 2006 that:

> Several Air Force officers were implicated in the incident, but they were not representing the Air Force as an institution .... I can even say that officers from other forces — the Army, the Navy, and the Police — were involved in the incident, but they didn't represent their own institutions, either.[28]

This is a remarkable statement given the elaborate efforts made by the Armed Forces History Centre to counter the Cornell Theory of the coup attempt as an internal military affair and their efforts to enforce the theory of the coup as a communist plot.

Suyanto's views do not, however, seem to reflect those of the military as a whole. In 2006, the Armed Forces History Centre, for example, still listed a link on its website to a brief history of "G30S/PKI". This acronym associating the coup attempt with the Indonesian Communist Party is still also used in the brief description provided of the coup attempt on the Centre's Sacred Pancasila webpages.[29] It is possible that the Armed Forces History Centre is struggling to keep up with changing views within the military, but other military leaders have also continued to warn of the dangers of resurgent communism. In March 2006, the Jakarta Military Commander, Major General Agustadi Sasongko Purnomo, warned the public to be on guard against the re-emergence of a Communist movement. He pointed to the cultural exhibition held by ex-communists at Taman Ismail Marzuki Arts Centre in Jakarta in February 2006 and intellectual discussions of the works of "old enemy" Pramoedya Ananta Toer, as evidence of this.[30] The opportunity provided by the fall of Suharto to ex-political prisoners to challenge New Order versions of history and to demand recognition of their suffering has provided further stimulus to anti-communism. It is thus too early to declare the end of anti-communist ideology in Indonesia and indeed other groups such as conservative Islamic organisations have also invested their own independent meanings in the discourse of anti-communism.

The pattern emerging in historical interpretation both within and outside the Indonesian military in the post-Suharto period is one of multiple and competing interpretations of the past, some of which challenge national constructions of the past and others which work within its boundaries.[31] Gerry Van Klinken suggests in the immediate transition period many officials and historians were reluctant to let go of the idea that a nationalist history was essential.[32] Adrian Vickers and I have also argued that a shortcoming of many new versions of the past produced in this period was their paramount search for new villains in Indonesian history, such as former President Suharto or the CIA.[33]

One of the clearest and not unfamiliar messages from this study of military-produced New Order historiography is that when only single versions of the past are allowed, history can become part of an ideological system of authoritarianism. During the New Order period, the military's historical representations of Indonesia's past were a central part of military justification for authoritarian mechanisms, such as a strong military role and repression of so-called "anti-Pancasila" forces. The persistence of the idea that history should be a tool for nation-building has so far prohibited critical examinations by Indonesians of the process by which national history has been constructed by different contributors over time. Such an examination would challenge the very authority upon which national history is reliant. One exception here is the work of Pramoedya Ananta Toer, which provides a potent counter history to New Order historical orthodoxy.[34] In a letter to his daughter written during his imprisonment and published many years later, Pramoedya eloquently highlights the ironies of Indonesia's supposedly great seafaring history as he travels from Jakarta to Buru Island on a crowded boat together with 800 other hungry prisoners in the most inhumane conditions.[35] The emergence of pluralism in interpretations of the past in Indonesia presents a major challenge to the Armed Forces History Centre, which saw itself as the official interpreter of the Indonesian past. If Indonesians decide that a national myth is a necessity for the future, some further questions that need to be addressed are: for whom and why, and who should be the authors and subjects of such histories?

Glossary and Abbreviations

1928 Generation (*Angkatan 28*): refers to persons involved with the Nationalist Movement; 1928 was the year in which the nationalist *Sumpah Pemuda* (Youth Oath) was declared

1945 Generation (*Angkatan 1945*): refers to those who had experienced the 1945–49 independence struggle against the Dutch

1945 values (*Nilai-Nilai* 1945): a term used to refer to the values imputed on the 1945 generation

1945–49 independence struggle (*perjuangan kemerdekaan* 1945–49): the struggle against the Dutch, who attempted to return to the Netherlands Indies after the defeat of the Japanese in World War II

1949 General Attack (*Serangan Umum* 1949): an attack launched by the Indonesian Army against the Dutch Army after the capture of the leaders of the Republic of Indonesia by the Dutch in 1948

1972 Army seminar on the transfer of values: aimed to address a perceived generation gap within the military by restating and transferring the military's core values

30 September Movement (*Gerakan* 30 September [G30S]): refers to the attempted coup itself and also to the group that carried out the coup attempt against the Army leadership on 30 September 1965

40 Hari Kegagalan "G-30-S" 1 Oktober–10 November: The Forty Day Failure of the 30 September Movement 1 October–10 November, the first published version of the 1965 coup attempt

ABRI (*Angkatan Bersenjata Republik Indonesia*): Armed Forces of the Republic of Indonesia

AKABRI (*Akademi ABRI*): Armed Forces Academy

alun-alun: town square

asas tunggal: sole foundation

badan perjuangan: struggle organisation

BAIS (*Badan Intelijen Strategis*): Strategic Intelligence Agency

Bakin (*Badan Koordinasi Intelijen Negara*): National Intelligence Co-ordinating Agency

Bakorstanas (*Badan Koordinasi Pemantapan Stabilitas Nasional*): Co-ordinating Agency for the Maintenance of National Stability

BIA (*Badan Intelijen ABRI*): Armed Forces Intelligence Agency

BKR (*Badan Keamanan Rakyat*): Body for the Protection of People's Security

BPS (*Badan Pendukung Sukarno*): Body to Support Sukarno

bapak: father, or a term of respect for an older man

bersih diri, bersih lingkungan: clean self, clean environment; refers to an anti-communist campaign commencing in the late 1980s

Badan Koordinasi Kemahasiswaan: Body for the Co-ordination of Student Affairs

Cakrabirawa: Sukarno's Presidential Guard

CGMI (*Consentrasi Gerakan Mahasiswa Indonesia*): Indonesian Student Movement Centre, a leftist student movement disbanded after the 1965 coup attempt

Cornell Paper: the paper produced by three researchers of Cornell University, which concluded that the 1965 coup attempt was the result of severe intra-Army conflicts

cungkup: a four-pillared pavilion structure often used to cover royal graves

dapur umum: communal kitchen; a form of temporary kitchen popular during the revolution

Darul Islam: House of Islam; refers to the armed movements in West-

and Central Java, South Sulawesi, South Kalimantan and Aceh aiming to establish an Islamic state in Indonesia

DI/TII Darul Islam /Tentara Islam Indonesia: Darul Islam/Islamic Army of Indonesia

Dewan Harian Nasional Angkatan 1945: National Council for the 1945 Generation

dharma: duty and sacrifice

diorama: a picture model often used in military museums to represent battle scenes

Diponegoro: a famous warrior-prince who led Javanese resistance in the Java War against the Dutch; Diponegoro is also the name of the central Java division of the Army

docu-drama: a dramatised film version of real events; a term used by Indonesian film-makers to describe the film *The Treachery of the 30 September Movement*

dokar: a horse-drawn cart

dwifungsi: the dual military and political functions of the Indonesian Armed Forces

G30S/PKI: a New Order acronym used to refer to the 30 September Movement as a PKI plot

GANEFO: Games of the New Emerging Forces

gapura: archway

garuda: the mythical bird mounted by Hindu god Vishnu; also the emblem of the Republic of Indonesia

Gerwani (*Gerakan Wanita Indonesia*): Indonesian Women's Movement; a women's organisation aligned with the Indonesian Communist Party

Golkar (*Golongan Karya*): organisational groups; denotes the New Order government's electoral vehicle

Guided Democracy: the period from 1959–65, during which Sukarno governed Indonesia under direct presidential rule made possible by his restoration of the 1945 Constitution

Hankamrata (*Pertahanan-Keamanan Rakyat Semesta*): Total People's Defence

Hari Kesaktian Pancasila: Sacred Pancasila Day

HMI (*Himpunan Mahasiswa Indonesia*): Islamic Students' Association

ICMI (*Institut Cendekiawan Muslim Indonesia*): Indonesian Muslim Intellectuals' Organisation

Indonesia Raya: the Indonesian national anthem

Ipoleksosbud (*Ideologi, Politik, Ekonomi, Sosial Budaya*): Ideology, Politics, Economy and Social Cultural Issues

Jalesveva Jayamahe: motto of the Indonesian Navy — "In the sea we are great"

jilbab: the Islamic head covering

KAMI (*Kesatuan Aksi Mahasiswa Indonesia*): Indonesian University Students' Action Front; the organisation that led the 1966 student demonstrations

karya bhakti: civic action or volunteer work

KASI (*Kesatuan Aksi Sarjana Indonesia*): Indonesian Graduates' Action Front

kaum buruh: workers, usually factory workers

kaum tani: farmers

kebaya: a tight-fitted long-sleeve Javanese style woman's top, often made of lace

kejawen: mysticism associated with the Javanese world

kejuangan: the "state of struggle"; a term used exclusively, it seems, by the military to refer to values of those who fought in the revolution

kekeluargaan: familism

kemanunggalan ABRI dan rakyat: the total integration of ABRI and the people

kentongan: a large, elongated traditional bell

keprajuritan: soldiership

Kesaktian Pancasila: Sacred Pancasila

keterbukaan: openness

keterpengaruhan: to be influenced by; a term used in anti-communist campaigns

kewilayahan: areal system

KNIL (*Koninklijk Nederlandsch-Indisch Leger*): Royal Netherlands Indies Army

KNPI (*Komite Nasional Pemuda Indonesia*): National Indonesian Youth Committee

kokutai: a Japanese term denoting "national essence"

komando jihad: Islamic holy war command

Konfrontasi: the armed campaign waged by Indonesia against the British and Malaysia in protest at the proposed formation of the new nation of Malaysia

Koordinasi Integrasi Sinkronisasi: Co-ordination, Integration and Synchronisation

Kopkamtib (*Komando Operasi Pemulihan Keamanan dan Ketertiban*): Operations Command to Restore Order and Security

Kostrad (*Komando Cadangan Strategis Angkatan Darat*): Army Strategic Reserve Command

lasykar: militia

LEKRA (*Lembaga Kebudayaan Rakyat*): Institute of People's Culture; a leftist cultural organisation comprised of artists and writers

Lembinmentra (*Lembaga Pembinaan Mental dan Tradisi ABRI*): ABRI Institute for the Traditions and Mental Upbuilding

Lemhanas (*Lembaga Ketahanan Nasional*): National Resilience Institute

Lembaga Penelitian Sejarah National UNTAG: Institute for National History Research of the Seventeenth of August University

LIPI (*Lembaga Ilmu Pengetahuan Indonesia*): Indonesian Institute of Sciences

Lubang Buaya (Crocodile Hole): the East Jakarta location where the corpses of the seven Army victims of the 1965 coup attempt were found

lurah: village head

Madiun Affair (*Peristiwa Madiun*): a 1948 revolt in which lower echelon PKI leaders, who were aggravated by Hatta's rationalisation of leftist troops from the military, supported the formation of a revolutionary government

Mahmillub (*Sidang Mahkamah Militer Luar Biasa*): Extraordinary Military Tribunal; the military-run trials of leading figures of the 30 September Movement

MPR (*Majelis Permusyawaratan Rakyat*): People's Consultative Assembly

MPRS (*Majelis Permusyawaratan Rakyat Sementara*): Provisional People's Consultative Assembly

makara: mythological beast with "an elephant's trunk, parrot's beak and fish's tail"

Manikebu (*Manifesto Kebudayaan Cultural Manifesto*): a manifesto issued in 1964 by a group of artists protesting against LEKRA's insistence that art follow politics

Manipol (*Manifesto Politik*): Political Manifesto, refers to the political manifesto outlined by Sukarno in his 1959 Independence Day speech.

Menwa (*Regimen Mahasiswa*): university military regiment

merdeka: freedom; a catchcry often associated with the 1945–49 independence struggle

Monas (*Monumen Nasional*): National Monument located in Jakarta, close to the Presidential Palace

musyawarah: deliberation through consensus

Murba: a party formed in 1948, under the leadership of Tan Malaka, and national-communist in orientation

Nahdlatul Ulama (NU): traditionalist Islamic association

Napak Tilas Panglima Besar Sudirman: The Commander for Life General Sudirman Walking Pilgrimage

national history: history produced for the purposes of nation-building

Nasakom (*Nasionalisme Agama Komunisme*): Nationalism, Religion and Communism, a Sukarnoist doctrine formulated in the early years of Guided Democracy to signal the ideal ideological mix of every institution

Nefos: Newly Emerging Forces; a term coined by President Sukarno to refer to "the forces for freedom, the forces for justice, the forces against imperialism, the forces against exploitation, the forces against capitalism"

NKK (*Normalisasi Kehidupan Kampus*): Normalisation of Campus Life, a decree promulgated in 1978 in response to anti-government student protests, which prohibited political activities on campus

Oldefos: Old Established Forces, the conservative and non-revolutionary forces, defined in opposition to Nefos

Orde Baru: New Order; a term used by the Suharto government to distinguish itself from Sukarno's regime; the term also refers to the period 1967–98

official memory: versions of the past that members of a nation have been encouraged to take on as their own memory of events

Opsus (*Operasi Khusus*): Special Operations, an interventionist, domestic intelligence agency dominated by Lieutenant General Ali Murtopo in the early New Order period

Organisasi Tanpa Bentuk: organisation without form, a New Order label for suspected communist organisations

pahlawan revolusi: Heroes of the Revolution; a title President Sukarno bestowed upon the seven Army victims of the 1965 coup attempt

Pancasila: Indonesia's national philosophy consisting of the five principles of belief in one God, humanitarianism, nationalism, democracy, and social justice

P4 *Pedoman Penghayatan dan Pengamalan Pancasila*: Upgrading Course on the Directives for the Realisation of Pancasila, courses aimed at associating the New Order with the Pancasila and creating bonds of loyalty between the people and the regime

patih: Chief Minister of the Regent

PBB (*Partai Bulan Bintang*): Muslim Crescent and Star Party, created in the reform era

PDI (*Partai Demokrasi Indonesia*): Indonesian Democratic Party; created in 1973 after the forced amalgamation of all nationalist parties

PPBN (*Pendidikan Pendahuluan Bela Negara*): Preliminary Education in National Defence

pelaku sejarah: historical actor

pejuang: independence fighter

Pemuda Rakyat: a Communist-aligned youth organisation

pemuda: youth

pendopo: a Javanese architectural structure that appears in royal courts and temples, also an audience hall or a large open structure

penggali: excavator

penumpasan: crushing

perjuangan: armed struggle

Permesta (*Piagam Perjuangan Semesta*): Charter of Total Struggle, a regional rebellion launched in 1957 by local military commanders in Sulawesi and Eastern Indonesia in opposition to the Republican government

pesantren: Islamic boarding school

Pesindo (*Pemuda Sosialis Indonesia*): Indonesian Socialist Youth

PETA (*Pembela Tanah Air*): Defenders of the Fatherland; the Japanese-created military organisation in which many *pejuang* received military training

Perusahaan Film Nasional (PFN): State Film Corporation

PGRS (*Pasukan Gerilya Rakyat Sarawak*): Sarawak People's Guerrilla Army

PKI (*Partai Komunis Indonesia*):   Indonesian Communist Party; founded in 1920 and banned in 1966

PMKRI (*Perhimpunan Mahasiswa Katolik Republik Indonesia*): Indonesian Catholic Students' Association

PPP (*Partai Persatuan Pembangunan*):   United Development Party, created in 1973 after the forced amalgamation of the leading Islamic parties

PRRI (*Pemerintah Revolusioner Republik Indonesia*):   Revolutionary Government of the Republic of Indonesia, a Sumatra-based rebellion against the Republican government launched in 1958 by local military commanders and leading to the establishment of a counter government in Bukitinggi, Sumatra

priyayi: elite Javanese

PSPB (*Pendidikan Sejarah Perjuangan Bangsa*):   History of the National Struggle; a history course introduced by Nugroho Notosusanto while he was Education Minister in 1984

PSI (*Partai Sosialis Indonesia*):   Indonesian Socialist Party

pusaka: heirloom

Pusjarah (*Pusat Sejarah ABRI*):   Armed Forces History Centre

PWI (*Persatuan Wartawan Indonesia*):   National Journalists Association

Raden Panji: a term of address somewhere between *Raden* (prince) and *Raden Mas* (son of nobility)

Rand Corporation: an organisation set up by the American Air Force at the conclusion of World War II to monitor international affairs, especially to monitor communist activity

rakyat: people

rekayasa: a fabricated event

renungan: reflection

Rute Gerilya Panglima Besar Jenderal Sudirman: Guerrilla Route of Sudirman, the Supreme Commander of the Armed Forces

sakti: sacred, supernatural, divine or magical

santri: devout Muslim

Sapta Usaha Tama (SUT):   Seven Endeavours education programme, introduced in 1960

sejarah: history

Sedjarah Pergerakan Nasional: History of the National Movement, a national history project that commenced in 1965 under the direction of the Vice-Secretary General of the National Front

seishin: Japanese term, denoting fighting spirit

Sejarah Nasional Indonesia: National History Textbook

Sedjarah Singkat Perdjuangan Bersendjata Bangsa Indonesia (SSPBBI):   A Concise History of the Armed Struggle of the Indonesian Nation, the first publication of the Armed Forces History Centre in 1964

Seri Bacaan Prajurit: Reading Series for Soldiers

Seskoad (*Sekolah Staf dan Komando Angkatan Darat*):   Army Staff and Command School

semangat: spirit

SOBSI (*Sentral Organisasi Buruh Seluruh Indonesia*):   Central Trade Union Organisation for Indonesian Workers

Supersemar (*Surat Perintah Sebelas Maret*):   Instruction of 11 March 1966; the instruction from President Sukarno to Major General Suharto to take all necessary measures for the restoration of security and order

syariah: Islamic law

tandu: a sedan chair

tapol (*tahanan politik*):   political prisoner

Tarpadnas: anti-communist indoctrination courses

Tentara Pelajar: Student Army, one of many struggle organisations founded during the independence struggle

TNI (*Tentara Nasional Indonesia*):   Indonesian National Army *tokoh*:   a prominent person

Transpolitisasi–Professionalisasi–Institutionalisasi: Trans-politicisation, Professionalisation and Institutionalisation

Treachery of the 30 September Movement (*Pengkhianatan Gerakan 30 September*):   the military-sponsored docu-drama on the 1965 coup attempt

Tritura (*Tri Tuntutan Rakyat*):   Three Demands of the People; the three demands in the 1966 student demonstrations for President Sukarno to lower prices, ban the Communist Party, and purge the Cabinet of Sukarnoists and Communists

Tri Ubaya Cakti: Doctrine of the Indonesian Army

Trisula: the 1968 military operation to crush communist resistance in South Blitar after the 1965 coup attempt

TVRI: Indonesian State Television Network

UUD 1945 (*Undang-undang Dasar 1945*):   1945 Constitution

USDEK: Five central ideas consisting of the 1945 Constitution, Indonesian-style socialism, Guided Democracy, Guided Economy and Indonesian identity

YPKP (*Yayasan Penelitian Korban Pembunuhan 1965–66*):   Institute for the Investigation into Victims of the 1965–66 Killings

Yayasan 18 September: 18 September Foundation, founded by victims of the 1984 Tanjung Priok Affair

wayang: Indonesian puppets, usually shadow puppets

wawasan nusantara: a military term referring to the need for an archipelagic outlook

waspada: vigilance

Notes

Preface

1   Tom Hewitt, "Diorama Presentation", *Journal of the Australian War Memorial*, no. 5 (October 1984): 29.

2   Because of the prohibitive costs, dioramas are rarely replaced or upgraded.

3   Walter Grasskamp, "Reviewing the Museum — or the Complexity of Things", *Nordisk Museologi*, no. 1 (1994): 65–74 from <http://www.umu.se/nordic.museology/NM/941/Grasskamp.html> [14 March 1996].

4   Ed Aspinall, "Opposition and Elite Conflict in the Fall of Soeharto", in Geoff Forrester and R.J. May (eds.), *The Fall of Soeharto* (Singapore: Select Books, 1999), p. 134.

5   *The Jakarta Post*, 1 and 6 October 1996.

Acknowledgements

1   The section on National Monument History Museum in Chapter 1 draws on my publication: "Representing the Indonesian Past: The National Monument History Museum from Guided Democracy to the New Order", *Indonesia*, no. 75 (April 2003): 91–122. Parts of my discussion on Nugroho in Chapters 2 and 5 draw on my publication "Nugroho Notosusanto: The Legacy of a Historian in the Service of an Authoritarian Regime", in Mary S. Zurbuchen (ed.), *Beginning to Remember: The Past in Indonesia's Present* (Singapore: Singapore University Press, 2005; Seattle: University of Washington Press), pp. 209–32. Sections of Chapters 3 and 6 have also been used in my article: "Commemoration of 1 October, *Hari Kesaktian Pancasila*: A Post-Mortem Analysis?", *Asian Studies Review* 26, no. 1 (March 2002): 39–72.

Introduction

1   Djoko Suyanto, "Krisis Nasional Hikmah di Balik Tragedi", in Agus Wirahadikusumah, *Indonesia Baru dan Tantangan TNI: Pemikiran Masa Depan* (Jakarta: Pustaka Sinar Harapan, 1999), pp. 232–42.

2   Hanif Sobari, "Djoko Suyanto Dinilai Lulus Ujian", *Suara Karya*, 2 February 2006.

3   Ibid. and Muninggar Sri Saraswati, "Suyanto Vows to Reform TNI", *Jakarta Post*, 10 February 2006.
4   Soeryo Winoto interview with Djoko Suyanto, "Military Must Have a Presence in the Regions", *The Jakarta Post*, 3 February 2006.
5   M. Fasabeni, "Aliansi Anti Militerisme Tolak Pengesahan RUU TNI", *Tempointeraktif.com*, 18 August 2004.
6   Heather Sutherland, "Professional Paradigms, Politics and Popular Practice: Reflections on 'Indonesian National History'", in Sri Kuhnt-Saptodewo, Volker Grabowsky and Martin Grossheim (eds.), *Nationalism and Cultural Revival in Southeast Asia: Perspectives from the Centre and Region* (Wiesbaden: Harrassowitz Verlag, 1997), p. 83.
7   Ulf Sundhaussen, *The Road to Power Indonesian Military Politics 1945–1967* (Kuala Lumpur: Oxford University Press, 1982), pp. 126–7.
8   Graeme Turner, *National Fictions: Literature and Film and the Construction of Australian Narrative* (Sydney: Allen & Unwin, 1986), p. 123.
9   Pierre Nora, "Between Memory and History: Les Lieux de Mémoire", translated by Marc Roudebush, *Representations*, no. 26 (Spring 1989): 8–11.
10 These works include *Les Cadres Sociaux de la Mémoire* (1925), *La Topographie Légendaire Évangiles en Terre Saint: Etude de Mémoire Collective* (1941) and *La Mémoire Collective* (1950). For an explanation as to how memory became a dominant category of analysis in the social sciences, see Kerwin Lee Klein, "On the Emergence of Memory in Historical Discourse", *Representations*, no. 69 (Winter 2000): 127–50.
11 Natalie Zemon Davis and Randolph Starn, "Introduction", *Representations*, no. 26 (Spring 1989): 2.
12 John R. Gillis, "Introduction: Memory and Identity: the History of a Relationship", in John R. Gillis (ed.), *Commemorations: the Politics of National Identity* (Princeton: Princeton University Press, 1994), p. 5.
13 Patricia Davison, "Museums and the Reshaping of Memory", in Sarah Nuttall and Carli Coetze (eds.), *Negotiating the Past: The Making of Memory in South Africa* (Cape Town: Oxford University Press, 1998), p. 145.
14 Amos Funkenstein, *Perceptions of Jewish History* (Berkeley: University of California Press, 1993), pp. 3, 6.
15 Blackburn and other feminist scholars have made this point. Susan Blackburn, "How Gender is Neglected in Southeast Asia Politics", in Maila Stivens (ed.), *Why Gender Matters in Southeast Asian Politics* (Clayton: Centre of Southeast Asian Studies, Monash University, 1991), p. 28 and Jean Gelman Taylor, "Official Photography, Costume and the Indonesian Revolution", in Jean Gelman Taylor (ed.), *Women Creating Indonesia: The First Fifty Years* (Clayton: Monash Asia Institute, 1997).
16 Cynthia Enloe, *Does Khaki Become You? The Militarisation of Women's Lives* (2nd edition) (London: Pandora, 1988), p. 13.
17 Ibid., p. 7.

18   Ibid., p. 212.
19   Karl G. Heider, *National Culture on Screen* (Honolulu: University of Hawaii Press, 1991); Krishna Sen, "Filming 'History' Under the New Order", in Krishna Sen (eds.), *Histories and Stories; Cinema in New Order Indonesia*, Winter Lecture Series (Clayton: Monash University, 1987), pp. 49–59; Hans Antlöv, "The Revolusi Represented — Contemporary Indonesian Images of 1945", *Indonesia Circle*, no. 68 (1996): 1–21; Klaus Schreiner, "History in the Showcase: Representations of National History in Indonesian Museums", in Sri Kuhnt-Saptodewo, Volker Grabowsky and Martin Grossheim (ed.), *Nationalism and Cultural Revival in Southeast Asia: Perspectives from the Centre and Region* (Wiesbaden: Harrassowitz Verlag, 1997), pp. 99–117.
20   Pusat Sejarah dan Tradisi ABRI, *30 Tahun Pusat Sejarah dan Tradisi ABRI*, Markas Besar Angkatan Bersenjata Republik Indonesia (Jakarta: Pusat Sejarah dan Tradisi ABRI, 1994), p. 100.
21   Major Herkusdianto, Director of the Sudirman Sasmitaloka Museum, interview by author, Yogyakarta, 3 March 1998.
22   Benedict Anderson, "Notes on Contemporary Indonesian Political Communication", *Indonesia*, no. 16 (October 1973): 39–80.
23   Katharine E. McGregor, "Museums and the Transformation from Colonial to Post-colonial Institutions in Indonesia: A Case Study of the National Museum, formerly Museum Batavia", in Fiona Kerlogue (ed.), *Performing Objects: Museums, Material Culture and Performance in Southeast Asia*, Contributions on Critical Museology and Material Culture Series (London: Horniman Museum, 2004), pp. 15–29.
24   See Susan Abeyasekere, *Jakarta A History* (Singapore and Oxford: Oxford University Press, 1987), p. 134.
25   Peter J. Nas, "Jakarta, City Full of Symbols: An Essay on Symbolic Ecology", in Peter J. Nas (ed.), *Urban Symbolism* (Leiden and New York: E.J. Brill, 1993), pp. 13–37.
26   Dinas Sejarah TNI AD, *Seri Monumen Sejarah Angkatan Darat* (Bandung: Dinas Sejarah TNI AD, 1978).
27   There are a few exceptions to this. Barbara Hatley, "Indonesian Ritual, Javanese Drama — Celebrating Tujuhbelasan", *Indonesia*, no. 34 (October 1982): 54–64. Budi Susanto and A Made Tony Supriatma, *ABRI Siasat Kebudayaan 1945–1995* (Yogyakarta: Seri Siasat Kebudayaan, Lembaga Studi Realino, 1995). Klaus H. Schreiner, *Politischer Heldenkult in Indonesien: Tradition und Moderne Praxis (The Cult of Political Heroes in Indonesia: Tradition and Modern Practices)* (Berlin: Reimer, 1995); and Keith Foulcher, "Sumpah Pemuda: The Making and Meaning of a Symbol of Indonesian Nationhood", *Asian Studies Review* 24, no. 3 (September 2000): 377–410.
28   Barry Schwartz, "The Social Context of Commemoration: A Study in Collective Memory", *Social Forces* 61, no. 2 (1982): 377 (my interpolation).

29   Anderson, *Imagined Communities: Reflections on the Origin and Spread of Nationalism*, pp. 117–8.

30   Robert Cribb, "Problems in the Historiography of the Killings in Indonesia", in Robert Cribb (ed.), *The Indonesian Killings of 1965–1966: Studies from Java and Bali*, Monash Papers on Southeast Asia No. 31 (Clayton: Centre of Southeast Asian Studies, Monash University, 1990), p. 13.

31   Schwartz, "The Social Context of Commemoration", p. 376.

32   Ibid., p. 396.

33   Asvi Warman Adam, "Pengendalian Sejarah Sejak Orde Baru", in Henri Chambert-Loir and Hasan Muarif Ambary (eds.), *Panggung Sejarah: Persembahan Kepada Prof. Dr. Denys Lombard* (Jakarta: Yayasan Obor Indonesia, 1999), pp. 567–77.

34   Departemen Pertahanan-Keamanan Pusat Sejarah ABRI, *Pedoman Penyelenggaraan Museum ABRI: Hasil Seminar Permuseuman ABRI 16–19 Juni 1973* (Jakarta: Departemen Pertahanan-Keamanan Pusat Sejarah ABRI, 1973), p. 3.

35   UNESCO, *UNESCO Statistical Yearbook 1974* (Paris: UNESCO, 1975), pp. 61–2.

36   Edhi Soenarso, interview by author at artist's home in Yogyakarta, 8 September 1997.

37   S. Broto, "Monumen Sebuah Ungkapan Penyaksian Sejarah Perjuangan Bangsa", *Senakatha: Media Komunikasi dan Informasi Sejarah*, January 1992, p. 43.

38   Colonel Sus Sri Hartani, interview by author, Jakarta, 27 February 1998.

39   Zainuddin, sound expert for the Armed Forces History Centre museums, interview by author, Yogyakarta, 8 September 1997.

40   Susan M. Pearce, *Museums, Objects and Collections: A Cultural Study* (Leicester and London: Leicester University Press), p. 234.

41   Georgina Born, "Public Museums, Museum Photography, and the Limits of Reflexivity", *Journal of Material Culture* 31 (2) (1998): 223–54. (Image p. 234.)

42   Schreiner, "History in the Showcase", p. 108.

43   Eilean Hooper-Greenhill, *Museums and their Visitors* (London: Routledge, 1994), p. 116.

44   ICOM suggests that all museums should present information in one of two recognised ICOM languages (French and English), in addition to the native language.

45   Susan Douglas, "Notes Toward a History of Media Audiences", *Radical History Review*, no. 54 (Fall 1992): 131.

46   Elaine Heumann Gurian, "Noodling Around with Exhibition Opportunities", in Ivan Karp and Stephen D. Lavine (eds.), *Exhibiting Cultures: The Poetics of Museum Display* (Washington and London: Smithsonian Institute Press, 1991), p. 181.

47   Arjun Appadurai and Carol A. Breckenridge, "Museums are Good to
       Think: Heritage on View in India", in Ivan Karp, Christine Mullen Kreamer
       and Stephen D. Lavine (eds.), *Museums and Communities: The Politics of
       Public Culture* (Washington and London: Smithsonian Institute Press, 1992),
       p. 45.
48   Crouch, *The Army and Politics in Indonesia*, pp. 273–303.
49   See for example, Malcolm Caldwell (ed.), *Ten Years Military Terror in
       Indonesia* (Nottingham: Bertrand Russell Peace Foundation Spokesman
       Books, 1975) and Julie Southwood and Patrick Flanagan, *Indonesia: Law,
       Propaganda and Terror* (London: Zed Press, 1983).
50   Departemen Pertahanan-Keamanan Pusat Sejarah ABRI, *Pedoman Penyeleng-
       garaan Museum ABRI*, p. 17.
51   Ibid., p. 36.
52   The two earliest such museums were the Struggle Museum in Bogor (*Museum
       Perjuangan Bogor*, 1957) and the Struggle Museum in Yogyakarta (*Museum
       Perjuangan Yogyakarta*, 1961). Regional branches of the National 1945
       Veterans' Association sometimes sponsor such museums. Museums in this
       category are the 45 Struggle Building (*Gedung Joang 45*) in Jakarta and the
       45 Struggle Museum (*Museum Juang 45*) in Medan.

Chapter 1

1   See, for example, Laura Hein and Mark Selden, "Learning Citizenship
       from the Past: Textbook Nationalism, Global Context and Social Change",
       Bulletin of Concerned Asian Scholars 30, no. 2 (1998): 3–15.
2   Stuart Macintyre and Anna Clark, *The History Wars* (Carlton: Melbourne
       University Press, 2004).
3   Harold Crouch, *The Army and Politics in Indonesia* (revised edition) (Ithaca:
       Cornell University Press, 1978), pp. 204–5.
4   The Games of the New Emerging Forces were held from 10–12 November
       1963 and all "progressive" world forces were invited. Ewa T. Pauker,
       "Ganefo 1: Sports and Politics in Djakarta", *Asian Survey* 4, no. 4 (April
       1965): 171–85.
5   Sukarno, *Djangan Sekali-kali Meninggalkan Sedjarah!* (Never Leave History)
       (Jakarta: Departemen Penerangan R.I.1966).
6   Mpu Prapañca, *Deśawarnana: (Nāgarakrtāgama)*, translated by Stuart
       Robson (Leiden: KITLV Press, 1995).
7   Heather Sutherland, "Notes on Java's Regent Families: Part 1", *Indonesia*,
       no. 16 (October 1973): 117.
8   Nugroho Notosusanto, *Sejarah dan Hankam* (2nd edition), Markas Besar
       Angkatan Bersenjata, Pusat Sejarah dan Tradisi ABRI, 1987, p. 10.
9   Sukarno, *Indonesia Accuses: Soekarno's Defence Oration in the Political Trial
       of 1930*, edited, translated and annotated by Roger K. Paget (Kuala Lumpur,
       New York: Oxford University Press, 1975), pp. 79–83.

10   George McT. Kahin, "Preface to Soedjatmoko", in Soedjatmoko, *An Approach to Indonesian History: Towards an Open Future, An Address before the Seminar on Indonesian History Gadjah Mada University Jogyakarta, December 14, 1957* (Ithaca: Southeast Asia Program, Cornell University, 1960), p. iv.

11   Geoffrey Barraclough, *Main Trends in History* (New York and London: Holmes and Meier Publishers, 1979), p. 149.

12   Herbert Passim, *Society and Education in Japan* (Tokyo and New York: Kodansha International, 1982), p. 107.

13   Soedjatmoko, *An Approach to Indonesian History*, p. 10.

14   Ruth McVey, "The Enchantment of the Revolution: History and Action in an Indonesian Communist Text", in Anthony Reid and David Marr (eds.), *Perceptions of the Past in Southeast Asia*, Asian Studies Association of Australia (Kuala Lumpur: Heinemann Educational Books (Asia), 1979), pp. 340–58.

15   Klaus H. Schreiner, "The Making of National Heroes: From Guided Democracy to New Order", in Henk Schulte Nordholt (ed.), *Outward Appearances: Dressing State and Society in Indonesia* (Leiden: KITLV Press, 1997), pp. 259–90.

16   H.A.J. Klooster, *Indonesiërs Schrijven hun Geschiedenis: De Ontwikkeling van de Indonesische Geschiedbeoefening in Theorie en Praktijk, 1900–1980* (Dordrecht: Foris Publications, 1985).

17   Barbara Leigh, "Making the Indonesian State: The Role of School Texts", *Review of Indonesian and Malaysian Studies* 25, no. 1 (Winter 1991): 17–43 and David Bourchier, "The 1950s in New Order Ideology and Politics", in D. Bourchier and J. Legge (eds.), *Democracy in Indonesia: 1950s and 1990s*, Monash Papers on Southeast Asia No. 31, Clayton, 1994, pp. 50–62.

18   Manipol-Usdek refers to the Political Manifesto of the Republic, the name given to Sukarno's 1959 Independence Day speech. Manipol was subsequently schematised into five central ideas (to which the term "*Usdek*" referred). These are the 1945 constitution, Indonesian socialism, Guided Democracy, Guided Economy and Indonesian identity. Rex Mortimer, *Indonesian Communism under Sukarno: Ideology and Politics, 1959–1965* (Ithaca: Cornell University Press, 1974), p. 95. See also Chapter 6.

19   Goenawan Mohamad, *The Cultural Manifesto Affair: Literature and Politics in Indonesia in the 1960s, A Signatory's View*, Centre of Southeast Asian Studies, Working Paper No. 45, Monash University, Clayton, 1988, pp. 2–3, 13, see also the Manifesto in the Appendix.

20   Keith Foulcher, *Social Commitment in Literature and the Arts: the Indonesian Institute of People's Culture 1950–1965* (Clayton: Centre of Southeast Asian Studies, Monash University, 1986), pp. 124–7.

21   Taufik Abdullah, *Sejarah Disiplin Ilmu: Rekonstruksi Masa Lalu*, Berita Pikiran, Proyek Pengkajian Dinamika Sosial Budaya dalam Proses Industrialisasi, LIPI, Jakarta, 1994–95, p. 202.

22   Ibid., pp. 202–3.

23   Tim ISAI, *Bayang Bayang PKI* (Jakarta: ISAI, 1996).

24   Oei Tjoe Tat, *Memoar Oei Tjoe Tat, Pembantu Presiden Sukarno* (Jakarta: Hasta Mitra, 1995) and *Merdeka,* 29 September 1995.

25   Redaktur, "Mengapa Dilarang?", *Media Kerja Budaya,* No. 3, February 1996, p. 9.

26   Hermawan Sulistyo, *The Forgotten Years: The Missing History of Indonesia's Mass Slaughters, Jombang-Kediri 1965–1966* (Arizona State University, 1997); and Iwan Gordono Sudjatmiko, *The Destruction of the Indonesian Communist Party: A Comparative Analysis of East Java and Bali,* Ann Arbor Microfilms International, 1992.

27   James T. Siegel, *Solo in the New Order: Language and Hierarchy in an Indonesian City* (Princeton: Princeton University Press, 1986), p. 145.

28   *Kompas,* 1 May 1999.

29   Gerry Van Klinken, "The Battle for History After Suharto: Beyond Sacred Dates, Great Men, and Legal Milestones", *Critical Asian Studies* 33, no. 3: 325.

30   The Murba Party, formed in 1948, under the leadership of Tan Malaka. Herbert Feith, *The Decline of Constitutional Democracy in Indonesia* (Ithaca: Cornell University Press, 1962), pp. 131–2.

31   The following section draws on a more detailed analysis of the Guided Democracy and New Order versions of this museum from my article "Representing the Indonesian Past: The National Monument History Museum from Guided Democracy to the New Order", *Indonesia,* no. 75 (April 2003): 91–122.

32   Panitia Museum Sedjarah Tugu Nasional, *Laporan Lengkap Lukisan Sedjarah Visuil Museum Sedjarah Tugu Nasional: Laporan Umum (Complete Report on Visual Descriptions of the History Scenes for the National Monument History Museum: General Report),* Djakarta, 1964 (hereafter *Laporan Umum*).

33   As per President Suharto's instruction, the scenes reflected the Pancasila and the decisions of the Fourth and Fifth General Sessions of the People's Consultative Assembly and the Special Session of the People's Consultative Assembly. Prajogo, *Tugu Nasional Laporan Pembangunan 1961–1978* (Jakarta: Pelaksana Pembina Tugu Nasional, 1978), p. 148. The museum guidelines were outlined in Presidential Decision No. 6, 1969.

34   Ali Moertopo, *Some Basic Thoughts on the Acceleration and Modernization of Twenty-five Years of Development* (Jakarta: Yayasan Proklamasi, Center for Strategic and International Studies, 1973), p. 35.

35   Benedict Anderson, *Imagined Communities: Reflections on the Origin and Spread of Nationalism* (2nd edition) (London: Verso, 1991), p. 184.

36   Nugroho Notosusanto, *Tercapainya Konsensus Nasional 1966–* (Jakarta: Balai Pustaka, 1985), p. 31.

37   *Laporan Umum,* p. 54.

38   The first publication of this work was Nugroho Notosusanto, *Naskah Proklamasi yang Otentik dan Rumusan Pantjasila yang Otentik (The Authentic Proclamation Document and the Authentic Formulation of the Pancasila)* (Jakarta: Pusat Sejarah dan Tradisi ABRI, 1971).

39   Sukarno's original formulation listed the five principles of nationalism, internationalism (humanitarianism), democracy (consent), social justice, and belief in one God. By 18 August, when the *Pancasila* was incorporated into the preamble to the 1945 Constitution, the principles were listed as belief in one God, humanitarianism, nationalism, democracy, and social justice.

40   See also Jean-Luc Maurer, "A New Order Sketchpad of Indonesian History", in Michael Hitchcock and Victor T. King (eds.), *Images of Malay-Indonesian Identity* (Kuala Lumpur: Oxford University Press, 1997), p. 219.

41   See my article, "Commemoration of 1 October, 'Hari Kesaktian *Pancasila*': A Post Mortem Analysis?", *Asian Studies Review* 36, no. 1 (March 2002): 39–72.

42   John R. Maxwell, "Soe Hok Gie: A Biography of a Young Intellectual" (PhD diss., Australian National University, Canberra, 1997), pp. 137–41.

43   Edward Aspinall, *Student Dissent in Indonesia in the 1980s* (Clayton: Centre of Southeast Asian Studies, Monash University, 1993), p. 7.

44   Badan Pengelola Monumen Nasional, *Monumen Nasional Dengan Museum Sejarah Nasionalnya* (Jakarta: Badan Pengelola Monumen Nasional di Jakarta, 1989), p. 62.

45   Jamie Mackie and Andrew MacIntyre, "Politics", in Hal Hill (ed.), *Indonesia's New Order: The Dynamics of Socio-Economic Transformation* (St. Leonards: Allen & Unwin, 1994), pp. 1–53.

46   R. William Liddle, "Soeharto's Indonesia: Personal Rule and Political Institutions", *Pacific Affairs* 58, no. 1 (Spring 1985): 72. Robert Lowry, *The Armed Forces of Indonesia* (St. Leonards: Allen & Unwin, 1996), p. 71. Donald K. Emmerson, "Understanding the New Order: Bureaucratic Pluralism in Indonesia", *Asian Survey* 23, no. 11 (November 1983): 1224.

47   David Bourchier, "Lineages of Organicist Political Thought in Indonesia" (PhD diss., Department of Politics, Monash University, Clayton, 1996), p. x.

48   Ibid., p. 8.

49   Ibid., pp. 161, 253–7.

50   Ibid., p. 164

51   Teruhisa Horio, *Educational Thought and Ideology in Modern Japan: State Authority and Intellectual Freedom*, edited and translated by Steven Platzer (Tokyo: University of Tokyo Press, 1988), p. 68.

52   Paul Brooker, *The Faces of Fraternalism: Nazi Germany, Fascist Italy, and Imperial Japan* (Oxford [England]: Clarendon Press; New York: Oxford University Press, 1991).

53   Bourchier, "Lineages of Organicist Political Thought in Indonesia", pp. 164, 239.
54   R.K. Hall (ed.), *Kokutai No Hongi: Cardinal Principles of the National Entity of Japan* (Cambridge: Harvard University Press, 1949), pp. 144–5 and Brooker, *The Faces of Fraternalism*, p. 257.
55   Horio, *Educational Thought and Ideology in Modern Japan*, p. 17.
56   Bourchier, "Lineages of Organicist Political Thought in Indonesia", pp. 229–36.
57   Mary Sheridan, "The Emulation of Heroes", *The China Quarterly* 33 (Jan.–Mar.1968).
58   William B. Husband, "Secondary School History Texts in the USSR: Revising the Soviet Past, 1985–1989", *Russian Review* 50(4) (1991): 458–80.
59   Charles D. Cary, "Martial-Patriotic Themes in Soviet School Textbooks", *Soviet Union* 6(1) (1979): 81–98 and Seungsook Moon, "Begetting the Nation: The Androcentric Discourse of National History and Tradition in South Korea", in Elaine H. Kim and Chungmoo Choi (eds.), *Dangerous Women: Gender and Korean Nationalism* (New York and London: Routledge, 1998), pp. 42–4.

Chapter 2

1   This chapter draws extensively on interviews and written communication with Irma Notosusanto, Onghokham, Arief Budiman, Hardoyo, Harold Crouch, Herb Feith, Robert Cribb, Ulf Sundhaussen and Jai Singh Yadava.
2   The term *Raden Panji* is a term of address somewhere between *Raden* (prince) and *Raden Mas* (son of nobility). Nugroho is listed as Raden Panji Noegroho Notosoesanto in Harsja W. Bachtiar, *Siapa Dia?: Perwira Tinggi Tentara Nasional Indonesia Angkatan Darat (TNI AD)* (Jakarta: Djambatan, 1988), p. 227.
3   Dutch East Indies Algemeene Secretarie, *Regeerings Almanak voor Nederlandsch-Indië*, Landsdrukkerij Weltevreden, Batavia, 1918 vol., p. 170; 1920 vol., p. 198.
4   Heather Sutherland, *The Making of a Bureaucratic Elite* (Singapore: Heinemann, 1979), p. 47.
5   Heather Sutherland, "Notes on Java's Regent Families, Part 1", *Indonesia*, no. 16 (October 1973): 132, 135–6.
6   *Star*, 3 December 1955.
7   Sutherland, "Notes on Java's Regent Families", p. 115.
8   Justus Maria van der Kroef, "Dutch Colonial Policy in Indonesia, 1900–1941" (PhD diss., Columbia University, University Microfilms International, Ann Arbor, Michigan, 1953), pp. 230, 234.
9   *Orang Indonesia yang Terkemoeka di Djawa*, Gunseikanbu, 1944 (2604), p. 13.

[10] Budi Darma, "Pengalaman Pribadi dengan Nugroho Notosusanto", *Horison*, no. 9 (1985): 342.

[11] Ibid., p. 343.

[12] Nugroho Notosusanto, "Some Effects of the Guerilla (1948–1949) on Armed Forces and Society", in Nugroho Notosusanto, *The National Struggle and the Armed Forces in Indonesia* (4th edition), Department of Defence and Security Centre for Armed Forces History, Jakarta, 1994, first presented at the Colloquium on the Indonesian Revolution as Social Transformation, Australian National University, 3–5 August 1973, p. 114.

[13] This explanation of the *Tentara Pelajar* is taken from Nugroho Notosusanto, "A New Generation (1952)", in Herbert Feith and Lance Castles (eds.), *Indonesian Political Thinking 1945–1965* (Ithaca and New York: Cornell University Press, 1970), p. 69 and Harsja W. Bachtiar, *Siapa Dia?: Perwira Tinggi Tentara Nasional Indonesia Angkatan Darat (TNI AD)*, 1988, p. 227.

[14] George Kahin, *Nationalism and Revolution in Indonesia* (Ithaca: Cornell University Press, 1952), p. 107.

[15] Nugroho Notosusanto, *Tentara Peta pada Jaman Pendudukan Jepang di Indonesia* (Jakarta: Gramedia, 1979).

[16] Notosusanto, "Some Effects of the Guerilla", p. 121.

[17] Ibid., pp. 121, 123.

[18] Ibid., p. 122.

[19] William Frederick, "The Appearance of Revolution", in Henk Schulte Nordholt (ed.), *Outward Appearances: Dressing State and Society in Indonesia* (Leiden: KITLV Press, 1997), p. 239.

[20] Ikrar Nusa Bhakti, "Prof Dr Nugroho Notosusanto Rektor UI yang Sejarahwan", *Mutiara*, no. 263 (3–16 March 1982): 6.

[21] Ian MacFarling, *The Dual Function of the Indonesian Armed Forces: Military Politics in Indonesia* (Canberra: Australian Defence Studies Centre, 1996), pp. 35–6.

[22] Nugroho Notosusanto, *Generations in Indonesia*, Department of Defence and Security (Jakarta: Centre for Armed Forces History, 1974), pp. 6–10.

[23] This is not the same sources as Indonesia's leading newspaper *Kompas*, which is cited later in this work, but rather an earlier publication of this name.

[24] The article dated 15 May 1952 was a response to the letter of a Dutch writer, Mr Jef Last, who had mistaken Nugroho for another Noegroho, whom he had met before the 1945–49 revolution, with seemingly more moderate views on teaching Dutch language in Indonesian secondary schools. Note this article was reprinted in English as Notosusanto, "A New Generation (1952)", in Feith and Castles (eds.), *Indonesian Political Thinking*, pp. 68–71.

[25] Ibid., pp. 68–9.

[26] Ibid., p. 70.

Notes to pp. 45–50

27   Notosusanto, *Tentara Peta pada Jaman Pendudukan Jepang di Indonesia*, p. 150.

28   Muharyo, "Nugroho Notosusanto Sahabatku dan Adikku", *Femina*, No. 24, 18 June 1985, p. 96.

29   Pamusuk Eneste, *Leksikon Kesusastraan Indonesia Modern* (revised edition) (Jakarta: Djambatan, 1990), p. 127.

30   *Riwayat Hidup Nugroho Notosusanto*, Pusat Dokumentasi Pusat Sejarah ABRI, No. 20, Code AD Nugroho Notosusanto.

31   A. Teeuw, *Modern Indonesian Literature* (The Hague: Martinus Nijhoff, 1967), p. 230.

32   Ibid., pp. 243–4.

33   Irma Nugroho Notosusanto, interview by author, Jakarta, 11 February 1998.

34   Nugroho Notosusanto, "Problems in the Study and Teaching of National History in Indonesia", *Journal of Southeast Asian History* 6, no. 1 (1964): 7.

35   Ibid.

36   Ibid.

37   See also ibid., p. 16, in which Nugroho discussed the subjectivity of knowledge.

38   Irma Nugroho Notosusanto, interview by author, Jakarta, 11 February 1998.

39   Herb Feith, discussion with author, Yogyakarta, 9 September 1997.

40   Irma Nugroho Notosusanto, interview by author, Jakarta, 11 February 1998.

41   Herbert Feith, "President Sukarno, The Army and the Communists: The Triangle Changes Shape", *Asian Survey* 4, no. 8 (August 1964): 969–75.

42   Departemen Pertahanan Keamanan Pusat Sejarah ABRI, *Sepuluh Tahun Pusat Sejarah dan Tradisi ABRI* (Jakarta: Departemen Pertahanan Keamanan Pusat Sejarah ABRI, 1964), p. 1.

43   Peter Christian Hauswedell, "Sukarno: Radical or Conservative? Indonesian Politics 1964–65", *Indonesia*, no. 15 (April 1973): 129.

44   Sukarno, *New Forces Build a New World*, Indonesian Policy Series of the Department of Foreign Affairs, 10th Anniversary 1st Asian African Conference, Executive Command, Jakarta, 1965, p. 16.

45   Herbert Feith, "President Sukarno, the Army and the Communists", p. 975.

46   I was unable to confirm whether this project went ahead because of the sensitivity in Indonesia of materials from this period. It was, of course, in the interests of the staff of the Armed Forces History Centre to suggest this volume had never been completed. However, it is possible that this project was underway, but was disrupted by the coup attempt.

47   *Harian Rakjat*, 23 February 1965.

48   Badan Pelaksana Pendidikan Kader Revolusi Angkatan Dwikora, *Sedjarah Pergerakan Nasional*, Badan Pendidikan/Peladjaran Badan Pelaksana Pendidikan Kader Revolusi Angkatan Dwikora, Djakarta, 1964.

49   Amongst the contributors to this volume were Arudji Kartawinata (Minister and Chairman of the DPR), Ali Sastroamidjojo, S.H. (Vice-Chairman of the People's Consultative Assembly), A. Anwar Sanusi (Vice-Secretary General of the National Front), Soemardjo (Head of the History and Anthropology Institute), Umar Bachsan (a member of the 1945 Generation), Wikana (Central Consultative Council of the 1945 Generation), General A.H. Nasution, Major General Wilujopuspojudo, Major General Sokowati and Sajuti Melik.

50   A. Anwar Sanusi, "Pengantar tentang Perdjuangan Angkatan Pendobrak", in Badan Pelaksana Pendidikan Kader Revolusi Angkatan Dwikora, *Sedjarah Pergerakan Nasional*, p. 2. (Note that the page numbers in this publication recommence for each contribution by a different author.)

51   Ibid.

52   Ruth McVey, "The Enchantment of the Revolution: History and Action in an Indonesian Communist Text", p. 348.

53   Sanusi, "Pengantar", p. 4.

54   Franklin B. Weinstein, *Indonesian Foreign Policy and the Dilemma of Dependence: From Sukarno to Soeharto* (Ithaca and London: Cornell University Press, 1976), pp. 320–5.

55   Sanusi, "Sedjarah Pergerakan Nasional", in Badan Pelaksana Pendidikan Kader Revolusi Angkatan Dwikora, *Sedjarah Pergerakan Nasional*, pp. 4–5.

56   Julie Southwood and Patrick Flanagan, *Indonesia: Law, Propaganda and Terror* (London: Zed Press, 1983), p. 10.

57   Sanusi, "Sedjarah Pergerakan Nasional", p. 10.

58   Sanusi, "Pengantar", p. 5.

59   Hauswedell, "Sukarno: Radical or Conservative?", p. 135.

60   McVey, "The Enchantment of the Revolution", p. 349.

61   Sanusi, "Pengantar", pp. 6–7.

62   Sanusi, "Sedjarah Pergerakan Nasional", p. 3.

63   He does, however, record this affair in the event-by-event chronology. The entry reads: "September 18, 1948 *Petjahnya Peristiwa Madiun* (The Outbreak of the Madiun Affair)". Sanusi, "Sedjarah Pergerakan Nasional", p. 7 (chronology).

64   See Ann Swift, *The Road to Madiun: The Indonesian Communist Uprising of 1948*, Cornell Modern Indonesia Project, Monograph Series No. 69, 1989, pp. 81–7.

65   Ibid., pp. 81–91.

66   Benedict Anderson, "Rewinding Back to the Future: The Left and Constitutional Democracy", in David Bourchier and John Legge (eds.), *Democracy in Indonesia 1950s and 1990s* (Clayton: Centre of Southeast Asian Studies, Monash University, 1994), p. 132.

67   Ibid.

68   Swift, *The Road to Madiun*, pp. 88–9.

69   Anderson, "Rewinding Back to the Future", p. 133.

70   The three publications released in 1964 were D.N. Aidit, *Buku Putih tentang Peristiwa Madiun*, Sekretariat Agitasi Propaganda CC PKI, Jakarta, 1964; D.N. Aidit, *Konfrontasi Peristiwa Madiun 1948, Peristiwa Sumatera 1956*, Pembaruan, Jakarta, 1964; and a reprint of Aidit's 1955 speech in front of the High Court in Jakarta in which he claimed the Madiun Affair involved provocation of the PKI. D.N. Aidit, *Aidit Menggugat Peristiwa Madiun* (*Pembelaan D.N. Aidit dimuka Pengadilan Negeri Djakarta, Tgl 24 Februari 1955*), Jajasan Pembaruan, Jakarta, 1964 (reprinted from 1955 and 1958).

71   C.L.M. Penders and Ulf Sundhaussen, *Abdul Haris Nasution: A Political Biography* (St. Lucia, London and New York: University of Queensland Press, 1985), p. 41.

72   Harold Crouch, *The Army and Politics in Indonesia* (revised edition) (Ithaca: Cornell University Press, 1988), pp. 52–3.

73   Although his eleven-volume history of the independence war, *Sekitar Perang Kemerdekaan Indonesia*, was not published until the 1970s, Klooster notes that Nasution wrote most of this work between 1952 and 1955. H.A.J. Klooster, *Indonësiers Schrijven hun Geschiedenis: De Ontwikkeling van de Indonesische Geschiedbeoefening in Theorie en Praktijk 1900–1980* (Dordrecht: Foris Publications, 1985), p. 133.

74   A.H. Nasution, "Pergerakan Nasional Dalam Segi Kebangkitan Kemiliteran", in Badan Pelaksana Pendidikan Kader Revolusi Angkatan "Dwikora", *Sedjarah Pergerakan Nasional*, p. 7.

75   Ibid., pp. 7–10.

76   Ibid., p. 7.

77   Arnold Brackman, *The Communist Collapse in Indonesia* (New York: Norton, 1969), pp. 118–9.

78   The original name of the Armed Forces History Centre was *Biro Khusus Urusan Sejarah Staf Angkatan Bersenjata* (Special Bureau for History, Armed Forces Staff). In January 1965, it became *Pusat Sejarah Angkatan Bersenjata* (Armed Forces History Centre). The Centre went through a number of other name changes. For the purposes of clarity, the Centre will be referred to hereafter as the Armed Forces History Centre. Departemen Pertahanan-Keamanan Pusat Sejarah ABRI, *Sepuluh Tahun Pusat Sejarah ABRI*, p. 22 and Pusat Sejarah dan Tradisi ABRI, *Seperempat Abad Pusjarah ABRI (5–10–1964 s.d 5–10–1989)*, Markas Besar Angkatan Bersenjata R.I. Pusat Sejarah dan Tradisi ABRI, Jakarta, 1989, pp. 3, 8, 15.

79   The project team consisted of the Army History Centre, History Section of the Department of the Navy, the Assistant Directorate for Information from the Department of the Air Force, the Directorate of Community Relations of the History Division of the Police and the University of Indonesia. The team was led by Major General A.J. Mokoginta.

[80] The University of Indonesia working team included Nugroho Notosusanto, Moela Marboen, M.P.B. Manus and Fuad Salim from the History Department in the Faculty of Letters at the University of Indonesia. Kelompok Kerdja Staf Angkatan Bersendjata, *Sedjarah Singkat Perdjuangan Bersendjata Bangsa Indonesia*, Staf Angkatan Bersendjata, Jakarta, 1964, p. xv.

[81] Ulf Sundhaussen, *The Road to Power: The Indonesian Military in Politics 1945–1967* (Kuala Lumpur: Oxford University Press, 1982), pp. 138–41.

[82] David Ransom, "Ford Country: Building an Elite for Indonesia", in Steve Wiseman (ed.), *The Trojan Horse: A Radical Look at Foreign Aid* (Palo Alto: Ramparts Press, 1975), especially pp. 93–103.

[83] Suwarto was Nugroho's uncle-in-law.

[84] Ulf Sundhaussen, *The Road to Power*, p. 99.

[85] Soe Hok Gie, *Catatan Seorang Demonstran* (Jakarta: LP3ES, 1983), p. 45.

[86] Goenawan Mohamad, discussion with author, Los Angeles, March 2001.

[87] Ruth McVey, "The Enchantment of the Revolution", p. 20.

[88] Peter Christian Hauswedell, "Sukarno: Radical or Conservative?", pp. 112–4, 129–41.

[89] John Maxwell, "Soe Hok Gie: A Biography of a Young Intellectual" (PhD diss., Australian National University, Canberra, 1997), p. 120.

[90] Garis Harsono, *Recollections of an Indonesian Diplomat in the Sukarno Era* (St. Lucia: University of Queensland Press, 1977), p. 300.

[91] *Harian Rakjat*, 19 February 1965 and 21 February 1965.

[92] Arief Budiman, discussion with author, Melbourne, 28 April 1998.

[93] Observations in this paragraph based on discussion with former CGMI member Hardoyo, discussion with author, Jakarta, 17 March 1998.

[94] Notosusanto, *Sejarah dan Hankam* (2nd edition), Markas Besar Angkatan Bersenjata, Pusat Sejarah dan Tradisi ABRI, 1987, p. 34 and Notosusanto, "Some Effects of the Guerilla", pp. 114–6.

[95] Kelompok Kerdja Staf Angkatan Bersendjata, *Sedjarah Singkat.*

[96] Departemen Pertahanan Keamanan Pusat Sejarah ABRI, *Sepuluh Tahun Pusat Sejarah ABRI*, p. 1.

[97] See, for example, D.N. Aidit *Kibarkan Tinggi Pandji Revolusi*, Jajasan Pembaruan, Jakarta, 1964 and *Revolusi Indonesia, Latar Belakang Sedjarah dan Hari Depannja* (materials for Revolutionary Cadres for Dwikora organised by the National Front), Jajasan Pembaruan, Djakarta and Iwa Kusumasumantri S.H., *Sedjarah Revolusi Indonesia: Masa Perdjuangan sebagai Perintis Revolusi* (Djakarta: Grafica, 1963).

[98] Kelompok Kerdja Staf Angkatan Bersendjata, *Sedjarah Singkat*, pp. 76–7.

[99] Howard Federspiel, "The Military and Islam in Sukarno's Indonesia", in Ahmad Ibrahim *et al.* (eds.), *Readings on Islam in Southeast Asia*, Social Issues in Southeast Asia (Singapore: Institute of Southeast Asian Studies, 1985), pp. 153–5.

[100] Hauswedell, "Sukarno: Radical or Conservative?", p. 138. See footnote 112 for publication details. Aidit, the Chairman of the PKI, also delivered

seminars to officers at Seskoad, along with other political leaders. C.H.A. East, "My Days at the Indonesian Army Staff and Command College", *News and Views: Indonesia Special Issue, Indonesia 20 Years' Nationhood 17.8.1945–17.8.1965*, Information Service Indonesia, Deakin (Canberra), 1965.

101 Irma Nugroho Notosusanto, interview by author, Jakarta, 11 February 1998.

102 Pusat Sejarah dan Tradisi ABRI, *30 Tahun Pusat Sejarah dan Tradisi ABRI*, Markas Besar Angkatan Bersendjata R. I Pusat Sejarah dan Tradisi ABRI, Jakarta, 1994, p. xvii.

Chapter 3

1 B.R.O'G. Anderson and Ruth McVey, *A Preliminary Analysis of the October 1, 1965 Coup in Indonesia* (Ithaca: Modern Indonesia Project, Cornell University, 1971).

2 Tim Institut Studi Arus Informasi (ISAI), *Bayang Bayang PKI* (Jakarta: ISAI, 1995).

3 A.C. Dake, *In the Spirit of the Red Banteng: Indonesian Communists between Moscow and Peking* (The Hague: Mouton, 1973).

4 W.F. Wertheim, "Suharto and the Untung Coup — The Missing Link", *Journal of Contemporary Asia*, no. 1 (1970): 50–7.

5 Oei Tjoe Tat personal notes on Sidang Paripurna Kabinet Ke-II at Bogor 6 November 1965. Oei Tjoe Tat, *Memoar Oei Tjoe Tat, Pembantu Presiden Soekarno* (Jakarta: Hasta Mitra, 1995), p. 174.

6 Pusat Sedjarah Angkatan Bersendjata, *40 Hari Kegagalan "G-30-S" 1 Oktober–10 November*, Staf Angkatan Bersendjata Pusat Sejarah Angkatan Bersendjata, Jakarta, 1965.

7 Ibid., p. 3.

8 The Editors, "Initial Statement of Lieutenant Colonel Untung", Selected Documents Related to the 30 September Movement, *Indonesia*, no. 1 (April 1966): 134.

9 Departemen Pertahanan-Keamanan Pusat Sejarah ABRI, *Sepuluh Tahun Pusat Sejarah dan Tradisi ABRI* (Jakarta: Departemen Pertahanan Keamanan Pusat Sejarah ABRI), p. 23.

10 Ibid.

11 John R. Maxwell, "Soe Hok Gie: A Biography of a Young Intellectual" (PhD diss., Australian National University, Canberra, 1997), pp. 133–4.

12 Soe Hok Gie, *Catatan Seorang Demonstran* (Jakarta: LP3ES, 1983), pp. 45, 159, 162.

13 Nugroho Notosusanto, *Tujuhbelas Tahun — Aksi Tritura Hakekat dan Hikmatnya*, Universitas Indonesia, Seri Komunikasi No. 11, Jakarta, 1983, p. 1.

14 Arief Budiman, discussion with author, Melbourne, 28 April 1998.
15 Pusat Sejarah dan Tradisi ABRI, *Seperempat Abad Pusjarah ABRI (5–10–1964 s.d. 5–10–1989)*, Markas Besar Angkatan Bersenjata R. I. Pusat Sejarah dan Tradisi ABRI, Jakarta, 1989, p. 128.
16 The original title of the work was "A Preliminary Analysis of the October 1, 1965 Coup in Indonesia". Because this document became the centre of a controversy, the researchers decided in 1971 to publish the original version with some added revisions and clarifications about this text's production. Benedict Anderson, "Scholarship on Indonesia and Raison D'État: Personal Experience", *Indonesia*, no. 62 (October 1996): 2, 5.
17 In 2001, the United States Government mistakenly released the documents "Foreign Relations of the United States, 1964–68, Volume XXVI: Indonesia; Malaysia, Singapore and the Philippines" which included details of US support for moves against the Communist Party in the wake of the coup attempt. This volume is now available at the US Department of State website: <http://www.state.gov/r/pa/ho/frus/johnsonlb/xxvi>.
18 Rand Corporation, *Selected Rand Abstracts*, Vol. 7, No. 4, January–December 1969 (Santa Monica: Rand Corporation, 1970).
19 Peter Dale Scott, "Exporting Military-Economic Development: America and the Overthrow of Sukarno, 1965–67", in Malcolm Caldwell (ed.), *Ten Years Military Terror in Indonesia* (Nottingham: Bertrand Russell Peace Foundation Spokesman Books, 1975), pp. 209–61. See also David Ransom, "Ford Country: Building an Elite for Indonesia", in Steve Wiseman and Members of the Pacific Studies Center and the North American Congress on Latin America (eds.), *The Trojan Horse: a Radical Look at Foreign Aid* (Palo Alto: Ramparts Press, 1975), pp. 101–2.
20 Many of these were also published in the journal *Asian Survey*. Rand Corporation, *Selected Rand Abstracts*, Vol. 7, No. 4, January–December 1969 (Santa Monica: Rand Corporation, 1970).
21 Scott, "Exporting Military-Economic Development", pp. 232–5, Ransom, "Ford Country", p. 102 and Ulf Sundhaussen, *The Road to Power: Indonesian Military Politics 1945–1967* (Kuala Lumpur: Oxford University Press, 1982), p. 228.
22 Irma Nugroho Notosusanto, interview by author, 11 February 1998.
23 Nugroho Notosusanto and Ismail Saleh, *The Coup Attempt of the "September 30 Movement" in Indonesia* (Jakarta: P.T. Pembimbing Masa, 1968).
24 Anderson, "Scholarship on Indonesia and Raison D'État", p. 3.
25 Notosusanto and Saleh, *The Coup Attempt of the "September 30 Movement"*, pp. 90–106. Several foreign scholars have questioned the reliability of evidence provided in these trials. Harold Crouch, *The Army and Politics in Indonesia* (revised edition) (Ithaca: Cornell University Press, 1988), pp. 103–8.
26 See Notosusanto and Saleh, *The Coup Attempt of the "September 30 Movement"*, pp. 8, 10–1, 19, 92–3, 141–51.

27 Ibid., p. 21.

28 Anderson and McVey, *A Preliminary Analysis of the Coup Attempt*, p. 10.

29 See for example Rex Mortimer, *Indonesian Communism under Sukarno: Ideology and Politics, 1959–1965* (Ithaca, New York: Cornell University Press, 1974), Appendix B (Interpreting the Coup), pp. 418–41.

30 Robert Elson, *Suharto: A Political Biography* (Cambridge: Cambridge University Press, 2001), pp. 110–1.

31 Departemen Pertahanan Keamanan Pusat Sejarah ABRI, *Sepuluh Tahun Pusat Sejarah ABRI*, p. 1.

32 Michael van Langenberg, "Gestapu and State Power in Indonesia", in Robert Cribb (ed.), *The Indonesian Killings of 1965–66: Studies from Java and Bali* (Clayton: Centre of Southeast Asian Studies, Monash University, 1990), p. 48.

33 Pusat Sedjarah Angkatan Bersendjata, *40 Hari Kegagalan*, pp. 34–41, 51.

34 Pipit Rochat, "Am I PKI or Non-PKI?" (translated with an afterword by Benedict Anderson), *Indonesia*, no. 40 (October 1985): 42.

35 Harold Crouch, *The Army and Politics in Indonesia*, p. 138.

36 Rochat, "Am I PKI or Non-PKI?", footnote 14, p. 44.

37 van Langenberg, "Gestapu and State Power in Indonesia", pp. 47–9.

38 An official instruction for the commencement of the monument project was issued from the Army on 2 December 1965 (Surat Perintah 517/12/65), Major General Soedjono, *Monumen Pancasila Cakti*, Jakarta, 1975, pp. 351–3.

39 Dinas Sejarah TNI Angkatan Darat, *Seri Monumen Sejarah TNI Angkatan Darat* (Jakarta: Dinas Sejarah TNI Angkatan Darat, 1977), p. 46.

40 Laurie J. Sears, *Shadows of Empire: Colonial Discourse and Javanese Tales* (Durham and London: Duke University Press, 1996), p. 49.

41 Pusat Sedjarah Angkatan Bersendjata, *40 Hari Kegagalan "G-30-S"*, p. 126.

42 Ibid., p. 44.

43 John Miksic, *Borobudur: Golden Tales of the Buddhas* (Singapore: Periplus Editions, 1997), p. 57.

44 Ibid., p. 51.

45 See Plates 47 and 74 in Bernet A.J. Kempers, *Ancient Indonesian Art* (Amsterdam: C.P.J. van der Peet, 1959).

46 See Dinas Sejarah TNI Angkatan Darat, *Seri Monumen Sejarah TNI*, pp. 40–7.

47 Timothy Lindsey, "Concrete Ideology: Taste, Tradition and the Javanese Past in New Order Public Space", in Virginia Matheson Hooker (ed.), *Culture and Society in New Order Indonesia*, South-east Asian Social Science Monographs (Kuala Lumpur: Oxford University Press, 1995), p. 170.

48 Harris Artamaya (Navy Colonel), "Mengenal lebih Dekat Mengenai Monumen *Pancasila* Sakti dan Museum Pengkhianatan PKI (Komunis)", *Senakatha: Media Komunikasi dan Informasi Sejarah*, no. 23 (1996): 35.

49 Benedict Anderson, *Language and Power: Exploring Political Cultures in Indonesia* (Ithaca and London: Cornell University Press, 1990), pp. 175–6.
50 I am grateful to Helen Pausacker, who has been trained as a *dalang* (*wayang* puppeteer), for many of the observations in the next section on *wayang* imagery.
51 H. Ulbricht, *Wayang Purwa: Shadows of the Past* (Kuala Lumpur: Oxford University Press, 1970), pp. 19–20.
52 Benedict Anderson, *Language and Power*, p. 28.
53 Ibid., p. 7.
54 Ibid.
55 Claire Holt, *Art in Indonesia: Continuities and Change* (Ithaca: Cornell University Press, 1967), p. 142.
56 Crouch, *The Army and Politics in Indonesia*, pp. 86–94.
57 Notosusanto and Saleh, *The Coup Attempt of the "September 30 Movement"*, pp. 141–5.
58 Saskia Wieringa, "The Politicization of Gender Relations in Indonesia" (PhD diss., Amsterdam University, Amsterdam, 1995), p. 301.
59 Holt, *Art in Indonesia*, p. 63.
60 Ibid., p. 98.
61 See Krishna Sen, *Indonesian Cinema: Framing the New Order* (London and New Jersey: Zed Books, 1994), p. 159 and Michael van Langenberg, "The New Order State: Language, Ideology, Hegemony", in Arief Budiman (ed.), *State and Civil Society in Indonesia*, Monash University Centre of Southeast Asian Studies, Monash Papers on Southeast Asia No. 22, Clayton, 1990, pp. 126–7.
62 Jacques LeClerc, "Girls, Girls, Girls and Crocodiles", in Henk Schulte Nordholt (ed.), *Outward Appearances: Dressing State and Society in Indonesia* (Leiden: KITLV Press, 1997), pp. 291–5, 303–5.
63 Holt, *Art in Indonesia*, p. 142.
64 Saskia Wieringa, "Sexual Metaphors in the Change from Soekarno's Old Order to Soeharto's New Order in Indonesia", *Review of Indonesian and Malaysian Affairs* 32, no. 2 (Summer 1998): 150–66.
65 Norma Sullivan, *Masters and Managers: A Study of Gender Relations in Urban Java*, Asian Studies Association of Australia, Women in Asia Publication Series (Clayton: Allen & Unwin, 1994), pp. 129–30.
66 Saskia Wieringa, "The Politicization of Gender Relations in Indonesia", p. 303 and Sailendri, "Shame", *Inside Indonesia* (June 1995): 10–1 and Amnesty International, *Indonesia: An Amnesty International Report* (Jakarta: Amnesty International, 1997), pp. 106–7.
67 van Langenberg, "Gestapu and State Power in Indonesia", p. 52 (my emphasis).
68 Fatima Mernissi, *Beyond the Veil: Male-Female Dynamics in Modern Muslim Society* (revised edition) (Bloomington and Indianapolis: Indiana University Press, 1987), p. 46.

69   Pusat Sejarah dan Tradisi ABRI, *30 Tahun Pusat Sejarah dan Tradisi ABRI*, Markas Besar Angkatan Bersenjata Pusat Sejarah dan Tradisi ABRI, Jakarta, 1994, p. 120.

70   Susan Selden Purdy, "Legitimation of Power and Authority in a Pluralistic State: Pancasila and Civil Religion in Indonesia" (PhD diss., Columbia University, 1984), pp. 230–8, 339–45.

71   Soedjono *Monumen Pancasila Cakti*, p. xiii (my emphasis).

72   John Echols and Hassan Shadily, *Kamus Indonesia Inggris: An Indonesian-English Dictionary* (3rd edition) (Jakarta: Gramedia, 1994), p. 474.

73   This point and others in this paragraph are drawn from Mark R. Woodward, *Islam in Java: Normative Piety and Mysticism in the Sultanate of Yogyakarta* (Tucson: Arizona University Press, 1989), pp. 166–7, 216, 225–33.

74   van Langenberg, "The New Order State", p. 134.

75   Anderson, *Language and Power*, p. 22.

76   See Denys Lombard, *Nusa Jawa: Silang Budaya Bagian 3 Warisan Kerajaan-Kerajaan Konsentris* (Jakarta: Gramedia Pustaka Utama, 1996), p. 146 and *Paguyuban Jawi* (Javanese Speaking Society), Programme for Ketoprak Ken Arok, performed at the Indonesian Consulate Melbourne, 8 June 1996.

77   Rex Mortimer, *Indonesian Communism under Sukarno*, p. 94.

78   See, for example, Muhammadiyah member Sastrosoewignyo's 1965 speech: Soerasto Sastrosoewignyo, "You Have Stabbed Us in the Back Again (1965)", in Herbert Feith and Lance Castles (eds.), *Indonesian Political Thinking 1945–1965* (Ithaca and London: Cornell University Press, 1970), pp. 373–6.

79   "Decree No. 1 on the Establishment of the Indonesian Revolution Council (text as read over Djakarta radio at approximately 2.00 p.m., 1 October 1965), Selected Documents Related to the September 30th Movement and Its Epilogue", *Indonesia*, no. 1 (1966): 136.

80   Ganis Harsono, *Recollections of an Indonesian Diplomat in the Sukarno Era* (St. Lucia: University of Queensland Press, 1977), p. 299.

81   Soeharto, "Sambutan Jenderal Soeharto Selaku Pejabat Presiden pada Peringatan: Hari Lahirnya *Pancasila* in Jakarta 1 June 1967", in Yayasan Pembela Tanah Air, *Garuda Emas Pancasila Sakti* (Jakarta: Yayasan Pembela Tanah Air, 1994), p. 17.

82   Nugroho first published *Naskah Proklamasi yang Otentik* in 1971 and then again in 1978. Nugroho Notosusanto, *Naskah Proklomasi Yang Otentik dan Rumusan Pancasila Yang Otentik* (Jakarta: Balai Pustaka, 1978).

83   Muhamad Yamin, *Naskah-persiapan Undang-Undang Dasar 1945* (Djakarta: Jajasan Prapantja, 1959–60).

84   See Abdoelmanap, *Republik Indonesia Menggugat*, pp. 77–169.

85   Karen Brooks, "The Rustle of Ghosts: Bung Karno in the New Order", *Indonesia*, no. 60 (1995): 71.

86   For a collection of these clippings, consult Yayasan Idayu, *Sekitar Tanggal dan Penggalinya: Guntingan Pers dan Bibliografi Tentang Pancasila* (Jakarta: Yayasan Idayu, 1981).

87   Bambang Bujono, "Perginya Seorang Bapak Asuh", *Tempo*, no. 15 (1985): 14–5.

88   Oey Hong Lee, *The Sukarno Controversies of 1980/81* (Clayton: Monash University Centre of Southeast Asian Studies, 1982), p. 23.

89   *Kompas*, 30 September 1970.

90   John Maxwell, *Soe-Hok Gie*, p. 275.

91   Robert Cribb, "Problems in the Historiography of the Killings in Indonesia", in Robert Cribb (ed.), *The Indonesian Killings of 1965–1966: Studies from Java and Bali* (Clayton: Monash University Centre of Southeast Asian Studies, 1990), p. 15.

92   *The Jakarta Post*, 1 October 1985.

93   Jacques Dumarçay, translated and edited by Michael Smithies, *The Palaces of South East Asia: Architecture and Customs* (Oxford: Oxford University Press, 1991), figure 45, p. 95.

94   Pusat Sejarah dan Tradisi ABRI, *Buku Panduan Monumen Pancasila Sakti Lubang Buaya Jakarta* (Jakarta: Pusat Sejarah dan Tradisi ABRI, 1997), p. 29.

95   Ariel Heryanto, "Where Communism Never Dies: Violence, Trauma and Narration in the Last Cold War Capitalist Authoritarian State", *International Journal of Cultural Studies* 2, no. 2: 156.

96   Ibid., pp. 23–4.

97   The museum is called The Ahmad Yani Revolutionary Hero Site (Sasmita Loka Pahlawan Revolusi Ahmad Yani), which implies that the site is a symbol of the "greatness" of Yani's spirit. For more on this museum see Anderson, *Language and Power*, pp. 182–3.

98   Pusat Sejarah dan Tradisi ABRI, *Buku Panduan Monumen Pancasila Sakti*, p. 26.

99   Ibid., pp. 23–9.

100   Interview with Zainuddin, P.T. Tiga Hasta Kreatif, Yogyakarta, 8 September 1997.

101   Sekretariat Negara Republik Indonesia, *30 Tahun Indonesia Merdeka* (6th edition) (Jakarta: PT Tira Pustaka, 1983), pp. 44–5.

102   Pusat Sejarah dan Tradisi ABRI, *30 Tahun Pusat Sejarah dan Tradisi ABRI*, p. 126.

103   Ibid., pp. 129–30.

104   Krishna Sen and David T. Hill, *Media, Culture and Politics in Indonesia* (Melbourne: Oxford University Press, 2000), p. 147.

105   Amaroso Katamsi (actor who played Suharto in the film), interview by author, Jakarta, 13 February 1997.

106   Saya S. Shiraishi, *Young Heroes: The Indonesian Family in Politics* (Ithaca: Cornell University Press, 1997), p. 77.

107   Sen, *Indonesian Cinema*, p. 159.
108   Notosusanto, *40 Hari Kegagalan "G-30-S"*, pp. 34–41. Notosusanto and
      Saleh, *The Coup Attempt of the "September 30 Movement"* , pp. 28–9.
109   Benedict Anderson, "How Did the Generals Die?", *Indonesia*, no. 43 (1987):
      113.
110   Ibid., pp. 109–34.
111   Pusat Sejarah dan Tradisi ABRI, *30 Tahun Pusat Sejarah dan Tradisi ABRI*,
      p. 130.
112   Poedhyarto Trisaksono, *Sosiodrama Pelengkap PSPB untuk Sekolah Dasar*,
      Jilid 4, untuk kelas VI. Tiga Serangkai, 1985, pp. 40–3.
113   Crouch, *The Army and Politics in Indonesia*, pp. 100–1.
114   Dinas Sejarah TNI Angkatan Darat, *Seri Monumen Sejarah TNI AD*,
      p. 14.
115   Tim ISAI, *Bayang Bayang PKI*, pp. iv–v.
116   See Amnesty International, *Indonesia: An Amnesty International Report*
      (London: Amnesty International Publications, 1997), pp. 102–8. See also
      the story of Christ Rumphium, "In Mother's Care: The Story of a Tapol
      Child", *Prisma*, no. 15 (1997): 12–9 and Wieringa's account of how an
      ex-Gerwani woman was forced to explain to her child that she had not been
      a whore as the child's school teacher had told him. Wieringa, "The
      Politicization of Gender Relations in Indonesia", p. xxxii.
117   *D&R*, 3 October 1998.
118   See Amnesty International, *Power and Impunity: Human Rights under the
      New Order* (London: Amnesty International, 1994), p. 94.
119   For this anecdote, I am grateful to Arief Budiman, discussion with author,
      Melbourne, 28 April 1998.
120   *Kompas*, 1 October 2000.
121   Charlie *apakabar* newslist, 1 October 1996.
122   Adrian Vickers, "Reopening Old Wounds: Bali and the Indonesian Killings
      — A Review Article", *The Journal of Asian Studies* 57, no. 3 (August 1998):
      781.
123   *The Australian*, 25 May 1998. This claim has been challenged by Harold
      Crouch and Bob Elson.
124   Two examples of magazines that made the "coup attempt" a special feature
      were "Suharto Dalam Konspirasi PKI", *Adil (Tabloid Berita Mingguan)*,
      30 September–6 October 1998 and "Kol. Latief: Suharto Tahu Rencana
      G-30-S/PKI", *Tajuk (Berita Investigasi dan Entertainmen)*, No. 15, 17
      September–30 September 1998.
125   *Kompas*, 1 May 1999.
126   *Tajuk*, No. 15, 17 September 1998.
127   Tim Penyusun koordinator Aristides Katoppo *et al.*, *Menyingkap Kabut
      Halim 1965* (Jakarta: Pustaka Sinar Harapan, 1999).
128   *Tajuk*, 17 September 1998 and *D&R*, 3 October 1998.

129   Saskia Eleonora Wieringa, *Penghancuran Gerakan Perempuan di Indonesia* (Jakarta: Arba Budaya and Kalyanamitra, 1999) and Sulami, *Perempuan, Kebenaran dan Penjara* (Jakarta: Cipta Lestari, 1999).

130   *The Jakarta Post,* 23 August 2000.

131   *Kompas,* 1 October 2000.

132   *Suara Merdeka,* 1 October 2000.

133   *The Jakarta Post,* 2 October 2000. For more on the fate of commemoration of 1 October after the fall of Suharto see my article, "Commemoration of 1 October, *Hari Kesaktian Pancasila*: A Post-Mortem Analysis", *Asian Studies Review* 26, no. 1 (March 2002).

134   Amongst other reasons people killed were fear, revenge, a sense of adventure, self-interest and self-defence. Cribb, "Problems in the Historiography of the Indonesian Killings", p. 15.

135   Hamdi Muluk, "Monumen Mempertanyakan Ingatan Kolektif", *Gatra* (7 October 2000): 92.

136   Andreas Huyssen, "Monument and Memory in a Postmodern Age", in James Young (ed.), *The Art of Memory: Holocaust Memorials in History* (Munich: Prestel Verlag, 1994), p. 9.

Chapter 4

1   On these divisions see Harold Crouch, *The Army and Politics in Indonesia* (revised edition) (Ithaca: Cornell University Press, 1988), pp. 79–80, 84–5, 237.

2   The Army first formed a history division, *Pusat Sedjarah Militer Angkatan Darat* (Pussemad) in 1954 in Bandung. The Navy's history division, *Seksi Sedjarah Angkatan Laut dan Maritim* was set up in 1960. The Air Force's history division was known as *Biro Budaya dan Sejarah Angkatan Udara* (Robudja). Nugroho Notosusanto, *Sejarah dan Hankam* (2nd edition), Markas Besar Angkatan Bersendjata, Pusat Sejarah dan Tradisi ABRI, Jakarta, 1987, p. 31.

3   Angkatan Bersendjata, *20 Tahun Indonesia Merdeka* (Jakarta: Departemen Penerangan Republik Indonesia, 1965), Vol. 3, p. 9.

4   Ibid., p. 524.

5   The 1950s insurrections and the campaigns of *Trikora* and *Dwikora* were the training grounds for both forces, given they lacked trained personnel and equipment during the struggle for independence. Robert Lowry, *The Armed Forces of Indonesia* (St. Leonards: Allen & Unwin, 1996), pp. 95–9, 101–6.

6   Krishna Sen, *Indonesian Cinema: Framing the New Order* (London and New Jersey: Zed Books, 1994), p. 82.

7   Pusat Sejarah ABRI, *30 Tahun Angkatan Bersenjata Republik Indonesia,* Departemen Pertahanan Keamanan, Pusat Sejarah ABRI, Jakarta, 1976.

8   Pusat Sejarah ABRI, *40 Tahun Angkatan Bersenjata Republik Indonesia*, Markas Besar Angkatan Bersenjata Republik Indonesia, Pusat Sejarah dan Tradisi ABRI, Jakarta, 1985.

9   Pusat Sejarah ABRI, *50 Tahun ABRI*, Pusat Sejarah dan Tradisi ABRI, Jakarta, 1995.

10   Crouch, *The Army and Politics in Indonesia*, pp. 237–9.

11   K.H. Ramadhan, *Soemitro: Dari Pangdam Mulawarman Sampai Pangkopkamtib* (Jakarta: Pustaka Sinar Harapan, 1994), pp. 174–82.

12   Crouch, *The Army and Politics in Indonesia*, p. 240.

13   Pusat Sejarah dan Tradisi ABRI, *Seperempat Abad Pusjarah ABRI (5–10–1964 s.d 5–10–1989)*, Markas Besar Angkatan Bersenjata R. I. Pusat Sejarah den Tradisi ABRI, Jakarta, 1989, pp. 3–4.

14   Departemen Pertahanan-Keamanan Pusat Sejarah ABRI, *Sepuluh Tahun Pusat Sejarah dan Tradisi ABRI*, Departemen Pertahanan-Keamanan Pusat Sejarah ABRI, Jakarta, 1964, p. 2.

15   These aims were set out in a document called *Naskah Rencana Pembinaan Sejarah Hankam dan ABRI yang integral* in Pusat Sejarah dan Tradisi ABRI, *Seperempat Abad Pusjarah ABRI*, p. 137.

16   Saleh A.D., interview by author, Jakarta, 12 January 1998.

17   Saleh A.D., interview by author, Jakarta, 12 January 1998, Amrin Imran (long-time employee of the Armed Forces History Centre) written responses to interview questions prepared by author, March 1998 and Rochmani Santoso, interview by author, Jakarta, 7 October 1997.

18   Nugroho Notosusanto, *Sedjarah dan Hankam*, p. 128.

19   Pusat Sejarah dan Tradisi ABRI, *Seperempat Abad Pusjarah ABRI*, p. 128.

20   Departemen Pertahanan-Keamanan Pusat Sejarah ABRI, *Sepuluh Tahun Pusat Sejarah*, p. 3.

21   Notosusanto, *Sedjarah dan Hankam*, pp. 35–6.

22   Departemen Pertahanan-Keamanan Pusat Sejarah ABRI, *Sepuluh Tahun Pusat Sejarah ABRI*, p. 6.

23   Ibid., pp. 14–5.

24   Departemen Pertahanan-Keamanan Pusat Sejarah ABRI, *Museum Pusat ABRI Satriamandala: Buku Panduan*, Departemen Pertahanan-Keamanan Pusat Sejarah ABRI, Jakarta, 1972, pp. 12, 16, 18–9.

25   Ibid., pp. 11, 17, 19.

26   Departemen Pertahanan-Keamanan Pusat Sejarah ABRI, *Sepuluh Tahun Pusat Sejarah ABRI*, p. 15.

27   Ibid.

28   From General M. Panggabean's speech at the opening of the museum addressed to President Suharto in ibid., p. 70.

29   This paragraph draws on Seskoad, *Karya Juang Seskoad 1951–1989*, Seskoad, 1989, pp. 97–8.

30   Feith, *The Decline of Constitutional Democracy in Indonesia* (Ithaca: Cornell University Press, 1962), pp. 246–302.

31 David Jenkins, *Suharto and his Generals: Indonesian Military Politics 1975–1983*, Monograph Series No. 64 (New York: Cornell Modern Indonesia Project, 1984), pp. 80–1, citing *Angkatan Bersenjata*, 12 November 1977.

32 *Doktrin Perdjuangan TNI-AD, Tri Ubaya Sakti: Buku Induk Seminar AD Ke-II Tanggal 25 s.d. 21 Agustus 1966 di Graha Wiyata Yudha*, Seskoad, Bandung, 1966, 1st edition, pp. 17–9.

33 Ibid.

34 Anthony Reid, *Indonesian National Revolution 1945–50* (Melbourne: Longman, 1974), pp. 51–3.

35 Roeslan Abdulgani, *Heroes Day and the Indonesian Revolution* (Bandung: Prapantja, 1964), p. 54.

36 Benedict Anderson, "The Pemuda Revolution: Indonesian Politics 1945–1946" (PhD diss., Cornell University, 1967), pp. 202–19. David Wehl, *The Birth of Indonesia* (London: George Allen & Unwin, 1948), p. 67.

37 William H. Frederick, "The Appearance of Revolution", in Henk Schulte Nordholt (ed.), *Outward Appearances: Dressing State and Society in Indonesia* (Leiden: KITLV Press, 1997), p. 203.

38 Reid, *The Indonesian National Revolution 1945–50*, p. 54.

39 John R.W. Smail, *Bandung in the Early Revolution 1945–1946: A Study of the Social History of the Indonesian Revolution*, Cornell Modern Indonesia Programme, Monograph Series (Ithaca and New York: Cornell University Press, 1964) and Benedict Anderson, *Java in a Time of Revolution, Occupation and Resistance 1944–46* (Ithaca: Cornell University Press, 1972). Frederick has however suggested that these new outlooks had earlier origins in the pre-war nationalist movement. William H. Frederick, *Visions and Heat: The Making of the Indonesian Revolution* (Athens: Ohio University Press, 1989), pp. 149–57, 294.

40 Frederick, *Visions and Heat*, pp. 149–57, 294.

41 George Kahin, *Nationalism and Revolution in Indonesia* (Ithaca: Cornell University Press, 1952), p. 107.

42 Anthony Reid, *The Blood of the People: Revolution and the End of Traditional Rule in Northern Sumatra* (Oxford, New York, Melbourne: Oxford University Press, 1979), p. 119.

43 Anthony Reid, "Indonesia: from briefcase to Samurai Sword", in Alfred McCoy (ed.), *Southeast Asia under Japanese Occupation* (New Haven: Yale University Southeast Asia Studies, 1980), p. 23.

44 Reid, *The Indonesian National Revolution, 1945–50*, p. 3.

45 William H. Frederick, "Reflections in a Moving Stream: Indonesian Memories of the War and the Japanese", in Remco Raben (ed.), *Representing the Japanese Occupation in Indonesia: Personal Testimonies and Public Images in Indonesia, Japan and the Netherlands* (Zwolle: Netherlands Institute for War Documentation and Waanders Publishers, 1999), pp. 20–1.

46   Ruth McVey, "The Post Revolutionary Transformation of the Indonesian Army", *Indonesia*, no. 11 (April 1971): 136.

47   Feith, *The Decline of Constitutional Democracy*, p. 516.

48   Adam Malik, *Riwayat Proklamasi Agustus 1945* (5th edition) (Djakarta: Widjaya, 1970).

49   See Willard A. Hanna, *Bung Karno's Indonesia: A Collection of 25 Reports Written for the American Universities Field Staff*, New York, 1960, no. 16, pp. 1–3.

50   Anderson, *Java in a Time of Revolution*, pp. 42–3, 51, 118–9.

51   Feith, *The Decline of Constitutional Democracy*, p. 516.

52   Ibid., p. 132.

53   *Anggaran Dasar dan Anggaran Rumah Tangga: Badan Penggerak Pembina Potensi Angkatan 1945 Keputusan MUBENAS X/1996*, Dewan Harian Nasional Angkatan 1945, Jakarta, 1996, p. 35.

54   Seskoad, *Karya Juang Seskoad 1951–1989*, p. 99.

55   *Dharma Pusaka 45, Hasil Seminar TNI-AD Ke-III Tanggal 13–18 Maret 1972, di Graha Wiyata Yudha, Seskoad Bandung*, Departemen Pertahanan-Keamanan Markas Besar Tentara Nasional Indonesia Angkatan Darat, Bandung, 1972, p. 2.

56   MacFarling notes that General Sudirman had originally espoused the 1945 Constitution as the basis of the politics of the Army. Ian MacFarling, *The Dual Function of the Indonesian Armed Forces: Military Politics in Indonesia*, Australian Defence Studies Centre, Canberra, 1996, p. 104.

57   *Dharma Pusaka 45, Hasil Seminar TNI-AD Ke-III*, p. 43.

58   From Ali Moertopo, *Strategi Pembangunan Nasional*, Centre for Strategic and International Studies, Jakarta, 1981, pp. 243–4 as provided in MacFarling, *The Dual Function of the Indonesian Armed Forces*, pp. 47–8.

59   Departemen Pertahanan-Keamanan Pusat Sejarah ABRI, *Pedoman Penyelenggaraan Museum ABRI, Hasil Seminar Permuseuman ABRI 16–19 Juni 1973*, Departemen Pertahanan-Keamanan Pusat Sejarah ABRI, Jakarta, 1973, pp. 57–8.

60   Michael van Langenberg, "Analysing Indonesia's New Order State: A Keywords Approach", *Review of Indonesian and Malaysian Affairs* 20, no. 2 (Summer 1986): 15.

61   Seskoad, *Karya Juang Seskoad 1951–1989*, p. 99.

62   *Dharma Pusaka 45, Hasil Seminar TNI-AD Ke-III*, pp. 20–1.

63   Ibid., p. 8.

64   Salim Said, *Genesis of Power: General Sudirman and the Indonesian Military in Politics 1945–1949* (Singapore: Institute of Southeast Asian Studies, 1992), p. 54.

65   Kementerian Penerangan Republik Indonesia, *Djenderal Soedirman: Pahlawan Sedjati*, Kementerian Penerangan Republik Indonesia, Yogyakarta, 1950.

66   Sekretariat Negara, *30 Tahun Indonesia Merdeka* (6th edition) (Jakarta: P.T. Tira Pustaka, 1983), p. 171. Vol. 3 (1965–73).

67   Departemen Pertahanan-Keamanan Pusat Sejarah ABRI, *Sepuluh Tahun Pusat Sejarah ABRI*, p. 28.

68   Dinas Sejarah TNI AD, *Seri Monumen Sejarah TNI Angkatan Darat*, Dinas Sejarah Angkatan Darat, Jakarta, 1977, p. 200.

69   Peter J. Nas, "Jakarta, City Full of Symbols: An Essay on Symbolic Ecology", in Peter J. Nas (ed.), *Urban Symbolism* (Leiden: E.J. Brill, 1993), p. 30.

70   Irma Nutosusanto, interview by author, Jakarta, 11 February 1998.

71   Robert Cribb, "Legacies of the Revolution 1945–50", in David Bourchier and John Legge (eds.), *Democracy in Indonesia 1950s and 1990s*, Monash Papers on Southeast Asia, No. 31, Clayton, 1994, p. 76.

72   Reid, *The Indonesian National Revolution 1945–50*, p. 155.

73   Nugroho Notosusanto, "Some Effects of the Guerilla on the Armed Forces and Society in Indonesia 1948–49", in Nugroho Notosusanto, *The National Struggle and the Armed Forces in Indonesia* (4th edition), Department of Defence and Security, Centre for Armed Forces History, Jakarta, 1994 (first presented at the Colloquium on the Indonesian Revolution as Social Transformation, Australian National University, 3–5 August 1973), pp. 7–8.

74   Tjokropranolo, *Panglima Besar TNI Jenderal Soedirman: Pemimpin Pendobrak Terakhir Penjajahan di Indonesia, Kisah Seorang Pengawal*, Marzuki Arifin (ed.) (Jakarta: P.T. Surya Persindo, 1992), p. 134.

75   Reid, *The Indonesian National Revolution 1945–50*, p. 152

76   John D. Legge, *Sukarno: A Political Biography* (London: The Penguin Press, 1972), p. 233.

77   "General Report from Banaran: Developments since December 19, 1948, Composed for the Government of the Republic of Indonesia By the staff of the Armed Forces", in T.B. Simatupang, *Report from Banaran: Experiences During the People's War*, translated by Benedict Anderson and Elizabeth Graves, Modern Indonesia Project, Southeast Asia Program, Cornell University, Ithaca, 1972, p. 128.

78   Reid, *The Indonesian National Revolution 1945–50*, p. 154.

79   C.L.M. Penders (ed.), *Muhammed Hatta: Indonesian Patriot Memoirs* (Singapore: Gunung Agung, 1981).

80   Legge, *Sukarno: A Political Biography*, p. 234.

81   See Tjokropranolo's account of the decision, *Jenderal Soedirman*, p. 135.

82   This paragraph is based on Reid, *The Indonesian National Revolution 1945–50*, pp. 160–1.

83   Alfred W. McCoy, "Same Banana: Hazing and Honor at the Philippine Military Academy", *The Journal of Asian Studies* 54, no. 3 (Aug. 1995): 691–2.

84   Departemen Pertahanan-Keamanan Pusat Sejarah ABRI, *Sepuluh Tahun Pusat Sejarah ABRI*, p. 31.

[85]   Ibid., p. 33.
[86]   *Buku Pedoman Tutor Napak Tilas Rute Gerilya Pangsar Jenderal Sudirman Bagi CAPRATAR, Penggal Yogyakarta-Bedoyo T.A. 1997/1998*, Tanggal 22–25 Oktober 1997, Akademi Militer Departemen Kejuangan, n.p., 1998 (hereafter *Buku Pedoman Tutor*), Appendix *Cuplikan Sudirman*, pp. 1–2.
[87]   "Pidato Radio Panglima Besar Jenderal Soedirman, 1949", in *Buku Pedoman Tutor*.
[88]   "Kata-kata Mutiara Panglima Besar Jenderal Soedirman", in *Cuplikan*, ibid.
[89]   "Amanat Panglima Besar Jenderal Soedirman Kepada Taruna Akademi Militer Yogyakarta Tahun 1948", in *Cuplikan*, ibid.
[90]   Ibid., Lampiran C, pp. 4–7 and *Rencana Latihan Napak Tilas Rute Gerilya Pangsar Jenderal Sudirman T.A. 1997/8*, Tanggal 22–25 Oktober 1997, AKMIL, 1997, pp. 8–12 (hereafter *Rencana Latihan Napak Tilas*).
[91]   The following observations are my own based on the 1997 *napak tilas*.
[92]   Ibid.
[93]   *Rencana Latihan Napak Tilas*, p. 12. This story is confirmed in Captain Supardjo's report in Simatapung, *Report from Banaran*, p. 153.
[94]   Alam Surawijaya (director), *Janur Kuning* 1979.
[95]   *Rencana Latihan Napak Tilas*, p. 12.
[96]   Major Herkusdianto, interview by author, Yogyakarta, October 1997.
[97]   Simatapung, *Report from Banaran*, pp. 153–5.
[98]   Simatapung, *Report from Banaran*, p. 47.
[99]   Reid, *The Indonesian National Revolution 1945–50*, p. 182.
[100] Peter Britton, "Indonesia's Neo-colonial Armed Forces", *Bulletin of Concerned Asian Scholars* 7, no. 3 (July–September 1975): 19.
[101] Ulf Sundhaussen, *The Road to Power: The Indonesian Military in Politics* (Kuala Lumpur: Oxford University Press, 1982), p. 173.
[102] Britton, "Indonesia's Neo-Colonial Armed Forces", p. 17.
[103] *Antara*, 7 November 1963 given in footnote 17, Chapter 7, Lee Kam Hing, *Education and Politics in Indonesia 1945–1965* (Kuala Lumpur: University of Malaya Press, 1995).
[104] Notosusanto, "Some Effects of the Guerilla (1948–1949) on Armed Forces and Society", p. 125.
[105] Ibid.
[106] See Captain Supardjo's account in Simatapung, *Report from Banaran*, pp. 151–9.
[107] *Buku Pedoman Tutor*, Lampiran A, pp. 6–7.

Chapter 5

[1]   As quoted in Departemen Pertahanan-Keamanan Pusat Sejarah ABRI, *Sepuluh Tahun Pusat Sejarah ABRI*, Departemen Pertahanan-Keamanan Pusat Sejarah ABRI, Jakarta, 1974, p. 46 (my emphasis).

2   Seskoad, *Karya Juang Seskoad 1951–1989*, Seskoad, 1989, p. 99.

3   AAGN Ari Dwipayana *et al.*, *Masyarakat Pascamiliter: Tantangan dan Peluang Demiliterisme di Indonesia* (Yogyakarta: Institute for Research and Empowerment [IRE], 2000), pp. 59–60.

4   Suharto, "Beherapa Pokok Pikiran mengenai Pewarisan Nilai-Nilai 45 kepada Generasi Muda Indonesia", *Himpunan Amanat Seminar TNI-Angkatan Darat Ke-III Tahun 1972*, Seskoad, Bandung, 13–18 March 1972, pp. 19, 28.

5   Robert W. Hefner, "Islam, State and Civil Society", *Indonesia*, no. 56 (October 1993): 13.

6   Benedict Anderson, *Language and Power: Exploring Political Cultures in Indonesia* (Ithaca and London: Cornell University Press, 1990), p. 186.

7   Julie Southwood and Patrick Flanagan, *Indonesia; Law, Propaganda and Terror* (London: Zed Press, 1983), p. 176.

8   Edward Aspinall, *Student Dissent in Indonesia in the 1980s* (Clayton: Centre of Southeast Asian Studies, Monash University, 1993), pp. 3–4.

9   Nugroho Notosusanto, *The Transfer of Values in the Indonesian Armed Forces*, Department of Defence and Security, Centre for Armed Forces History, Jakarta, 1994.

10   The following discussion where not otherwise noted draws on material from *Dharma Pusaka 45, Hasil Seminar TNI-AD Ke-III Tanggal 13–18 Maret 1972, Di Graha Wiyata Yuddha, Seskoad Bandung*, Departemen Pertahanan-Keamanan Markas Besar Tentara Nasional Indonesia Angkatan Darat, 1972.

11   *Sejarah Taman Makam Pahlawan Nasional Kalibata*, Dep. Sosial, 1993/94 and Pusat Sejarah dan Tradisi ABRI, *Seperempat Abad Pusjarah ABRI*, Markas Besar Angkatan Bersenjata Republik Indonesia, Pusat Sejarah dan Tradisi ABRI, p. 148.

12   Dinas Sejarah TNI Angkatan Darat, *Seri Monumen Sejarah TNI Angkatan Darat*, Dinas Sejarah TNI Angkatan Darat, Jakarta, 1977.

13   Seskoad, *Himpunan Amanat Seminar TNI-Angkatan Darat Ke-III*, Seskoad, Bandung 13–18 March 1972, pp. 166, 168.

14   A.H. Nasution, *Memenuhi Panggilan Tugas* (Jakarta: Gunung Agung, 1982).

15   Some examples are: Soeharto, *Soeharto: Pikiran, Ucapan, dan Tindakan Saya: Otobiografi seperti dipaparkan kepada G. Dwipayana dan Ramadhan K.H.* (Jakarta: Citra Lamtoro Gung Persada, 1989); Pour, Julius, *Benny Moerdani: Profil Prajurit Negarawan*, Yayasan Kejuangan Panglima Besar Sudirman, 1993; Ramadhan K.H., *Bang Ali: Demi Jakarta (1966–1977): Memoar* (Jakarta: Pustaka Sinar Harapan, 1992); Maraden Panggabean, *Berjuang dan Mengabdi* (Jakarta: Pustaka Sinar Harapan, 1993); Soemitro, *Soemitro, Mantan Pangkopkamtib: Dari Pengdam Mulawarman sampai Pangkomkmatib* (Jakarta: Pustaka Sinar Harapan, 1994).

16   Budi Susanto and Made Toni Supriatma, *ABRI Siasat Kebudayaan 1945–1995*, Seri Siasat Kebudayaan, Lembaga Studi Realino, Yogyakarta, 1995, pp. 121–2, 124.

17   See David Jenkins, *Suharto and His Generals: Indonesian Military Politics 1975–1983*, Monograph Series No. 64 (Ithaca, New York: Cornell University Press, 1984), pp. 162–4.

18   Adam Malik, *In the Service of the Republic* (Singapore: Gunung Agung, 1980), pp. 173–8.

19   Angus McIntyre, *Suharto's Composure: Considering the Biographical and Autobiographical Accounts*, Monash Centre of Southeast Asian Studies, Working Paper No. 97, Monash Asia Institute, Clayton, 1996, p. 11. Translations as provided by McIntyre from Soeharto, *Soeharto: Pikiran, Ucapan dan Tindakan Saya Otobiografi*, p. xii.

20   For example, Sekretariat Negara Republik Indonesia, *30 Tahun Indonesia Merdeka* (6th edition) (Jakarta: PT Tira Pustaka, 1983).

21   *Himpuan Amanat Seminar TNI-Angkatan Darat Ke-III*, pp. 168–9.

22   Salim Said, *Shadows on the Silver Screen: A Social History of Indonesian Film*, translated by Toenggoel P. Siagian with a foreword by Karl Heider, John H. McGlynn and Janet P. Boileau (eds.) (Jakarta: Lontar Foundation, 1991), pp. 59–75.

23   Krishna Sen, *Indonesian Cinema: Framing the New Order* (London: Zed Books, 1994), p. 82.

24   Budi Irawanto, *Konstruksi Relasi Sipil-Militer dalam Sinema Indonesia Kajian Semiotik tentang Representasi Relasi Sipil-Militer dalam Film Enam Jam di Yogya, Janur Kuning dan Serangan Fajar*, Skripsi Fakultas FISIPOL, UGM, 1995, pp. 153–8.

25   This paragraph is based on Departemen Pertahanan-Keamanan Pusat Sejarah ABRI, *Pedoman Penyelenggaraan Museum ABRI, Hasil Seminar Permuseuman ABRI 16–19 Juni 1973*, Departemen Pertahanan-Keamanan Pusat Sejarah dan Tradisi ABRI, Jakarta, 1973, pp. 1, 8, 10.

26   Departemen Pertahanan-Keamanan Pusat Sejarah ABRI, *Sepuluh Tahun Pusat Sejarah ABRI*, p. 16.

27   Ibid., pp. 56, 58.

28   Nugroho Notosusanto, *Sejarah dan Hankam* (2nd edition), Markas Besar Angkatan Bersendjata, Pusat Sejarah dan Tradisi ABRI, 1987, p. 18. He notes that there is equally a need for ABRI museums.

29   Nugroho Notosusanto, Foreword to Departemen Pertahanan-Keamanan Pusat Sejarah ABRI *Museum Pusat ABRI Satriamandala: Buku Panduan*, Departemen Pertahanan-Keamanan Pusat Sejarah ABRI, Jakarta, 1972, p. 6.

30   Departemen Pertahanan-Keamanan Pusat Sejarah dan Tradisi ABRI, *Museum Pusat ABRI Satriamandala*, p. 15.

31   Cynthia Enloe, *Does Khaki Become You? The Militarisation of Women's Lives* (2nd edition) (London: Pandora, 1988), pp. 1–3.

32   It should also be noted that the caption to the initial diorama was also updated to emphasise other roles of women, such as nursing and providing

supplies. Pusat Sejarah dan Tradisi ABRI, *Mengenal Museum ABRI Satriamandala,* Pusat Sejarah dan Tradisi ABRI, Jakarta, 1994, p. 74.

33 Ibid., pp. 73–4.

34 Sekretariat Negara Republik Indonesia, *30 Tahun Indonesia Merdeka,* Vol. 1 (1945–49), p. 27.

35 Susan Blackburn, "Gender Interests and Indonesian Democracy", in David Bourchier and John Legge (eds.), *Democracy in Indonesia: 1950s and 1990s,* Monash Papers on Southeast Asia, Centre of Southeast Asian Studies, Clayton, p. 174.

36 Colonel Sus Sri Hartani of the Air Force served as Deputy Head of the museum between 1972 and 1978.

37 Robert Lowry, *The Armed Forces of Indonesia* (St. Leonards: Allen & Unwin, 1996), p. 128.

38 See, for example, New Order issues of *Jurnal Perempuan,* in which frequent critiques were made of New Order gender ideology.

39 *Dharma Pusaka,* p. 86.

40 Lowry, *The Armed Forces of Indonesia,* p. 202.

41 AAGN Ari Dwipayana *et al., Masyarakat Pascamiliter,* p. 60.

42 Team Pembinaan Penatar dan Bahan Penataran Pegawai Republik Indonesia, *Bahan Penataran Penghayatan dan Pengalaman Pancasila, Undang-Undang Dasar 1945, Garis-Garis Besar Haluan Negara,* Jakarta, 1978, pp. 178–82.

43 Lee Kam Hing, *Education and Politics in Indonesia 1945–1965* (Kuala Lumpur: University of Malaya Press, 1995), pp. 179–81.

44 Departemen Pertahanan-Keamanan Pusat Sejarah ABRI, *Sepuluh Tahun Pusat Sejarah ABRI,* p. 34.

45 Markas Besar Angkatan Bersenjata Republik Indonesia Pusat Sejarah dan Tradisi ABRI, *Seperempat Abad Pusjarah ABRI,* p. 130.

46 Sartono Kartodirdjo, Marwati Djoened Poesponegoro and Nugroho Notosusanto (eds.), *Sejarah Nasional Indonesia,* Departemen Pendidikan dan Kebudayaan, Jakarta, 1976.

47 Onghokham, discussion with author, Jakarta, 29 September, 1997.

48 Herb Feith, discussion with author, Yogyakarta, 9 September 1997.

49 Arief Budiman, discussion with author, Melbourne, 28 April 1998.

50 *Merdeka,* 8 April 1976.

51 *Merdeka,* 8 April 1976.

52 Pusat Sejarah dan Tradisi ABRI, *30 Tahun Pusat Sejarah dan Tradisi ABRI,* Markas Besar Angkatan Bersenjata R.I. Pusat Sejarah dan Tradisi ABRI, Jakarta, 1994, p. 161.

53 Broad Guidelines on State Policy, 1983 as given in David Bourchier, "The 1950s in New Order Ideology and Politics", in D. Bourchier and J.D. Legge (eds.), *Democracy in Indonesia, 1950s and 1990s,* Monash Papers on Southeast Asia, No. 31, Clayton, 1994, pp. 51–2.

54   Kartodirdjo, Poesponegoro and Notosusanto, *Sejarah Nasional Indonesia*, Vol. 6, pp. 17–8.
55   Zainal Arifin, "Memilih Bahan Mengakar PSPB di Sekolah Dasar", *Suara Karya*, 20 March 1984.
56   Bambang Suseno, "Menumbuhkan Motivasi Murid Belajar Sejarah", *Suara Karya*, 3 April 1984.
57   *Suara Karya*, 17 November 1984.
58   "Pendidikian Sejarah Perjuangan Bangsa Penyusun Buku Pelajaran Sejarah Hendaknya Bertolak dari Strategi Pendidikan", *Suara Karya*, 15 November 1984.
59   "PSPB Bukan Pelajaran Sejarah", *Antara*, 21 November 1984.
60   Nugroho Notosusanto, *Tentara Peta pada Jaman Pendudukan Jepang di Indonesia*, Gramedia, Jakarta, 1979, p. 151.
61   "Mendikbud Fuad Hassan: Diperhatikan Usul dan Pendapat mengenai PSPB", *Kompas*, 11 September 1985.
62   "Induk Karangan Soal PSPB", *Merdeka*, 13 September 1985.
63   Fuad Hassan, "Mengimbau Semua Pihak Meredakan Polemik tentang PSPB", *Sinar Harapan*, 19 September 1985.
64   *Sinar Harapan*, 17 September 1985.
65   Hassan, "Mengimbau Semua Pihak".
66   "Akan Ada Perbaikan dan Buku PSPB Baru Sudah Dipersiapkan", *Sinar Harapan*, 11 September 1985.
67   Harsya W. Bachtiar, "Buku Sejarah Nas Tak akan Dimusnahkan", *Pelita*, 17 September 1985.
68   B.M. Diah, "Buku Sejarah Nasional Harus Ditulis Kembali: Tidak Kena Kalau Diperbaiki Saja", *Merdeka*, 17 September 1985.
69   "Demonstran Bakar Buku Sejarah Nasional", *Kompas*, 3 May 2001.
70   Kartodirdjo, Poesponegoro and Notosusanto (eds.), *Sejarah Nasional Indonesia*, Vol. 6, p. 62.
71   Ibid., p. 108.
72   Nugroho Notosusanto, "Regenerasi dan Motivasi", speech for *Hari Pendidikan Nasional* (National Education Day), 2 May 1985, Departemen Pendidikan dan Kebudayaan.
73   Romo Mangunwijaya, "Saya Cuma Pastor Desa tentang Disiplin Pendidikan, Hadiah Nobel dan Korupsi", *Matra*, December 1996, pp. 21, 23.
74   Arief Budiman, discussion with author, Melbourne, 28 April 1998.
75   Soe Hok Gie, *Catatan Seorang Demonstran* (Jakarta: LP3ES, 1983), pp. 187, 191.
76   Ikrar Nusa Bhakti, "Prof Dr Nugroho Notosusanto: Rektor UI yang Sejarahwan", *Mutiara*, no. 263 (3 March 1982): 9.
77   His appointment clearly came from above. Discussion with Onghokham, 29 September 1997.

78 Valina Muchtar, "Selamat Jalan Pak Nug: Saya Selalu Ingat Sosoknya yang Gagah dan Selalu Tersenyum", *Pikiran Rakyat*, 4 June 1985.

79 Bujono, "Perginya Seorang Bapak Asuh", *Tempo*, No. 15, 1985, pp. 14–5.

80 Bisry Hasanuddin, "In Memoriam Prof Dr Nugroho Notosusanto yang Terlalu Cepat", *Singgalang*, 1 July 1985.

81 Herb Feith, discussion with author, Yogyakarta, 9 September 1997.

82 Sartono Kartodirdjo, interview by author, Yogyakarta, September 1997.

83 Robert Cribb, discussion with author, Jakarta, 29 May 1997.

84 Notosusanto, *Sejarah dan Hankam*, p. 33.

85 Based on Arief's recollections of his brother Soe Hok Gie's respect for Nugroho as a lecturer. Arief Budiman, discussion with author, Melbourne, 28 April 1998.

86 Louis Gottschalk, *Understanding History: A Primer of Historical Method* (New York: Knopf, 1950).

87 Notosusanto, *Sejarah dan Hankam*.

88 The former Foreign Minister, Soenario, used the term "quasi-academic" to refer to Nugroho's work on Pancasila. *Merdeka*, 4 August 1981.

89 Christianto Wibisono, "Nugroho Tentang Demokrasi", *Sinar Harapan*, 5 June 1985, p. 6.

90 H.A.J. Klooster, *Indonesiërs Schrijven hun Geschiedenis: De Ontwikkeling van de Indonesische Geschiedbeoefening in Theorie en- Praktijk, 1900–1980* (Dordrecht: Foris Publications, 1985), p. 134.

91 Notosusanto, *Sejarah dan Hankam*.

92 Majalah Tempo, *Apa dan Siapa Sejumlah Orang Indonesia 1985–1986* (Jakarta: Grafiti Pers, 1985), p. 603.

93 Satyagraha Hoerip, "Sebelum Mas Nug Pergi", *Sinar Harapan*, 7 June 1985.

94 Irma Nugroho Notosusanto, interview by author, Jakarta, 11 February 1998.

95 Nugroho Notosusanto, "Saya Ingin Mengungkap Simpati terhadap Manusia Kecil", *Optimis*, 24 December 1981.

96 Nugroho Notosusanto, *The Dual Function of the Indonesian Armed Forces Especially Since 1966*, Department of Defence and Security, Armed Forces History Centre, Djakarta, 1970, footnote 5, p. 9.

97 Ibid.

98 Notosusanto, *The Transfer of Values*, p. 14.

99 Notosusanto, "Saya Ingin Mengungkap Simpati", p. 46.

100 David Reeve, discussion with author, Melbourne, November 2005

101 Letter from Nugroho Notosusanto to Herbert Feith, Rawamangun, 31 July 1969, Monash University Archives, *Herbert Feith Files 1948–1987*.

102 Letter from Herbert Feith to Stephanie Grant of Amnesty International, London 22 March 1970, Monash University Archives, *Herbert Feith Files 1948–1987*.

103 See Soe Hok Gie, *Orang Orang di Persimpangan Kiri Jalan: Kisah Pemberontakan Madiun, September 1948*, Yayasan Bentang Budaya, Yogyakarta 1997. This was published many years after the thesis was accepted.

104 These impressions of Nugroho are based on a compilation of comments from discussions and interviews with people who met and knew him.

105 Arief Budiman, discussion with author, Melbourne, 28 April 1998.

106 Muharyo, "Nugroho Notosusanto Sahabatku dan Adikku", p. 95.

Chapter 6

1 Armed Forces History Centre Staff (Pak Saleh, Pak Amrin Imran, Ibu Rochmani Santoso, Colonel Sus Sri Hartini), interviews by author, Jakarta, October 1997 to January 1998

2 Ikrar Nusa Bhakti, "Prof Dr Nugroho Notosusanto: Rektor UI yang Sejarahwan", *Mutiara*, no. 263 (1982).

3 The Editors, "Current Data on the Indonesian Military Elite", *Indonesia*, no. 37 (April 1984): 150.

4 Harsja W. Bachtiar, *Siapa Dia? Perwira Tinggi Tentara Nasional Indonesia Angkatan Darat (TNI-AD)* (Jakarta: Djambatan, 1988), pp. 206–7.

5 Irma Nugroho Notosusanto, interview by author, Jakarta, 11 February 1998.

6 John Pemberton, *On the Subject of "Java"* (Ithaca: Cornell University Press, 1994), pp. 152–3.

7 "Museum Keprajuritan Nasional", *Senakatha Media Komunikasi dan Informasi Sejarah*, no. 1 (1986): 16–7.

8 Irma Nugroho Notosusanto, interview by author, Jakarta, 11 February 1998.

9 Pusat Sejarah dan Tradisi ABRI, *30 Tahun Pusat Sejarah dan Tradisi ABRI*, p.140.

10 L.B. Moerdani, "Sambutan Panglima Angkatan Bersenjata Republik Indonesia", *Museum Keprajuritan Indonesia: Taman Mini Indonesia*, Markas Besar Angkatan Bersenjata Republik Indonesia, Pusat Sejarah dan Tradisi ABRI, Jakarta, 1987, p. 6.

11 Benedict Anderson, "Current Data on the Indonesian Military Elite", *Indonesia*, no. 45 (1988): 138.

12 Kelompok Kerja Staf Angkatan Bersendjata, *Sedjarah Singkat Perdjuangan Bersendjata Bangsa Indonesia*, Staf Angkatan Bersendjata, Jakarta, 1964, pp. 4–26.

13 *Doktrin Perdjuangan TNI-AD Tri Ubaya Sakti: Buku Induk Seminar AD Ke-II Tanggal 25 s.d. 21 Agustus 1966 di Graha Wiyata Yudha*, Seskoad Bandung, 1966, 1st edition, p. 63.

14 Ulf Sundhaussen, *The Road to Power: Indonesian Military Politics 1945–1967* (Kuala Lumpur: Oxford University Press, 1982), p. 46.

15   Ali Moertopo, *Some Basic Thoughts on the Acceleration and Modernization of 25 Years Development,* Yayasan Proklamasi, Centre for Strategic and International Studies, Jakarta, 1973, pp. 10–1.

16   Ibid., p. 451.

17   Jun Honna, "Military Ideology in Response to Democratic Pressure during the late Soeharto Era: Political and Institutional Contexts", *Indonesia,* no. 67 (April 1999): 79–81.

18   Anderson, "Current Data on the Indonesian Military Elite", p. 136. The original source was Murdani's statement as given in *Tempo,* 4 May 1985.

19   R. William Liddle, "Indonesia 1977: The New Order's Second Parliamentary Election", *Asian Survey* 18, no. 2 (February 1978): 181.

20   Richard Tanter, "Intelligence Agencies and Third World Militarization: A Case Study of Indonesia, 1966–1989" (PhD diss., Department of Politics, Monash University, 1991), p. 319.

21   Al-Chaidar and Amnesti Internasional, *Bencana Kaum Muslimin di Indonesia, 1980–2000* (Yogyakarta: Wihdah Press, 2000), pp. 55–6.

22   Tanter, "Intelligence Agencies and Third World Militarization", p. 320 and Richard Tanter, discussion with author, May 2001.

23   For this and the following points, see C. van Dijk, "Survey of Major Developments in Indonesia in the First Half of 1981: The Plane Hijacking and Suharto's Referendum Proposal", *Review of Indonesian and Malaysian Affairs* 15, no. 2 (1981): 138–9.

24   See Guy Sacerdoti, "The Extremists Exorcised", *Far Eastern Economic Review* (10 April 1981): 29.

25   Ibid., p. 28.

26   Pracoyo Wiryoutomo, "Luka itu Bernama Priok, Lampung ...", *Panji Masyarakat,* no. 9 (17 June 1998): 18.

27   van Dijk, "Survey of Major Developments in Indonesia in the First Half of 1981", p. 138.

28   Julius Pour, *Benny Moerdani: Profil Prajurit Negarawan,* Yayasan Kejuangan Panglima Besar Sudirman, 1993, p. 446.

29   Ibid., pp. 410–48.

30   International Crisis Group Report, *Al Qaeda in Southeast Asia: The Case of the Ngruki Network in Indonesia,* Asia report No. 20, available at <http://www.crisisgroup.org/home/index> [8 August 2002].

31   Richard Tanter, "The Totalitarian Ambition: Intelligence and Security Agencies in Indonesia", in Arief Budiman (ed.), *State and Civil Society in Indonesia,* Monash Papers on Southeast Asia, No. 22, Centre of Southeast Asian Studies, Monash University, Clayton, 1994, p. 235 from Seskoad, *Vademecum: Pengetahuan Pertahanan Keamanan,* Markas Besar TNI-AD, Seskoad, Bandung, 2nd edition, 1982.

32   John Esposito, *The Islamic Threat Myth or Reality?* (New York: Oxford University Press, 1999), p. 119.

33 van Dijk, "Survey of Major Developments in Indonesia in the First Half of 1981", p. 144.
34 Esposito, *The Islamic Threat Myth or Reality?*, p. 172.
35 Kuntowijoyo, *Paradigma Islam: Interpretasi untuk Aksi* (Bandung: Mizan, 1991), pp. 370–1.
36 David Jenkins, *Suharto and his Generals: Indonesian Military Politics 1975–1983*, Cornell Indonesia Project, Ithaca, 1984, p. 158.
37 *Kompas*, 8 April 1980. This speech clearly recycled many of the themes of Ali Murtopo's thinking.
38 Amnesty International, *Indonesia Muslim Prisoners of Conscience* (London: Amnesty International, 1986), p. 5.
39 The original cause of trouble in the Tanjung Priok episode was the entrance of local military officers to the As'Sa'adah prayer house, without removing their shoes and using dirty water to remove a poster advertising an Islamic youth seminar from the prayer-house wall. Several days later, outsiders set fire to the officer's motorcycle. *Indonesia Reports — Politics Supplement — — November 15*, Indonesia Publications, College Park, 1984.
40 "Merekayasa Peristiwa Berdarah", *Panji Masyarakat*, 17 June 1998, pp. 19–20. See also 15 November 1984 in *The Petition of 50 and the Tanjung Priok Incident*, Indonesia Publications, 1987.
41 Ibid., pp. 6–7.
42 Amnesty International, *Indonesia Muslim Prisoners of Conscience*, pp. 4–5, 8–14.
43 Pusat Sejarah dan Tradisi ABRI, *Mengenal Museum ABRI Satrimandala*, Pusat Sejarah dan Tradisi ABRI, Jakarta, 1994, pp. 45–6.
44 Pusat Sejarah dan Tradisi ABRI, *30 Tahun Pusat Sejarah dan Tradisi ABRI*, p. 150.
45 Liddle, "The Islamic Turn in Indonesia", p. 629.
46 "Jenderal yang Dianggap Musuh", *Panji Masyarakat*, 17 June 1998, p. 22.
47 Colonel Murtini (Head of Museum Waspada Purbawisesa), interview by author, Jakarta, September 1997.
48 *Kompas*, 11 November 1987 (my emphasis).
49 Hayun Ugaya, "Museum Waspada Purbawisesa", *Senakatha: Media Komunikasi dan Informasi Sejarah*, no. 12 (1991): 28
50 *Kompas*, 11 November 1987.
51 Pusat Sejarah dan Tradisi ABRI, *Museum Waspada Purbawisesa: Buku Panduan*, Pusat Sejarah dan Tradisi ABRI, Jakarta, 1997, p. 1.
52 Kelompok Kerdja Staf Angkatan Bersendjata, *Sedjarah Singkat Perdjuangan Bersendjata Bangsa Indonesia*, pp. 97–108.
53 Anne Marie The, *Darah Tersimbah di Djawa Barat*, Staf Angkatan Bersendjata, Djakarta, 1965; Yusmar Basri, *GOM VI: Untuk Menumpas DI/TII di Jawa Tengah*, Staf Angkatan Bersendjata, Jakarta, 1965 and Zanaibun Harahap, *Operasi-operasi Militer Menumpas Kahar Muzakar*, Staf Angkatan Bersendjata, Djakarta, 1965.

54   See Dinas Sejarah TNI AD, *Seri Monumen Sejarah TNI AD*, Dinas Sejarah TNI AD, Bandung, 1977, pp. 9, 11.

55   Sedjarah Militer Kodam VI Siliwangi, *Siliwangi dari Masa Kemasa*, Fakta Mahjuma, Jakarta, 1968, pp. 502–57.

56   Pusat Sejarah dan Tradisi ABRI, *Museum Waspada Purbawisesa Buku Panduan*, p. iii.

57   This paragraph draws on ibid., pp. iii–12.

58   Karl G. Heider, *Indonesian Cinema: National Culture on Screen* (Honolulu: University of Hawaii Press, 1991), p. 105.

59   Kelompok Kerdja Staf Angkatan Bersendjata, *Sedjarah Singkat Perdjuangan Bersendjata Bangsa Indonesia*, pp. 94.

60   Karl D. Jackson, *Traditional Authority, Islam and Rebellion: A Study of Indonesian Political Behaviour* (Berkeley: University of California Press, 1980), p. 17.

61   Ibid., p. 13.

62   This and the following paragraph draw on Pusat Sejarah dan Tradisi ABRI, *Museum Waspada Purbawisesa: Buku Panduan*, pp. 32–4.

63   Audrey and George Kahin, *Subversion as Foreign Policy: The Secret Eisenhower and Dulles Debacle in Indonesia* (New York: The New Press, 1995), p. 54.

64   van Djik, "Survey of Major Developments in Indonesia in the First Half of 1981", p. 9.

65   Pusat Sejarah dan Tradisi ABRI, *30 Tahun Pusat Sejarah dan Tradisi ABRI*, p. 152.

66   Pracoyo, "Luka Itu Bernama Priok, Lampung …", pp. 15–6.

67   "Jenderal yang Dianggap Musuh", p. 22.

68   Pusat Studi dan Pengembangan Informasi, *Tanjung Priok Berdarah Tanggung Jawab Siapa? Kumpulan Fakta dan Data*, Gema Insani, Jakarta, 1998, p. 140.

69   See Al-Chaidar Tim Peduli Tapol Amnesti International, *Bencana Kaum Muslimin di Indonesia 1980–2000*, pp. 31–98.

70   Ibid., p. 26.

71   Douglas E. Ramage, *Politics in Indonesia: Democracy, Islam, and the Ideology of Tolerance* (London and New York: Routledge, 1997), p. 148.

72   Questionnaire responses from Head of Museum, Colonel Murtini, September 1997.

73   Colonel Murtini, interview by author, September 1997.

74   Liddle, "The Islamic Turn in Indonesia", p. 625.

75   Colonel Murtini, interview by author, September 1997.

76   Ugaya, "Museum Waspada Purbawisesa", p. 28

77   Ibid., p. 29.

78   Liddle, "The Islamic Turn in Indonesia", p. 614.

79   See Marcus Mietzner, "Godly Men in Green", *Inside Indonesia*, No. 53, January–March 1998, pp. 8–9.

80 "Islam Bukan Ancaman", *Republika*, 30 January 1993, p. 1 as cited in Ramage, *Politics in Indonesia*, p. 132.
81 Honna, "Military Ideology in Response to Democratic Pressure during the Late Suharto Era", pp. 94–5.
82 Feisal Tanjung, *ABRI— Islam Mitra Sejati* (Jakarta: Pustaka Sinar Harapan, 1997).
83 See Kenneth M. George, "Designs on Indonesia's Muslim Communities", *The Journal of Asian Studies* 51, no. 3 (1998): 693–713.
84 *Kompas*, 13 August 2000.
85 See, for example, the publications Al-Chaidar and Amnesti Internasional, *Bencana Kaum Muslimin di Indonesia, 1980–2000* and Al-Chaidar, *Lampung Bersimbah Darah: Menelusuri Kejahatan "Negara Intellijen" Orde Baru dalam Peristiwa Jamaáh Warsidi* (Jakarta: Madani Press, 2000).
86 Frances Raillon, "The New Order and Islam or the Imbroglio of Faith and Politics", *Indonesia*, no. 57 (April 1994): 215. Andi Faisal Bakti, "Rebel Rises from the Dead", *Inside Indonesia* (October 2001): 13–5.
87 Honna, "Military Ideology in Response to Democratic Pressure during the Late Suharto Era", pp. 96–100.
88 Jean van de Kok *et al.*, "1965 and All That: History in the Politics of the New Order", *Review of Indonesian and Malaysian Affairs* 25, no. 2 (Summer 1991): 88.
89 "Bersih Lingkungan, Menyaring Masa Lalu", *Tempo*, 17 September 1988, p. 33 and Vatikiotis, *Indonesian Politics under Suharto*, p. 87.
90 Gordon R. Hein, "Indonesia in 1988: Another Five Years of Suharto", *Asian Survey* 29, no. 2 (February 1989): 121.
91 See Goodfellow, *Api Dalam Sekam*, pp. 23–6.
92 Michael Vatikiotis, *Indonesian Politics under Suharto: Order Development and Pressure for Change* (London and New York: Routledge, 1993), p. 86.
93 Herb Feith Interview, "Suharto under Pressure", *Inside Indonesia*, no. 19 (April 1989): 2.
94 Hein, "Indonesia in 1988", p. 121.
95 Honna, "Military Ideology in Response to Democratic Pressure during the Late Suharto Era", p. 85.
96 Harold Crouch, "An Ageing President, An Ageing Regime", in Harold Crouch and Hal Hill (eds.), *Indonesia Assessment 1992: Political Perspectives on the 1990s*, Proceedings of Indonesia Update Conference August 1992, Department of Social and Political Change, Research School of Pacific Studies, Australian National University, Canberra 1992, p. 54.
97 Max Lane, *Openness, Political Discontent and Succession in Indonesia: Political Developments in Indonesia, 1989–91* (Nathan: Griffith University, 1991), p. 55.
98 *Far Eastern Economic Review*, 6 December 1990.
99 Edward Aspinall, "Students and the Military: Regime Friction and Civilian Dissent in the Late Suharto Period", *Indonesia*, no. 59 (April 1995): 28.

100   Goodfellow, *Api Dalam Sekam*, p. 26.

101   Ibid., pp. 27, 31.

102   *Far Eastern Economic Review*, 2 August 1990.

103   Goodfellow, *Api Dalam Sekam*, p. 13.

104   *Jakarta Post*, 29 September 1990.

105   *Suara Pembaruan*, 29 September 1990.

106   *Angkatan Bersenjata*, 29 September 1990.

107   Ibid.

108   Ibid.

109   *Angkatan Bersenjata*, 29 September 1990.

110   *Suara Pembaruan*, 3 October 1990.

111   *Kompas*, 2 October 1992.

112   "Mengenal Lebih Dekat mengenai Monumen *Pancasila* Sakti Museum Pengkhianatan PKI (Komunis)", *Senakatha: Media Komunikasi dan Informasi*, no. 23 (1996): 35.

113   "Monumen *Pancasila* Sakti dalam Usianya Yang ke-30", *Senakatha: Media Komunikasi dan Informasi*, no. 26 (1997): 32.

114   Pusat Sejarah ABRI, *Bahaya Laten Komunisme di Indonesia*, Pusat Sejarah ABRI, Jakarta, Vols. 1–4B, 1991–95.

115   "Mengenal Lebih Dekat Monumen *Pancasila* Sakti dan Museum Pengkhianatan PKI (Komunis)", pp. 35–6.

116   Pusat Sejarah dan Tradisi ABRI, *Buku Panduan Monumen Pancasila Sakti Lubang Buaya Jakarta*, p. 9.

117   Ann Swift, *The Road to Madiun: The Indonesian Communist Uprising of 1948* (Ithaca: Cornell University Press, 1989), pp. 72–4. See also David Charles Anderson, "The Military Aspects of the Madiun Affair", *Indonesia*, no. 21 (April 1976): 1–64.

118   For commentary on this theory, see Swift, *The Road to Madiun*, pp. 75, 87–8. On the Madiun Affair, see also Soe Hok Gie, *Orang Orang di Persimpangan Kiri Jalan: Kisah Pemberontakan Madiun, September 1948*, Yayasan Bentang Budaya, Yogyakarta 1997.

119   Pusat Sejarah dan Tradisi ABRI, *Buku Panduan Monumen Pancasila Sakti*, p. 11.

120   For a description of the tragedy of this period, see Pramoedya Ananta Toer, "Acceptance" (translated by William H. Frederick) in *Reflections on Rebellion: Stories from the Indonesian Upheavals of 1948 and 1965*, Papers in International Studies Southeast Asia No. 60, Ohio University, Athens, 1983, pp. 7–48.

121   See Rex Mortimer, *The Indonesian Communist Party and Land Reform 1959–1965* (Ithaca: Cornell University Press, 1972), pp. 26–33, 48–55.

122   Pusat Sejarah dan Tradisi ABRI, *Buku Panduan Monumen Pancasila Sakti*, p. 18.

123   "Monumen *Pancasila* Sakti Dalam Usianya Yang Ke-30", p. 26.

124 Pusat Sejarah dan Tradisi ABRI, *Buku Panduan Monumen Pancasila Sakti*, pp. 19–20.

125 Crouch, *The Army and Politics in Indonesia*, pp. 140–1.

126 John R. Maxwell, "Soe Hok Gie: A Biography of a Young Intellectual" (PhD diss., Australian National University, Canberra, 1997), p. 195.

127 Carmel Budiardjo, "Repression and Political Imprisonment", in Malcolm Caldwell (ed.), *Ten Years' Military Terror in Indonesia* (Nottingham: Spokesman Books, 1975), p. 101.

128 Greg Fealy, *The Release of Indonesia's Political Prisoners: Domestic Versus Foreign Policy, 1975–1979*, Centre of Southeast Asian Studies, Working Paper 94, Monash University Centre for Southeast Asian Studies, 1995, p. 56.

129 This paragraph draws on ibid., pp. 7–8, 38.

130 Pusat Sejarah dan Tradisi ABRI, *Bahaya Laten Kommunisme di Indonesia: Penumpasan Pemberontakan PKI dan Sisa-Sisanya*; and Sekretariat Negara, *30 Tahun Indonesia Merdeka* (3rd edition) (Jakarta: P.T. Tira Pustaka, 1983), Vol. 3 (1965–73), pp. 82–3.

131 Justus M. van der Kroef, "Indonesian Communism since the 1965 Coup", *Pacific Affairs* 43, no. 1 (Spring 1970): 49–50.

132 Brian May, *The Indonesian Tragedy* (London and Boston: Routledge and K. Paul, 1978), p. 203.

133 Maskun Iskandar and Jopie Lasut (translated by Robert Cribb), "The Purwodadi Affair: Two Accounts", in Robert Cribb (ed.), *The Indonesian Killings of 1965–1966: Studies from Java and Bali*, Monash Papers on Southeast Asia No. 21 (Clayton: Centre of Southeast Asian Studies, Monash University, 1990), p. 195.

134 van der Kroef, "Indonesian Communism since the 1965 Coup", pp. 52–3; and Maskun Iskandar and Jopie Lasut, "The Purwodadi Affair", p. 198.

135 van der Kroef, "Indonesian Communism since the 1965 Coup", p. 35.

136 Ken Young, "Local and National Influences in the Violence of 1965", in Cribb (ed.), *The Indonesian Killings of 1965–1900: Studies from Java and Bali*, pp. 81–2.

137 Cribb does however suggest that the passivity of victims may have been exaggerated in accounts. Robert Cribb, "Introduction", in Cribb (ed.), *The Indonesian Killings of 1965–1900: Studies from Java and Bali*, pp. 34–5.

138 Pusat Sejarah dan Tradisi ABRI, *Buku Panduan Monumen Pancasila Sakti Lubang Buaya Jakarta*, p. 21 (my emphasis).

139 Oei Tjoe Tat, *Memoar Oei Tjoe Tat, Pembantu Presiden Soekarno* (Jakarta: Hasta Mitra, 1995), p. 191.

140 For a description of some of the killing campaigns, see Julie Southwood and Patrick Flanagan, *Indonesia: Law, Propaganda and Terror* (London: Zed Press, 1983), pp. 75–9. Brian May, *The Indonesian Tragedy*, pp. 122–3, Young, "Local and National Influences in the Violence of 1965", p. 80,

Pipit Rochijat, "Am I PKI or non-PKI?" (translated with an afterword by Benedict Anderson), *Indonesia*, no. 40 (October 1985): 37–56 and Anonymous, "Additional Data on Counter-Revolutionary Cruelty in Indonesia, Especially in East Java", in Cribb (ed.), *The Indonesian Killings of 1965–1900: Studies from Java and Bali*, pp. 169–76.

141 Pusat Sejarah dan Tradisi ABRI, *Bahaya Laten Komunisme di Indonesia: Penumpasan Pemberontakan PKI dan Sisa-Sisanya*, Jilid IVB, pp. 215–8.

142 Ibid., p. 215.

143 *Tempo*, 18 June 1988.

144 For more on this phenomenon, see Anton Lucas, "Land Disputes, the Bureaucracy, and Local Resistance in Indonesia", in Jim Schiller and Barbara Martin-Schiller (eds.), *Imagining Indonesia: Cultural Politics and Political Culture*, Ohio University for International Studies, Monographs in International Studies, Southeast Asian Series, Number 97, Athens, 1997, pp. 229–60.

145 "Aksi Mahasiswa: Dengan Isu Local Membentuk Opini Nasional", *Tempo* (22 April 1989): 72–3.

146 Adam Schwarz, *A Nation in Waiting: Indonesia's Search for Stability* (2nd edition) (St. Leonards: Allen & Unwin, 1999), p. 303.

147 Aspinall, "Students and the Military", pp. 35–9.

148 "Museum Waspada Purbawisesa", *Senakatha: Media Komunikasi dan Informasi Sejarah*, no. 12 (1991): 30.

149 See, for example, her discussion of the film *Max Havelaar* in Krishna Sen, "Filming 'History' under the New Order", in Krishna Sen *et al.* (eds.), *Histories and Stories; Cinema in New Order Indonesia*, Winter Lecture Series (Clayton: Monash University, 1987), pp. 54, 56.

150 Ariel Heryanto, "Ethnic Identities and Erasure: Chinese Indonesians in Public Culture", in Joel S. Kahn (ed.), *Southeast Asian Identities: Culture and the Politics of Representation in Indonesia, Malaysia, Singapore and Thailand* (Singapore: Institute of Southeast Asian Studies; New York: St. Martin's Press, 1998), p. 97.

151 "Mengenal Lebih Dekat Monumen *Pancasila* Sakti dan Museum Pengkhianatan PKI (Komunis)", *Senakatha: Media Komunikasi dan Informasi Sejarah*, no. 23 (1996): 36.

152 Geoff Simons, *Indonesia: The Long Oppression* (New York: St. Martin's Press, 2000), p. 61.

153 Honna, "Military Ideology in Response to Democratic Pressure during the late Suharto Era", pp. 79–86.

154 William Liddle and Rizal Mallarangeng, "Indonesia in 1996: Pressures from Above and Below", *Asian Survey* 17, no. 2 (1997): 168, 170.

155 Krishna Sen and David Hill, *Media, Culture and Politics in Indonesia* (Melbourne: Oxford University Press, 2000), pp. 149–50.

156 "Jangan Ada Komunis di Antara Kita", *Tajuk*, no. 15 (1–17 September 1998): 24–8.

157 *Suara Pembaruan*, 22 May 2000.
158 Stanley, "Opening that Dark Page", *Inside Indonesia*, July–September 2000.
159 Sulami, *Perempuan-Kebenaran dan Penjara* (Jakarta: Cipta Lestari, 1999).
160 "Trisula dan Kemiskinan yang Tersisa", *Gatra*, 9 October 1999, p. 89.
161 *Jakarta Post*, 8 April 2000.
162 *Duta*, 29 March 2000.
163 Ibid.
164 *Jakarta Post*, 15 April 2000.
165 Stanley, "Opening that Dark Page".
166 Umar Said, "Pemakaman-Kembali Kerangka Korban 65 Digagalkan", *Soeara Kita*, no. 14 (April 2001): 4–7.
167 *Tempo*, 16 April 2000, p. 23.
168 *Bernas*, 21 November 2000.
169 Katharine E. McGregor, "Commemoration of 1 October, *Hari Kesaktian Pancasila*: A Post Mortem Analysis?" *Asian Studies Review* 26, no. 1 (March 2002).
170 Honna, "Military Ideology in Response to Democratic Pressure during the Late Suharto Era", p. 95.

Afterword

1 For more on these organisations or people, see International Crisis Group Briefing Paper, *Al-Qaeda in Southeast Asia: the Case of the "Ngukri Network" in Indonesia*, Jakarta/Brussels, 8 August 2002.
2 These figures are calculated on the basis of visitor figures provided in Pusat Sejarah dan Tradisi ABRI, *30 Tahun Pusat Sejarah dan Tradisi ABRI*, pp. 116, 135, 149, 157.
3 Edward Aspinall, *Student Dissent in Indonesia in the 1980s* (Clayton: Centre of Southeast Asian Studies, Monash University, 1993), pp. 4–9, 30–2.
4 David Jenkins, *Suharto and his Generals: Indonesian Military Politics 1975–1983*, Monograph Series no. 64 (Ithaca, New York: Cornell Modern Indonesia Project, Cornell University, 1984), p. 76.
5 *Hasil Seminar Dharma Pusaka 45 PASISI SUSREG ke-VI SESKO ABRI Bagian Darat, Laut, Udara dan Kepolisian 1979–1980*, 31 Maret 1980–6 April 1980 di Bandung, Departemen Pertahanan-Keamanan, pp. 26–7, 64–6.
6 Lynn Hunt, "History as Gesture: or the Scandal of History", in Jonathan Arac and Barbara Johnson (eds.), *Consequences of Theory* (Baltimore: John Hopkins University Press, 1991), pp. 102–3.
7 Kees Koonings and Dirk Kruijt, "Military Politics and the Mission of Nation Building", in Kees Koonings and Dirk Kruijt (eds.), *Political Armies: The Military and Nation Building in the Age of Democracy* (London and New York: Zed Books, 2002), p. 19.

8   Mary P. Callahan, "Cracks in the Edifice? Military Society Relations in Burma since 1988", in Mortern B. Pederson, Emily Rudland and Ronald J. May, *Burma Myanmar: Strong Regime Weak State* (Adelaide: Crawford House Publishing, 2000), p. 33.

9   Martin Smith, "Army Politics as a Historical Legacy", in Koonings and Kruijt (eds.), *Political Armies: The Military and Nation Building in the Age of Democracy*, pp. 278–82.

10   Callahan, "Cracks in the Edifice?", p. 33.

11   Celso Castro, "The Military and Politics in Brazil, 1964–2000", in Koonings and Kruijt (eds.), *Political Armies: The Military and Nation Building in the Age of Democracy*, pp. 106–7.

12   Ibid., p. 107.

13   Morris Janowitz, *The Military in the Political Development of New Nations: An Essay in Comparative Analysis* (Chicago: University of Chicago Press, 1964), pp. 63–4.

14   Ariel Heryanto and Sumit K. Mandal, *Challenging Authoritarianism in Southeast Asia: Comparing Indonesia and Malaysia* (London and New York: Routledge Curzon, 2003), p. 2.

15   See Adrian Vickers and Katharine McGregor, "Public Debates about History: Comparative Notes from Indonesia", *History Australia* 2, no. 2 (June): 44.1–44.13.

16   In the 20 August 1998 edition of *Tajuk*, for example, each of these cases of human rights abuses was discussed.

17   *Gatra*, 10 October 1998.

18   The Editors, "Changes in Civil-Military Relations since the Fall of Suharto", *Indonesia*, no. 70 (October 2000): 133, 138.

19   *Undang-Undang Republik Indonesia: Tentara Nasional Indonesia, Pertahanan Negara, Kepolisian Negara Republik Indonesia* (Jakarta: BP Panca Usaha, 2005), p. 50. The following discussion of this law draws on this publication.

20   Riwanto Tirtosudarmo, "The Mystification of the Unitary State of Indonesia", *Jakarta Post*, 14 October 2005.

21   See Jemma Purdey, *Anti-Chinese Violence in Indonesia 1996–1999*, Asian Studies Association of Australia Southeast Asia Publications Series (Singapore: Singapore University Press, 2006); George Aditjondro, "Guns, Pamphlets and Handie-talkies: How the Military Exploited Ethno-religious Tensions in Maluku to Preserve their Political and Economic Privileges", in Ingrid Wessel and Georgia Winhofer, *Violence in Indonesia* (Hamburg: Abera Verlag, 2001), pp. 100–28.

22   Nico Schulte Nordholt, "The Janus Face of the Indonesian Armed Forces", in Kees Koonings and Dirk Kruijt (eds.), *Political Armies: The Military and Nation Building in the Age of Democracy*, p. 156.

23   Tim Imparsial, *Menuju TNI Profesional [Perjalanan Advokasi RUU TNI]*, Imparsial, Koalisi Keselamatan Masyarakat Sipil, Lembaga Studi Pers dan Pembangunan, Jakarta, 2005, pp. 18–9.

24 M. Fasabeni, "Aliansi Anti Militerisme Tolak Pengesahan RUU TNI", *Tempointeraktif.com*, 18 August 2004. Muhammad Fasabeni, "Koalisi Perempuan Tolak RUU TNI", *Tempointeraktif.com*, 24 August 2004. Muhammad Fasabeni, "Barisan Oposisi Rakyat Tolak RUU TNI", *Tempointeraktif.com*, 2 September 2004. Sunariah, "UU TNI Sogokan Politik kepada TNI", *Tempointeraktif.com*, 29 September 2004. Bibin Bintariadi, "Mahasiswa Malang Tuntut Jabatan Panglima TNI Dihapus", *Tempointeraktif.com*, 30 September 2004.

25 Tim Imparsial, *Menuju TNI Profesional.*

26 Ibid., p. 17.

27 Kees Koonings and Dirk Kruijt, "Military Politics and the Mission of Nation Building", in Koonings and Kruijt (eds.), *Political Armies: The Military and Nation Building in the Age of Democracy*, p. 31.

28 Tiarma Siboro, "Of Officer Camaraderie, Friendships", *The Jakarta Post*, 3 February 2006.

29 <http://www.sejarahtni.mil/index> [2 March 2006].

30 M. Rizal Maslan, *Detik.com*, 7 March 2006.

31 Gerry van Klinken, "The Battle for History after Suharto: Beyond Sacred Dates, Great Men, and Legal Milestones", *Critical Asian Studies* 33, no. 3 (2001): 323–50.

32 Ibid., p. 330.

33 Vickers and McGregor, "Public Debates about History", pp. 44.2–44.3.

34 Key works of Pramoedya include: *Bumi Manusia* (1981), *Anak Semua Bangsa* (1981), *Jejak Langkah* (1985) and *Rumah Kaca* (1988).

35 Pramoedya Ananta Toer, *Nyanyi Sunyi Seorang Bisu; Catatan-Catatan dari Pulau Buru*, Hasta Mitra, Jakarta, 2000. For more on Pramoedya's works as forms of counter history see Razif Bahari, "Remembering History, W/Righting History: Piecing the Past in Pramoedya Ananta Toer's Buru Tetralogy", *Indonesia* 75 (April 2003): 62–90.

Bibliography

OFFICIAL HISTORY SOURCES

Abdullah, Taufik *et al.* (ed.), *50 Tahun Indonesia Merdeka*, Vol. 1 (1945–65). Jakarta: P.T. Citra Media Persada, 1997.

Aidit, D.N., *Aidit Menggugat Peristiwa Madiun: (Pembelaan D.N. Aidit dimuka Pengadilan Negeri Djakarta, Tgl 24 Februari 1955)*. Jakarta: Jajasan Pembaruan, 1964 (reprinted from 1955 and 1958).

———, *Buku Putih Tentang Peristiwa Madiun*, Sekretariat Agitasi Propaganda CC PKI, Jakarta, 1964.

———, *Kibarkan Tinggi Pandji Revolusi*. Jakarta: Jajasan Pembaruan, 1964.

———, *Konfrontasi Peristiwa Madiun 1948, Peristiwa Sumatera 1956*. Jakarta: Pembaruan, 1964.

———, *Revolusi Indonesia: Latar Belakang Sedjarah dan Hari Depannja*. Djakarta: Aidit Jajasan Pembaruan, 1964.

———, "Sedjarah Pergerakan Nasional", in *Revolusi Indonesia, Latar Belakang Sedjarah dan Hari Depannja*. Djakarta: Jajasan Pembaruan, 1964.

Akademi Militer Departemen Kejuangan, *Buku Pedoman Tutor Napak Tilas Rute Gerliya Pangsr Jenderal Sudirman Bagi Capratar Yogyakarta–Bedoyo 1997/98, 22–25 October 1997*, n.p., 1998.

Anggaran Dasar dan Anggaran Rumah Tangga, Badan Penggerak Pembina Potensi Angkatan 1945 Keputusan MUBENAS XI/1996, Dewan Harian Nasional Angkatan 1945, Jakarta, 1996.

Angkatan Bersendjata, "Tentara Nasional Indonesia–Angkatan Darat 1945–1965", in Panitia Penjusun Naskah Buku "20 Tahun Indonesia Merdeka", *20 Tahun Indonesia Merdeka*, Departemen Penerangan Republik Indonesia, Jakarta, 1965.

Atmouiloto, Arswendo, *Pengkhianatan G30 S/PKI*, Pustaka Sinar Harapan, Jakarta, 1994.

Badan Pengelola Monumen Nasional di Jakarta, *Monumen Nasional Dengan Museum Sejarah Nasionalnya*, Badan Pengelola Monumen Nasional di Jakarta, Jakarta, 1989.

Badan Pelaksana Pendidikan Kader Revolusi Angkatan Dwikora, *Sedjarah Pergerakan Nasional*, Badan Pendidikan/Peladjaran Badan Pelaksana Pendidikan Kader Revolusi Angkatan Dwikora, Djakarta, 1964.

Buku Pedoman Tutor Napak Tilas Rute Gerilya Pangsar Jenderal Sudirman Bagi
  CAPRATAR, Penggal Yogyakarta–Bedoyo T. A. 1997/1998, Akademi Militer
  Departemen Kejuangan, Tanggal 22–25 Oktober 1997, 1998.

Departemen Angkatan Darat, "Tentara Nasional Indonesia–Angkatan Darat
  1945–1965", in *20 Tahun Indonesia Merdeka*, Jilid III, Bagian 2.

Departemen Penerangan, *Album Lukisan Revolusi Rakjat Indonesia 1945–1949*,
  Departemen Penerangan, Jakarta, 1949.

Departemen Pertahanan-Keamanan Pusat Sejarah ABRI, *Museum Pusat ABRI*
  Satriamandala: Buku Panduan, Departemen Pertahanan-Keamanan Pusat
  Sejarah ABRI, Jakarta, 1972.

_____, *Pedoman Penyelenggaraan Museum ABRI: Hasil Seminar Permuseuman*
  ABRI 16–19 Juni 1973, Departemen Pertahanan-Keamanan Pusat Sejarah
  ABRI, Jakarta, 1973.

_____, *Sepuluh Tahun Pusat Sejarah dan Tradisi ABRI*, Departemen Pertahanan-
  Keamanan Pusat Sejarah ABRI, Jakarta, 1974.

Dharma Pusaka 45, Hasil Seminar TNI–AD Ke-III Tanggal 13–18 Maret 1972,
  di Graha Wiyata Yudha, Seskoad Bandung, Departemen Pertahanan-
  Keamanan Markas Besar Tentara Nasional Indonesia Angkatan Darat,
  Bandung, 1972.

Dinas Museum dan Sejarah Ibukota Jakarta, *Monumen dan Patung di Jakarta*,
  Pemerintah Daerah Khusus Ibukota Jakarta, Dinas Museum dan Sejarah,
  Jakarta, 1993.

Dinas Sejarah TNI Angkatan Darat, *Museum Pusat TNI-AD Dharma Wiratama*,
  Dinas Sejarah TNI Angkatan Darat, n.p., 1982.

_____, *Seri Monumen Sejarah Angkatan Darat*, Dinas Sejarah TNI AD,
  Bandung, 1978.

Disjarahad (Dinas Sejarah AD), *Sasmitaloka Panglima Besar Jenderal Sudirman*,
  Disjarahad, 1983.

Doktrin Perdjuangan TNI-AD Tri Ubaya Sakti: Buku Induk Seminar AD Ke-II
  Tanggal 25 s.d. 21 Agustus 1966 di Graha Wiyata Yudha, Seskoad, Bandung,
  1966, 1st edition.

Fajar Orde Baru (Lahirnya Orde Baru): Dokumentasi Sejarah dan Latarbelakang
  Kebangkitan Orde Baru beserta Laporan Pembangunan Indonesia Dalam
Satu Dasawarna Menjelang Tahun Pertama Repelita III, Alda, Jakarta, 1979.

Hasil Seminar Dharma Pusaka 45 PASIS SUSREG KE-VI SESKO ABRI
  Bagian Darat, Laut, Udara dan Kepolisian 1979–1980, 31 Maret 1980–
  6 April 1980 di Bandung, Departemen Pertahanan-Keamanan, n.p.

Harahap, Zanaibun, *Operasi-operasi Militer Menumpas Kahar Muzakar*, Staf
  Angkatan Bersendjata, Djakarta, 1965.

Harris Artamaya, "Mengenal lebih Dekat Mengenai Monumen Pancasila Sakti
  dan Museum Pengkhianatan PKI (Komunis)", *Senakatha: Media Komuni-*
  kasi dan Informasi Sejarah, no. 23 (1996): 35.

Kartodirdjo, Sartono, Marwati Djoened Poesponegoro and Nugroho Notosusanto (eds.), *Sejarah Nasional Indonesia*, Departemen Pendidikan dan Kebudayaan, Jakarta, 1975.

Kelompok Kerdja Staf Angkatan Bersendjata, *Sedjarah Singkat Perdjuangan Bersendjata Bangsa Indonesia*, Staf Angkatan Bersendjata, Jakarta, 1964.

Kementerian Penerangan Republik Indonesia, *Djenderal Soedirman: Pahlawan Sedjati*, Kementerian Penerangan Republik Indonesia, Yogyakarta, 1950.

Kusumasumantri, Iwa, *Sedjarah Revolusi Indonesia*, Grafika, Djakarta, 1963, Jilid II-III.

Lembaga Pembinaan Mental dan Tradisi ABRI, Monumen Pancasila Sakti, *Proyek Monumen Pancasila Sakti*, Jakarta, Lembaga Pembinaan Mental dan Tradisi ABRI, Monumen Pancasila Sakti, 1975.

Moerdani, L.B., "Sambutan Panglima Angkatan Bersendjata Republik Indonesia", *Museum Keprajuritan Indonesia: Taman Mini Indonesia*, Markas Besar Angkatan Bersenjata Republik Indonesia, Pusat Sejarah dan Tradisi ABRI, Jakarta, 1987.

"Monumen Pancasila Sakti dalam Usianya Yang ke-30", *Senakatha: Media Komunikasi dan Informasi Sejarah*, no. 26 (1997): 24–6, 31–3.

"Museum Keprajuritan Nasional", *Senakatha: Media Komunikasi dan Informasi Sejarah*, no. 1 (1986): 16.

Nasution, A.H. "Pergerakan Nasional Dalam Segi Kebangkitan Kemiliteran", in Badan Pelaksana Pendidikan Kader Revolusi Angkatan Dwikora, *Sedjarah Pergerakan Nasional*, Badan Pelaksana Pendidikan Kader Revolusi Angkatan Dwikora, Djakarta, 1964.

Notosusanto, Nugroho and Ismail Saleh, *The Coup Attempt of the "September 30 Movement" in Indonesia*. Jakarta: P.T. Pembimbing Masa, 1968.

Notosusanto, Nugroho *et al.* (eds.), *Pejuang dan Prajurit: Konsepsi Implementasi Dwifungsi ABRI*. Jakarta: Sinar Harapan, 1984.

Notosusanto, Nugroho, *The Dual Function of the Indonesian Armed Forces Especially since 1966*, Department of Defence and Security, Armed Forces History Centre, Djakarta, 1970.

————, *Naskah Proklamasi yang Otentik dan Rumusan Pantjasila yang Otentik*, Pusat Sejarah dan Tradisi ABRI, Jakarta, 1971.

————, *Tentara Peta pada Jaman Pendudukan Jepang di Indonesia* (Jakarta: Gramedia, 1979).

————, *Sejarah dan Hankam* (2nd edition), Markas Besar Angkatan Bersenjata, Pusat Sejarah dan Tradisi ABRI, Jakarta, 1987.

————, *The National Struggle and the Armed Forces in Indonesia* (4th edition), Department of Defence and Security, Centre for Armed Forces History, Jakarta, 1994.

————, "Some Effects of the Guerrilla (1948–1949) on Armed Forces and Society", in Nugroho Notosusanto, *The National Struggle and the Armed Forces in Indonesia*, Department of Defence and Security Centre for Armed

Forces History, Jakarta, 1994 (4th edition) (first presented at the Colloquium on the Indonesian Revolution as Social Transformation, Australian National University, 3–5 August 1973), pp. 109–28.

————, *The Transfer of Values in the Indonesian Armed Forces*, Department of Defence and Security, Centre for Armed Forces History, Jakarta, 1994.

Panduan Museum Pusat TNI Angkatan Udara Dirgantara Mandala dalam Informasi, Yogyakarta, 1994.

Panitia Museum Sedjarah Tugu Nasional, *Laporan Lengkap Lukisan Sedjarah Visuil Museum Sedjarah Tugu Nasional: Hasil Penelitian C Menudju Sosialisme Indonesia*, Panitia Museum Sedjarah Tugu Nasional, Djakarta, 1964.

————, *Laporan Lengkap Lukisan Sedjarah Visuil Museum Sedjarah Tugu Nasional: Laporan Umum*, Panitia Museum Sedjarah Tugu Nasional, Djakarta, 1964.

Panitia Penjusun Naskah Buku "20 Tahun Indonesia Merdeka", *20 Tahun Indonesia Merdeka*, Departemen Penerangan Republik Indonesia, Jakarta, 1965.

"Pidato Radio Panglima Besar Jenderal Soedirman, 1949", in *Buku Pedoman Tutor Napak Tilas Rute Gerilya Pangsar Jenderal Sudirman Bagi CAPRATAR, Penggal Yogyakarta–Bedoyo T. A. 1997/1998*, Tanggal 22–25 Oktober 1997, Akademi Militer Departemen Kejuangan, 1998.

Poedhyarto Trisaksono, *Sosiodrama Pelengkap PSPB untuk Sekolah Dasar*, Jilid 4, untuk kelas VI. Tiga Serangkai, Solo, 1985.

Prajogo, *Tugu Nasional Laporan Pembangunan 1961–1978*, Pelaksana Pembina Tugu Nasional, Jakarta, 1978.

Pusat Sedjarah Angkatan Bersendjata, *40 Hari Kegagalan "G-30-S" 1 Oktober– 10 November*, Staf Angkatan Bersendjata Pusat Sejarah Angkatan Bersendjata, Jakarta, 1965.

Pusat Sejarah ABRI, *30 Tahun Angkatan Bersenjata Republik Indonesia*, Markas Besar Angkatan Bersenjata Republik Indonesia, Pusat Sejarah dan Tradisi ABRI, Jakarta, 1976.

————, *40 Tahun Angkatan Bersenjata Republik Indonesia*, Markas Besar Angkatan Bersenjata Republik Indonesia, Pusat Sejarah dan Tradisi ABRI, Jakarta, 1985.

————, *Bahaya Laten Komunisme di Indonesia: Perkembangan Gerakan dan Pengkhianatan Komunisme di Indonesia (1913–1948)*, Pusat Sejarah ABRI, Jilid I, Jakarta, 1991.

————, *Bahaya Laten Komunisme di Indonesia: Penumpasan Pemberontakan PKI (1948)*, Pusat Sejarah ABRI, Jilid II, Jakarta, 1992.

————, *Bahaya Laten Komunisme di Indonesia: Konsolidasi dan Infiltrasi PKI (1950–1959)*, Pusat Sejarah ABRI, Jilid III, Jakarta, 1992.

————, *Bahaya Laten Komunisme di Indonesia: Pemberontakan G30S/PKI dan Penumpasannya*, Pusat Sejarah ABRI, Jilid IV A, Jakarta, 1994.

————, *50 Tahun ABRI*, Pusat Sejarah dan Tradisi ABRI, Jakarta, 1995.

————, *Bahaya Laten Komunisme di Indonesia: Penumpasan Pemberontakan PKI dan Sisa-Sisanya*, Pusat Sejarah ABRI, Jilid IV B, Jakarta, 1995.

Pusat Sejarah dan Tradisi ABRI, *Seperempat Abad Pusjarah ABRI (5–10–1964 s.d 5–10–1989)*, Markas Besar Angkatan Bersenjata R. I. Pusat Sejarah dan Tradisi ABRI, Jakarta, 1989.

————, *30 Tahun Pusat Sejarah dan Tradisi ABRI*, Markas Besar Angkatan Bersenjata R. I Pusat Sejarah dan Tradisi ABRI, Jakarta, 1994.

————, *Biografi Pahlawan Nasional dari Lingkungan ABRI*, Pusat Sejarah dan Tradisi ABRI, Jakarta, 1994.

————, *Mengenal Museum ABRI Satriamandala*, Markas Besar Angkatan Bersenjata R.I. Pusat Sejarah dan Tradisi ABRI, Jakarta, 1994.

————, *Buku Panduan Monumen Pancasila Sakti Lubang Buaya Jakarta*, Pusat Sejarah dan Tradisi ABRI, Jakarta, 1997.

————, *Museum Waspada Purbawisesa Buku Panduan*, Pusat Sejarah dan Tradisi ABRI, Jakarta, 1997.

Rencana Latihan Napak Tilas Rute Gerilya Pangsar Jenderal Sudirman T. A. 1997/ 1998, Tanggal 22–25 Oktober 1997, AKMIL, 1997.

S. Broto, "Monumen Sebuah Ungkapan Penyaksian Sejarah Perjuangan Bangsa", *Senakatha: Media Komunikasi dan Informasi Sejarah*, no. 13 (January 1992): 41–9.

Sanusi, A. Anwar, "Pengantar: Tentang Perjuangan Angkatan Pendobrak", in Badan Pelaksana Pendidikan Kader Revolusi Angkatan Dwikora, *Sedjarah Pergerakan Nasional*, Badan Pendidikan/Peladjaran Badan Pelaksana Pendidikan Kader Revolusi/Peladjaran Badan Pelaksana Pendidikan Kader Revolusi Angkatan Dwikora, Jakarta, 1964

————, "Sedjarah Pergerakan Nasional", in Badan Pelaksana Pendidikan Kader Revolusi Angkatan Dwikora, 1–5, *Sedjarah Pergerakan Nasional*, Badan Pendidikan/Peladjaran Badan Pelaksana Pendidikan Kader Revolusi Angkatan Dwikora, Jakarta, 1964.

Sedjarah Militer Kodam VI Siliwangi, *Siliwangi dari Masa Kemasa*, Fakta Mahjuma, Jakarta, 1968.

Sekretariat Negara Republik Indonesia, *30 Tahun Indonesia Merdeka*, Vols. 1–4 (6th edition). Jakarta: PT Tira Pustaka, 1983.

Seskoad, *Serangan Umum 1 Maret 1949 di Yogyakarta: Latar Belakang dan Pengaruhnya*, Seskoad. Jakarta: P.T. Citra Lamtoro Gung Persada, 1989.

Soedjono (Maj. Gen. TNI), *Monumen Pancasila Cakti*, Pusat Sejarah dan Tradisi ABRI, Jakarta, 1975.

Soerjono, R.H. *et al.* (eds.), *Sewindu Monumen Yogya Kembali 1989–1997*, Yayasan Monumen Yogya Kembali, Yogyakarta, 1997.

Sri Hartani, "Sadar Museum Harus Dimulai sejak Balita", *Senakatha: Media Komunikasi dan Informasi Sejarah*, no. 14 (April 1992): 14–8.

The, Anne Marie, *Darah Tersimbah di Djawa Barat*, Staf Angkatan Bersendjata, Djakarta, 1965.

Ugaya, Hayun, "Museum Waspada Purbawisesa", *Senakatha: Media Komunikasi dan Informasi Sejarah*, no. 12 (1991): 28.
Yusmar Basri, *GOM VI: Untuk Menumpas DI/TII di Jawa Tengah*, Staf Angkatan Bersendjata, Djakarta, 1965.

FILMS

Jakarta 66: Sejarah Perintah 11 Maret, 1986 (director Arifin C. Noor)
Janur Kuning, 1979 (director Surawijaya, Alam)
Pengkhianatan Gerakan 30 September, 1980 (director Arifin C. Noor)

THESES, BOOKS, ACADEMIC ARTICLES AND OTHER ARTICLES

Abdoelmanap, Soerowo, *Republik Indonesia Menggugat*. Jakarta: Pustaka Grafiksi, 1997.
Abdulgani, Roeslan, *Heroes Day and the Indonesian Revolution*. Jakarta: Prapantja Publishing House, 1964.
⸻, *Nationalism, Revolution and Guided Democracy in Indonesia*. Clayton: Centre of Southeast Asian Studies, Monash University, 1973.
Abdullah, Taufik, *Sejarah Disiplin Ilmu: Rekonstruksi Masa Lalu, Berita Pikiran*. Jakarta: Proyek Pengkajian Dinamika Sosial Budaya dalam Proses Industrialisasi-LIPI, 1994–95.
Abeyasekere, Susan, *Jakarta: A History*. Singapore and Oxford: Oxford University Press, 1987.
Adam, Asvi Warman, "Pengendalian Sejarah sejak Orde Baru", in Henri Chambert-Loir and Hasan Muarif Ambary (eds.), *Panggung Sejarah: Persembahan kepada Prof. Dr. Denys Lombard*. Jakarta: Yayasan Obor Indonesia, 1999, pp. 567–77.
Aditjondro, George, "Guns, Pamphlets and Handie-talkies: How the Military Exploited Ethno-religious Tensions in Maluku to Preserve their Political and Economic Privileges", in Ingrid Wessel and Georgia Winhofer, *Violence in Indonesia*. Hamburg: Abera Verlag, 2001, pp. 100–28.
Al-Chaidar and Amnesti Internasional, *Bencana Kaum Muslimin di Indonesia, 1980–2000*. Yogyakarta: Wihdah Press, 2000.
Al-Chaidar, *Lampung Bersimbah Darah: Menelusuri Kejahatan "Negara Intellijen" Orde Baru dalam Peristiwa Jamaáh Warsidi*. Jakarta: Madani Press, 2000.
Amnesty International, *Indonesia Muslim Prisoners of Conscience*. London: Amnesty International, 1986.
⸻, *Power and Impunity: Human Rights under the New Order*. London: Amnesty International, 1994.
⸻, *Indonesia: An Amnesty International Report*. London: Amnesty International Publications, 1997.

Anderson, Benedict and McVey, Ruth, *A Preliminary Analysis of the October 1, 1965 Coup in Indonesia*. Ithaca: Cornell University Modern Indonesia Project, 1971.

Anderson, Benedict, "The Pemuda Revolution: Indonesian Politics 1945–1946". PhD diss., Cornell University, 1967.

————, *Java in a Time of Revolution, Occupation and Resistance 1944–46*. Ithaca: Cornell University Press, 1972.

————, "Notes on Contemporary Indonesian Political Communication", *Indonesia*, no. 16 (October 1973): 39–80.

————, "How Did The Generals Die?", *Indonesia*, no. 43 (April 1987): 109–34.

————, "Current Data on the Indonesian Military Elite", *Indonesia*, no. 45 (April 1988): 137–59.

————, "Current Data on the Indonesian Military Elite", *Indonesia*, no. 48 (October 1989): 65–96.

————, *Language and Power: Exploring Political Cultures in Indonesia*. Ithaca and London: Cornell University Press, 1990.

————, *Imagined Communities: Reflections on the Origin and Spread of Nationalism*, (2nd edition). London and New York: Verso, 1991.

————, "Rewinding Back To The Future: The Left and Constitutional Democracy", in David Bourchier and John Legge (eds.), *Democracy in Indonesia: 1950s and 1990s*. Clayton: Centre of Southeast Asian Studies, Monash University, 1994, pp. 128–42.

————, "Scholarship on Indonesia and Raison d'État: Personal Experience", *Indonesia*, no. 62 (October 1996): 1–18.

Anderson, David Charles, "The Military Aspects of the Madiun Affair", *Indonesia*, no 21 (April 1976): 1–64.

Anonymous, "Additional Data on Counter-Revolutionary Cruelty in Indonesia, Especially in East Java", in Robert Cribb (ed.), *The Indonesian Killings of 1965–1966: Studies from Java and Bali*. Clayton: Monash Papers on Southeast Asia No. 21, Centre of Southeast Asian Studies, Monash University, 1990, pp. 169–76.

Anonymous, "Akan Ada Perbaikan dan Buku PSPB Baru Sudah Dipersiapkan", *Sinar Harapan*, 11 September 1985.

Anonymous, "Aksi Mahasiswa: Dengan Isu Lokal Membentuk Opini Nasional", *Tempo*, 22 April 1989, pp. 72–3.

Anonymous, "Bersih Lingkungan, Menyaring Masa Lalu", *Tempo*, 17 September 1988, p. 33.

Anonymous, "Demonstran Bakar Buku Sejarah Nasional", *Kompas*, 3 May 2001.

Anonymous, "Indonesia the Land the Communists Lost", *Time: The Australian Edition*, 16 July 1966, p. 38.

Anonymous, "Induk Karangan Soal PSPB", *Merdeka*, 13 September 1985.

Anonymous, "Jangan Ada Komunis di Antara Kita", *Tajuk*, No. 15, 1–17 September 1998, pp. 24–8.
Anonymous, "Jenderal yang Dianggap Musuh", *Panji Masyarakat*, 17 June 1998, p. 22.
Anonymous, "Kami Golongan yang 35 Tahun Digenjet", *Tempo Interaktif*, 5 April 2000.
Anonymous, "Kesimpulan Seminar Sejarah Nasional Untag PSPB Produk Nugroho Almarhum Jatuhkan Nama Soekarno Hatta", *Sinar Harapan*, 7 June 1985.
Anonymous, "Kisah Pengangkatan Jenazah 7 Pahlawan Revolusi", *Pelita*, 28 September 1990.
Anonymous, "Kol. Latief: Suharto Tahu Rencana G-30-S/PKI", *Tajuk (Berita investigasi dan Entertainmen)*, No. 15, 17 September–30 September 1998.
Anonymous, "Medikbud Fuad Hassan: Diperhatikan Usul dan Pendapat Mengenai PSPB", *Kompas*, 11 September 1985.
Anonymous, "Merekayasa Peristiwa Berdarah", *Panji Masyarakat*, 17 June 1998, pp. 19–20.
Anonymous, "Pendidikan Sejerah Perjuangan Bangsa Penyusun Buku Pelajaran Sejerah Hendaknya Bertolak dari Strategi Pendidikan", *Suara Karya*, 15 November 1984.
Anonymous, "Penemuan Jenazah Pahlawan Revolusi Buka Tabir Kebiadaban G30S/PKI", *Angkatan Bersenjata*, 2 October 1990.
Anonymous, "PSPB Bukun Pelajaran Sejarah", *Antara*, 21 November 1984.
Anonymous, "Suharto Dalam Konspirasi PKI", *Adil (Tabloid Berita Mingguan)*, 30 September–6 October 1998.
Anonymous, "Thirty-four Years of Co-operation between Unesco and ICOM", *Museums* 32 (1980): 154–62.
Anonymous, "Trisula dan Kemiskinan yang Tersisa", *Gatra*, 9 October 1999, pp. 88–9.
Anonymous, "Uncovering the Cemeteries of Truth", *Jakarta Post*, 7 April 2000.
Antlöv, Hans, "The Revolusi Represented: Contemporary Indonesian Images of 1945", *Indonesia Circle*, no. 68 (1996): 1–21.
Appadurai, Arjun and Carol A. Breckenridge, "Museums are Good to Think: Heritage on View", in Ivan Karp, Christine Mullen Kreamer and Steven D. Lavine (eds.), *Museums and Communities: The Politics of Public Culture*. Washington and London: Smithsonian Institute Press, pp. 34–55.
Ariffadhillah, "The Recent Situation in Aceh after the Joint Understanding on a Humanitarian Pause for Aceh", in Ingrid Wessel and Georgina Wimhöfer (eds.), *Violence in Indonesia*. Hamburg: Abera Verlag Markus Voss, 2001, pp. 317–34.
Arifin, Zainal, "Memilih Bahan Mengakar PSPB di Sekolah Dasar", *Suara Karya*, 20 March 1984.
Aspinall, Edward, *Student Dissent in Indonesia in the 1980s*. Clayton: Centre of Southeast Asian Studies, Monash University, 1993.

————, "Students and the Military: Regime Friction and Civilian Dissent in the Late Suharto Period", *Indonesia*, no. 59 (April 1995): 21–44.

Bachtiar, Harsja W., *Siapa Dia?: Perwira Tinggi Tentara Nasional Indonesia Angkatan Darat (TNI AD)*. Jakarta: Djambatan, 1988.

Bahari, Razif, "Remembering History, W/Righting History: Piecing the Past in Pramoedya Ananta Toer's Buru Tetralogy", *Indonesia* 75 (April 2003): 62–90.

Bakti, Andi Faisal, "Rebel Rises from the Dead", *Inside Indonesia*, no. 67 (October 2001): 13–5.

Bambang Bujono, "Perginya Seorang Bapak Asuh", *Tempo*, no. 15 (1985): 14–5.

Barraclough, Geoffrey, *Main Trends in History*. New York and London: Holmes and Meier Publishers, 1979.

Benda, Harry J. and Ruth McVey (eds.), *The Communist Uprising of 1926–1927 in Indonesia: Key Documents*, Translation Series. Ithaca, New York: Modern Indonesia Project, Southeast Asia Program, Cornell University, 1960.

Bennett, Tony, *The Birth of the Museum*. London and New York: Routledge, 1995.

Berger, John, *Ways of Seeing*. London: British Broadcasting Corporation and Penguin Books, 1987.

Bibin Bintariadi, "Mahasiswa Malang Tuntut Jabatan Panglima TNI Dihapus", *Tempointeraktif.com*, 30 September 2004.

Blackburn, Susan, "How Gender is Neglected in Southeast Asia Politics", in Maila Stivens (ed.), *Why Gender Matters in Southeast Asian Politics*. Clayton: Centre of Southeast Asian Studies, Monash University, 1991, pp. 25–42.

————, "Gender Interests and Indonesian Democracy", in David Bourchier and John Legge (eds.), *Democracy in Indonesia: 1950s and 1990s*. Clayton: Monash Papers on Southeast Asia No. 31, Centre of Southeast Asian Studies, Monash University, 1994, pp. 168–81.

Boland, B.J., *The Struggle of Islam in Modern Indonesia*, (revised reprint). The Hague: KITLV, 1982.

Born, Georgina, "Public Museums, Museum Photography, and the Limits of Reflexivity", *Journal of Material Culture* 3, no. 2 (1998): 223–54.

Bosch, F.D.K., *The Golden Germ: An Introduction to Indian Symbolism*. The Hague: Mouton, 1960.

Bourchier, David, *Dynamics of Dissent in Indonesia: Sawito and the Phantom Coup*, Interim Report Series, No. 63. New York: Cornell Modern Indonesia Project, Southeast Asia Program, Cornell University, 1984.

————, "The 1950s in New Order Ideology and Politics", in D. Bourchier and J. Legge (eds.), *Democracy in Indonesia: 1950s and 1990s*. Clayton: Monash Papers on Southeast Asia No. 31, Centre of Southeast Asian Studies, Monash University, 1994, pp. 50–62.

————, "Lineages of Organicist Political Thought in Indonesia". PhD diss., Department of Politics, Monash University, Clayton, 1996.

Brackman, Arnold C., *Indonesian Communism: A History*. New York: Praeger, 1963.

Britton, Peter, "Military Professionalism in Indonesia: Javanese and Western Military Traditions in Army Ideology to the 1970s". MA Thesis, Department of Politics, Monash University, 1987.

————, "The Indonesian Army: 'Stabiliser and Dynamiser'", in Rex Mortimer (ed.), *Showcase State: The Illusion of Indonesia's Accelerated Modernisation*. Sydney: Angus and Robertson, 1973, pp. 51–66.

————, "Indonesia's Neo-colonial Armed Forces", *Bulletin of Concerned Asian Scholars* 7, no. 3 (July–September 1975): 14–21.

Brongtodiningrat, K.P.H., *Arti Kraton Yogyakarta*, translated by R. Murdani Hadiatmaja, Museum Kraton Yogyakarta, Yogyakarta, 1978.

Brooker, Paul, *The Faces of Fraternalism: Nazi Germany, Fascist Italy, and Imperial Japan*. Oxford and New York: Oxford University Press, 1991.

Brooks, Karen, "The Rustle of Ghosts: Bung Karno in the New Order", *Indonesia*, no. 60 (1995): 61–100.

Brown, Colin, "Sukarno on the Role of Women in the Nationalist Movement", *Review of Indonesian and Malaysian Affairs* 15, no. 1 (1981): 68–92.

Bruinessen, M. van, "State-Islam Relations in Contemporary Indonesia, 1915–1990", in C. van Dijk and A. H. de Groot (eds.), *State and Islam*. Leiden: CNWS Publications, 1995, pp. 96–114.

Budiardjo, Carmel, "Repression and Political Imprisonment", in Malcolm Caldwell (ed.), *Ten Years' Military Terror in Indonesia*. Nottingham: Spokesman Books, 1975, pp. 95–105.

Budi Darma, "Pengalaman Pribadi dengan Nugroho Notosusanto", *Horison*, no. 9 (1985).

Budi Susanto, and A. Made Tony Supriatma, *ABRI Siasat Kebudayaan 1945–1995*, Seri Siasat Kebudayaan, Lembaga Studi Realino, Yogyakarta, 1995.

Budiman, Arief, "Indonesian Politics in the 1990s", in Harold Crouch and Hal Hill (eds.), *Indonesia Assessment 1992: Political Perspectives on the 1990s*, Proceedings of Indonesia Update Conference August 1992, Department of Social and Political Change, Research School of Pacific Studies, Australian National University, Canberra 1992, pp. 130–9.

Bunnell, Frederick P., "Guided Democracy Foreign Policy 1960–1965: President Sukarno Moves from Non-Alignment to Confrontation", *Indonesia*, no. 2 (October 1966): 37–76.

Caldwell, Malcolm (ed.), *Ten Years' Military Terror in Indonesia*. Nottingham: Spokesman Books, 1975.

Callahan, Mary P., "Cracks in the Edifice? Military Society Relations in Burma since 1988", in Pederson, Mortern B., Rudland, Emily and May, Ronald J., *Burma Myanmar: Strong Regime, Weak State*. Adelaide: Crawford House Publishing, 2000.

Cameron, Duncan, "The Museum: A Temple or the Forum?", *Curator* 14, no. 1 (1971): 11–24.

————, "The Pilgrim and the Shrine: The Icon and the Oracle, A Perspective on Museology for Tomorrow", *Museum Management and Curatorship* 14, no. 1 (1995): 47–55.

Carey, Peter B.R., "Raden Saleh, Dipanagara and the Painting of the Capture of Dipanagara at Magelang, 28 March 1830", *Journal of the Malaysian Branch of the Royal Asiatic Society* 55, no. 242 (1982): 1–25.

Cary, Charles D., "Martial-Patriotic Themes in Soviet School Textbooks", *Soviet Union* 6 (1) (1979): 81–98.

Castles, Lance, "Socialism and Private Business: The Latest Phase", *Bulletin of Indonesian Economic Studies* 1, no. 1 (June 1965): 13–45.

Castro, Celso, "The Military and Politics in Brazil, 1964-2000", in Koonings, Kees and Kruijt, Dirk (eds.), *Political Armies: The Military and Nation Building in the Age of Democracy*, pp. 90–110.

Chauvel, Richard, *Nationalists, Soldiers and Separatists: The Ambonese Islands from Colonialism to Revolt 1880–1950*. Leiden: KITLV Press, 1990.

Choi, Jin-Tai, *Aviation Terrorism: Historical Survey, Perspectives and Responses*. New York: St. Martin's Press, 1994.

Clark, Toby, *Art and Propaganda in the Twentieth Century: The Political Image in the Age of Mass Culture*. London: Weidenfeld and Nicolson, 1997.

Conde, Anne Marie, "A Marriage of Sculpture and Art: Dioramas at the Memorial", *Journal of the Australian War Memorial*, no. 5 (October 1984, 1985): 56–9.

Crane, Susan, "Memory and Distortion, History in the Museum", *History and Theory* 36, no. 4 (1997): 44–63.

Cribb, Robert and Colin Brown (eds.), *Modern Indonesia: A History since 1945*. London and New York: Longman, 1995.

Cribb, Robert, "Problems in the Historiography of the Killings in Indonesia", in Robert Cribb (ed.), *The Indonesian Killings of 1965–1966: Studies from Java and Bali*. Clayton: Centre of Southeast Asian Studies, Monash University, 1990, pp. 1–44.

————, *Gangsters and Revolutionaries: The Jakarta People's Militia and the Indonesian Revolution, 1945–1949*. Honolulu: University of Hawaii Press, 1991.

————, *Historical Dictionary of Indonesia*. Metuchen, NJ and London: The Scarecrow Press, 1992.

————, "Legacies of the Revolution 1945–50", in David Bourchier and John Legge (eds.), *Democracy in Indonesia: 1950s and 1990s*. Clayton: Monash Papers on Southeast Asia, No. 31, Centre of Southeast Asian Studies, 1994, pp. 74–8.

Crouch, Harold. *The Army and Politics in Indonesia*, (revised edition). Ithaca: Cornell University Press, 1988.

————, "An Ageing President, An Ageing Regime", in Harold Crouch and Hal Hill (eds.), *Indonesia Assessment 1992: Political Perspectives on the 1990s*, Proceedings of Indonesia Update Conference August 1992, Department of Social and Political Change, Research School of Pacific Studies, Australian National University, Canberra, 1992, pp. 43–62.

————, "Democratic Prospects in Indonesia", in David Bourchier and John Legge (eds.), *Democracy in Indonesia: 1950s and 1990s*. Clayton: Monash Papers on Southeast Asia No. 31, Centre of Southeast Asian Studies, Monash University, 1994, pp. 115–27.

Dake, A.C., *In the Spirit of the Red Banteng: Indonesian Communists between Moscow and Peking*. The Hague: Mouton, 1973.

Davis, Natalie Zemon and Randolph Starn, "Introduction", *Representations*, no. 26 (Spring 1989): 1–6.

Davison, Patricia, "Museums and the Reshaping of Memory", in Sarah Nuttall and Carli Coetze (eds.), *Negotiating the Past: The Making of Memory in South Africa*. Cape Town: Oxford University Press, 1998, pp. 143–60.

"Decree No. 1 on the Establishment of the Indonesian Revolution Council (Text as read over Djakarta radio at approximately 2.00pm, October 1 1965) Selected Documents Related to the September 30th Movement and Its Epilogue", *Indonesia*, no. 1 (1966): 136–8.

Department of Education and Culture Directorate General for Culture, *Directory of Museums in Indonesia*, Museums Development Project, English edition, Jakarta, 1999.

Departemen Sosial, *Sejarah Taman Makam Pahlawan Nasional Kalibata*, Departemen Sosial-Direktorat Jenderal Bina Pembinaan Kepahlawanan dan Keperintisan, Jakarta, 1993.

Diah, B.M., "Buku Sejarah Nasional Harus Ditulis Kembali: Tidak Kena Kalau Diperbaiki Saja", *Merdeka*, 17 September 1985.

Dijk, C. van, "Survey of Major Developments in Indonesia in the First Half of 1981: The Plane Hijacking and Suharto's Referendum Proposal", *Review of Indonesian and Malaysian Affairs* 15, no. 2 (1981): 136–59.

Dinas Sejarah TNI AD, "Crushing the G30S/PKI Central Java", in Robert Cribb (ed.), *The Indonesian Killings of 1965–1966: Studies from Java and Bali*. Clayton: Monash Papers on Southeast Asia No. 21, Centre of Southeast Asian Studies, 1990, pp. 159–67.

Djiwandono, J. Soedjati and Yong Mun Cheong (eds.), *Soldiers and Stability in Southeast Asia*, Regional Strategic Studies Programme. Singapore: Institute of Southeast Asian Studies, 1988.

Dobbin, Christine, "The Search for Women in Indonesian History", in Ailsa Thomson Zainu'ddin *et al.* (eds.), *Kartini Centenary: Indonesian Women Then and Now*, Papers given at Annual Public Lectures on Indonesia, Centre of Southeast Asian Studies, August 1979, Monash University, Clayton, 1980, pp. 56–68.

Douglas, Stephen A., "Women in Indonesian Politics: The Myth of Functional Interest", in Sylvia A. Chipp and Justin J. Green (eds.), *Asian Women in Transition*. University Park: Pennsylvania State University Press, 1980, pp. 152–81.

Douglas, Susan, "Notes Toward a History of Media Audiences", *Radical History Review*, no. 54 (Fall 1992): 127–38.

Dumarçay, Jacques (translated and edited by Michael Smithies), *The Palaces of South East Asia: Architecture and Customs*. Oxford: Oxford University Press, 1991.

Dutch East Indies, Algemeene Secretarie, *Reegerings Almanak voor Nederlandsch-Indië*, Landsdrukkerij Weltevreden, Batavia, 1918 and 1920.

Dwipayana, AAGN Ari *et al.*, *Masyarakat Pascamiliter: Tantangan dan Peluang Demiliterisme di Indonesia*. Yogyakarta: Institute for Research and Empowerment (IRE), 2000.

East, C.H.A., "My Days at the Indonesian Army Staff and Command College", *News and Views Indonesia Special Issue, Indonesia 20 Years' Nationhood 17.8.1945–17.8.1965*, Information Service Indonesia, Deakin, 1965.

Echols, John M. and Hassan Shadily, *Kamus Indonesia Inggris: An Indonesian–English Dictionary* (3rd edition). Jakarta: Gramedia, 1994.

The Editors, "Changes in Civil-Military Relations since the Fall of Suharto", *Indonesia*, no. 70 (October 2000): 133, 138.

————, "Current Data on the Indonesian Military Elite", *Indonesia*, no. 37 (April 1984): 145–69.

————, "Initial Statement of Lieutenant Colonel Untung", Selected Documents Related to the 30 September Movement, *Indonesia*, no. 1 (April 1966): 134–5.

Eliade, Mircea, *Ideas, Images and Symbols*. New York: Sheed and Ward, 1961.

Elson, Robert E., *Suharto: A Political Biography*. New York: Cambridge University Press, 2001.

Emmerson, Donald K., "Understanding the New Order: Bureaucratic Pluralism in Indonesia", *Asian Survey* 23, no. 11 (November 1983): 1220–37.

Eneste, Pamusuk, *Leksikon Kesusastraan Indonesia Modern* (3rd edition). Jakarta: Djambatan, 1990.

Enloe, Cynthia, *Does Khaki Become You? The Militarization of Women's Lives* (2nd edition). London: Pandora, 1988.

Errington, Shelly, "The Cosmic Theme Park of the Javanese", *Review of Indonesian and Malaysian Affairs* 31, no. 1 (June 1997): 7–36.

Esposito, John, *Islam and Democracy*. New York: Oxford University Press, 1996.

————, *The Islamic Threat Myth or Reality?* New York: Oxford University Press, 1999.

Fasabeni, Muhammad, "Aliansi Anti-Militerisme Tolak Pengesahan RUU TNI", *Tempointeraktif.com*, 18 August 2004.

————, "Koalisi Perempuan Tolak RUU TNI", *Tempointeraktif.com*, 24 August 2004.

_____, "Barisan Oposisi Rakyat Tolak RUU TNI", *Tempointeraktif.com*, 2 September 2004.

Fealy, Greg, *The Release of Indonesia's Political Prisoners: Domestic Versus Foreign Policy, 1975–1979*. Clayton: Working Paper 9, Centre of Southeast Asian Studies, Monash University, 1995.

Federspiel, Howard M., "The Military and Islam in Sukarno's Indonesia", in Ahmad Ibrahim, Sharon Siddique and Yasmin Hussain (compilers), *Readings on Islam in Southeast Asia*, Social Issues in Southeast Asia. Singapore: Institute of Southeast Asian Studies, 1985, pp. 151–7.

_____, *A Dictionary of Indonesian Islam*. Athens, Ohio: Ohio University, Center for International Studies, Monographs in International Studies, Southeast Asia Series No. 94, 1995.

Feillard, Andrée, "Traditionalist Islam and the Army in Indonesia's New Order: The Awkward Relationship", in Greg Barton and Greg Fealy (eds.), *Nahdlatul Ulama, Tradition Islam and Modernity in Indonesia*. Clayton: Monash Asia Institute, Monash University, 1996, pp. 42–67.

Feith, Herbert, Letter to Stephanie Grant of Amnesty International, London 22 March 1970, Monash University Archives, *Herbert Feith Files 1948–1987*.

_____, *The Decline of Constitutional Democracy in Indonesia*. Ithaca: Cornell University Press, 1962.

_____, "President Sukarno, The Army and the Communists: The Triangle Changes Shape", *Asian Survey* 4, no. 8 (August 1964): 969–80.

_____, "Suharto's Search for a Political Format", *Indonesia*, no. 6 (1968): 88–105.

_____, "Suharto under Pressure", *Inside Indonesia*, no. 19 (April 1989): 2.

_____, *Soekarno-Militer dalam Demokrasi Terpimpin*. Jakarta: Pustaka Sinar Harapan, 1995.

Foulcher, Keith, *Social Commitment in Literature and the Arts: the Indonesian Institute of People's Culture 1950–1965*. Clayton: Centre of Southeast Asian Studies, Monash University, 1986.

_____, "Sumpah Pemuda: The Making and Meaning of a Symbol of Indonesian Nationhood", *Asian Studies Review* 24, no. 3 (September 2000): 377–410.

Fox, James J., "Ziarah Visits to the Tombs of the Wali, the Founders of Islam on Java", in M.C. Ricklefs (ed.), *Islam in the Indonesian Social Context*. Clayton: Centre of Southeast Asian Studies, Monash University, 1991, pp. 19–38.

Frederick, William H., "The Appearance of Revolution", in Henk Schulte Nordholt (ed.), *Outward Appearances: Dressing State and Society in Indonesia*. Leiden: KITLV Press, 1997, pp. 199–248.

_____, *Visions and Heat: The Making of the Indonesian Revolution*. Athens: Ohio University Press, 1989.

_____, "Reflections in a Moving Stream: Indonesian Memories of the War and the Japanese", in Remco Raben (ed.), *Representing the Japanese*

Occupation in Indonesia: Personal Testimonies and Public Images in Indonesia, Japan and the Netherlands. Zwolle: Netherlands Institute for War Documentation and Waanders Publishers, 1999, pp. 16–35.

Funkenstein, Amos, *Perceptions of Jewish History.* Berkeley: University of California Press, 1993.

"General Report from Banaran: Developments since December 19, 1948", composed for the Government of the Republic of Indonesia by the staff of the Armed Forces, in T.B. Simatupang, *Report from Banaran: Experiences During the People's War,* translated by Benedict Anderson and Elizabeth Graves. Ithaca: Modern Indonesia Project, Southeast Asia Program, Cornell University, 1972.

George, Kenneth M., "Designs on Indonesia's Muslim Communities", *The Journal of Asian Studies* 51, no. 3 (1998): 693–713.

Gillis, John R., "Introduction: Memory and Identity: the History of a Relationship", in John R. Gillis (ed.), *Commemorations: The Politics of National Identity.* Princeton: Princeton University Press, 1994, pp. 3–24.

Goenawan Mohamad, *The Cultural Manifesto Affair: Literature and Politics in Indonesia in the 1960s A Signatory's View.* Clayton: Working Paper No. 45, Centre of Southeast Asian Studies, Monash University, 1988.

Goodfellow, Robert, *Api Dalam Sekam: The New Order and the Ideology of Anti-communism.* Clayton: Working Paper No. 95, Centre of Southeast Asian Studies, Monash University, 1995.

Grasskamp, Walter, "Reviewing the Museum or the Complexity of Things", *Nordisk Museologi* 1994, No. 1, pp. 65–74, <http://www.umu.se/nordic.museology/NM/941/Grasskamp.html> [14 March 1996].

Groys, Boris, "The Role of Museums When the Nation State Breaks Up", ICOM General Conference Stavanger, Norway, 1 July 1995, <http://www.umu.se/nordicmuseology/NM/Groys1995.html> [14 March 1996].

Gurian, Elaine Heumann, "Noodling Around with Exhibition Opportunities", in Ivan Karp and Stephen D. Lavine (eds.), *Exhibiting Cultures: The Poetics of Museum Display.* Washington and London: Smithsonian Institute Press, 1991, pp.176–90.

Hall, R.K. (ed.), *Kotukai No Hongi: Cardinal Principles of the National Entity of Japan.* Cambridge, Massachusetts: Harvard University Press, 1949.

Hall, Terence H. and Gavin W. Jones, "Fertility Decline in the New Order Period: The Evolution of Population Policy", in Hal Hill (ed.), *Indonesia's New Order: The Dynamics of Socio-Economic Transformation.* St. Leonards: Allen & Unwin, 1994, pp. 123–45.

Hamdi Muluk, "Monumen Mempertanyakan Ingatan Kolektif", *Gatra,* 7 October 2000, p. 92.

Hanna, Willard A., *Bung Karno's Indonesia: A Collection of 25 Reports Written for the American Universities Field Staff,* The American Universities Field Staff, New York, 1960.

Hardjowirogo, *Sedjarah Wayang Purwa* (5th edition). Djakarta: Balai Pustaka, 1968.

Harsono, Ganis, *Recollections of an Indonesian Diplomat in the Sukarno Era.* St. Lucia: University of Queensland Press, 1977.

Harvey, Barbara, *Tradition and Islam and Rebellion, South Sulawesi 1950–1965.* Ann Arbor, Michigan, 1974.

Hasanuddin, Bisry, "In Memoriam Prof Dr Nugroho Notosusanto yang Terlalu Cepat", *Singgalang,* 1 July 1985.

Hasil-Hasil Sidang Umum ke-IV MPRS Ketetapan-Ketetapan MPRS No. IX/ MPRS/1966 s/d No. XXXII/MPRS/1966, Pradnja Paramita, Djakarta, 1969.

Hassan, Fuad, "Mengimbau Semua Pihak Meredakan Polemik tentang PSPB", *Sinar Harapan,* 19 September 1985.

Hatley, Barbara, "Indonesian Ritual, Javanese Drama — Celebrating Tujuhbelasan", *Indonesia,* no. 34 (October 1982): 54–64.

Hatta, Mohammad, "Oil and Water Do Not Mix (1957)", in Herbert Feith and Lance Castles (eds.), *Indonesian Political Thinking 1945–1965.* Ithaca and London: Cornell University Press, 1970, pp. 365–8.

————, "A Revolution Should Not Last Too Long (1956)", in Herbert Feith and Lance Castles (eds.), *Indonesian Political Thinking 1945–1965.* Ithaca and London: Cornell University Press, 1970, pp. 94–97.

Hauswedell, Peter Christian, "Sukarno: Radical or Conservative? Indonesian Politics 1964–65", *Indonesia,* no. 15 (April 1973): 109–44.

Hefner, Robert. W., "The Politics of Popular Art: Tayuban Dance and Culture in East Java", *Indonesia,* no. 43 (1987): 75–94.

————, "State and Civil Society; ICMI and the Struggle for the Indonesian Middle Class", *Indonesia,* no. 56 (October 1993): 1–35.

Heider, Karl G., *Indonesian Cinema: National Culture on Screen.* Honolulu: University of Hawaii Press, 1991.

Hein, Gordon R., "Indonesia in 1988: Another Five Years of Suharto", *Asian Survey* 29, no. 2 (February 1989): 119–28.

————, "Indonesia in 1989: A Question of Openness", *Asian Survey* 30, no. 2 (February 1990): 221–5.

Hein, Laura and Mark Selden, "Learning Citizenship from the Past: Textbook Nationalism, Global Context and Social Change", *Bulletin of Concerned Asian Scholars* 30, 2 (1998): 3–15.

Heryanto, Ariel and Mandal, Sumit K., *Challenging Authoritarianism in Southeast Asia: Comparing Indonesia and Malaysia.* London and New York: Routledge Curzon, 2003.

Heryanto, Ariel, "Ethnic Identities and Erasure: Chinese Indonesians in Public Culture", in Joel S. Kahn (ed.), *Southeast Asian Identities: Culture and the Politics of Representation in Indonesia, Malaysia, Singapore and Thailand.* Singapore: Institute of Southeast Asian Studies; New York: St. Martin's Press, 1998, pp. 95–114.

————, "Where Communism Never Dies: Violence, Trauma and Narration in the Last Cold War Capitalist Authoritarian State", *International Journal of Cultural Studies* 2, no. 2 (August 1999): 147–77.

Hewitt, Tom, "Diorama Presentation", *Journal of the Australian War Memorial,* no. 5 (October 1984): 29–35.

Hildson, Anne-Marie, *Madonnas and Martyrs: Militarism and Violence in the Philippines.* Women in Asia Publication Series, Allen & Unwin, 1995.

Hiromitsu, Inokuchi and Nozaki Yoshiko. "Japanese Education, Nationalism and Ienaga Saburo's Court Challenges", in Laura Hein and Mark Selden (eds.), *Censoring History: Citizenship and Memory in Japan, Germany and the United States.* New York and London: ME Sharpe, 2000.

Hitchcock, Michael, "Indonesia in Miniature", in Michael Hitchcock and Victor T. King (eds.), *Images of Malay-Indonesian Identity.* Kuala Lumpur, Oxford, New York: Oxford University Press, 1997, pp. 227–35.

Hobsbawm, Eric, *Age of Extremes: The Short Twentieth Century 1914–1991.* London: Abacus, 1994.

Holt, Claire, *Art in Indonesia: Continuities and Change.* Ithaca: Cornell University Press, 1967.

Honna, Jun, "The Military and Democratisation in Indonesia: The Developing Civil-Military Discourse during the Late Soeharto Era". PhD diss., Department of Political and Social Change, Australian National University, Canberra, 1999.

————, "Military Ideology in Response to Democratic Pressure during the Late Suharto Era: Political and Institutional Contexts", *Indonesia,* no. 67 (April 1999): 77–126.

Hoop, A.N.J. Th. a Th. van der, *Korte Gids voor het Museum,* Koninklijk Bataviaasch Genootschap van Kunsten en Wetenschappen, Batavia, 1948.

Hooper-Greenhill, Eilean, *Museums and their Visitors.* London: Routledge, 1994.

Horio, Teruhisa, *Educational Thought and Ideology in Modern Japan: State Authority and Intellectual Freedom* (edited and translated by Steven Platzer). Tokyo: University of Tokyo Press, 1988.

Hughes, John, *Indonesian Upheaval.* New York: David Mc Kay Company, 1967.

Hunt, Lynn, "History as Gesture: or, the Scandal of History", in Jonathan Arac and Barbara Johnson (eds.), *Consequences of Theory.* Baltimore: John Hopkins University Press, 1991, pp. 91–107.

Husband, William B., "Secondary School History Texts in the USSR: Revising the Soviet Past, 1985–1989", *Russian Review* 50(4) (1991): 458–80.

Huyssen, Andreas, "Monument and Memory in a Postmodern Age", in James Young (ed.), *The Art of Memory: Holocaust Memorials in History.* Munich: Prestel Verlag, 1994, pp. 9–17.

Igarashi, Yoshikuni, *Bodies of Memory: Narratives of War in Postwar Japanese Culture.* Princeton and Oxford: Princeton University Press, 2000.

Ikrar Nusa Bhakti, "Prof Dr Nugroho Notosusanto: Rektor UI yang Sejarahwan", *Mutiara*, no. 263 (3–16 March 1982).

Imparsial, Tim, *Menuju TNI Profesional [Perjalanan Advokasi RUU TNI]*, Imparsial, Koalisi Keselamatan Masyarakat Sipil, Lembaga Studi Pers dan Pembangunan, Jakarta, 2005.

Indonesia Reports — Politics Supplement — November 15, Indonesia Publications, Lanham-Seabrook, College Park, 1984.

Indra, Muhammad Ridhwan, *The 1945 Constitution: A Human Creation*, Muhammad Ridhwan Indra, Jakarta, 1990.

International Crisis Group Briefing Paper, *Al-Qaeda in Southeast Asia: The Case of the "Ngukri Network" in Indonesia*, Jakarta/Brussels, 8 August 2002.

International Crisis Group Report, *Al Qaeda in Southeast Asia: The Case of the Ngruki Network in Indonesia*, Asia report No. 20. <http://www.crisisgroup. org/home/index> [8 August 2002].

Irawanto, Budi, *Konstruksi Relasi Sipil-Militer dalam Sinema Indonesia: Kajian Semiotik tentang Representasi Relasi Sipil-Milter dalam Film Enam Jam di Yogya, Janur Kuning dan Serangan Umum*, Skripsi Fakultas Fisipol, Universitas Gadjah Mada, Yogakarta, 1995.

Iskandar, Maskun and Jopie Lasut (translated by Robert Cribb), "The Purwodadi Affair: Two Accounts", in Robert Cribb (ed.), *The Indonesian Killings of 1965–1966: Studies from Java and Bali*. Clayton: Monash Papers on Southeast Asia, No. 21, Centre of Southeast Asian Studies, 1990, pp. 195–226.

Jackson, Karl D., *Traditional Authority, Islam and Rebellion: A Study of Indonesian Political Behaviour*. Berkeley: University of California Press, 1980.

Janowitz, Morris, *The Military in the Political Development of New Nations: An Essay in Comparative Analysis*, Phoenix Books. Chicago: University of Chicago Press, 1964.

_____, *Military Institutions and Coercion in the Developing Nations*. Chicago: University of Chicago Press, 1977.

Jassin, H.B., *Kesusatraan Indonesia dalam Kritik dan Esai*. Djakarta: Gunung Agung, 1967.

Johnson, John J. (ed.), *The Role of the Military in Underdeveloped Countries*. Princeton, New Jersey: Princeton University Press, 1962.

Jenkins, David, *Suharto and His Generals: Indonesian Military Politics 1975–1983*. Ithaca, New York: Monograph Series No. 64, Cornell Modern Indonesia Project, Cornell University, 1984.

Kaeppler, Adrienne I., "Paradise Regained: The Role of Pacific Museums in Forging National Identity", in Kaplan, Flora E.S. (ed.), *Museums and the Making of "Ourselves": The Role of Objects in National Identity*. London and New York: Leicester University Press, 1994, pp. 19–44.

Kahar Muzakar, "Down With the New Majapahitism!", in Herbert Feith and Lance Castles (eds.), *Indonesian Political Thinking, 1945–1965*. Ithaca: Cornell University Press, 1960, pp. 330–4.

Kahin, Audrey and George, *Subversion as Foreign Policy: The Secret Eisenhower and Dulles Debacle in Indonesia.* New York: The New Press, 1995.

Kahin, Audrey (ed.), *Regional Dynamics of the Indonesian Revolution: Unity from Diversity.* Honolulu: University of Hawaii Press, 1985.

Kahin, George Mc T., *Nationalism and Revolution in Indonesia.* Ithaca: Cornell University Press, 1952.

————, "Preface to Soedjatmoko", in Soedjatmoko, *An Approach to Indonesian History: Towards an Open Future*, An Address before the Seminar on Indonesian History, Gadjah Mada University, Jogyakarta, 14 December 1957. Ithaca: Cornell University, Southeast Asia Program, 1960, pp. iii–v.

Kammen, Douglas and Siddharth Chandra, *A Tour of Duty: Changing Patterns of Military Politics in Indonesia in the 1990s.* Ithaca: Cornell Modern Indonesia Project, 1999.

Kaplan, Flora E.S. (ed.), *Museums and the Making of "Ourselves": The Role of Objects in National Identity.* London and New York: Leicester University Press, 1994.

Karp, Ivan, Christine Mullen Kreamer and Steven D. Lavine (eds.), *Museums and Communities: The Politics of Public Culture.* Washington: Smithsonian Institute Press, 1992.

Karp, Ivan and Steven D. Lavine (eds.), *Exhibiting Cultures: the Poetics and Politics of Museum Display.* Washington: Smithsonian Institute Press, 1991.

Karp, Ivan, "Introduction", in Ivan Karp, Christine Mullen Kreamer and Steven D. Lavine (eds.), *Museums and Communities: The Politics of Public Culture.* Washington: Smithsonian Institute Press, 1992, pp. 1–17.

Kartodirdjo, Sartono, "Some Problems on the Genesis of Nationalism in Indonesia", *Journal of Southeast Asian History* 3, no. 1 (March 1962): 67–94.

————, "Historical Study and Historians in Indonesia Today", *Journal of Southeast Asian History* 4, no. 1 (1963): 22–9.

Kates, Gary, *The French Revolution: Recent Debates and New Controversies.* London and New York: Routledge, 1998.

Katoppo, Aristides *et al.*, *Menyingkap Kabut Halim 1965.* Jakarta: Pustaka Sinar Harapan, 1999.

Kavanagh, Gaynor, *Museums and The First World War.* London and New York: Leicester University Press, 1994.

Kelleher, Catherine McArdle, *Political Military Systems: Comparative Perspectives.* Beverly Hills: Sage Publications, 1974.

Kempers, Bernet A.J., *Ancient Indonesian Art.* Amsterdam: C.P.J. van der Peet, 1959.

Kennedy, Gavin, *The Military in the Third World.* London: Duckworth, 1974.

Ketetapan-Ketetapan MPRS Hasil-Hasil Sidang Umum ke-IV, Tahun 1967, Pantjuran Tudjuh, Jakarta, 1967.

Klein, Kerwin Lee, "On the Emergence of *Memory* in Historical Discourse", *Representations*, no. 69 (Winter 2000): 127–50.

Klinken, Gerry Van, "The Battle for History After Suharto: Beyond Sacred Dates, Great Men, and Legal Milestones", *Critical Asian Studies* 33, no. 3: 323–50.

Klooster, H.A.J., *Indonesiërs Schrijven hun Geschiedenis: De Ontwikkeling van de Indonesische Geschiedbeoefening in Theorie en Praktijk, 1900–1980* (*Indonesians Write Their History: The Development of Indonesian Historiography in Theory and Practice, 1900–1980*). Dordrecht: Foris Publications, 1985.

Koentjaraningrat, *Javanese Culture*. Singapore: Institute of Southeast Asian Studies and Oxford University Press, 1990.

Kok, Jean van de, Robert Cribb and M Heins, "1965 and all That: History in the Politics of the New Order", *Review of Indonesian and Malaysian Studies* 25, no. 2 (Summer 1991): 84–94.

Koonings, Kees and Kruijt, Dirk, "Military Politics and the Mission of Nation Building", in Koonings, Kees and Kruijt, Dirk (eds.), *Political Armies: The Military and Nation Building in the Age of Democracy*. London and New York: Zed Books, 2002, pp. 9–34.

Koopmans, Ype, "Koloniale Expansie en de Nederlandse Monumentale Sculptuur", *Tijdschrift voor Geschiedenis*, no. 105 (1992): 383–406.

Kreps, Christina, "The Paradox of Cultural Preservation in Museums (The Politics of Culture and the Museum)", *Journal of Arts Management, Law and Society* 23, no. 4 (Winter 1994): 291–306.

Kuntowijoyo, *Paradigma Islam: Interpretasi untuk Aksi*. Bandung: Mizan, 1991.

Lane, Max, *Openness, Political Discontent and Succession in Indonesia: Political Developments in Indonesia, 1989–91*. Nathan: Griffith University, 1991.

Langill, Richard, "Military Rule and Developmental Policy in Indonesia under the New Order, 1966–1974". Unpublished PhD diss., The American University, Washington, University Microfilms International, Ann Arbor, 1979.

Lavine, Steven and Ivan Karp, "Introduction Museums and Multiculturalism", in Steven Lavine and Ivan Karp (eds.), *Exhibiting Cultures: The Poetics of Museum Display*. Washington and London: Smithsonian Institute Press, 1991, pp. 1–8.

LeClerc, Jacques, "Mirrors and the Lighthouse: A Search for Meaning in the Monuments and Great Works of Sukarno's Jakarta, 1960–1966", in Peter J. Nas (ed.), *Urban Symbolism*. Leiden and New York: E.J. Brill, 1993, pp. 38–58.

_____, "Girls, Girls, Girls and Crocodiles", in Henk Schulte Nordholt (ed.), *Outward Appearances: Dressing State and Society in Indonesia*. Leiden: KITLV Press, 1997, pp. 291–305.

Lee Kam Hing, *Education and Politics in Indonesia, 1945–1965*. Kuala Lumpur: University of Malaya Press, 1995.

Leifer, Michael, *Indonesia's Foreign Policy*. London, Boston: Published for Royal Institute of International Affairs by Allen & Unwin, 1983.

Leigh, Barbara, "Making the Indonesian State: The Role of School Texts", *Review of Indonesian and Malaysian Studies* 25, no. 1 (Winter 1991): 17–43.

————, "Female Heroes in School Examinations: Traditions and Tensions in Creating a Gendered State", *Asian Studies Review* 17, no. 3 (April 1994): 23–33.

Legge, John, *Sukarno: A Political Biography*. New York: Praeger Publications, 1972.

Lev, Daniel, *The Transition to Guided Democracy: Indonesian Politics 1957–1959*. Ithaca: Modern Indonesia Project, Southeast Asia Program, Cornell University, 1966.

Levy, Curtis, *Riding the Tiger* (videorecording), Australian Film Finance Corporation and Olsen Levy Productions, written by Curtis Levy and Christine Olsen, 1992.

Liddle, William and Rizal Mallarangeng, "Indonesia in 1996: Pressures from Above and Below", *Asian Survey* 37, no. 2 (1997): 167–74.

Liddle, R. William, "Indonesia 1977: The New Order's Second Parliamentary Election", *Asian Survey* 18, no. 2 (February 1978): 175–85.

————, "Soeharto's Indonesia: Personal Rule and Political Institutions", *Pacific Affairs* 58, no. 1 (Spring 1985): 68–90.

————, "The Islamic Turn in Indonesia: A Political Explanation", *The Journal of Asian Studies* 55, no. 3 (August 1996): 613–34.

Lindsey, Timothy C., "Concrete Ideology: Taste, Tradition and the Javanese Past in New Order Public Space", in Virginia Matheson Hooker (ed.) *Culture and Society in New Order Indonesia*, South-east Asian Social Science Monographs. Kuala Lumpur: Oxford University Press, 1995, pp. 166–82.

Lombard, Denys, *Nusa Jawa: Silang Budaya Kajian Sejarah Terpadu, Bagian 1: Batas-Batas Pembaratan*. Jakarta: Gramedia Pustaka Utama, 1996.

————, *Nusa Jawa: Silang Budaya Bagian 3 Warisan Kerajaan-Kerajaan Konsentris*, Gramedia Pustaka Utama, Jakarta, 1996.

Lord, Laura Woolsey, "The Uses of History in Contemporary Indonesia". MA Thesis, Faculty of Graduate School, Cornell University, 1959.

Lowry, Robert, *The Armed Forces of Indonesia*. St. Leonards: Allen & Unwin, 1996.

Lucas, Anton and Robert Cribb, "Women's Roles in the Indonesian Revolution: Some Historical Reflections", in Taufik Abdullah (ed.), *The Heartbeat of the Indonesian Revolution*. Jakarta: Gramedia, 1997, pp. 70–93.

Lucas, Anton. *One Soul One Struggle: Region and Revolution in Indonesia*. Sydney: Allen & Unwin, 1991.

————, "Images of Women During the Indonesian Revolution", in Jane Drakard and John Legge (eds.), *Indonesian Independence Fifty Years on 1945–1995*, Annual Indonesia Lecture Series No. 20, Clayton, 1996, pp. 47–72.

————, "Land Disputes, the Bureaucracy, and Local Resistance in Indonesia", in Jim Schiller and Barbara Martin-Schiller (eds.), *Imagining Indonesia: Cultural Politics and Political Culture*, Ohio University for International Studies, Monographs in International Studies, Southeast Asian Series, Number 97, Athens, 1997, pp. 229–60.

Lüsebrink, Hans Jürgen and Rolf Reichardt, *The Bastille: A History of a Symbol of Despotism and Freedom*. Durham and London: Duke University Press, 1997.

MacFarling, Ian, *The Dual Function of the Indonesian Armed Forces: Military Politics in Indonesia*, Australian Defence Studies Centre, Canberra, 1996.

McCoy, Alfred W. "Same Banana: Hazing and Honor at the Philippine Military Academy, *The Journal of Asian Studies* 54, no. 3 (August 1995): 689–726.

McGregor, Katharine E., "The Struggle Captured: Commemorating the Indonesian Independence Struggle in 1975". Honours Thesis, History Department, Melbourne University, 1995.

————, "Museums and the Transformation from Colonial to Post-colonial Institutions in Indonesia: A Case Study of the National Museum, formerly Museum Batavia", in Fiona Kerlogue (ed.), *Performing Objects: Museums, Material Culture and Performance in Southeast Asia*, Contributions on Critical Museology and Material Culture Series (London: Horniman Museum, 2004), pp. 15–29.

————, "Representing the Indonesian Past: The National Monument History Museum from Guided Democracy to the New Order", *Indonesia*, no. 75 (April 2003): 91–122.

————, "Commemoration of 1 October, *Hari Kesaktian Pancasila*: A Post-Mortem Analysis?", *Asian Studies Review* 26, no. 1 (March 2002).

————, "Nugroho Notosusanto: The Legacy of a Historian in the Service of an Authoritarian Regime", in Mary S. Zurbuchen (ed.), *Beginning to Remember: The Past in Indonesia's Present*. Singapore: Singapore University Press; Seattle: University of Washington Press, 2005, pp. 209–32.

McIntyre, Angus, "Sukarno: Abandoned by History" (unpublished manuscript).

————, "Sukarno as Artist Politician", in Angus McIntyre (ed.), *Indonesian Political Biography: In Search of Cross Cultural Understanding*. Clayton: Centre of Southeast Asian Studies, Monash Papers on Southeast Asia, Monash University, 1993, pp. 161–209.

————, *Soeharto's Composure: Considering the Biographical and Autobiographical Accounts*. Clayton: Monash Asia Institute, 1996.

Macintyre, Stuart and Anna Clark, *The History Wars*. Carlton: Melbourne University Press, 2004.

McKernan, Michael, *Here is Their Spirit: A History of the Australian War Memorial 1917–1990*. St. Lucia: University of Queensland Press in Association with the Australian War Memorial, 1991.

McMichael, Heathcote, "Indonesia's Political Prisoners: A Source of Legitimacy for the Suharto Regime". Honours Thesis, Melbourne University, 1980.

McVey, Ruth, "The Post Revolutionary Transformation of the Indonesian Army", *Indonesia*, no. 11 (April 1971): 131–76.

_____, "The Post Revolutionary Transformation of the Indonesian Army Part II", *Indonesia*, no. 13 (April 1972): 147–82.

_____, "The Enchantment of the Revolution: History and Action in an Indonesian Communist Text", in Anthony Reid and David Marr (eds.), *Perceptions of the Past in Southeast Asia*, Asian Studies Association of Australia. Kuala Lumpur: Heinemann Educational Books (Asia), 1979, pp. 340–58.

_____, "Faith as the Outsider: Islam in Indonesian Politics", in James P. Piscatori (ed.), *Islam in the Political Process*. Cambridge: Cambridge University Press, 1983, pp. 199–225.

Mackie, Jamie and Andrew MacIntyre, "Politics", in Hal Hill (ed.), *Indonesia's New Order: The Dynamics of Socio-Economic Transformation*. St. Leonards: Allen & Unwin, 1994, pp. 1–53.

Majalah Tempo, *Apa dan Siapa Sejumlah Orang Indonesia 1982–1983*. Jakarta: Grafiti Pers, 1982.

_____, *Apa dan Siapa Sejumlah Orang Indonesia 1985–1986*. Jakarta: Grafiti Pers, 1985.

Maklai, Brita, "New Streams, New Visions: Contemporary Art since 1966", in Virginia Matheson Hooker (ed.), *Culture and Society in New Order Indonesia*. Kuala Lumpur: Oxford University Press, 1995, pp. 70–83.

Malik, Adam, *Riwayat Proklamasi Agustus 1945* (5th edition). Djakarta: Widjaya, 1970.

_____, *In the Service of the Republic*. Singapore: Gunung Agung, 1980.

Mallarangeng, Rizal and R. William Liddle, "Indonesia in 1995: The Struggle for Power and Policy", *Asian Survey* 36, no. 2 (February 1996): 109–16.

Maluddin Anwar *et al.*, "Menghapus Kisah Heroik Soeharto", *Gatra*, 17 October 1998, pp. 92–3.

Mangunwijaya, Y.B., "Saya Cuma Pastor Desa tentang Disciplin Pendidikan, Hadiah Nobel dan Korupsi", *Matra*, December 1996.

_____, *Gerundelan Orang Republik*. Yogyakarta: Pustaka Pelajar, 1995.

Marianto, Martinus Dwi, "Surrealist Painting in Yogyakarta". PhD diss., Faculty of Creative Arts, University of Wollongong, 1995.

Maslan, M. Rizal, *Detik.com*, 7 March 2006.

Maurer, Jean-Luc, "A New Order Sketchpad of Indonesian History", in Michael Hitchcock and Victor T. King (eds.), *Images of Malay-Indonesian Identity*. Kuala Lumpur, Oxford and New York: Oxford University Press, 1997, pp. 209–26.

Maxwell, John R., "Soe Hok Gie: A Biography of a Young Intellectual". PhD diss., Australian National University, Canberra, 1997.

May, Brian, *The Indonesian Tragedy*. London and Boston: Routledge and Kegan Paul, 1978.

Maynard, Harold, "A Comparison of Military Elite Role Perceptions in Indonesia and the Philippines". Unpublished PhD diss., The American University, Washington, University Microfilms International, Ann Arbor, 1976.

Mernissi, Fatima, *Beyond the Veil: Male-Female Dynamics in Modern Muslim Society* (revised edition). Bloomington and Indianapolis: Indiana University Press, 1987.

Mietzner, Marcus, "Godly Men in Green", *Inside Indonesia*, no. 53 (January–March 1998): 8–9.

Miksic, John, *Borobudur: Golden Tales of Buddhas*. Hong Kong: Periplus Editions, 1997.

Moertopo, Ali, *Some Basic Thoughts on the Acceleration and Modernisation of 25 Years' Development*. Jakarta: Centre for Strategic and International Studies, Yayasan Proklamasi, 1973.

_____, *Strategi Pembangunan Nasional*. Jakarta: Centre for Strategic and International Studies, 1981.

Moon, Seungsook, "Begetting the Nation: The Andocentric Discourse of National History and Tradition in South Korea", in Elaine H. Kim and Chun Moo Choi (eds.), *Dangerous Women: Gender and Korean Nationalism*. New York and London: Routledge, 1998, pp. 42–4.

Moore, Kevin, *Museums and Popular Culture*. London and Washington: Cassel, 1997.

Morales-Moreno, Luis Gerardo, "History and Patriotism in the National Museum of Mexico", in Flora E.S. Kaplan, *Museums and the Making of "Ourselves": The Role of Objects in National Identity*. London and New York: Leicester University Press, 1994, pp. 171–91.

Morfit, Michael, "Pancasila: The Indonesian State Ideology according to the New Order Government", *Asian Survey* 21, no. 8 (1981): 838–51.

Mortimer, Rex, *The Indonesian Communist Party and Land Reform, 1959–1965*. Clayton: Centre of Southeast Asian Studies, Monash Papers on Southeast Asia No. 1, Monash University, 1972.

_____, *Indonesian Communism Under Sukarno: Ideology and Politics, 1959–1965*. Ithaca: Cornell University Press, 1974.

Moser, Stephanie, "The Dilemma of Didactic Displays: Habitat Dioramas, Life-Groups and Reconstructions of the Past", in Nick Merriman (ed.), *Making Early Histories in Museums*. London and New York: Leicester University Press, 1999, pp. 95–116.

Mosse, George, *Fallen Soldiers: Reshaping the Memory of the World Wars*. New York: Oxford University Press, 1990.

Mrazek, Rudolf, "Sjahrir at Boven Digoel: Reflections on Exile in the Dutch East Indies", in Daniel S. Lev and Ruth McVey (eds.), *Making Indonesia.* Ithaca: Cornell University Press, 1996, pp. 41–65.

Muchtar, Valina, "Selamat Jalan Pak Nug: Saya Selalu Ingat Sosoknya yang Gagah dan Selalu Tersenyum", *Pikiran Rakyat,* 4 June 1985.

Muharyo, "Nugroho Notosusanto Sahabatku dan Adikku", *Femina,* no. 24 (18 June 1985): 94–6.

Najmabadi, Afsaneh, "Hazards of Modernity and Morality: Women, State and Ideology in Contemporary Iran", in Albert Hourani *et al.* (eds.), *The Modern Middle East: A Reader.* Berkeley and Los Angeles: University of California Press, 1993, pp. 677–82.

Nas, Peter J., "Jakarta, City Full of Symbols: An Essay on Symbolic Ecology", in Peter J. Nas (ed.), *Urban Symbolism.* Leiden and New York: E.J. Brill, 1993, pp. 13–37.

Nasution, A.H., *Memenuhi Panggilan Tugas.* Jakarta: Gunung Agung, 1982.

Noer, Deliar, "Yamin and Hamka Two Routes to an Indonesian Identity", in Anthony Reid and David Marr (eds.), *Perceptions of the Past in Southeast Asia.* Kuala Lumpur: Heinemann Educational Books (Asia), 1979, pp. 249–62.

Nora, Pierre, "Between Memory and History: *Les Lieux de Mémoire*", translated by Marc Roudebush, *Representations,* no. 26 (Spring 1989): 7–25.

Notosusanto, Nugroho, "Problems in the Study and Teaching of National History in Indonesia", *Journal of Southeast Asian History* 6, no. 1 (1965): 1–16.

——————, "A New Generation (1952)", in Herbert Feith and Lance Castles (eds.), *Indonesian Political Thinking, 1945–1965.* Ithaca and New York: Cornell University Press, 1970, pp. 68–70.

——————, *Generations in Indonesia.* Jakarta: Department of Defence and Security, Centre for Armed Forces History, 1974.

——————. Letter from Nugroho Notosusanto to Herbert Feith, Rawamangun, 31 July 1969, Monash University Archives, *Herbert Feith Files 1948–1987.*

——————, *Tentara Peta Pada Jaman Pendudukan Jepang di Indonesia.* Jakarta: Gramedia, 1979.

——————. "Saya Ingin Mengungkap Simpati Terhadap Manusia Kecil", *Optimis,* 24 December 1981.

——————. *Tujuhbelas Tahun Aksi Tritura Hakekat dan Hikmatnya,* Universitas Indonesia, Seri Komunikasi No. 11, Jakarta, 1983.

——————, "Regenerasi dan Motivasi", speech for *Hari Pendidikan Nasional* (National Education Day), 2 May 1985, Departemen Pendidikan dan Kebudayaan.

——————, *Tercapainya Konsensus Nasional 1966–1969.* Jakarta: Balai Pustaka, 1985.

Oei, Tjoe Tat, *Memoar Oei Tjoe Tat, Pembantu Presiden Sukarno*. Jakarta: Hasta Mitra, 1995.

Oey, Hong Lee, *The Sukarno Controversies of 1980/81*. Clayton: Centre of Southeast Asian Studies, Monash University, 1982.

Onghokham, "Pemalsuan dan Ilmu Sejarah", *Tempo*, 5 September 1981.

Orang Indonesia yang Terkemoeka di Djawa, Gunseikanbu, n.p., 1944 (2604).

Paget, Roger K., "Djakarta Newspapers, 1965–1967: Preliminary Comments", *Indonesia*, no. 4 (1967): 211–6.

_____, "The Military in Indonesian Politics: The Burden of Power", *Pacific Affairs* 11, nos. 3 and 4 (1967–8): 294–314.

Paguyuban Jawi (Javanese Speaking Society), Programme for Ketoprak Ken Arok, performed at the Indonesian Consulate Melbourne, 8 June 1996.

Panggabean, Maraden, *Berjuang dan Mengabdi*. Jakarta: Pustaka Sinar Harapan, 1993.

Passim, Herbert, *Society and Education in Japan*. New York: Kodansha International, 1982.

Pauker, Ewa T., "Ganefo 1: Sports and Politics in Djakarta", *Asian Survey* 4, no. 4 (April 1965): 171–85.

Pauker, Guy, "Indonesia the Year of Transition", *Asian Survey* 7, no. 2 (February 1967): 138–50.

Pausacker, Helen, "Limbuk Wants to be a Dalang", *Inside Indonesia*, no. 9 (December 1986): 30–1.

Pearce, Susan M., *Museum Objects and Collections: A Cultural Study*. Leicester and London: Leicester University Press, 1992.

Pemberton, John, *On the Subject of "Java"*. Ithaca: Cornell University Press, 1994.

Penders, C.L.M. and Ulf Sundhaussen, *Abdul Haris Nasution: A Political Biography*. St. Lucia, London and New York: University of Queensland Press, 1985.

Penders, C.L.M., *The Life and Times of Sukarno*. London: Sidgwick and Jackson, 1974.

_____ (ed.), *Mohammed Hatta Indonesian Patriot Memoirs*. Singapore: Gunung Agung, 1981.

Pipit Rochijat, "Am I PKI or Non-PKI?" (translated with an afterword by Benedict Anderson), *Indonesia*, no. 40 (October 1985): 37–56.

Pour, Julius, *Benny Moerdani: Profil Prajurit Negarawan*, Yayasan Kejuangan Panglima Besar Sudirman, 1993.

Pracoyo Wiryoutomo, "Luka itu Bernama Priok, Lampung ...", *Panji Masyarakat*, no. 9, Thn 2 (17 June 1998): 15–8.

Pramoedya Ananta Toer, "Acceptance" (translated by William H Frederick), in *Reflections on Rebellion: Stories from the Indonesian Upheavals of 1948 and 1965*, Papers in International Studies Southeast Asia No. 60, Ohio University, Athens, 1983, pp. 7–48.

_____, *Nyanyi Sunyi Seorang Bisu: Catatan-Catatan dari Pulau Buru*. Jakarta: Hasta Mitra, 2000.

Prapañca, Mpu, *Deśawarnana: (Nāgarakrtāgama)*, translated by Stuart Robson. Leiden: KITLV Press, 1995.

Purdey, Jemma, *Anti-Chinese Violence in Indonesia 1996–1999*, Asian Studies Association of Australia Southeast Asia Publications Series. Singapore: Singapore University Press, 2006.

Purdy, Susan Selden, "Legitimation of Power and Authority in a Pluralistic State: Pancasila and Civil Religion in Indonesia". PhD diss., Columbia University, 1984.

Pusat Studi dan Pengembangan Informasi, *Tanjung Priok Berdarah Tanggung Jawab Siapa? Kumpulan Fakta dan Data*, Gema Insani, Jakarta, 1998.

Raben, Remco (ed.), *Representing the Japanese Occupation in Indonesia: Personal Testimonies and Public Images in Indonesia, Japan and the Netherlands*. Zwolle: Netherlands Institute for War Documentation and Waanders Publishers, 1999.

Rachman, Erlita, *Jakarta 50 Tahun dalam Pengembangan dan Penataan Kota*, Dinas Tata Kota Daerah Khusus Ibu Kota, Jakarta, 1995.

Raillon, François, "The New Order and Islam or the Imbroglio of Faith and Politics", *Indonesia*, no. 57 (April 1994): 197–217.

Ramage, Douglas E., *Politics in Indonesia: Democracy, Islam, and the Ideology of Tolerance*. London and New York: Routledge, 1997.

Ramadhan K.H., *Bang Ali demi Jakarta (1966–1977): Memoar*. Jakarta: Pustaka Sinar Harapan, 1992.

_____, *Soemitro: Dari Pangdam Mulawarman sampai Pangkopkamtib*. Jakarta: Pustaka Sinar Harapan, 1994.

_____, *Soemitro: Former Commander of the Indonesian Security Apparatus*. Jakarta: Pustaka Sinar Harapan, 1996.

Rand Corporation, *Selected Rand Abstracts, Vol. 7, No. 4, January–December 1969*. Santa Monica: Rand Corporation, 1970.

Ransom, David, "Ford Country: Building an Elite for Indonesia", in Steve Wiseman and Members of the Pacific Studies Center and the North American Congress on Latin America (eds.), *The Trojan Horse: a Radical Look at Foreign Aid*. Palo Alto: Ramparts Press, 1975, pp. 93–116.

Redaktur, "Mengapa Dilarang?", *Media Kerja Budaya*, no. 3 (February 1996): 4–9.

Reid, Anthony and David Marr (eds.), *Perceptions of the Past in Southeast Asia*, Asian Studies Association of Australia. Singapore, Kuala Lumpur and Hong Kong: Heinemann Educational Books, 1979.

Reid, Anthony, *Indonesian National Revolution 1945–50*. Melbourne: Longman, 1974.

_____, *The Blood of the People: Revolution and the End of Traditional Rule in Northern Sumatra*. Oxford, New York, Melbourne: Oxford University Press, 1979.

_____, "The Nationalist Quest for an Indonesian Past", in Anthony Reid and David Marr (eds.), *Perceptions of the Past in Southeast Asia*, Asian Studies Association of Australia. Singapore, Kuala Lumpur and Hong Kong: Heinemann Educational Books, 1979, pp. 281–98.

_____, "Indonesian Historiography — Modern", in D.R. Woolf (ed.), *A Global Encyclopaedia of Historical Writing*, Vols. A–J. New York: Garland Publishers, 1998, pp. 465–67.

_____, "The Victory of the Republic", in C. Wild and P. Carey (eds.), *Born in Fire: The Indonesian Struggle for Independence An Anthology*. Athens: Ohio University Press, 1986, pp. 178–83.

Ricklefs, Merle C., *A History of Modern Indonesia Since c. 1200* (3rd edition). Hampshire: Palgrave, 2001.

Riza Sofyat and Wahyudi El Panggabean, "Sejarah dalam Bayang-Bayang Kekuasaan", *Forum Keadilan*, 14 December 1998, p. 57.

Robison, Richard, "Indonesia Tensions in State and Regime", in Kevin Hewison, Richard Robison and Garry Rodan (eds.), *South-East Asia in the 1990s: Authoritarianism, Democracy and Capitalism*. Sydney: Allen & Unwin, 1993, pp. 39–74.

Roeder, O.G., *Who's Who in Indonesia: Biographies of Prominent Indonesian Personalities in all Fields* (2nd edition), compiled by O.G. Roeder and Mahiddin Mahmud. Singapore: Gunung Agung, 1980.

Roem, Mohammad *et al.* (ed.), *Tahta untuk Rakyat: Celah-celah Kehidupan Sultan Hamengku Buwono IX.* Jakarta: Gramedia, 1982.

Rumphium, Christ, "In Mother's Care: The Story of a Tapol Child", *Prisma*, no. 15 (1997): 12–9.

Rutherford, Danilyn, "Unpackaging a National Heroine: Two Kartinis and their People", *Indonesia*, no. 55 (April 1993): 23–40.

Sacerdoti, Guy, "The Extremists Exorcised", *Far Eastern Economic Review* (10 April 1981): 28–30.

Said, Julinar and Triana Wulandari, *Ensiklopedia Pahlawan Nasional*, Sub-Direktorat Sejarah Direktorat Sejarah dan Nilai Tradisional, Direktorat Jenderal Kebudayaan, Jakarta, 1995.

Said, Salim, *Shadows on the Silver Screen: A Social History of Indonesian Film;* translated by Toenggoel P. Siagian with a foreword by Karl Heider; John H. McGlynn and Janet P. Boileau (eds.). Jakarta: Lontar Foundation, 1991.

_____, *Genesis of Power: General Sudirman and the Indonesian Military in Politics 1945–49*. Singapore: Institute of Southeast Asian Studies, 1991.

_____, "Suharto's Armed Forces: Building a Power Base in New Order Indonesia, 1966–1998", *Asian Survey* 39, no. 6 (June 1998): 535–52.

Said, Umar, "Pemakaman-Kembali Kerangka Korban 65 Digagalkan". *Soeara Kita*, no. 14 (April 2001): 4–7.

Sailendri, "Shame", *Inside Indonesia*, no. 43 (June 1995): 10–1.

Sastrosoewignyo, Soerasto, "You Have Stabbed Us in the Back Again (1965)", in Herbert Feith and Lance Castles (eds.), *Indonesian Political Thinking 1945–1965*. Ithaca and London: Cornell University Press, 1970, pp. 373–6.

Satyagraha Hoerip, "Sebelum Mas Nug Pergi", *Sinar Harapan*, 7 June 1985.

Schreiner, Klaus H., *Politischer Heldenkult in Indonesien: Tradition und Moderne Praxis* (*The Cult of Political Heroes in Indonesia: Tradition and Modern Practices*). Berlin: Reimer, 1995.

————, "History in the Showcase: Representations of National History in Indonesian Museums", in Sri Kuhnt-Saptodewo, Volker Grabowsky and Martin Grossheim (eds.), *Nationalism and Cultural Revival in Southeast Asia: Perspectives from the Centre and Region*. Wiesbaden: Harrassowitz Verlag, 1997, pp. 99–117.

————, "The Making of National Heroes: From Guided Democracy to New Order", in Henk Schulte Nordholt (ed.), *Outward Appearances: Dressing State and Society in Indonesia*. Leiden: KITLV Press, 1997, pp. 259–90.

Schulte, Nico Nordholt, "The Janus Face of the Indonesian Armed Forces", in Koonings, Kees and Kruijt, Dirk (eds.), *Political Armies: The Military and Nation Building in the Age of Democracy*, pp. 135–61.

Schwarz, Adam, *A Nation in Waiting: Indonesia's Search for Stability* (2nd edition). St. Leonards: Allen & Unwin, 1999.

Schwarz, Barry, "The Social Context of Commemoration: A Study in Collective Memory", *Social Forces* 61, no. 2 (1982): 374–402.

Scott, Peter Dale, "Exporting Military-Economic Development — America and the Overthrow of Sukarno, 1965–67", in Malcolm Caldwell (ed.), *Ten Years' Military Terror in Indonesia*. Nottingham: Spokesman Books, 1975, pp. 209–64.

Sears, Laurie J., *Shadows of Empire: Colonial Discourse and Javanese Tales*. Durham and London: Duke University Press, 1996.

Sen, Krishna and David T. Hill, *Media, Culture and Politics in Indonesia*. Melbourne: Oxford University Press, 2000.

Sen, Krishna, "Filming 'History' under the New Order", in Krishna Sen (ed.), *Histories and Stories: Cinema in New Order Indonesia*. Clayton: Winter Lecture Series, Monash University, 1987, pp. 49–59.

————, *Indonesian Cinema: Framing the New Order*. London: Zed Books, 1994.

Seskoad, *Himpunan Amanat Seminar TNI-Angkatan Darat Ke-III, 1979*. Seskoad, n.p., 1979.

————, *Karya Juang Seskoad 1951–1989*. Seskoad, n.p., 1989.

Sheridan, Mary, "The Emulation of Heroes", *The China Quarterly* 33 (January–March 1968).

Siboro, Tiarma, "Of Officer Camaraderie, Friendships", *The Jakarta Post*, 3 February 2006.

Shiraishi, Saya S., *Young Heroes: The Indonesian Family in Politics*. Ithaca: Cornell University Press, 1997.

Siegel, James T., *Solo in the New Order: Language and Hierarchy in an Indonesian City*. Princeton: Princeton University Press, 1986.

Simatupang, T.B., *Report from Banaran: Experiences During the People's War* (translated by Benedict Anderson and Elizabeth Graves). Ithaca: Modern Indonesia Project, Southeast Asia Program, Cornell University Press, 1972.

Simons, Geoff, *Indonesia: The Long Oppression*. New York: St. Martin's Press, 2000.

Smail, John R.W., *Bandung in the Early Revolution 1945–1946: A Study of the Social History of the Indonesian Revolution*. Ithaca and New York: Cornell Modern Indonesia Program, Monograph Series, Cornell University Press, 1964.

Smith, Martin, "Army Politics as a Historical Legacy", in Koonings, Kees and Kruijt, Dirk (eds.), *Political Armies: The Military and Nation Building in the Age of Democracy*. London and New York: Zed Books, 2002, pp. 270–96.

Soedjatmoko, *An Approach to Indonesian History: Towards an Open Future*, An Address before the Seminar on Indonesian History, Gadjah Mada University, Jogyakarta, 14 December 1957. Ithaca: Cornell University, Southeast Asia Program, 1960.

————, "The Indonesian Historian and His Time", in Soedjatmoko *et al.* (eds.), *An Introduction to Indonesian Historiography*. Ithaca: Cornell University Press, 1965, pp. 404–15.

Soe Hok Gie, *Catatan Seorang Demonstran*. Jakarta: LP3ES, 1983.

————, *Orang Orang di Persimpangan Kiri Jalan: Kisah Pemberontakan Madiun, September 1948*. Yogyakarta: Yayasan Bentang Budaya, 1997.

Soeharto, *Pikiran, Ucapan dan Tindakan Saya: Otobiografi*, seperti dipaparkan kepada G. Dwipayana dan Ramadhan K.H., Citra Lamtoro Gung Persada, Jakarta, 1989.

————, "Sambutan Jenderal Soeharto Selaku Pejabat Presiden pada Peringatan: Hari Lahirnya *Pancasila* in Jakarta 1 June 1967", in Yayasan Pembela Tanah Air, *Garuda Emas Pancasila Sakti*. Jakarta: Yayasan Pembela Tanah Air, 1994.

Soekmono, R., "Archaeology and Indonesian History", in Soedjatmoko *et al.* (eds.), *An Introduction to Indonesian Historiography*. Ithaca: Cornell University Press, 1965, pp. 36–46.

Soemitro, *Soemitro, Mantan Pangkopkamtib: Dari Pangdam Mulawarman sampai Pangkopkamtib*. Jakarta: Pustaka Sinar Harapan, 1994.

Sola, Tominslav, "The Future of Museums and the Role of Museology", *Museum Management and Curatorship* 12 (1992): 393–400.

Southwood, Julie and Patrick Flanagan, *Indonesia: Law, Propaganda and Terror*. London: Zed Press, 1983.

Sri Suko, "Sekilas Tentang Monumen *Pancasila* Sakti", *Senakatha: Media Kommunikasi dan Informasi Sejarah*, Jakarta, 1986.

Stam, Deidre C., "The Informed Muse: The Implications of "The New Museology for Museum Practice", *Museum Management and Curatorship* 12 (1993): 267–83.

Stanley, "Opening that Dark Page", *Inside Indonesia*, July–September 2000.

Stivens, Maila, "Why Gender Matters in Southeast Asian Politics", in Maila Stivens (ed.), *Why Gender Matters in Southeast Asian Politics*. Clayton: Centre of Southeast Asian Studies, Monash University, 1991, pp. 9–24.

Strassler, Karen, "Material Witnesses: Reformasi Photographs and Popular Memory", Paper Given at UCLA History and Memory Conference in Contemporary Indonesia, UCLA, April 2001.

Sudjatmiko, Iwan Gordono, "The Destruction of the Indonesian Communist Party (PKI): A Comparative Analysis of East Java and Bali". PhD diss., Harvard University, Ann Arbor Microfilms International, 1992.

Suharto, "Beberapa Pokok Pikiran mengenai Pewarisan Nilai-Nilai 45 kepada Generasi Muda Indonesia", *Himpunan Amanat Seminar TNI-Angkatan Darat Ke-III Tahun 1972*, Seskoad, Bandung 13–18 March 1972, pp. 11–30.

————, "State Address of Acting President Suharto on the Occasion of Independence Day, 1967", Ministry of Information, Jakarta as provided in Suharto, "Suharto: The New Order, the Panca Sila, and the 1945 Constitution [August 16, 1967]", in Roger M. Smith (ed.), *Southeast Asia: Documents of Political Development and Change*. Ithaca: Cornell University Press, 1974, pp. 219–21.

————, "Kata Sambutan", in Kongres Wanita Indonesia, *Setengah Abad Pergerakan Wanita Indonesia*. Jakarta: Balai Pustaka, 1978.

————, "The Destruction of the PKI in 1965–66", Paper for conference *Memandang Tragedi Nasional 1965 Secara Jernih*, 8 September 1999, Kampus PUSPIPTEK Serpong sponsored by Masyarakat Sejarawan Indonesia, 1999.

Sukarno, *Reflections upon the Indonesian Revolution*, speech published by the Department of Foreign Affairs, Government of Indonesia, Djakarta, 1964.

————, "Nation Building and Character Building", in *Indonesian Policy Series: New Forces Build a New World, 10th Anniversary 1st Asian African Conference 1965*. Jakarta: Department of Foreign Affairs, 1965.

————, *New Forces Build a New World*, Indonesian Policy Series of the Department of Foreign Affairs, Republic of Indonesia, 10th Anniversary First Asian African Conference, Executive Command, Djakarta, 1965.

————, *Reach to the Stars! A Year of Self-Reliance*. Jakarta: Department of Information, Republic of Indonesia, 1965.

————, *Djangan Sekali-kali Meninggalkan Sedjarah! (Never Leave History!)*. Jakarta: Departemen Penerangan R.I., 1966.

————, "Returning to the Rails of the Revolution (1959)", in Herbert Feith and Lance Castles (eds.), *Indonesian Political Thinking, 1945–1965*. Ithaca and London: Cornell University Press, 1970, pp. 99–109.

————, *Indonesia Accuses: Soekarno's Defence Oration in the Political Trial of 1930*, edited, translated and annotated by Roger K. Paget. Kuala Lumpur, New York: Oxford University Press, 1975.

Sulami, *Perempuan Kebenaran dan Penjara*. Jakarta: Cipta Lestari, 1999.

Sulistyo, Hermawan, *The Forgotten Years: The Missing History of Indonesia's Mass Slaughters: Jombang-Kediri 1965–1966*. Arizona State University, 1997.

Sullivan, Norma, "Gender and Politics in Indonesia", in Maila Stivens (ed.), *Why Gender Matters in Southeast Asian Politics*. Clayton: Monash Papers on Southeast Asia No. 23, Centre of Southeast Asian Studies, Monash University, 1991, pp. 61–86.

————, *Masters and Managers: A Study of Gender Relations in Urban Java*, Asian Studies Association of Australia, Women in Asia Publication Series. St. Leonards: Allen & Unwin, 1994.

Sunariah, "UU TNI Sogokan Politik kepada TNI", *Tempointeraktif.com*, 29 September 2004.

Sundhaussen, Ulf, *The Road to Power Indonesian Military Politics, 1945–1967*. Kuala Lumpur: Oxford University Press, 1982.

————, "The Inner Contraction of the Suharto Regime: A Starting Point for a Withdrawal to the Barracks", in David Bourchier and John Legge (eds.), *Democracy in Indonesia, 1950s and 1990s*. Clayton: Centre of Southeast Asian Studies, Monash University, 1994, pp. 272–85.

Sunindyo, Saraswati, "Murder, Gender and the Media: Sexualising Politics and Violence", in Laurie Sears (ed.), *Fantasizing the Feminine*. Durham and London: Duke University Press, 1996, pp. 120–39.

————, "When the Earth is Female and the Nation is Mother: Gender, the Armed Forces and Nationalism in Indonesia", *Feminist Review*, no. 58 (Spring 1998): 1–21.

Supomo, S., "The Image of Majapahit in Later Javanese and Indonesian Writing", in Anthony Reid and David Marr (eds.), *Perceptions of the Past in Southeast Asia*, Asian Studies Association of Australia. Singapore, Kuala Lumpur and Hong Kong: Heinemann Educational Books, 1979, pp. 171–85.

Supreme Advisory Council, "The Political Manifesto as a General Programme of the Revolution (1959)", in Herbert Feith and Lance Castles (eds.), *Indonesian Political Thinking, 1945–1965*. Ithaca and London: Cornell University Press, 1970, pp. 109–11.

Suryadinata, Leo, *Prominent Indonesian Chinese: Biographical Sketches*. Singapore: Institute of Southeast Asian Studies, 1995.

Suryakusuma, Julia, "State Ibuism: The Social Construction of Womanhood in the Indonesian New Order". MA Thesis, Institute of Social Studies, The Hague, 1987.

————, "The State and Sexuality in New Order Indonesia", in Laurie Sears (ed.), *Fantasizing the Feminine in Indonesia*. Durham and London: Duke University Press, 1996, pp. 92–119.

Suseno, Bambang, "Menumbuhkan Motivasi Murid Belajar Sejarah", *Suara Karya*, 3 April 1984.

Sutaarga, Moh. Amir, *A Short Guide to the Museum Nasional Jakarta*, n.p., Jakarta, 1972.

————, "Masalah Museum di Indonesia", in Moh. Amir Sutaarga, *Persoalan Museum di Indonesia*, Direktorat Museum Dit-Djen. Kebudayaan Departemen Pendidikan dan Kebudayaan, 1971 (originally published in *Siasat* No. 2 May, June, July, August and September 1958).

————, *Museografi dan Museologi: Kumpulan Karangan tentang Ilmu Permuseuman*, Direktorat Museum Diretorat Djenderal Kebudayaan Departemen Pendidikan dan Kebudayaan, 1971.

Sutherland, Heather, "Notes on Java's Regent Families: Part 1", *Indonesia*, no. 16 (October 1973): 113–48.

————, "Professional Paradigms, Politics and Popular Practice: Reflections on 'Indonesian National History'", in Sri Kuhnt-Saptodewo, Volker Grabowsky and Martin Grossheim (eds.), *Nationalism and Cultural Revival in Southeast Asia: Perspectives from the Centre and Region*. Wiesbaden: Harrassowitz Verlag, 1997, pp. 83–98.

————, *The Making of a Bureaucratic Elite*. Singapore: Heinemann, 1979.

Sutton, R. Anderson, "Who is the Pesindhen? Notes on the Female Singing Tradition in Java", *Indonesia*, no. 37 (April 1984): 119–33.

Suyanto, Djoko "Krisis Nasional Hikmah di Balik Tragedi", in Agus Wirahadikusumah, *Indonesia Baru dan Tantangan TNI: Pemikiran Masa Depan*. Jakarta: Pustaka Sinar Harapan, 1999, pp. 232–42.

Swift, Ann, *The Road to Madiun: The Indonesian Communist Uprising of 1948*. Ithaca: Cornell Modern Indonesia Project, Monograph Series No. 69, Cornell University Press, 1989.

Tanjung, Feisal, *ABRI — Islam Mitra Sejati*. Jakarta: Pustaka Sinar Harapan, 1997.

Tanter, Richard, "Intelligence Agencies and Third World Militarization: a Case Study of Indonesia, 1966–1989". PhD diss., Department of Politics, Monash University, 1991.

————, "The Totalitarian Ambition: Intelligence and Security Agencies in Indonesia", in Arief Budiman (ed.), *State and Civil Society in Indonesia*. Clayton: Monash Papers on Southeast Asia No. 22, Centre of Southeast Asian Studies, Monash University, 1994, pp. 215–88.

Taylor, Jean Gelman, "Images of the Indonesian Revolution", in Jane Drakard and John Legge (eds.), *Indonesian Independence Fifty Years on 1945–1995*, Annual Indonesia Lecture Series No. 20, Clayton, 1996, pp. 13–36.

_____, "Official Photography, Costume and the Indonesian Revolution", in Jean Gelman Taylor (ed.), *Women Creating Indonesia: The First Fifty Years.* Clayton: Monash Asia Institute, 1997.

Taylor, Paul Michael, "The *Nusantara* Concept of Culture: Local Traditions and National Identities as Expressed in Indonesia's Museums", *Fragile Traditions: Indonesian Art in Jeopardy.* Honolulu: University of Hawaii Press, 1994, pp. 71–90.

Team Pembinaan Penatar dan Bahan Penataran Pegawai Republik Indonesia, *Bahan Penataran Penghayatan dan Pengalaman Pancasila, Undang-Undang Dasar 1945, Garis-Garis Besar Haluan Negara* (2nd edition), Team Pembinaan Penatar dan Bahan Penataran Pegawai Republik Indonesia, 1981.

_____, *Bahan Penataran Penghayatan dan Pengalaman Pancasila, Undang-Undang Dasar 1945, Garis-Garis Besar Haluan Negara,* Jakarta, 1978.

Teeuw, A., *Modern Indonesian Literature.* The Hague: Martinus Nijhoff, 1967.

Tétreault, Mary Ann, "Women and Revolution: What Have We Learned?", in Mary Ann Tétreault (ed.), *Women and Revolution in Africa, Asia, and the New World.* Columbia: University of South Carolina Press, 1994, pp. 426–41.

Tim ISAI, *Bayang Bayang PKI.* Jakarta: ISAI, 1996.

Tim Imparsial, *Menuju TNI Profesional [Perjalanan Advokasi RUU TNI],* Imparsial, Koalisi Keselamatan Masyarakat Sipil, Lembaga Studi Pers dan Pembangunan, Jakarta, 2005.

Tirtosudarmo, Riwanto, "The Mystification of the Unitary State of Indonesia", *Jakarta Post,* 14 October 2005.

Tjokropranolo, *Panglima Besar TNI Jenderal Soedirman: Pemimpin Pendobrak terakhir Penjajahan di Indonesia, Kisah Seorang Pengawal,* Marzuki Arifin (ed.). Jakarta: PT. Surya Persindo, 1992.

Turner, Graeme, *National Fictions: Literature and Film and the Construction of Australian Narrative.* Sydney: Allen & Unwin, 1986.

Ulbricht, H., *Wayang Purwa: Shadows of the Past.* Kuala Lumpur: Oxford University Press, 1970.

Undang-Undang Republik Indonesia Tentara Nasional Indonesia Pertahanan Negara Kepolisian Negara Republik Indonesia. Jakarta: BP Panca Usaha, 2005.

UNESCO, *UNESCO Statistical Yearbook 1973.* Paris: UNESCO, 1974.

_____, *UNESCO Statistical Yearbook 1974.* Paris: UNESCO, 1975.

Utrecht, Ernst, *The Indonesian Army: A Socio-political Study of An Armed, Privileged Group in Developing Countries.* Townsville: South East Asian Monograph Series, No. 4, James Cook University of North Queensland, 1980.

Van der Kroef, Justus Maria, "Dutch Colonial Policy in Indonesia, 1900–1941". PhD diss., Columbia University, University Microfilms International, Ann Arbor, Michigan, 1969.

———, "Indonesian Communism since the 1965 Coup", *Pacific Affairs* 43, no. 1 (Spring 1970): 34–60.

———, *The Communist Party of Indonesia: Its History, Programme and Tactics.* Vancouver: University of British Colombia, 1985.

Van Langenberg, Michael, "Analysing Indonesia's New Order State: A Keywords Approach", *Review of Indonesian and Malaysian Affairs* 20, no. 2 (Summer 1986): 1–47.

———, "Gestapu and State Power in Indonesia", in Robert Cribb (ed.), *The Indonesian Killings of 1965–1966: Studies from Java and Bali.* Clayton: Monash University, Centre of Southeast Asian Studies, 1990, pp. 45–62.

———, "The New Order State: Language, Ideology, Hegemony", in Arief Budiman (ed.), *State and Civil Society in Indonesia.* Clayton: Monash University, Centre of Southeast Asian Studies, Monash Papers on Southeast Asia No. 22, 1990, pp. 121–49.

Vatikiotis, Michael, "Chain of Command", *Far Eastern Economic Review*, 17 March 1988, pp. 38–39.

———, *Indonesian Politics under Suharto: Order Development and Pressure for Change.* London and New York: Routledge, 1993.

Vergo, Peter (ed.), *The New Museology.* London: Reaktion Books, 1989.

Vickers, Adrian and Katharine McGregor, "Public Debates about History: Comparative Notes from Indonesia", *History Australia* 2, no. 2 (June): 44.1–44.13.

Vickers, Adrian, "Reopening Old Wounds: Bali and the Indonesian Killings — A Review Article", *The Journal of Asian Studies* 57, no. 3 (August 1998): 774–85.

Vreede-de Stuers, Cora, *The Indonesian Woman: Struggles and Achievements.* 's-Gravenhage: Mouton and Co., 1960.

Walsh, Kevin, *The Representation of The Past: Museums and Heritage in The Post-Modern World.* London and New York: Routledge, 1992.

Wanner, Catherine, *Burden of Dreams: History and Identity in Post-Soviet Ukraine.* Pennsylvania: Pennsylvania State University Press, 1998.

Ward, Ken, "Indonesia's Modernisation: Ideology and Practice", in Rex Mortimer (ed.), *Showcase State: The Illusion of Indonesia's Accelerated Modernisation.* Sydney: Angus and Robertson, 1973, pp. 67–82.

Weatherbee, Donald E., *Ideology in Indonesia: Sukarno's Indonesian Revolution.* New Haven: Yale University, 1966.

Wehl, David, *The Birth of Indonesia.* London: George Allen & Unwin, 1948.

Weinstein, Franklin, *Indonesian Foreign Policy and the Dilemma of Dependence: From Sukarno to Soeharto.* Ithaca and London: Cornell University Press, 1976.

Wertheim, W.F., "Suharto and the Untung Coup — The Missing Link", *Journal of Contemporary Asia*, no. 1 (1970): 50–7.

Wibisono, Christianto, "Nugroho Tentang Demokrasi", *Sinar Harapan*, 1985.

Wieringa, Saskia Eleonora, *Penghancuran Gerakan Perempuan di Indonesia*. Jakarta: Arba Budaya and Kalyanamitra, 1999.

————, "The Politicization of Gender Relations in Indonesia". PhD diss., Amsterdam University, Amsterdam, 1995.

————, "Sexual Metaphors in the Change from Soekarno's Old Order to Soeharto's New Order in Indonesia", *Review of Indonesian and Malaysian Affairs* 32, no. 2 (Summer, 1998): 150–66.

Woodcroft-Lee, Carlien Patricia, "Separate but Equal: Indonesian Muslim Perceptions of the Roles of Women", in Lenore Manderson (ed.), *Women's Work and Women's Roles: Economics and Everyday Life in Indonesia, Malaysia and Singapore*. Canberra: Australian National University, 1983, pp. 173–92.

Woodward, Mark R., *Islam in Java: Normative Piety and Mysticism in the Sultanate of Yogyakarta*. Tucson: Arizona University Press, 1989.

Yamaguchi, Masao, "The Poetics of Exhibition in Japanese Culture", in Ivan Karp and Steven D. Lavine (eds.), *Exhibiting Cultures: the Poetics and Politics of Museum Display*. Washington: Smithsonian Institute Press, 1991, pp. 57–67.

Yamin, Muhamad, *Pembahasan Undang-undang Dasar Republik Indonesia*. Djakarta: Jajasan Prapantja, 1960.

Yayasan Idayu, *Sekitar Tanggal dan Penggalinya: Guntingan Pers dan Bibliografi Tentang Pancasila*. Jakarta: Yayasan Idayu, 1981.

Young, Ken, "Local and National Influences in the Violence of 1965", in Robert Cribb (ed.), *The Indonesian Killings of 1965–1966: Studies from Java and Bali*. Clayton: Monash Papers on Southeast Asia No. 21, Centre of Southeast Asian Studies, 1990, pp. 63–100.

Zainu'ddin, Ailsa Thomson, "Kartini — Her Life, Work and Influence", in Ailsa Thomson Zainu'ddin *et al.* (eds.), *Kartini Centenary Indonesian Women Then and Now*. Papers given at the annual public lectures on Indonesia, Australia-Indonesia Association and the Centre of Southeast Asian Studies prior to independence day August 1979, Monash University, 1980, pp. 1–29.

Index

Panjaitan, Lieutenant Colonel L.
   Sintong, 188
Parman, Major General TNI S., 93,
   95, 97, 99, 101
Pauker, Guy, 65–6, *see also* Rand
   Corporation
pejuang, 2, 42, 43, 120, 145, 224–5
pemuda, 44, 120, 148
Pemuda Rakyat, 67
pendopo, 70, 133
penumpasan, 206, 208
People's Consultative Assembly
   1966 Special Decree, 212
People's Democratic Party, 211
Permesta/PRRI rebellions, 43, 113,
   173
PETA, 41, 111, 121, 133, 157
PKI, *see* Communist Party of
   Indonesia
Poesponegoro, Marwati Djoened, 193
Police Force, Indonesian, 18, 114,
   116, 224
Political prisoners, 62, 88, 104, 106,
   109, 170, 206, 212, 221, 228
post-coup killings, *see* killings
   1965–68
post-Suharto era, 1–2, 105–8, 179,
   188, 212–4, 217, 224–8
PPP, *see* United Development Party
Prapañca, Mpu, 22
Prawiranegara, Sjafruddin, 128
Prawirasoebrata, Major General
   Soebijakto, 43
Prawirosudirjo, Professor Garnadi,
   124
Preliminary Education in National
   Defence course, 152
Princen, Haji J.C., 206
priyayi class, 40, 42
Priyono, Education Minister, 26,
   48, 60, 153
Provisional People's Consultative
   Assembly, 21, 28, 122, 208

PSI, 56
pusaka, 85, 88, 125

Rand Corporation, 65–6
Ransom, David, 55
Reading Series for Soldiers, 115, 146,
   165
Red Cross, 119, 150
Reid, Anthony, 120, 128, 129
Renville agreement, 128–9, 161
Resilience Institute, 43, 91
Return of Yogyakarta Museum, *see*
   Museums
Revolution Monument, 9

Sadli, Dr Ir. Mohamad, 56, 124
Sahal, Ahmad, 213
Saleh, Chaerul, 122, 146
Saleh, Ismail, 66, 109
Sanusi, A. Anwar, 49–52, 54–5, 59
Sapta Marga, see Military ideology,
   Soldier's Oath
Sarawak People's Guerrilla Army,
   207
Sarwo Edhie, General, 75, 80, 96
Satriamandala Armed Forces
   Museum, *see* Museums
Schreiner, Klaus, 12, 23
Schwartz, Barry, 10
Sen, Krishna, 100, 113, 147, 210–1
Seskoad, 4, 28, 55–6, 64–6, 124, 142
Shadows of the PKI, 25
Shiraishi, S., 99
Siegel, James, 25
Simatupang, Lieutenant General
   T.B., 137
Sjamsuddin, 122
Smail, John R.W., 120
Soemohardjo, Lieutenant General
   Oerip, 129
Soenarso, Edhi, 12, 198